Samuel Wiseman's *Book of Record*

Samuel Wiseman's
Book of Record

The Official Account of Bacon's Rebellion in Virginia

Edited by
Michael Leroy Oberg

LEXINGTON BOOKS
Lanham • Boulder • New York • Toronto • Oxford

LEXINGTON BOOKS

Published in the United States of America
by Lexington Books
An imprint of The Rowman & Littlefield Publishing Group, Inc.
4501 Forbes Boulevard, Suite 200, Lanham, Maryland 20706

PO Box 317
Oxford
OX2 9RU, UK

British Library Cataloguing in Publication Information Available

Library of Congress Cataloging-in-Publication Data Available

ISBN 0-7391-0711-9 (hardcover : alk. paper) ISBN 978-0-7391-0711-9

Printed in the United States of America

♾™ The paper used in this publication meets the minimum requirements of American
National Standard for Information Sciences—Permanence of Paper for Printed Library
Materials, ANSI/NISO Z39.48–1992.

Contents

Acknowledgements

I first became aware of Samuel Wiseman's *Book of Record* in 1993, when I was completing work on my doctoral dissertation at Syracuse University. Over the decade that has passed since, I had hoped to publish the document. I frequently taught the history of Bacon's Rebellion, the colonial uprising that Wiseman chronicled, and always believed that having Wiseman's *Book* in an accessible format would enrich my courses. Teaching at a small college in Montana with few library resources, Wiseman's detailed compilation I believed could provide the basis for a workable student research project. Historians of colonial America, I believed, would benefit as well by having Wiseman's record available to them in an accessible format. There were all sorts of reasons, then, to undertake the challenge of editing so large a manuscript, but a heavy teaching load at my first institution, and then other research projects, kept me from devoting the time that I felt it deserved.

At long last I have now finished the project, and I could not have done so without the assistance of a number of friends and colleagues. At Geneseo, Jim Williams and Bill Cook, historians of the classical world and medieval Italy respectively, helped me with Latin translations. Joe Cope, my colleague in the history of Stuart Ireland, took the time from his own busy schedule to read the manuscript and offer some important suggestions. I told Jim Rice about this project at the annual Conference on Iroquois Research, and he willingly volunteered to read the manuscript and offer me his sage advice. Warren Billings, the leading expert on the history of seventeenth-century Virginia, was gracious enough to provide me with a copy of his biography of Sir William Berkeley in advance of its publication, and to read and comment on the manuscript while overseeing several search committees in his department. Stephen Saunders Webb, whose advice led me to Samuel Wiseman in the first place, read the manuscript, helped me track down information on some of the obscure individuals mentioned in Wiseman's text, and has enthusiastically supported the project since I first mentioned it to him. The staff of the Virginia Historical Society has been extraordinarily helpful. Susan Danforth at the John Carter Brown library helped obtain permissions for the map from the *Blathwayt Atlas*, and Rebekka Brooks at Lexington has been a great person to work with. The staff of Magdalene College library graciously extended permission for me to reprint Wiseman's important document, and without their consent, this book simply could not exist. Finally, without the support of a family willing to allow me to take off to Richmond, and pile books, papers, and notecards around the house, this book simply would not have been possible.

Introduction

In January of 1677 Samuel Wiseman arrived in Virginia. A clerk, scribe, and secretary, Wiseman accompanied the three royal commissioners, Herbert Jeffreys, Sir John Berry, and Francis Moryson, as well as "a Complete Regiment of a thousand men," charged with "carrying on the Warr against the Kings Enemies, and suppressing the Present Rebellion."[1] Bacon's Rebellion, the uprising in question, had ended by the time Wiseman and the commissioners arrived. Wiseman would nonetheless assist the commissioners, all of them military officers, in investigating the causes of the rebellion, a brief but violent "tumult" which reveals much about the social structure of one of England's most important colonies and that most historians agree dramatically impacted the development of Virginia.

Samuel Wiseman diligently fulfilled his duties to the commissioners, and "behaved himself with great honesty and unwearied industry."[2] He compiled documents and a record of the commissioners' proceedings for future reference. As a result, Wiseman's "Book of Record," the chronicle of his and the commissioners' investigation, is a remarkable document, a vivid depiction of a colonial society in turmoil, one that had struggled through the dangers of race war, the crisis of internal rebellion, the repression that immediately followed, and a lengthy campaign to restore order. It provides us with a great deal of information about the structure of the Restoration Empire, the sources of discontent in the king's Old Dominion, and the place of Virginia in the English Atlantic world.

I

To understand Nathaniel Bacon's Rebellion against the authority of the king's governor of Virginia, Sir William Berkeley, one must look closely at the seven decades of history that preceded the uprising. Virginia, like many of the early English attempts at colonization, began its life as a commercial venture. In 1606 King James I chartered the Virginia Company of London, granting to a select group of the king's "loving subjects" the right "to make habitacion plantacion and to deduce a Colonie of sondrie of our people into that parte of America commonly called Virginia."[3] Profits ranked high on the company's list of priorities and its leaders conceived of their settlement as a business operation. Colo-

---

1. Certificate of the Commissioners of Virginia to the Committee for Trade and Plantations, 3 January 1678, Entry Book of Letters, Commissions, Instructions, Charters, Warrants, Patents and Grants Concerning Virginia, and Especially the Rebellion of Nathaniel Bacon There and the Governorships of Berkeley and Culpeper and Lt. Governor Jeffreys, 1675-1682, C.O. 5/1355, 247-248 (Virginia Colonial Records Project, Virginia Historical Society, Richmond, VA [hereafter VCRP]).
2. Ibid.

nists would search for precious metals, open a lucrative trade with the Indians, and, the company's promoters hoped, discover a passage through the continent to the riches of Asia. If these activities failed to generate profits, the company's investors were willing to settle for the fruits of more earthy pursuits: the production of iron, glass, potash, pitch, and tar. If the colony provided a refuge for those in England dislocated by rapid economic and social change, and provided as well an opportunity to convert the Indians to Christianity, all the better.[4]

The Virginia Company, however, failed to attain any of its initial objectives, and in its early years the colony it planted at Jamestown struggled to survive. Factional squabbling among the colony's leaders, the extraordinarily unhealthful location chosen for the settlement, and endemic fighting with the neighboring Powhatan chiefdom of Indians rendered life in the fledgling colony miserable at best.[5] Few colonists survived the critical "seasoning" period where they accustomed themselves to Virginia's harsh environment.

A measure of prosperity arrived in the colony only in 1614. The colonist John Rolfe married Pocahontas, the daughter of Powhatan, who had been held captive at Jamestown for nearly a year. The marriage initiated a tenuous peace between natives and newcomers, bringing to a close over five years of attack and reprisal. Peace, however, brought new problems. In the wake of Rolfe's first successful attempt at the cultivation of tobacco, the earliest samples of which he shipped to England in March of 1614, Virginia's long-suffering settlers began eagerly and energetically to exploit the first profitable commodity produced in the colony. Englishmen fanned out along the James and York rivers to plant a crop with a voracious appetite for Indian land. Company attempts to curtail the colonists' devotion to tobacco never succeeded. In 1616, for example, only 2,300 pounds of tobacco had been shipped from Virginia. Two years later the total surpassed 41,000 pounds. By 1622, the figure had tripled, reaching more than 120,000 pounds.[6] Indians from the Powhatan Chiefdom found themselves driven from their traditional lands along the James River and its tributaries.

Angered by English settlers extracting their livelihood from Powhatan soil, alienated by the cultural arrogance of Englishmen determined to convert them,

3. Philip L. Barbour, ed., *The Jamestown Voyages Under the First Charter, 1606-1609*, 2 vols., *Works Issued by the Hakluyt Society*, Series II, vols. 136-137 (Cambridge: Cambridge University Press, 1969), 24.

4. Michael Leroy Oberg, *Dominion and Civility: English Imperialism and Native America, 1585-1685* (Ithaca, N.Y.: Cornell University Press, 1999), 50-54; James R. Perry, *The Formation of Society on Virginia's Eastern Shore, 1615-1655* (Chapel Hill: University of North Carolina Press, 1990), 11.

5. On the early years at Jamestown, see Edmund S. Morgan, *American Slavery, American Freedom: The Ordeal of Colonial Virginia* (New York: Norton, 1975), 71-91; Carville V. Earle, "Environment, Disease and Mortality in Early Virginia," in *The Chesapeake in the Seventeenth Century*, eds. Thad Tate and David C. Ammerman (New York: Norton, 1979), 96-125; Helen C. Rountree, *Pocahontas's People: The Powhatan Indians of Virginia Through Four Centuries* (Norman: University of Oklahoma Press, 1990); Oberg, *Dominion and Civility*, 54-59.

6. Irene W. D. Hecht, "The Virginia Colony, 1607-1640: A Study in Frontier Growth," (PhD diss., University of Washington, 1969), 356.

and threatened by the aggressive territorial expansion of English settlement, the Indians responded. Powhatan's successor, Opechancanough, and his allies descended upon the colonists in March of 1622 "like violent lightening" in a devastating surprise attack. In a matter of hours, 347 English men, women, and children lay dead, almost a third of the colony's population. The Indians, one chronicler reported, "basely and barbarously murthered, not sparing eyther age or sexe, man, woman or childe; so sodaine in their cruell execution, that few or none discerned the weapon or blow that brought them to destruction." Those settlements placed most recently in Powhatan territory suffered the heaviest casualties.[7]

Opechancanough's attack upon the English settlers doomed the Virginia Company of London's colonial venture. Throughout its existence Virginia had consumed thousands of English lives. That less than 1,000 English settlers lived in a colony to which over 7,000 had emigrated demonstrated clearly to officials at home in London that the Virginia Company could be considered nothing less than a failure.[8] No monarch, however irresponsible, could condone the shipment of his subjects across the Atlantic to nearly certain death. Accordingly, James I extinguished the charter of the Virginia Company of London and made Virginia a royal colony in 1624.[9]

James, and his successor, Charles I (r. 1625-1649), needed an orderly Virginia. Customs revenue on Chesapeake tobacco could grant the Stuart sovereigns a vital measure of independence from Parliament and, according to Sir John Harvey, who governed the colony from 1630 to 1635, make Virginia "as Sicilye to Rome, the Granarie to his Majesties Empire, especiallie to all our Northerne Plantations."[10] With energy, Harvey pursued a program of reform

---

7. Edward Waterhouse, *A Declaration of the State of the Colony and Affaires in Virginia, with a Relation of the Barbarous Massacre,* (London, 1622), 14, 17; Joseph Mead to Sir Martin Stuteville, 13 July 1622, in Robert C. Johnson, ed., "The Indian Massacre of 1622: Some Correspondence of the Rev. Joseph Mead," *Virginia Magazine of History and Biography,* 71 (October 1963), 408-409; Oberg, *Dominion and Civility,* 68-80; J. Frederick Fausz, "The Powhatan Uprising of 1622: A Historical Study of Ethnocentrism and Cultural Conflict" (PhD diss., College of William and Mary, 1977).
8. Morgan, *American Slavery, American Freedom,* 101-102.
9. Ibid.
10. Wilcomb E. Washburn, *Virginia Under Charles I and Cromwell, 1625-1660* (Williamsburg, VA: Jamestown 350th Anniversary Commemoration Committee, 1957), 17; Harvey to Secretary Dorchester, 2 April 1631, W. Noel Sainsbury, ed., *Calendar of State Papers, Colonial Series, America and West Indies, 1574-1660,* (London: Longman, Green, Longman and Roberts, 1860) 129 (hereafter *CSP Col, 1574-1660*); Harvey to Lords of the Council, 9 March 1632, in Robert C. Johnson, ed., "Virginia in 1632," *Virginia Magazine of History and Biography,* 65 (October 1957), 459. Harvey's policies in Virginia are consistent with the activities of Charles's appointees in Ireland at the same time in that, there too, the king worked to bring order and stability to the dark corners of the realm and more efficiency to the collection of customs revenue. See Kevin Sharpe,

designed to bring order and prosperity to Virginia. He tried to prevent contact between Indians and whites and the unnecessary and provocative encroachment of settlers upon Indian lands. To do so, he built a palisade across the peninsula between the James and York rivers. Indians would be kept out; Englishmen, and their livestock, kept in. Harvey also concluded a peace with the Powhatan Indians so that, by 1633, he could report to the Privy Council that "the country is on good termes with the Indians." Harvey also worked to diversify Virginia's economy and reduce the colonists' reliance upon tobacco. He implemented as well the county court system to improve the efficiency of colonial administration at the local level.[11]

Harvey met opposition from colonists who hoped to open native land to English settlement and exploitation, and who opposed his support, at the king's request, of Maryland's hated Catholics. In April of 1635, one year after the settlement of Maryland, the governor's opponents overthrew him. Harvey and his adversaries promoted distinctly different views of the Anglo-American frontier, and of the place of the frontier within the empire. This, more than any other factor, explains his ouster. Harvey tried to manage the colony's growth and prevent the colonial population from expanding onto Indian land. In his view, a peaceful Virginia meant a profitable colony for the Crown. During his tenure as governor, for instance, Harvey granted only 98 patents for land. During the interim tenure of John West from 1635 to 1636, by contrast, 309 patents were issued. With the "thrusting-out" of Governor John Harvey, frontier interests had prevailed in Virginia.[12]

The forces of frontier aggression that undermined Governor Harvey confounded as well Sir William Berkeley, who arrived in the colony as governor in February of 1642. Like Harvey, Berkeley worked to improve the colony's defenses and to prevent a scattered pattern of settlement. The governor's skills quickly faced a formidable test when, in April of 1644, Opechancanough led his second, and final, great rising against the English, killing 400 colonists in a matter of hours.

Berkeley successfully executed the resulting war against the Powhatans. By the spring of 1646 the governor recognized "the almost impossibility of a further revenge upon them." By the end of the summer of that year, Opechancanough had been captured and then killed, murdered in his jail cell by an Indian-hating soldier. The death of Opechancanough, coupled with the effectiveness of Berkeley's raids, led to the surrender of the Powhatan Indians to the English in October of 1646. Opechancanough's successor, Necotowance, acknowledged English dominion over the Powhatan chiefdoms. In return, the English agreed to defend

The Personal Rule of Charles I (New Haven, CT: Yale University Press, 1992), p. 126-129. I am indebted to Joseph Cope for bringing Sharpe's work to my attention.
11. "Governor Harvey's Report, (1624)," in "The Aspinwall Papers," *Collections of the Massachusetts Historical Society*, 4th ser., 9 (1871), 69-72; Washburn, *Virginia Under Charles I*, 5-6, 10.
12. See Nell Marion Nugent, comp., *Cavaliers and Pioneers: Abstracts of Virginia Land Patents and Grants, 1623-1800* (Richmond, VA: Dietz Print Company, 1934), 14-53; Oberg, *Dominion and Civility*, 177-179.

the Powhatans "against any rebells or other enemies whatsoever." Necotowance ceded to the English all lands between the York and James rivers, from the falls to the Chesapeake Bay, and acceded to the draconian English demand that "it shall be lawfull for any person to kill any such Indian" who entered the region. Berkeley recognized the Powhatans' right "to inhabit and hunt on the north-side of Yorke River, without any interruption from the English."[13]

The agreement of 1646, bringing to a close what some historians have called the "Third Anglo-Powhatan War," would provide the foundation for Berkeley's Indian policy for the next three decades.[14] The governor recognized that Opechancanough's rising had been provoked by English territorial aggression, and that no order could exist along the colony's frontiers unless Indians were guaranteed possession of their lands free from English interference. For the health of both colony and empire, Berkeley knew he must control the English frontier population.

This was, indeed, no easy task. Over the course of the quarter century following the royalization of Virginia, living conditions in the colony slowly, but steadily, improved. A continuous rise in the European demand for tobacco, despite falling prices, brought increased wealth to Virginia, which in turn encouraged considerable immigration. Some of these newcomers were men of means, the younger sons of English gentry and well-to-do urban families, seeking to earn a living in the production and marketing of tobacco. More of the immigrants, however, arrived as indentured servants: young men and women attracted to the Chesapeake by the hope of someday acquiring land, servants, and a plantation of their own.[15] In the middle decades of the century, those who managed to survive their terms of servitude usually succeeded in establishing themselves as small-scale tobacco farmers.[16] But in order to do so, they needed land. And as the population of Virginia grew, approaching 25,000 by 1660,

13. Robert Beverley, *The History of the Present State of Virginia,* ed. Louis B. Wright (Chapel Hill: University of North Carolina Press, 1947), 63; Grand Assembly of Virginia to the House of Commons, 17 March 1646, in *Proceedings and Debates of the British Parliaments Respecting North America,* ed. Leo Francis Stock, 2 vols. (Washington, D.C.: Carnegie Foundation, 1924), 1: 182.

14. The first Anglo-Powhatan war lasted from 1609 until 1614. The second commenced with the attack in 1622, and lasted intermittently until 1633. See Rountree, *Pocahontas's People,* 84-87; J. Frederick Fausz, "An Abundance of Blood Shed on Both Sides: England's First Indian War, 1609-1614," *Virginia Magazine of History and Biography,* 98 (January 1990), 3-56.

15. See James Horn, *Adapting to a New World: English Society in the Seventeenth Century Chesapeake* (Chapel Hill: University of North Carolina Press, 1994), 24-31; Jack P. Greene, *Pursuits of Happiness: The Social Development of Early Modern British Colonies and the Formation of American Culture* (Chapel Hill: University of North Carolina Press, 1988).

16. Russell Menard, "From Servant to Freeholder: Status Mobility and Property Accumulation in Seventeenth-Century Maryland," *William and Mary Quarterly,* 3d ser., 30 (January 1973), 37-64.

Berkeley recognized that land hunger and soil exhaustion could threaten frontier order. Tobacco was a hard crop on the land, quickly robbing the soil of its nutrients. After three years, on average, a planter would require new soil. Old tobacco fields might support the cultivation of corn, but only for an additional three years, and then the land would have to lie fallow for two decades before it regained its fertility.[17] Settlers moved often, then, constantly pressing upon Indian land, constantly threatening native subsistence patterns and, consequently, endangering the peace of the king's Old Dominion.

Berkeley tried to ease tensions wherever possible between Indians and Englishmen. The governor recognized, for instance, that the enslavement of tributary Indians, those remnants of the Powhatan chiefdom who had accepted English dominion in 1646, would not conduce to the safety and prosperity of the colony. He called upon the colony's assembly, the House of Burgesses, to enact legislation prohibiting the "theft" of Indian children and requiring that those apprenticed voluntarily to the English not be sold, or treated, like slaves. Berkeley also called for the repeal of that provision in the 1646 agreement which permitted English settlers to kill Indians who entered the English reserve between the James and York rivers. He feared that the colony would suffer "through the Rashness and unadvicedness of Divers persons whoe by such Act Rather vindicate some private mallice, then provide for theire owne, or the Publick Indempnitye."[18]

Berkeley directed his Indian policy toward meeting the difficult problems posed by expanding and aggressive English settlements. He hoped to relieve the nearly constant tension and violence which had characterized the Virginia frontier. Despite his efforts, however, conflict and competition between natives and newcomers over access to and control of the land nearly was inevitable. English planters, in general, chose sites for tobacco plantations with three criteria in mind. They needed navigable water to transport the crop to market. They needed freshwater springs for drinking water. Finally, they would locate the ideal tobacco plantation on high-quality silty and sandy loam soils suitable for hoe cultivation. Similar considerations were involved in the selection of sites for Powhatan villages. Settlers and Indians thus grappled for control of identical tracts of land that they employed in different and incompatible ways.[19]

---

17. Lois Green Carr, "Rural Settlements in the Seventeenth Century Chesapeake," in *Settlements in the Americas: Cross-Cultural Perspectives*, ed. Ralph Bennett (Newark: University of Delaware Press, 1993), 178.

18. Warren M. Billings, ed., "Some Acts Not In Hening's Statutes: The Acts of Assembly, April 1652, November 1652, and July 1653," *Virginia Magazine of History and Biography*, 83 (January 1975), 64.

19. Stephen R. Potter, *Commoners, Tribute and Chiefs: The Development of Algonquian Culture in the Potomac Valley* (Charlottesville: University Press of Virginia, 1993), 220-221. Also useful on this point is Lewis Binford, *Cultural Diversity among Aboriginal Cultures of Coastal Virginia and North Carolina* (New York: Garland, 1991); Timothy Silver, *A New Face on the Countryside: Indians, Colonists and Slaves in the South Atlantic Forests, 1500-1800* (Cambridge: Cambridge University Press, 1990).

Sir William Berkeley's surrender of the government of Virginia in the spring of 1652 was a product of Puritan victories in the English Civil War. Berkeley remained in the colony at his plantation at Green Spring and watched as the Commonwealth regime that replaced him largely continued his policies and confronted challenges similar to those he had faced. When a respectful assembly recalled him in 1660, however, a few months before Charles II was restored to the throne of England, Berkeley renewed his search for stability and order in the king's Old Dominion.

II

Early in 1662, the Virginia assembly, under the direction of Berkeley's lieutenant, Francis Moryson, completed a codification of the colony's laws. Under the new code, according to one contemporary, "the Church of England was confirmed the established Religion, the Charge of Government sustain'd, Trade and Manufactures were encouraged, a Town projected, and all the Indian Affairs settled."[20]

Indeed, much of the new code attempted to solve the colony's long-standing problem of Indian-white relations. Berkeley and Moryson recognized that "the mutuall discontents, complaints, jealousies, and feares of English and Indian proceed chiefly from the violent intrusions of diverse English made into their lands." Consequently, both sides suffered injury, and a cycle of "reports and rumours are spread of the hostile intentions of each to the other, tending infinitely to the disturbance of the peace of his majestys country." The 1662 enactment reveals clearly Virginians seeking to maintain order over an aggressively expanding and, at times, tumultuous colonial frontier.[21]

Earlier "laws prohibiting the purchase of any Indians lands," the codification read, were "made fruitles and ineffectuall" because it was as "easy to affright [the Indians] to a publique as well as a private acknowledgement" of the sale. "Corrupt interpreters" added "to this mischiefe by rendering [the Indians] willing to surrender when indeed they intended to have received a confirmation of their owne rights, and redresse of their wrong." Allowing these abuses to continue would involve the colony in "an inevitable and destructive warre." The governor, council, and assembly, all of whom approved the codification, thus

---

20. Beverley, *History and Present State of Virginia*, 66. The House of Burgesses had been created by the Virginia Company of London in 1619, part of a program of administrative reforms designed to improve the quality of life in the colony, encourage emigration to Virginia, and bring profits to investors. The burgesses were only one part of the Virginia assembly, which after 1643 included the governor, the governor's council, and the House of Burgesses. I am indebted to Warren Billings for making this point clear to me.

21. William Waller Hening, ed., *The Statutes at Large; Being a Collection of All the Laws from the First Session of the Legislature in the Year 1619*, 2nd ed., vol. 2 (Richmond, VA: R & W & G Bartow, 1823), 138.

declared that "for the future noe Indian king or other upon any pretence alien and sell, nor noe English for any cause or consideration whatsoever purchase or buy any tract or parcell of land now justly claymed or actually possest by any Indian or Indians whatsoever; all such bargaines and sales hereafter made or pretended to be made being hereby declared invalid, voyd and null, any acknowledgement, surrender, law or custome formerly used to the contrary notwithstanding; and further that the Indians properties of their goods be hereby assured and confirmed to them, and their persons soe secured that whoever shall defraud or take from them their goods and doe hurt and injury to their persons shall make such satisfaction and suffer such punishment as the laws of England or this country doe inflict, if the same had bine done to an Englishman."[22]

The body of laws required that Englishmen settled on Indian land without proof of title vacate their claims. The new laws empowered the governor to appoint "such uninterested persons as he shall think fitt, to enquire into and examine the severall claimes made to any part of our neighboring Indians land." Englishmen settled near Indian villages, moreover, must "helpe the Indians to fence in a corne field proportionable to the number of persons the said Indian towne doth consist off." The laws allowed unarmed Indians to fish and to gather shellfish and wild fruits for "the better reliefe of the poor Indians whome the seating of the English hath forced from their wonted conveniences," a reflection of the environmental strain placed upon native villagers by expanding English settlements. Finally, the body of laws outlawed acts of vigilante justice committed upon Indians.[23]

In the years following the codification Berkeley continued to call upon the House of Burgesses to enact legislation designed to prevent disorder along the frontier. The assembly required that tributary Indians, the remnants of Powhatan's chiefdom, assist in the apprehension of natives who had committed crimes against Englishmen, an attempt on the governor's part to secure justice quickly while eliminating the incentive for vengeful frontiersmen to commit bloody acts of vigilantism. The assembly strictly prohibited the sale of arms to Indians, and the assembly, as well, attempted to prevent a vulnerable pattern of settlement by requiring that no "frontier plantations" be seated unless the party included "fowre able hands well armed."[24]

Sir William Berkeley wanted peaceful relations with Virginia's Indians. He recognized that the endemic disorder he faced on the colony's frontiers resulted primarily from English pressure on Indian land, and that frontier aggression could disrupt both economic activity on his side of the Atlantic and the king's customs revenue on the other. The governor recognized as well that a disorderly frontier reduced the likelihood that any Indians would convert to Christianity.[25]

---

22. Ibid., 138-139.

23 Ibid., 139-141, 155-156; Oberg, *Dominion and Civility*, 188-189.

24. Hening, ed., *Statutes*, 2: 209, 215, 218-219, 237.

25. Wilcomb Washburn, *The Governor and the Rebel: A History of Bacon's Rebellion* (Chapel Hill: University of North Carolina Press, 1957), 160-162; On Christianity, see "Virginia's Cure," in *Tracts and Other Papers Relating Principally to the Origin, Settle-*

The governor believed strongly in his ability to govern the Virginia frontier, and he remained a firm believer in the colony's potential. With a properly diversified economy, Berkeley believed that Virginia could play a vital role in securing the prosperity of the Restoration Empire. Like the king, Berkeley hoped the settlers would gather in towns. There, artisans could establish their crafts and find a market for their wares. A population settled in towns would require food and give planters an economic incentive to plant corn and grain for townsfolk. Berkeley, moreover, would encourage those willing to try their hands at iron-working, glass-making, spinning and weaving, raising silkworms, and building ships. He would insulate settlers from the vagaries of an unpredictable tobacco market, while increasing the profitability of tobacco by reducing the supply.[26]

Berkeley failed, however, to reduce the colonists' devotion to tobacco culture. Between 1637 and 1640, an average of 1,395,063 pounds of tobacco had been exported annually to England. In 1669, that figure exceeded nine million pounds. Ever since the 1630s, frontier barons had turned their attention towards the accumulation of large tracts of land for speculation and tobacco culture. Berkeley had proposed in 1663 that taxes be levied on this land in an attempt to discourage the engrossment of large tracts for speculation, as well as to relieve pressure on Indian fields and hunting grounds, but even in this he failed to overcome the opposition of frontier planters. Plans to orchestrate, along with Maryland, a one-year moratorium on tobacco planting, designed to increase demand and prices for the crop, also came to nothing.[27]

Overproduction of tobacco ensured that the price offered for the crop in English ports would remain low. Restrictions on colonial trade passed under both the Commonwealth and the restored monarchy made matters worse. The Navigation Acts, which required that colonists ship their goods to English ports aboard English vessels with English crews, eliminated legal opportunities for English planters to avoid low prices and high customs duties at home by selling their produce directly to the Dutch. Designed to ensure that the wealth of the colonies enriched only the empire, the Navigation Acts forced Virginians to dump their tobacco in a glutted English market. [28]

ment, and Progress of the Colonies in North America, vol. 3, ed. Peter Force (Washington D. C., W. Q. Force, 1836), 15, 7.

26. Morgan, *American Slavery, American Freedom*, 187-188; John C. Rainbolt, *From Prescription to Persuasion: Manipulation of Eighteenth Century Virginia Economy* (Port Washington, NY: Kennikat Press, 1971), 6.

27. Lewis Cecil Gray, *History of Agriculture in the Southern United States to 1860*, (Washington, DC: The Carnegie Institution of Washington, 1933), 1: 213; Jon Kukla, "Order and Chaos in Early America: Political and Social Stability in Pre-Restoration Virginia," *American Historical Review*, 90 (April 1985), 285; Morgan, *American Slavery, American Freedom*, 193.

28. Warren M. Billings, John E. Selby, and Thad W. Tate, *Colonial Virginia: A History* (White Plains, NY: KTO Press, 1986), 78-79.

War with the Dutch from 1664 to 1667, and again from 1672 to 1674, further damaged the tobacco trade, as tobacco ships either were captured on the high seas, converted to military use in England, or burned at anchor in Virginia by Dutch raiders. The reduction in the size of the fleet drove up shipping costs, while the produce of many planters rotted at dockside for want of transport. Crown policies during the war did not help. Charles II and his councilors ordered Berkeley to build an expensive fort at Point Comfort, at the mouth of the James River. The governor argued unsuccessfully that such a fort was useless, because "the Entrance into the Province is so large that any enemys ship may ride out of all possible danger to the greatest cannon in the world." Berkeley's prediction proved correct when, in July of 1763, a small Dutch fleet destroyed the tobacco ships lying at anchor in the James River.[29]

The king's grant of the Northern Neck in 1663 to a number of investors, and his proprietary grant of all the colony's public lands to Lords Culpeper and Arlington in 1674, further added to Virginia's considerable fiscal woes. The two grants threw land titles throughout the colony into confusion and forced Berkeley to levy a tax to send "agents to addresse the King to vacate those Grants." Berkeley thus faced the humiliation of having to levy taxes to buy back, from court favorites, the land he governed in the king's name.[30]

Against this backdrop of economic crisis, Virginia began to acquire a new social structure. Throughout the seventeenth century, the number of English servants surviving their terms of servitude in the colony increased. As they became free, they looked for land of their own. The growing ranks of freedmen found it increasingly difficult to obtain land suitable for tobacco culture that had not already been claimed, so they moved to the frontiers, where they competed with Indians for control of the land.[31]

Life here was difficult. While some small farmers, through a combination of luck and determination, might join the ranks of wealthy planters, for the vast majority, profits were meager. James Horn has pointed out that "monotonous, hard physical labor in the fields year after year was the lot of most men and many women who settled in Maryland and Virginia during the seventeenth century." Few of the former servants, Horn notes, would have wished to return to the poverty of England. Still, the economic independence they acquired was often tenuous at best.[32] In Gloucester County in the second half of the seventeenth century, for instance, less than 20% of those individuals whose initial land patents were for less than 200 acres managed to obtain additional land in the county. Of those who patented between 200 and 399 acres, only about one

29. Berkeley and Council in Virginia to Secretary Lord Arlington, 13 July 1666, *Calendar of State Papers, Colonial Series, America and West Indies, 1661-1668*, ed. W. Noel Sainsbury (London: Longman, Green, Longman and Roberts, 1880), 396.

30. Beverley, *History and Present State of Virginia*, 75; Morgan, *American Slavery, American Freedom*, 245; Sister Jean de Lourdes Leonard, "Operation Checkmate: The Birth and Death of a Virginia Blueprint for Progress," *William and Mary Quarterly*, 3d ser., 24 (January 1967), 69-71.

31. Morgan, *American Slavery, American Freedom*, 218-232.

32. Horn, *Adapting to a New World*, 292.

quarter obtained additional holdings.[33] The increase in taxation to pay for useless forts and castles, the king's careless generosity, and the collapse of tobacco prices at home caught small farmers on the frontier in a mounting cycle of debt, which forced many of them back into the tenantry or servitude they had hoped to escape.[34] The tax burden alone amounted to a figure somewhere between a quarter and a half of the average planter's income, making living even at a subsistence level difficult. With more stringent trade regulations, falling tobacco prices, and the elimination of the Dutch as an alternative to crushing English customs duties, the future for Virginia's tobacco planters looked bleak.[35]

Governor Berkeley, who operated during these turbulent years with little effective imperial oversight, bore the brunt of the growing popular discontent. Henry Norwood, a loyal supporter of the Crown and Virginia's treasurer, as early as 1667 could complain of "extream and grievous taxes" that colonists "ly under Continually and yet the tobbaccoes that are Raised not Expended to the desired end." Few of Virginia's former servants, it appears, respected the governor. The political system seemed unresponsive to the needs of ordinary settlers. Since 1661, no election had been held for seats in the House of Burgesses. The governor maintained the same group in power, periodically proroguing the assembly when it suited his needs. This assembly worked with the governor to exclude the heavily-taxed former servants from power. In 1670, the Burgesses voted to disfranchise those "who having little interest in the country, doe oftner make tumults at a election to the disturbance of his majesties peace, then by their discretions in their votes provide for the conservation thereof, by making choice of persons fitly qualifyed for the discharge of soe greate a trust." Thereafter only property-holders were entitled to vote.[36] Forts that brought no security; a closed provincial elite headed, in the eyes of aspiring planters, by a corrupt and avaricious governor intent upon engrossing the wealth of men of moderate and limited means; a political system unresponsive to local needs; a general constriction in opportunity—all served to weaken Berkeley's position in the colony at a time when he needed badly the support of the people.[37]

As the colony sunk into social and economic turmoil, the English failed to notice changes occurring on the other side of the frontier. Ever since the final defeat of Opechancanough in 1646, the Indian groups scattered along the peripheries of English settlement—members of the component bands that once had constituted Powhatan's chiefdom—were marginalized, as English settlement

33. Rainbolt, *From Prescription to Persuasion*, 17.

34. Morgan, *American Slavery, American Freedom*, 227.

35. Stephen Saunders Webb, *1676: The End of American Independence* (New York: Knopf, 1984), 19; Rainbolt, *From Prescription to Persuasion*, 18.

36. Hening, ed., *Statutes*, 2: 280.

37. Richard L. Morton, *Colonial Virginia* (Chapel Hill: University of North Carolina Press, 1960), 219-220; Billings, Selby and Tate, *Colonial Virginia*, 79-81; Horn, *Adapting to a New World*, 373-374.

advanced up the rivers. Some, by 1660 at least, were serving as slaves for life. [38]
Even though growing numbers of natives slowly were becoming Anglicized as
English settlements surrounded their own, the intensification of competition for
control of land on the frontier produced increasingly harsh assessments of Indian
character.[39] At the same time other tribes, stronger than the Powhatan remnants,
began moving into the region, refugees fleeing Iroquois aggression. The strongest of these groups, the Susquehannocks, by the mid-1670s had nowhere else to
go, caught in a vise between the Maryland English, the Virginia frontier, and the
Iroquois.[40] The Susquehannocks, and another powerful Potomac Valley group
known as the Doegs, had no choice but to resist increasing frontier pressure
upon their lands. At stake was their survival as autonomous peoples.

By the middle of the 1670s the Susquehannocks had taken up residence
along the Potomac, where they settled on the north side of the river in an abandoned fort well below the falls. Here they found themselves in close quarters
with frontiersmen from Maryland and Virginia. These settlers would pressure
the Susquehannocks as they had pressed the Powhatans before them. The results
would devastate both Indian and white societies in Virginia.[41]

III

The immediate origins of Bacon's Rebellion lay along Virginia's Potomac frontier. In July of 1675, "certaine Doegs & Susquehanok Indians on the Maryland
side" of the river "stole" some hogs from Thomas Mathew, a Northern Neck
planter who had "abused and cheated them, in not paying for such Indian trucke
as he had formerly bought of them." Mathew gathered together a small force,
pursued the responsible Indians across the river, and killed several in a ham-
fisted effort to reclaim his livestock. To the Doegs and Susquehannocks, this
was merely one more example of how Mathew treated his neighbors, and to
retaliate, a Doeg "Warr Capt. with some Indians came over to Potomake and
kill'd two of Mathews his servants, and came also a second time and kill'd his
sonne."[42]

Upon learning of the Doeg attack, local militia forces under the command
of Giles Brent and George Mason set off in pursuit of the killers. Both Brent and
Mason had a long history of handling Indians roughly, and this time would be
no different. At a fork in the trail, Brent and Mason split their forces. Within a
mile, Brent stumbled across a Doeg village. He called the Indians to parley. The
Doeg leader "came Trembling forth and would have fled" had not Brent grasped
his scalplock. The Doeg leader denied any knowledge of the attack on Mathew's
farm. When the Doeg leader slipped free from Brent's grasp, the militia leader

38. Hening, ed., *Statutes*, 2: 155; W. Stitt Robinson, Jr., "Tributary Indians in Colonial
Virginia," *Virginia Magazine of History and Biography*, 67 (January 1959), 49-64.
39. Rountree, *Pocahontas's People*, 89.
40. Webb, *1676*, 4.
41. Oberg, *Dominion and Civility*, 194-198.
42. British Public Record Office, Kew, England, Colonial Office: America and West
Indies 5, Original Correspondence, 1606-1807, CO 5/1371, 188 (VCRP).

shot and killed him. A brief but bloody firefight ensued which left another ten Indians dead. Meanwhile, the noise of the gunfire "awakened the Indians in the Cabin which Coll: Mason had Encompassed." When the surprised Indians rushed out, the frontiersmen opened fire, killing fourteen Susquehannocks before Mason realized that he had the wrong Indians.[43]

With confusing reports flowing in from the Northern Neck, Berkeley quickly ordered John Washington and Isaac Allerton to undertake "a full & thorough inquisition . . . of ye True Causes of ye severall Murthers & Spoyles & by what Nation or Nations donne." After completing their investigation, Berkeley ordered Washington and Allerton to "demand satisfaction and take such further course in this Exegency as shall be thought requisite and necessary."[44]

Instead of investigating, Washington, Allerton, and the militia forces they led joined late in September with a force from Maryland. The Doegs by this time had fled into the backcountry, but the Susquehannocks had gathered themselves in their Potomac fortress. Washington and Allerton resolved to lay siege to the Susquehannock stronghold, which they lacked the firepower to knock down. Five Susquehannock headmen came out to parley with the English. The militia leaders, in one of the all-too-common demonstrations of stupidity and viciousness which characterized life along the early Anglo-Indian frontier, "caused the [Indian] Comissioners braines to be knock'd out," an action "being Diametricall to the Law of Arms."[45]

Frontier planters would pay for this treachery with their lives. With the militia conducting "a negligent siege," the entire native garrison escaped from the fortress in mid-October and then "resolved to imploy there liberty in avenging their Commissioneres blood, which they speedily effected in the death of sixty inosscent soules." Then, "forsaking Maryland," the Susquehannocks crossed the Potomac and "thence over the heads of Rappahannock and York Rivers, killing whom they found on the upmost Plantations untill they came to the Head of James River, where . . . they Slew Mr. Bacon's Overseer whom He much Loved, and one of his Servants, whose Blood Hee Vowed to Revenge if possible."[46] Having avenged their losses, the Susquehannocks sent messengers to Governor Berkeley offering to conclude a peace. Berkeley refused to treat with them. The

43. C.O. 5/1371, 188 (VCRP); "Mathew's Narrative," in *Narratives of the Insurrections, 1675-1690*, ed. Charles M. Andrews (New York: Charles Scribner's Sons, 1915), 17.
44. Westmoreland County Records, Deeds and Wills, fol. 232, printed in the *William and Mary Quarterly*, 1ˢᵗ ser., 4 (1895-1896), 86.
45. "The History of Bacon's and Ingram's Rebellion," in *Narratives*, ed. Andrews, 47-48; See also "Mathew's Narrative," *Ibid.*, 18-19; Westmoreland County Deeds and Wills, 1665-1677, fol. 288, printed in *William and Mary Quarterly*, 1ˢᵗ ser., 2 (1893-1894), 39-40.
46. "Mathew's Narrative," in *Narratives*, ed. Andrews, 19-20; "Bacon's and Ingram's Rebellion," *Ibid.*, 48-49.

Susquehannocks then gradually withdrew in small numbers into the backcountry.[47]

Berkeley faced enormous demands to avenge his colony's losses. He commissioned his lieutenant governor, Sir Henry Chicheley, to raise troops against "the Murtherers." Before the troops marched, however, Berkeley thought better, countermanded his order, and disbanded the force. Frontier planters, he ordered, should now draw together, ten men in a house, in order to defend themselves from Indian attack. They were on their own. The recall of Chicheley stunned the colony, angered a frontier population who had hoped that help was on its way, and further damaged the governor's credibility. Berkeley appeared, at best, indecisive, and at worst, a coward.[48]

The Indian warfare on Virginia's frontier held for Berkeley a frightening prospect. The governor believed that because of King Philip's War to the north "the New England men will not recover their wealth and Townes they have lost this twenty coming yeares." One hundred miles of territory had been devastated in New England, and many towns burned, for want of secure defenses along the frontier. New Englanders had added to their problems, in Berkeley's view, by marching out recklessly in search of Indians, falling victim in due course to well-planned Indian ambushes. Berkeley thought it possible that "the beginning of the New England troubles were the cause of ours," and that he faced, with the New Englanders, a massive Indian uprising aimed at eliminating the English presence in North America, and that threatened the very existence of the king's new world possessions.[49]

Berkeley's own experience in crushing Opechancanough's final uprising in the 1640s, along with the ominous prospect posed by the current crisis in New England, militated against an offensive strategy. Berkeley proposed to the House of Burgesses a set of measures designed to remove control of the war from the hands of thugs like Brent, Mason, and Washington, to secure the allegiance of the tributary Indians, and to construct a series of forts at the heads of the major rivers. Five hundred men would man the forts, with troops constantly ranging between them in search of natives. In order to prevent another disaster like Mason's and Brent's attack, the assembly ordered that no Englishman attack any "fort, habitations, or number of the enemy settled or fortifyed" without permission from the governor.[50]

47. "Bacon's and Ingram's Rebellion," in *Narratives*, ed. Andrews, 49.

48. C.O. 5/1371, 189 (VCRP); Washburn, *Governor and the Rebel*, 25-26.

49. Berkeley to Secretary of State Joseph Williamson, 1 April 1676, quoted in the *Virginia Magazine of History and Biography*, 20 (1912), 245-246; Berkeley to Mr. Ludwell, 1 April 1676, C.O. 1/36, 67-68 (VCRP); Washburn, *Governor and the Rebel*, 25-26. On King Philip's War, see Douglas Edward Leach, *Flintlock and Tomahawk: New England in King Philip's War* (New York: Norton, 1958); Webb, *1676*, 221-244; Oberg, *Dominion and Civility*, 113-173. For an intellectual history of the consequences of King Philip's War, see Jill Lepore, *The Name of War: King Philip's War and the Origins of American Identity* (New York: Knopf, 1998).

50. Hening, ed., *Statutes*, 2: 327, 330-332; Papers Relating to the American Colonies, 1657-1676, Egerton MSS 2395, fol. 539 (VCRP).

Western settlers found little to their liking in the governor's plan. The scattered forts, Berkeley's opponents argued, could not stop Indian incursions and the enemy, after learning "where these Mouse-traps were sett, and for what purpose," would bypass them, "which they might easily enough do, without any detriment to theire designes." For a population already overburdened with taxes, the additional levies required to support construction of the forts seemed like a useless waste of money, or worse, a "Designe of the Grandees to engrosse all their Tobacco into their owne hands." Thus at a time when Berkeley most needed the support of the frontier population, "the sense of this oppression and the dread of a common approaching calamity made the giddy-headed multitude madd, and precipitated them upon that rash overture of Running out upon the Indians themselves."[51]

Berkeley received petitions from the frontier counties in the spring of 1676, requesting commissions to attack the Indians. "The poore distressed subjects in the upper parts of the James River" asked the governor to allow them to appoint officers and "to take armes in defence of our lives and estates which without speedy prevention lie liable to the Injury of such insulting enimmies."[52] Nathaniel Bacon shared these concerns.

We know disappointingly little about the man who would lead Virginia into rebellion. According to one partisan account, Nathaniel Bacon was "indifferent tall but slender, blackhair'd and of an ominous, pensive, melancholly Aspect, of a pestilent and prevalent logical discourse tending to athiesme in most companyes." He was "not given to much talke, or to make suddaine replyes, of a most imperious and dangerous hidden Pride of heart, despising the wisest of his neighbours for their Ignorance, and very ambitious and arrogant."[53] He was in his mid-20s when he came to Virginia, shipped to the plantations after having "broken into some extravagancies" involving an attempt to defraud a neighboring youth of part of his inheritance. A cousin both to Governor Berkeley and Nathaniel Bacon, Sr., one of the king's councilors in Virginia, Bacon was honored with appointment to the governor's council. He received, as well, ample assistance in establishing himself at "Curles," a plantation just east of the fall

51. "Bacon's and Ingram's Rebellion," in *Narratives*, ed. Andrews, 50; C.O. 5/1371, 189 (VCRP); Berkeley and Council to Charles II, 25 January 1676, Letters and Papers Concerning American Plantations, 1 June 1676–7 October 1676, C.O. 1/37, 33 (VCRP). For defenses of Berkeley's policies see the Answer of Alexander Culpeper to the Objections Against Sir William Berkeley, 4 December 1677, Entry Book of Letters, Commissions, Instructions, Citations, Warrants, Patents and Grants Concerning Virginia, and Especially the Rebellion There of Nathaniel Bacon, 1675-1682, C.O. 5/1355, 230-239 (VCRP); William Sherwood to Joseph Williamson, 1 June 1676, in *Virginia Magazine of History and Biography*, 1 (1893), 168-169; and especially, Washburn, *Governor and the Rebel*, 31-32.
52. Letters and Papers Concerning American Plantations, 7 March 1675/6-30 May 1676, C.O. 1/36, fol. 139, (VCRP).
53. Washburn, *Governor and the Rebel*, 18.

line along the James River. There he engaged himself in planting and, with the governor's license, trading with neighboring Indians.[54]

We know little else. As historian Warren Billings wrote, "there are no Bacon pictures, no Bacon archive, no Bacon diaries: only fragments remain." These scraps, however, have been "pliant enough to shape him into the patriot who struck the first blow for American Independence, into the Indian-hating opportunist who ruined the reputation of a popular governor, or into someone else." The commissioners who traveled to Virginia to put down the rebellion knew nothing firsthand about Governor Berkeley's opponent.[55]

We do know that in April of 1676 Bacon had gathered with several of his friends at his plantation in Henrico County to drink and make "the Sadnesse of the times their discourse." These men persuaded Bacon to cross the James into Charles City County "to goe over and see" the volunteers then gathering for a march against the Susquehannocks. The backcountry settlers, afraid of the Indians, implored Bacon, one of the most prominent men along the James, to "becom there Guardian Angle, to protect them from the cruilties of the Indians."[56]

Bacon's supporters tried to obtain a commission for him, but the governor refused. Bacon, the governor's supporters argued, simply had no business criticizing Berkeley's policies. The governor advised Bacon against becoming a mutineer, and when Bacon refused to abandon his preparations for a campaign against the Indians, Berkeley proclaimed him a rebel on May 10. The next day Berkeley dissolved the assembly, which had sat for fourteen years, and called for new elections. The new burgesses, he said, would deal with the Indian problem and air any grievances against his administration. Berkeley promised that if the policies pursued by his administration were the principal source of discontent in the colony, he would petition the king to recall him from service in Virginia.[57]

By this point, Bacon already had commenced his march against the Indians. He had little interest in engaging the powerful Susquehannocks and Doegs. Instead, he chased the Pamunkeys, one of the constituent nations of the Powhatan Chiefdom and tributaries of the colony since 1646, into the Dragon Swamp. The Pamunkeys were no threat to the English, but Bacon's forces, "coveting the good land" they occupied, attacked them anyway. Bacon and his rebel force next came to the village of the Occaneechees, "a nation . . . who were ever friends to the English and seated in an Island very well-fortified by nature."[58]

Aggressive and energetic traders, and accustomed to dealing with Englishmen, the Occaneechees likely expected to participate in exchange with the rebels. The Occaneechee *weroance*, or leader, Posseclay, fed Bacon's men and

---

54. Ibid., 17-18.

55. Billings, Selby and Tate, *Colonial Virginia*, 85.

56. "Commissioners' Narrative," in *Narratives*, ed. Andrews, 123..

57. William Sherwood to Joseph Williamson, 1 June 1676, C.O. 1/37, 1 (VCRP); Egerton MSS 2395, 546 (VCRP).

58. William Berkeley to Sir Henry Coventry, 2 February 1677, in Wilcomb E. Washburn, ed., "Sir William Berkeley's 'A History of Our Miseries,'" *William and Mary Quarterly*, 3d ser., 14 (July 1957), 407; Washburn, *Governor and the Rebel*, 37.

then offered to attack, for the rebels, a group of Susquehannocks encamped 20 miles from the village. The Occaneechees returned from the attack victorious, and they brought "in Divers prisoners most which the Indians Knockt in the head in the sight and instance of the Inglish." With the prisoners, the Occaneechees also brought "in a considerable quantity of beavor and a considerable quantity of Beads the only Indian Coyne."[59] Bacon claimed the treasure, to which "the Indians modestly replied that . . . they had got it with the hazard of their lives and that they knew not how any one besides themselves could pretend any title to it." The rebels opened fire. "About 50 Indians were blown up in their Cabins, [and] some killed in the fort" into which the Occaneechees retired. Now clearly aware of Bacon's manners in treating with Indians, the Occaneechees fought back fiercely. With "Night approaching," the rebels withdrew, "leaveing a drum and some men behinde and soe Mr. Bacon and those of his men which were left, retired in a disorderly manner, Eleven of his Company being killed, and severall mortally wounded."[60]

Bacon's attack upon the Occaneechess and Pamunkeys, the governor's supporters believed, destroyed Berkeley's Indian policy. Because of Bacon, Philip Ludwell wrote, "we have not now, that we know of, hardly 100 friend Indians on all our Borders Round, & at least 1500 enemies more than wee needed to have had." Bacon's activity exhausted Berkeley, throwing the aged governor into such fits of despondency and frustration that he could write, in mid-May, "to spare none that has the name of an Indian for they are now all our enemies." Two days before the convening of the new assembly in June, Berkeley informed Secretary of State Henry Coventry "that I am not able to support my selfe at this Age six months longer and therefore on my Knees I beg his sacred majesty would send a more Vigorous Governor."[61]

Supporters of Nathaniel Bacon packed the new assembly that gathered in Jamestown on June 5, 1676. Like the rebel, these men feared the prospect of Indian attack and resented exorbitant taxes that bought them no protection. Bacon himself had been elected as burgess from Henrico County, though he did not come to claim his seat and challenge openly the governor's proclamation from the previous month. He did sneak into town the night of the sixth, however, to confer with supporters. He was captured the next morning. On bended knee, he admitted his errors and begged Berkeley for a pardon. Aware that perhaps as

59. Washburn, ed., "Sir William Berkeley," 407. For Occaneechee trade activities, see H. Trawick Ward and R. P. Stephen Davis, Jr., "The Archaeology of the Historic Occaneechi Indians," *Southern Indian Studies*, 36-37 (1988), 1-128.

60. "Virginia's Deploured Condition," in "The Aspinwall Papers," 167.

61. Ludwell to Joseph Williamson, 28 June 1676, in *Virginia Magazine of History and Biography*, 1 (1893), 180; Berkeley to Thomas Goodrich, 15 May 1676, quoted in Morgan, *American Slavery, American Freedom*, 260; Berkeley to Henry Coventry, 3 June 1676, quoted in *The Old Dominion in the Seventeenth Century: A Documentary History of Virginia, 1606-1689*, ed. Warren M. Billings (Chapel Hill: University of North Carolina Press, 1975), 272.

many as 2,000 of Bacon's well-armed supporters had entered the town, "armed and resolved to rescue him out of our hands," the governor prudently pardoned Bacon, and on the tenth restored him to the council. Four days later, Bacon left town.[62]

During Bacon's absence, Berkeley lectured the burgesses on the foolishness of attacking indiscriminately all Indians. The assembly conceded that a distinction may exist between Indian enemies and Indian friends, but they allowed the governor little else. "Forasmuch as wee are not altogether satisfied that all Indians are combined against us, and are our enemies," and that "wee are taught as well by the rules of our sacred religion, as those of humanitie, that we ought not to involve the innocent with the guiltie," the assembly declared "that all such Indians shall be accounted and prosecuted as enemies that either already have, or hereafter shall forsake theire usuall and accustomed dwelling townes without licence obtained first from the honourable governor . . . as alsoe such indians as shall refuse upon demand to deliver up into the hands of the English all such armes and ammunition of what kind or nature soever." Indians who fled from armed Englishmen, along with Indians who resisted their English assailants, together were accounted enemies by the June Assembly.[63]

Other than an act by the burgesses petitioning the Crown to continue Berkeley in office, June was a disastrous month for the governor's Indian policy. The Baconian assembly ordered several of the forts established by the act of the March assembly abandoned, and their garrisons redistributed. The assembly ordered that a force of 1,000 men, "whereof the one eighth part to be horsemen and dragoones be forthwith raised in order to the prosecuting this Indian warr." Furthermore, the assembly prohibited all trade with Indians, ordered the enslavement of Indians captured in war, and the sale of land abandoned by the Indians to defray the costs of the war. Friendly Indians were disarmed and permitted to hunt only with bows and arrows. In addition to legalizing all-out warfare against Indians, the assembly addressed another source of discontent in the colony by permitting all freemen to vote for burgesses, thus repealing the 1670 enactment that limited the franchise to freeholders.[64] And finally, after storming the capital with "att least 400 foote ye Scum of the Country, & 120 horse," Bacon extracted from Berkeley, at gunpoint, a commission to raise volunteers to march against the Indians.[65]

Bacon now had governmental sanction, however violently obtained, for his crusade against the Indians. Berkeley, who recognized that "I could doe the King little service by dying for him," had been powerless to resist. Sir William Berkeley, exhausted and defeated by the frontier interests he had sought to contain for 34 years, retired to his plantation at Green Spring. Indeed, the governor, frequently ill during the final year he spent in the colony, and who died shortly

---

62. Washburn, *Governor and the Rebel*, 51-52; Webb, *1676*, 32.

63. Hening, ed., *Statutes*, 2: 341-342.

64. Ibid., 351-352, 356-357.

65. Ibid., 341-348, 350-351, 351-352; William Sherwood to Joseph Williamson, 28 June 1676, in *Virginia Magazine of History and Biography*, 1 (1893), 171.

after his return to England in 1677, may have been suffering from a terminal illness.[66]

The governor, however, whatever ailed him, could not remain inactive for long. Late in July he received a petition from the residents in Gloucester County, complaining of Bacon's appropriation of horses and weapons "to the great disturbance of the peace of this county." Berkeley, energized by what he believed was a hint of support, granted the county the right to resist Bacon, and denied that Bacon's commission had any validity.[67] The governor's attempt to raise forces in the county failed, however, when the recruits realized they were to march against Bacon instead of Indians. The troops opposed the notion of attacking Bacon, for he had engaged "the comon enimy, who had in a most barberous manner murthered som hundreds of our deare Brethren and Country Men." Finding no one to support him, and aware that rebel forces were on the way, Berkeley once again defiantly proclaimed Bacon a rebel and then fled across the bay to the Eastern Shore.[68]

With Berkeley gone, Bacon consolidated his control over the colony. In response to Berkeley's declaration proclaiming him a rebel, Bacon issued his "Declaration in the Name of the People" from Middle Plantation on June 30. Bacon condemned the governor for his "greate unjust taxes" which bought no security, for monopolizing the Indian trade through his licensing practices, and "for having protected, favoured, & Imboldened the Indians against his Majesties loyall subjects, never contriveing, requireing, or appointeing any due or proper meanes of satisfaction for their many Invasions, Robbories, & Murthers comitted upon us." Bacon denounced as well the recall of Chicheley's force from its Indian targets, "when we might with ease have distroyed them." For these crimes, Bacon condemned Berkeley and his supporters "as Traytors to ye King & Countrey."[69]

In his "Manifesto," issued shortly thereafter, Bacon made clear the foundations of his campaign against the governor. A "main article of our Giult," Bacon declared, "is our open & manifest Aversion of all, not onely the Foreign but the protected & Darling Indians, this wee are informed is Rebellion of a deep dye." Bacon asserted that all Indians were

> Wholly unqualifyed for the benefitt and Protection of the Law, For That the law does reciprocally protect and punish, and that all people offending must either in person or Estate make equivalent satisfaction Or Restitution according to the manner and merit of ye Offences, Debts or Trespasses; Now since the Indians cannot according to the tenure and forme of any law to us known be prose-

66. Berkeley to Sir Henry Coventry, 2 February 1677, in "Miseries," ed. Washburn, 409.
67. Humble Petition of the County of Gloster, "Aspinwall Papers," 181-183; The Governors Answere to that Petition," Ibid., 183.
68. "Bacon's and Ingram's Rebellion," in *Narratives*, ed. Andrews, 56; Isle of Wight County Grievances, C.O. 1/39, 223-224 (VCRP).
69. C.O. 1/37, 128-129 (VCRP).

cuted, Seised, or Complained against, Their Persons being difficulty distinguished or known, Their many nations languages, and their subterfuges such as
makes them incapable to make us Restitution or satisfaction would it not be
very giulty to say They have bin unjustly defended and protected these many
years.[70]

Bacon complained as well of the colony's high taxes and the corruption of
Berkeley's regime, where greedy "sponges have suckt up the Publique Treasure" and distributed it to "unworthy Favourites and juggling Parasites whose
tottering Fortunes have bin repaired and supported at the Publique chardg."[71]

After rallying the countryside against Berkeley, and securing oaths of allegiance to support him against both Berkeley and the Crown, Bacon sent his
"navy," commanded by Giles Bland, to Accomack County on the Eastern Shore
to apprehend the governor, while he marched off in search of Indians.

Bacon led his forces again toward the falls of the James in search of the
Susquehannocks. He did not find his prey, so he turned next toward "the Freshes
of Yorke," to fall once again upon the Pamunkeys, who had taken refuge in the
Dragon Swamp. Bacon's forces killed several and took 45 prisoners, in addition
to plundering the village of "Indian matts, Basketts, matchcotes, parcells of
Wampampeag and Roanoke . . . in Baggs, skins, Furrs, Pieces of Lynnen, Broad
cloth, and divers sorts of English goods (which the Queene had much value
for)." The Queen of Pamunkey, Cockacoeske, fled to the woods where she
struggled to survive.[72]

While Bacon had busied himself scattering the Pamunkeys, however, his
naval forces had been captured on the Eastern Shore, enabling Berkeley to return to Jamestown early in September with troops recruited in Accomack
County. Bacon regrouped his followers, and with their loot and Indian prisoners
advanced toward Jamestown, where they arrived on the evening of September
13. The governor's forces outnumbered those of Bacon by at least two to one.
Nonetheless, the rebels dug trenches and settled into a siege of Jamestown.
Berkeley's ships' cannon failed to dislodge them from their positions on the
mainland side of the isthmus, and the rebels easily turned back a half-hearted
sortie launched by Berkeley's soldiers.[73]

Bacon and his followers subsequently began a concentrated assault upon
Berkeleyan morale. First, Bacon took "the wives and female Relations of such
Gentlemen as were in the Governor's Service against him," and placed "them in
the Face of his Enemy, as Bulwarkes for their Battery."[74] Then Bacon put the
captured Pamunkeys up on the entrenchments, reminding everyone in Jamestown that they risked their lives for an Indian lover.[75] Combined with the effect
of Baconian artillery fire, morale in the town reached a critical ebb. Berkeley's

70. Ibid., 179.
71. Ibid.
72. "Commissioners' Narrative," in *Narratives*, ed. Andrews, 123, 127.
73. Ibid., 132-134; "Bacon's and Ingram's Rebellion," *Ibid.*, 70.
74. "Commissioners' Narrative," in *Narratives*, ed. Andrews, 135.
75. Webb, *1676*, 63.

forces drifted away, until "only some 20 gentlemen" could be found willing to stand by him. Once again Bacon forced the governor to abandon the provincial capital in favor of refuge on the Eastern Shore.[76] Bacon entered the town unopposed on September 19. That night he set the town on fire.

Reports of Indian warfare, "extreme and grievous taxes," and planters unable to grow their tobacco flooded the office of the king's secretaries of state, and other powerful men close to the Crown. From these letters, imperial officials in England found it difficult to escape the conclusion that royal authority in Virginia faced a serious challenge in the form both of Indian warfare and internal rebellion.[77] To fulfill their absolutist aspirations and rule without parliament, the Stuart sovereigns needed the £100,000 in customs revenue collected on Virginia tobacco. By causing "the neglect of one year's planting there," Bacon's Rebellion struck to the heart of the Stuart imperial design.[78]

In September of 1676 the king directed Secretary of State Sir Henry Coventry to allow "Sir William Barkley's petition to give him leave to retire for his ease and recovery of his strength." This constituted royal recognition that "the age and infirmities" of the governor rendered him "totally unsuitable to the execution of so weighty a charge as the management of the King's affairs."[79] Charles then appointed Herbert Jeffreys, Sir John Berry, and Francis Moryson to a royal commission to investigate the causes of the rebellion. 1,100 English troops, sent to secure order in Virginia, accompanied the commissioners.[80]

The commissioners all brought important experience to their charge. Berry, by 1676 a famous commander in the king's navy, had fought heroically against the empire's enemies in the Caribbean and the Mediterranean. Moryson knew Virginia well: a royalist military officer, he had fled to the colony in 1649 after the execution of Charles I. He flourished in Virginia. He became Speaker of the House of Burgesses in 1656 and he joined the governor's council in 1660 when the assembly recalled Berkeley. During Berkeley's absence from the colony in 1661 and 1662, Moryson acted in his stead. In 1663, he arrived in England to serve as the colony's agent. During the 13 years that followed, Moryson's views on the place of Virginia within the empire evolved. He became an ardent advocate of Stuart imperialism and an enemy of provincial autonomy. So, too,

76. "Commissioners' Narrative," in *Narratives*, ed. Andrews, 135.

77. Webb, *1676*, 210.

78. Ibid., 189; Stephen Saunders Webb, *The Governors-General: The English Army and the Definition of Empire, 1569-1681* (Chapel Hill: University of North Carolina Press, 1979), 342; Washburn, *Governor and the Rebel*, 93.

79. Secretary Sir Henry Coventry to the Attorney General, 16 September 1676, *Calendar of State Papers, Colonial Series, America and West Indies, 1674-1675*, ed. W. Noel Sainsbury, (London: Longman, Green, Longman and Roberts, 1893), 449.

80. Commission of Charles II to Herbert Jeffreys and Others, 3 October 1676, C.O. 5/1355, 83-85, (VCRP); Washburn, *Governor and the Rebel*, 95. On the equipment and uniforms of these soldiers, see H. Charles McBarron, "Military Dress: Jeffery's Regiment of Foot, 1676-1682," *Military Collector and Historian*, 14 (Spring 1962), 11-12.

with Herbert Jeffreys, the commander in chief of the expedition. A career military man, he was the king's choice to succeed Sir William Berkeley.[81]

Berry and Moryson arrived at the port at Kecoughton late in January of 1677. They discovered that Bacon had died the preceding October from disease. After vicious fighting along Virginia's rivers, and nearly constant raids and counter-raids, the rebels had been defeated. Governor Berkeley, rather than restoring order, had since occupied himself in the plunder of his enemies' estates, and in the execution of former rebels. In some cases he did so without trial. The commissioners informed Berkeley of their arrival, and requested his assistance in provisioning the English force, reestablishing peace with the neighboring Indians, and following the orders they had received from the Crown. Even a cursory glance at Wiseman's *Book of Record* reveals the gaping differences in perception that separated the governor from his enemies. Bacon's Rebellion began in a deeply polarized colonial society rife with problems the king's commissioners wanted to rectify. Samuel Wiseman's *Book of Record* chronicles the commissioners' efforts, as they attempted to learn just what happened in Virginia.

IV

Generations of American historians have found in the Nathaniel Bacon's rebellion against the king's governor of Virginia a compelling story laden with immense significance for understanding the subsequent development of the English colonies in America. For Thomas Jefferson Wertenbaker, a proud son of Virginia, Bacon was "the torchbearer of the Revolution," leading his impoverished, naked, and distressed followers in rebellion against a corrupt, authoritarian, and oppressive governor. Bacon and his followers faced unjust laws and extreme taxes. Bacon rebelled, consequently, "to redress those wrongs and to end misgovernment."[82] So noble a rebellion "gave birth in the breasts of many brave men . . . a desire to resist by all means possible the oppression of the Stuart kings. It stirred," Wertenbaker continued, "the people to win, in their legislative halls, victories for the cause of liberty, as real as those which Bacon and his followers had failed to secure on the field of battle."[83]

Wilcomb Washburn, who published *The Governor and the Rebel* in 1957, strongly disagreed with these findings. In Washburn's view, Bacon's Rebellion was about hating Indians. Bacon and his followers, hard-pressed and living on a remote frontier, needed access to Indian land. The governor, however, wanted to maintain peace along the colony's marchlands, and he worked to keep Indians and whites apart. The "real grievance" against Berkeley, Washburn argued, was not that he failed to defend the colony against Indian attack, as Bacon's rebels charged. Rather, Berkeley contended against "the tyranny of temporarily enraged frontiersmen." They rose against him when "he refused to authorize the slaughter and dispossession of the innocent as well as the 'guilty'" among

81. Webb, *Governors-General,* 336-337, 428.
82. Thomas Jefferson Wertenbaker, *Virginia Under the Stuarts* (Princeton, NJ: Princeton University Press, 1915), 155.
83. Ibid., 194.

neighboring Indians. There was little that was democratic or patriotic in Bacon's Rebellion.[84]

Bacon as patriot or Indian-hating thug; Berkeley as a governor grown bitter, inept, and tyrannical, or a far-sighted imperial administrator trying carefully to manage the growth of a rapidly developing colony. The qualities of the governor and his principal antagonist always have figured largely in historical interpretations of Bacon's Rebellion.[85] Historians, however, have not exclusively focused so heavily on the personalities involved. Many have examined the impact of Bacon's Rebellion, and what it reveals to subsequent generations about the social and political development of seventeenth-century Virginia.

For Bernard Bailyn, Bacon's Rebellion was "symptomatic of a profound disorganization of European society in its American setting." Berkeley and the tight provincial elite dependent upon him met opposition from substantial planters whose discontent "stemmed to a large extent from their own exclusion from privileges they sought." Newcomers like Bacon and Giles Bland, both of gentle birth in England, found their paths to upward mobility blocked by the governor and his circle, an elite that in their view simply lacked the conditions and qualities necessary for respect in England. In this sense, Bacon was not a democrat but an elitist. His ambitions were stifled by a calcified colonial political system, and so he rejected the claims of the Berkeley group to legitimately rule the king's Old Dominion.[86]

While Bailyn emphasized the volatility of a divided elite in an unstable and developing society, Edmund S. Morgan, in *American Slavery, American Freedom,* focused his attention on the colony's lower orders. In the closing weeks of the rebellion, Morgan argued, many servants and slaves began to rally around Bacon's banner. Most of the rebel's followers were, in fact, former servants. Morgan realized that the colony's prosperity always had depended upon bound labor, and the white servants who had provided the backbone for Virginia's economic explosion had proven themselves a disorderly lot. Increasingly able to survive their terms of servitude as the period of "seasoning" passed, the ex-servants provided the basis for a restless, hard-drinking, and well-armed class of landless tenants. Furthermore, after 1660 especially, the exploitation by planters of the previously little-utilized headright system made it increasingly difficult for ex-servants to find land suitable for tobacco culture. The best lands along the rivers already had been snatched up. Consequently, the former servants were left with the unsavory option of either moving further to the west, where a marginal

84. Washburn, *Governor and the Rebel,* 162-163.
85. Warren M. Billings' forthcoming study, *Sir William Berkeley: A Virginian's Biography* (Baton Rouge: University of Louisiana Press) will provide by far the most balanced portrayal of Governor Berkeley.
86. Bernard Bailyn, "Politics and Social Structure in Virginia," in *Colonial America: Essays in Politics and Social Development,* ed. Stanley N. Katz, John M. Murrin, and Douglas Greenberg, 4th ed. (New York: McGraw-Hill, 1993). For a refutation of Bailyn's thesis, see Kukla, "Order and Chaos," 275-298.

was made even less appealing by the menace of Indian attack, or sinking back into tenantry. Virginia, Morgan argued, was following a policy could easily lead to disaster.[87]

These social tensions reached the breaking point in 1676, when ex-servants and frontier planters became rebels under Bacon's leadership. For Morgan, the most important lesson to emerge from the rebellion was that hostility to an inferior race could be transformed into a more powerful form of hostility than that directed towards the upper classes. White indentured servants had always been a tumultuous lot, and Virginia planters increasingly felt the need to keep them under strict control. Their policy, however, of keeping English servants under increasingly tight discipline for ever-longer periods of time, created a serious threat to Virginia's social system The Virginia gentry, Morgan argued, thus made a decision to move towards a new social order—one that would "nourish the freeman's freedom and at the same time make possible the unlimited exploitation of labor."[88]

To Morgan, Bacon's Rebellion offered a persuasive explanation for Virginia's rapid move toward African slavery in the last quarter of the seventeenth century. After the rebellion, planters made an easy decision to convert to chattel slavery. Aware of the dangers involved in keeping white servants oppressed, planters simply bought slaves instead of servants. Bacon's Rebellion taught that upper- and lower-class whites could unite "in the systematic oppression of men who seemed not quite human." Racism in Virginia, Morgan concluded, absorbed the fear and contempt that upper-class men in England would have normally directed toward the lower classes, and vice-versa. By lumping Indians, mulattoes, and Africans in a single pariah caste, Virginians paved the way for a similar lumping of small and large planters in a single master class. Thus was freedom for whites intimately associated in the minds of Virginians with the enslavement of blacks.[89]

While Morgan was interested in Bacon's Rebellion primarily for its explanatory power in accounting for the evolution of African slavery in Virginia, Stephen Saunders Webb saw the rebellion as a critical event in the history of the Anglo-American empire. The king, Webb argued, needed an orderly Virginia. The customs revenue collected on Virginia tobacco provided the margin of royal independence from Parliament. Bacon's Rebellion was a significant blow to that system. Acting on information acquired mostly from Bacon's lieutenant, Giles

87. Morgan, *American Slavery, American Freedom*, passim. For a similar approach treating Maryland, see Russell P. Menard, "From Servant to Freeholder: Status Mobility and Property Accumulation in Seventeenth-Century Maryland," *William and Mary Quarterly*, 3d ser., 30 (January 1973), 37-69.

88. Kathleen M. Brown, in *Good Wives, Nasty Wenches and Anxious Patriarchs: Gender, Race and Power in Colonial Virginia,* (Chapel Hill: University of North Carolina Press, 1996), 139, believed that the rebellion pitted "two distinct cultures of masculinity" against one another. In Brown's view, "the militant and superficially populist ethos of ordinary men . . . confronted the elite masculine culture of honor held so dear by the colony's wealthy planters."

89. Morgan, *American Slavery, American Freedom*, 234, 344, 328.

Bland, Charles II arrived at the conclusion that Sir William Berkeley had badly misgoverned the colony. "To replace the aged governor and his corrupt coterie, to put down the rebels, to find out what was going on in Virginia so that the crown could govern there, and then to impose garrison government on the hitherto autonomous colony," Webb wrote, "the king chose tried instruments of his authority," the experienced military commissioners whom Samuel Wiseman accompanied as clerk, scribe, and secretary, to America. In the wake of the rebellion, "the crown was determined to crush both misgovernors and rebels and to replace them by authentic and direct royal rule in the public interest of the empire." This new imperial oversight, Webb contends, was pervasive, and constituted the "end of American Independence."[90]

Webb's "Garrison Government" thesis has been controversial, but he may well be right, for King Charles II expressed tremendous concern upon learning of Virginia's problems. The rebellion began in the spring of 1676, the result of a dispute between the governor and frontier settlers over the conduct of the Susquehannock War. By the time it reached its conclusion, it had evolved into a movement directed against the authority of the king's governor of Virginia. The supporters of William Berkeley could not appreciate the fears and pressures that drove frontiersmen to take up arms against the governor. The Berkeleyans could only conclude that the rebellion had "not proceeded from any real fault in ye Government but rather from the lewd dispositions of some persons, of desperate fortunes, lately sprung up amongst us."[91]

V

Sadly, we know little about Samuel Wiseman, the man who so ably served the commissioners, and who so diligently transcribed their proceedings. We know nothing of his family. Though there were prominent men close to Charles II— namely, the surgeon Richard Wiseman and the "Clerk of the Kitchen" for Lord Shaftesbury, John Wiseman—with whom he shared a surname, there is no evidence of a family relation. Samuel Wiseman, it seems, saw the position as clerk to the commissioners as an avenue to advancement, a means of improving his station in the world. The commissioner Francis Moryson claimed in a 1678 letter to William Blathwayt that he had succeeded in persuading Wiseman to take the job upon the assurance of Secretary of State Joseph Williamson "that

90. Webb, *Governors-General*, 331-333, 358; Webb, *1676*. See also Horn, *Adapting to a New World*, 378-379. For a critique of Webb's work, see Richard A. Johnson, "The Imperial Webb: The Thesis of Garrison Government in Early America Reconsidered," *William and Mary Quarterly*, 3d ser., 43 (October 1986), 408-430. Also useful is the discussion in John M. Murrin, "Political Development," in *Colonial British America: Essays in the New History of the Early Modern Era,* ed. Jack P. Greene and J. R. Pole (Baltimore: Johns Hopkins University Press, 1984).
91. Philip Ludwell to Mr. Secretary Coventry, 14 April 1677, C.O. 5/1355, 152-155 (VCRP).

this employment should be but an earnest to a better." In this sense, Wiseman must have been bitterly disappointed. Upon the return of Wiseman, Berry, and Moryson to England late in the summer of 1677, his employers pleaded in his behalf for payment. Wiseman, according to Jeffreys, in 1678 was in such dire straits "that he cannot have a sixpence."[92]

Samuel Wiseman's *Book of Record* has not been previously published. I have relied on the copy housed in the Pepsyian Library at Magdalene College, Cambridge. Samuel Pepys (1633-1703), the noted diarist, began to serve as the Secretary to the Lord Commissioners of the Admiralty in England in 1673. In that capacity, with the small staff at his disposal, Pepys revolutionized the Admiralty. He laid the foundations for a professional class of naval officers, oversaw the construction of a much larger navy, and introduced an atmosphere of discipline and diligence to the naval service. Pepys was a copious compiler, and likely requested from Wiseman a copy of his and the commissioners' proceedings in Virginia. Samuel Wiseman's *Book of Record* was among the 3,000 books and manuscripts bequeathed by Pepys to Magdalene College in 1703. Archivists employed by the Virginia Colonial Records Project made a microfilm copy of this version in the 1950s. Wiseman's book has been abstracted by John Neville, and bits and pieces of the document appeared late in the nineteenth and early in the twentieth centuries in the *Virginia Magazine of History and Biography* and the first series of the *William and Mary Quarterly*.[93] In editing the document, I have made a number of editorial decisions designed to improve the general readability of Wiseman's *Book of Record*. All superscript characters signifying abbreviations have been lowered to the line, and all abbreviations silently expanded. I have added punctuation, when necessary, to improve the clarity of the documents Wiseman transcribed. Not all the documents in Wiseman's *Book* are in chronological order; I have decided to leave them in the order which Wiseman placed them. Furthermore, I have divided Wiseman's book into seven chapters, an editorial strategy that I hope will allow readers to digest better Wiseman's diligent record-keeping. The first section, "Preliminaries," deals with the legal background of the commissioners' expedition to Virginia, and the powers they were granted by the Crown to restore order in the king's Old Dominion. The second section, "The Commissioners and Sir William Berkeley," contains a wealth of information on the dispute that quickly developed between the commissioners and the discredited governor of the colony, who went to great pains to justify his policies toward the colony's Indian population and the defeated rebels. Chapter 3, "The Treaty of Middle Plantation," includes the Treaty of May of 1677, the agreement which formalized peace between the Powhatan Indians of Virginia and the colony. The document is marvelous for the extent to

---

92. Moryson to Blathwayt, in W. Noel Sainsbury and J. W. Fortescue, eds., *Calendar of State Papers, Colonial Series, America and West Indies, 1677-1680*, (London, 1896), p. 203.

93. See John Davenport Neville, *Bacon's Rebellion: Abstracts of Materials in the Colonial Records Project*, (Williamsburg: The Jamestown Foundation, n.d.); Virginia Colonial Records Project, Survey Report No. 06618, (Virginia Historical Society, Richmond, Virginia).

which it demonstrates the crises confronting native peoples in the face of expanding English settlements. The fourth chapter, "The Commissioners' Narrative," includes their report to the king on the causes and consequences of Bacon's Rebellion. Chapter 5, "The Commissioners' Resolve," traces the commissioners' attempt to integrate Virginia firmly into the Restoration Empire, and the consequences of that consolidation for the colony's inhabitants. Chapter 6, "The Counties' Grievances," is a fascinating collection of grievances, collected by Wiseman from the various county courts, along with the commissioners' replies. The members of the county courts explained to the commissioners the conditions that led to their participation in the rebellion; the commissioners' responses show their vision of how the colony should fit into the empire. Finally, Chapter 7, "The Price of Loyalty: Personal Grievances," shows dramatically the rebellion's human costs in terms of property destroyed and lives ruined. Individuals who lost all in the rebellion appealed to the commissioners for aid and assistance. My hope is that this book, as edited, will be useful for researchers, for advanced history majors, and for students newly introduced to the field of early American history. I have tried to make the work as easy to read as possible, without compromising in any way Wiseman's incredible compiling of information.

1 Preliminaries

Document 1

The Names of ye Severall Counties within his Majesties Collony of Virginia; are as follows: viz

James Citty	Gloster
Charles Citty	Middlesex
Henrico	Rappahanock
Isle of Wight	Lancaster
Nancymond	Stafford
Lower Norfolke	Westmerland
Kiquotan alias	Northumberland
Elizabeth City County	
Warwick	Accomac
Yorke	Northampton
New Kent	

Document 2
30 December 1676

An Oath of Secrecy

I Samuel Wiseman doe hereby Voluntarily make Oath and Sweare, that I will not reveale, make knowne, or divulge unto any person or persons whatsoever, any matter or thing, in writing or otherwise, Instrusted and comitted to mee with charge of Secrecy and close-keeping by You, **Herbert Jeffery Esquire, Sir John Berry** Knt, and **Francis Morison** Esquire, his Majesties Honorable Commissioners for this present Expedicion to **Virginia**, or any of you, But that I shall and will conceale and hold secret whatsoever you the said Commissioners shall from time to time soe charge and intrust mee with: And I doe also sweare Faithfully to observe and execute all such further Orders and Directions, to mee to be by You given, in all things as by my Place and Trust of Principall Clerke to You the Honorable Commissioners aforesaid, I stande obliged and ought to doe. Soe helpe mee God.

Samuel Wiseman, Esq.

Jurat 30 die Decembris

Anno Dni. 1676, a° Gr

Regni R. Caroli sedi,
Xxviii coram nobis[1]
John Berry
Francis Moryson

Document 3
10 October 1676

His Majestyes Grant & Declaracion
In favour of his Subjects inhabiting in Virginia.

Charles the Second, by the grace of God King of England, Scotland, France and Ireland, Defendor of the Faith, etc. **To** all to whome these presents shall come Greeting. **Know yee** that wee of our especiall grace, certaine knowledge and meere motion have declared and granted, And by these presents doe for us our heires and successors declare and grant, That all the Subjects of Us our heires and Successors from tyme to tyme Inhabiting within our Colony and Plantation of **Virginia** shall have their immediate Dependance upon the Crowne of England, under the Rule and Government of such Governour or Governours as Wee, our heires or Successors shall from tyme to tyme apoint in that behalfe, and of or upon noe other person or persons whatsoever. **And Further,** that the Governor for the time being shalbe Resident in that Countrey, Except Wee or our heires shall at anytime Commaund his Attendance in England or elswhere, in which case a Deputie shall be chosen to continue during the absence of such Governour in manner as hath formerly beene used; unlesse Wee our Heires or Successors shall thinke fitt to Nominate such Deputie. And further, if any Governour shall happen to dye, then another Governour shall and may be chosen as hath beene formerly used; to continue untill Wee our Heires or Successors shall appoint a New Governour. **And Moreover,** that all lands now possessed by the severall and respective Planters or Inhabitants of **Virginia** are and shall be Confirmed and established to them and their heires for Ever, where the property of any particular mans Interest in any Lands there shall not be altered or prejudiced by reason thereof. **And** our further will and pleasure is, And wee doe hereby of our further grace and favour Declare and Grant, that for the Encouragement of such our Subjects as shall from time to time goe to dwell in the said Plantacion, there shall be assigned out of the Lands (not already appropriated) to every person soe coming to dwell Fiftie Acres, according as hath beene used and allowed

---

1. "Sworn on the 30th of December, Year of our Lord 1676, Before Charles the Second, in the 28th Year of his Reign." Charles II dated the beginning of his reign in 1649, the year in which Puritan forces executed his father, Charles I, at the close of the English Civil War.

since the first Plantacion, to be held by us, our Heires and Successors, as of our mannor of **East Greenwich** in the County of Kent, in free and common Soccage.[2] **And further** that all Lands possessed by any Subject inhabiting in Virginia which is Escheated or shall Escheate unto Us our Heires or Successors, shall and may bee enjoyed by such Inhabitant or Possessor, his Heires and Assignes for ever, Paying twoe poundes of Tobacco Composicion for every Acre, which is the rate sett by our Governour according to the Instruccions to him in that behalf:[3] And further that the Governour and Councell of Virginia for the time being, And in the absence of the Governour, the Deputy Governour and Councell, or any five, or more of them (whereof the Governour and his Deputye to be alwayes one) shall and hereby have full power and authority to heare and determine all Treasons, Murders, Felonyes and other Offences to be comitted or done within the said Government, soe as they proceede therein as neere as may be to the Lawes and Statutes of this our Kingdome of England. **And Lastly - -** Know yee that wee being of our Royall goodnesse graciously inclined to favour the Subjects of Us, our Heires and Successors, which now doe or hereafter shall Inhabite in the said Countrey of Virginia and to give the more liberall & ample Encouragement to Plantacions there, Doe hereby declare our Royall Will and pleasure to be that all and every Clause, Article and sentence in these our Letters patents conteined shall be from tyme to tyme ever hereafter, as often as any ambiguity, Doubt or Question shall or may happen to arise thereupon, expounded, construed, deemed and taken to bee by us meant and intended, and shall enure[4] and take effect in the most beneficiall and avayleable sence to all intents and purposes for the profitt and advantage of the Subjects of us, our heires and Successors of Virginia aforesaid, as well against Us our Heires and Successors, as against all and every other person or persons whatsoever: Any Law, Statute, Custome or Usage to the contrary thereof in anywise notwithstanding. **In Witnes** whereof wee have caused these our Letters to bee made Patents.[5] **Witnes**

---

2. "*free and common socage.*" A type of land tenure in England where land was held by the tenant in exchange for services other than military service. This was the ordinary form of holding real estate in England.

3. "*escheat.*" A reversion of property to the state in consequence of a want of any individual competent to inherit. See Henry Campbell Black, *Black's Law Dictionary*, 5th ed. (St. Paul, MN: West Publishing Company, 1979), 488.

4. "*enure.*" To come into operation, to take place, to have effect. *Oxford English Dictionary*, (hereafter *OED*).

5 "*letters patent.*" "Open letters, as distinguished from letters close. An Instrument proceeding from the government, and conveying a right, authority, or grant to an individual." *Black's Law Dictionary*, 1013.

ourself att Westminster, the tenth day of October, in the Eight and twentyeth yeare of our Raigne.

Samuel Wiseman

Document 4
10 October 1676

A **Pardon** granted unto the Governour and Assembly of his Majesties Plantation of **Virginia** for passing certaine Acts, being under a **Force:**[6]

Charles the Second by the grace of God King of England, Scotland, France and Ireland Defendor of the Faith &c. **To** all to whome these presents shall come, Greeting. **Whereas** Nathaniel Bacon the Younger of our Plantacion of Virginia, combineing with divers indigent and seditious persons, did in the month of June, last past Trayterously levy Warr against Us and Our Government. And the said Nathaniel Bacon and his Complices (to the number of about five hundred persons) did in a violent and hostile manner besett and encompasse our Governour and Assembly of our said Plantacion (being then Assembled and mett together) in the **Statehouse** within our Towne called **James Citty**, to consult about and debate the publick Affaires of our said Plantacion. And the said Rebells and Traytors holding up their Musquetts ready charged and cockt, did threaten to kill and murder the said Governor and Assembly unlesse they would grant such a Commission to the said Nathaniel Bacon, as was by him desired, for the constituting him Commander in Chiefe of certaine Forces to be raised within the said Plantacion. And unlesse they would passe and enact certaine pretended acts and Lawes which were prepared and offered to them by the said Nathaniel Bacon and his said Adherents and Complices. And more particularly one pretended Act, whereby the said Rebells and Traytors might be Pardoned and indempnified for their said Treason and Rebellion. All which said Acts they the said Governour and Assembly were (for feare of their lives and by the terror of the said threats and violence) compelled to passe accordingly. And though wee are sufficiently satisfied That our said Governour and Assembly were not guilty of any presumption or ill affection towards Us in passing the said pretended Acts, but were constrained out of pure Feare, and for safety of their Lives to doe therein; Yett to the intent that they the said Governor and Assembly may not be Subject to any Question or bee in danger of any Punishment for such their assent to, or concurrence in the passing the said pretended Acts, or in granting the said pretended Commission. **Wee doe** hereby of our especiall grace, certaine knowledge

6. "*a Force.*" In other words, Charles II is pardoning Sir William Berkeley and the members of the June Assembly for their actions on the grounds that Bacon forced them to take the actions in question.

and meere motion Pardon and Release unto the said Governour and Assembly, and every of them (in as full and ample manner as if their names were herein particularly mentioned and expressed) All and all manner of Crimes, Misprisions,[7] Contempts and Misdemeanors by them or any of them committed or done in or about the passing, assenting to, or concurring in the said pretended Acts or in granting the said pretended Commission. **And** doe for us our heires and Successors freely and absolutely Discharge, Pardon and Forgive the said Governour and Assembly and every of them (in as full and ample manner as if their Names were herein particularly inserted) all punishments, paines, Forfeitures and Advantages which wee our heires or Successors might have or take against them, or any of them, for or by reason of the premisses, Soe that they, or any of them shall not at any time hereafter bee in anywise impeached, questioned, or proceeded against for the same.

And our will and pleasure is That these our Letters Patents shall be taken most favourable for the discharging, Indempnifying and Pardoning the said Governoour and Assembly and every of them for and concerning the premisses. Notwithstanding the not nameing the said Governour and Assembly by their Christian-Names, Sir-Names, Places of abode, or addicions. **And** Nothwithstanding the not reciteing or not true reciteing or expressing the particular Offences, Crimes, Forfeitures, Penaltyes & Advantages hereby released, pardoned, remissed and forgiven, or any Law, Statute, or Usage to the contrary hereof in any wise notwithstanding. **In Witnes** whereof Wee have caused these our Letters to be made Patents. **Witnes** Ourselfe att Westminster, the Tenth day of October in the Eight and twentieth yeare of our Raigne.

Concordat cum Originali[8]

Samuel Wiseman

Document 5
10 October 1676
A Commission, Giving Power to the Governor of Virginia to Pardon Offences.

Charles the Second by the grace of God King of England Scotland France and Ireland, Defendor of the Fayth &c. **To** our trusty and welbeloved **Sir William Berkeley** Knight, Our Governour of our Plantacion of Virginia, Greeting. **Whereas** Nathaniel Bacon the Younger and divers other ill-disposed persons his

---

7. "*misprision.*" Contempt or scorn, particularly against the sovereign.
8. "In accordance with the original."

Complices and Adherents, have raised a **Rebellion** and went to Warr against us within our said Plantacion. **Wee** being graciously inclined and willing to extend our Royall Compassion to such of our Subjects as have acted in, and bee guilty of, or shall act in and be guilty of the said Warre and Rebellion; who (being sensible and repenting of their Disloyalty and Disobedience to us and our Government) shall humbly implore our Grace and Mercy, and shall returne to their due obedience and duty **Have** thought fitt to give and grant, and doe by these presents give and grant full power and authority to you our said Governour for us, and in our name to Pardon Release and Forgive unto all such of our Subjects (other then the said Nathaniel Bacon) as you shall thinke fitt and convenient for our service, All Treasons, Felonyes, and other Crimes and Misdemeanors by them or any of them acted, done, or committed, or which shall be acted, done, or committed by them, or any of them during and relating to this present Warr and Rebellion, with full Restitution to the persons, soe by you to be Pardoned, their Heires, Executors and Administrators of their Estates, as well reall as personall. **And** our will and Pleasure is, that all and every such Pardon and Pardons by you to bee granted, pursuant to the Power and authority hereby to You given, shall bee to all intents and purposes as good and effectuall in Law and shall be pleadable and allowed in all our Courts and before and by all our Justices, Magistrates, and Officers whatsoever, In as full and ample manner, as if the same had beene graunted by us, and had passed under our Great Seale of England. **In witnes** whereof wee have caused these our Letters to be made patents. **Witnes** Ourself att Westminster the tenth day of October in the Eight and twentieth yeare of Our Raigne.

Convenit cum Originali[9]
Sa. Wiseman

Document 6
10 October 1676

A Commission Graunted unto Herbert Jeffrey Esquire, Sir John Berry Knight, and Francis Morison Esquire, to Inquire into the Grievances of his Majesties Plantacion of Virginia.

Charles the Second by the grace of God King of England, Scotland France and Ireland, Defender of the Faith &c. **To** our Trusty and Welbeloved Subjects **Herbert Jeffery** Esquire, **Sir John Berry** Knight and **Francis Morison** Esquire, Greeting. **Whereas** it hath come to our knowledge that divers great divisions and distractions have arisen, and sundry great disorders have beene committed within our Plantation of Virginia, to the disturbance of that Peace and Tranquil-

---

9. "In Harmony with the Original."

ity which our good Subjects of that Plantacion have long enjoyed under our happy Government; And wee having beene informed that the Evills aforesaid have in great measure beene occasioned by divers Grievances, which our good Subjects there have of late laine under; the particulars whereof are yett to us unknowne. And because by reason of the great distance of the said Plantacion from our usuall Place of residence, our good Subjects of the said Plantacion cannot soe easily make knowne unto us their respective Grievances as other our Subjects may, who live at a neerer distance. Wee being willing to be informed of all and singuler the Premisses, to the end wee may thereunto apply fitt and speedy Remedyes. And having great Confidence in Your Wisdomes, Industry and Loyalty, Doe by these presents appoint you the said Herbert Jeffery, Sir John Berry, and Francis Morison to bee our **Commissioners**, to Enquire into, and Report unto us, All such Grievances and Pressures, which any of our Loving Subjects within the Plantacion aforesaid have suffered, or layne under, or doe suffer and lye under, and more especially such Grievances and all other causes matters and things which have occasioned the late Divisions, Distraccions and Disorders there. **And** for the better Execucion of our Royall Will and Pleasure in this behalfe, Wee doe hereby give unto You, or to any Two of you, full Power and Authority not onely to receive such Informacions & Advertisements[10] as shall be brought unto you by or from any of our Subjects touching the premisses, but also to enquire by Examination of Witnesses upon Oath, which we doe hereby give full power and authority to you, or any Two of you to Administer or by such other wayes or meanes as you, or any two of you, in your Discretions shall think fitt, into all such Grievances and Pressures, as aforesaid, and all other matters, things and causes which have occasioned the said late Divisions, Distractions, and Disorders, and to Report the same to Us, with all convenient Speede, together with the Opinion of You, or any two of you touching the Premisses, to the end that wee may give such Orders for the Redresse of all such Grievances and Pressures and for the future well-government of the said Plantacion, as Wee in Our Royall Wisdome shall thinke fitt and convenient. **And** Wee doe hereby give unto You or any two of you full Power and Authority to send for such Persons, Papers and Records, as may bee usefull unto You, or any two of you for the better carrying on of our service hereby intended. **Willing** and Requiring Our Governor of our said Plantacion, for the tyme being his Deputy Governor, and all and every other our Officers and Subjects within the said Plantacion to bee in all things helpful, ayding and assisting to You and every of

10. *"Advertisement."* Information.

You in the Execucion of this our Royall Commission.[11] **And Lastly** Our will & Pleasure is, that in the Execucion & performance of the Authorityes to You hereby Given, You and every of you doe carefully observe, and conforme your selves unto such Instruccions as have beene, or shall be by Us given or sent unto you in Writing, under our Royall Signett and Signe Manuall. **In Witnes** whereof wee have caused these our Letters to bee made Patents. **Witnes** Ourselfe att Westminster the Tenth day of October, in the Eight & twentieth yeare of our Raigne.

Convenit cum Originali.
Sa. Wiseman

Document 7
9 November 1676

The Privy Seale
Affixed here.

Charles R.[12]
Instructions for Our Trusty and Welbeloved Herbert Jeffreys Esqr., Sir John Berry Knight, and Francis Morison, Esqr. Whome Wee have appointed Our Commissioners for Our Colony of Virginia.

1. You shall with the first convenience Embarque your selves upon Our good Ship Bristoll (and with what speede you can (wind and weather permitting) transport Yourselves to Our said Colony of Virginia.

2. Being arrived there, You shall in the first place take all the convenient wayes you can of informing Yourselves truly and thoroughly of the State of Affairs in that Our Colony; And as often as you shall judge it

11. Sir Henry Chicheley served as deputy governor. For background on his career, see Stephen Saunders Webb, *The Governors-General: The English Army and the Definition of Empire* (Chapel Hill: University of North Carolina Press, 1979), 509. The king had learned, correctly, that Chicheley had been imprisoned by the rebels. As a result, he commissioned Jeffreys to serve as deputy governor until Berkeley returned home. Sir John Berry, who arrived in the colony before Jeffreys, delivered to the governor a letter from Secretary of State Henry Coventry which explained the new state of affairs. Charles II, Coventry wrote, "hath given a commission to Col. Jefferies to act in your Stead under the title of Lieutenant Governor, which Letter and Commission will be delivered and shewed you by Colonel Jeffries himself, upon which his Majestie expects your return hither, and that he should from that time act in your stead." See Henry Coventry to Sir William Berkeley, 15 November 1676, Correspondence of the Board of Trade, 1676–1677, C.O. 389/6, 177-178 (VCRP).

12. as in Charles Rex, King of England.

necessary, make use of those Powers allowed you in Our Commission given you.

3. You shall bee assistant to Our Lieutentant Governor or Commander in chiefe there with your councell and advice whensoever he shall demand it; and particularly in that affaire of renewing a Peace with the Neighbour Indians,[13] in which Wee doe particularly order him to demaund your assistance.

4. You shall have delivered to You a Copy of the Instruccions given to Sir William Berkeley Our then Governor of that our Colony at Our first coming to the exercise of Our Royall Authority in England, and you shall informe yourselves how those Instruccions have beene pursued, and wherein there hath beene any failer, and upon what grounds, and by whose neglect and wilfull fault.[14]

5. You shall informe Yourselves of all Grievances in generall, but particularly of that which the people seem so much concerned in, the great Salary paid to the Members of the Assembly: And You shall bee Assistant with Your Advice to Our Lieutenant Governor in causing an immediate redresse of it.

6. You shall take all the opportunityes you can to possesse[15] Our Subjects of that Colony, That as Wee are and ever wilbe severe in punishing such as shall wilfully violate Our Lawes and Royall Authority, and shall presume to Encourage or abett Tumults and Rebellions, Soe shall Wee be noe less indulgent to the just Complaints of Our oppressed people, and as soone as informed of their Grievances direct proportionable redresse for them, and take such resentment upon the authors and continuers of them, as the quality of the Offence shall require; And this You may lett them know was the chiefe cause of Our sending you thither.

7. You shall make particular acquaintance with those of Our Councill there; and that not onely in generall as a Council, but seperately, and in their particular persons, both in order to a cleerer and more impartiall

---

13. A reference to the remnants of the Powhatan Chiefdom, who had surrendered to the English in 1646 and become tributaries of the colony. See Helen C. Rountree, *Pocahontas's People: The Powhatan Indians of Virginia through Four Centuries* (Norman: University of Oklahoma Press, 1990), Chapters 4-5; W. Stitt Robinson, "Tributary Indians in Colonial Virginia," *Virginia Magazine of History and Biography*, 67 (January 1959), 49-64.

14. See Document 8, below.

15. "*possesse.*" To inform, make clear to.

information of yourselves of Affaires in Generall, and likewise to render Yourselves more capable of informing Us of the Capacity & dispositions of those that compose the Councill; and how farr fitted and qualified for such a trust.

8.   You shall likewise make a particular Enquiry into the Militia of that Countrey, the quality, disposition and capacity of the Officers, soe that at your returne (or sooner) Wee may have from You a thorough Information of the Strength, and alsoe of the defects of that Government.[16]

9.   The like Enquiry you shall make into the Lawes of that place, of which you are to return to Us a Copie to be inspected here, together with your Remarks upon them, and which and why you think inconvenient, and fitt to be altered or abrogated.

10.   You shall upon all occasions give unto Us, or to one of our Principall Secretaryes of State,[17] an Account of all Your Proceedings, and of the Condicion of Affaires there. **Given** att Our Court att Whitehall the 9th day of November 1676 in the 28th yeare of Our Raigne.

C. R.

Document 8
12 September 1662

Instructions to Our Trusty and Welbeloved Sir William Berkeley Knight Our Governor of Our Colony of **Virginia**

1.   That Almightie God may bee more inclined to bestow his Blessing upon Us and you in the improvement of that Our Colony, You shall in the first place take speciall care that Hee bee Devoutly and duly served in all the Government, the Booke of Common Prayer as it is now Established be Read each Sunday and Holy-day, and the Blessed Sacrament administered according to the Rites of the Church of England: You shall be carefull that the

---

16. On the militia, see William L. Shea, *The Virginia Militia in the Seventeenth Century* (Baton Rouge: Louisiana State University Press, 1983), 108. According to Shea, many militiamen took part in the rebellion, aiding Bacon in his march against the Indians. At the outset of the rebellion all of Bacon's followers were militia men, and in some cases complete units rallied around his banner. The militia, says Shea, provided poor whites on the frontier with organization, a chance to meet their neighbors, and training in the use of arms. Through July of 1676 the "rebellion had been largely a test of will between Berkeley and Bacon over control and use of the provincial militia in the Susquehannock War."

17. In 1676, the principal secretaries of state were Henry Coventry and Joseph Williamson. Neither was a powerful secretary. The power of the office of the Secretaries of State was growing during the later Stuart period, gaining power at the expense of the king's Privy Council. This power, however, can be overstated. Secretaries and councilors alike served at the pleasure of the king.

Churches already built there be well and orderly kept, and more Built, as the Colony shall by God's Blessing be improved. And that besides a competent maintenance to be Assigned to the Minister of each Church, out of the fruits and producions of the Earth, and labour of Planters, that a convenient House be built at the Common Charge for each Minister neare each Church, and one hundred Acres of Lande assigned unto him for a Glebe,[18] and exercise of his Industry.

2. That you shall within one Moneth after your arrival, or sooner if you think fitt, call a Generall Assembly, according to the usuage & Custome of that Our Colony: And at the opening thereof you shall Declare unto them, That Wee are graciously pleased to grant a free and generall Act of Pardon and Oblivion unto all Our Subjects of what Degree and Quality soever of that Our Colony, of all Crimes, Offence and Misdemeanours committed since (blank) Excepting such persons who are Attainted[19] by Act of Parliament in this Our Kingdom for the Horrid Murther of Our Deare Father of Blessed Memory,[20] if any of which persons shall at present be with that Our Colony, or shall hereafter repaire thither, hee or they shall be forthwith Apprehended and sent hither to receive condigne punishment, provided that you and the Assembly take present care for the Repeale of all Lawes and Orders made during the late time of Rebellion and Usurpation against our Crowne and Dignitie, and derogatory to the Obedience which all our Subjects of that Our Colony doe give unto Us, and to our Government, and which Wee presume they are willing to pay Us.

3. You shall lett that Assembly know that Wee do Expect from You and them, that you Establish good and wholesome Rules and Orders, and Execute them accordingly, for the punishment, discountenanceing and suppressing of all Vice, Debauchery and Idlenesse, of which, as all good Christians ought to be ashamed in all Places, so in New Plantacions if farr from their owne Country, and when they are exposed to soe many dangers, inconveniencyes and wants, that without an extraordinary wonderfull Protection and Assistance from God Almightie they are in daily hazard of perishing, the

18. "*glebe.*" A parcel of land assigned to a clergyman as part of his benefice. In 1661 the House of Burgesses provided that "there be glebes provided for every parrishe with convenient housing and stockes upon the same." See William Waller Hening, ed., *The Statutes at Large; Being a Collection of All the Laws from the First Session of the Legislature in 1619* (Richmond: R. & W. & G. Barton, 1823), 2: 30.

19. "*attainted.*" To Condemn to death, corruption of blood, and extinction of all civil rights and capacities." OED.

20. The king's opponents executed Charles I on 30 January 1649.

same ought to be more abominated: And that they likewise Establish all necessary encouragement of Virtue and industry and Obedience, and for whatsoever else may advance the Wealth, Honour, and Reputation of that our Colony, and of every Member thereof. In Order to which Wee doe very heartily commend to your and theire care and Consideration.

1.   First, that care be taken to dispose the Planters to bee willing to build Townes upon every River, which must tend very much to their Security, and in time to theire benefit, of which they cannot have a better Evidence and Example than from their Neighbours of New England, who obliging themselves to that order, have in few yeares raysed that Colony to breed Wealth and reputation and Security; Wishing there may be at least one Towne in every River, and that you begin at **James River**, which being first Seated, Wee desire to give all Countenance, and to settle the Government there: And therefore as Wee doe expect that you give good Examples yourselfe by building some houses there, which will in short time turne to your benefit: Soe you shall in Our Name lett the Councellors of that our Colony know, that Wee will take itt very well at their Hands, if they will every of them build one or more Houses there; And you shall give a particular account by a Letter to Ourselfe of the Successes of this Our Designe, what Orders are made by Our Assembly for the advancement thereof, and what particular Persons doe engage themselves to build upon this Our recommendation.

2.   That all possible endeavours be used, and encouragement given to advance the Plantacion of Silke, Flax, Hempe, Pitch and Pott-Ashes, for which Wee are well assured that Climate and Soyle is very proper, Wee Ourself having made experience of the Silke growing there, and finding it to be equall to any Wee have seene, and yett that seemes to be most difficult of any of the rest . . Wee Expect upon the review of what is already Established for the encouragement of these particulars, new and greater rewards and encouragements be given thereunto in proportion to the greate benefit that Our Colony would in a short time reape thereby.

3.   Whereas Wee have beene moved to putt some restraint on the Planting of Tobacco in that Our Col-

ony, both for the advancing of other Comodities. We have recommended to you, and because the price thereof falls soe low, by the great Quantityes brought in from Our other Plantations, that the same in a short tyme will not be valuable to the Planters or Merchants: And whereas Wee have beene likewise moved to make some order for the Limmiting of the Shipps which Trade thither, that they shall not lade and returne from thence, but from and during some time benefit; At all which debates you have beene present, and in all which Our Privy Councill have forborne to give any determination, by reason of the difference of opinions between the Merchants and Planters, and Masters of Ships, noe one partye which seeme to be of the same mind and opinion.

Wee doe recommend the consideracion and debate of the whole to you, and to Our Assembly, to the end that upon the due deliberation of what is best for that Our Colony (Wee meane for the generall good and future advancement thereof, not the particular benefit of a few lesse industrious persons) such good Rules may be Established, as may be for the Publique benefitt.

And because what shall be found necessary to be settled in these particulars will require that the same provision be likewise made in Mary-land, Wee doe direct you that some Commissioners be appointed to Treate with others of Mary-Land to that purpose, and a fitt Place agreed upon for the same, in order whereunto Wee are well assured the Lord Baltimore[21] will send Directions to those who are trusted by him; and if any thing should be insisted on by them contrary to

---

21. Cecilius Calvert, the second Lord Baltimore (1605-1675), inherited his father's dream of planting a religiously tolerant colony on American shores. By the time that Governor Berkeley had received his instructions from the restored King in 1663, Lord Baltimore's colony, Maryland, had begun to flourish. See Russell R. Menard and Lois Green Carr, "The Lords Baltimore and the Colonization of Maryland," in *Early Maryland and the Wider World*, ed. David Beers Quinn (Detroit, MI: Wayne State University Press, 1982), 167-185.

reason, and prejudicial to Our Colony of Virginia,
upon representation thereof to Us, Wee shall give
such Determination therein as shall be just.

Whereas there hath beene presented to Us an Order
of Our Councill for the Colony concerning Two shillings imposed by the Assembly upon every Hogshead[22] of Tobacco exported out of that Our Colony,
upon which some Limitations have been offered by
the Masters of Ships. Wee are well contented to Confirme the said Imposition of Two shillings as aforesaid, or any other Imposition Our Assembly shall
judge fitt and reasonable to make for the good of Our
Colony, support for Our Government there, and the
bringing in and Planting the Comodities aforesaid:
And Wee are graciously pleased, that out of the said
Money, soe imposed One Thousand pounds per Annum; be constantly issued to Our Governor there for
the tyme being; And the remainder thereof, whatsoever it shall amount unto, shall be disposed towards
the Encouragement of the Plantacion of the Comodities aforesaid; a true Account whereof shall be
yearely Transmitted to Our Councill of Plantacions
residing here, by You Our Governor, and such as
shall be appointed to Manage the same.

4. Whereas Wee have certaine knowledge that there is great Endeavours used
of the Fruite and benefit that would benefit by the Act of Assembly concerning Navigation, if the same were carefully and faithfully Executed and
observed, and that very much Tobacco was Shipt in that Our Colony in
Dutch Vessells, wherein some few English Mariners are Entertained by the
ill Arts of some, and Negligence of others, to Defraud Us and the Kingdome
for that purpose, And that very much which is putt on board some English
Vessells is not yet brought into England, and entered here, as by the same
Act ought to be, insoemuch as the quantity of Tobacco brought into this
Kingdome is noe Degree proportionable to the quantitie yearely Transported out of that Our Colony; Wee doe hereby require that a very account
you doe cause to bee Entred there, and Transmitted to Our Commissioners
Farmers of Our Customs here, of all the Tobacco which shall be Shipt from
that Our Colony in English Vessells, and that you suffer none other to be
shipt from thence, with the time when the same was shipped, the name of
the Ship, and of the Master, and to what place hee, or they bound; to the end

22. *"hogshead."* A cask or barrel.

a Discovery being thus made, care may be taken for the severe prosecution and punishment of those who shall transgresse the said Act of Parliament.

5. Wee being informed, that the Grant of Our Royal Father of Blessed Memory, heretofore made to that Our Colony, to Exempt the Planters from paying Quitt-Rents for the first Seaven yeares, hath turned to the greate prejudice of that Our Colony, and that many have abused that Grace, and taken occasion thereby to take and create to themselves a Title to such quantityes of Land which they never intended to, or in truth can occupy and Cultivate, but thereby onely keepe out others who would Plant and Manure the same; Wee do therefore Revoke all such Grants, as contrary to the intention of Our late Royall Father, and to the good of the People, And doe Appoint you, by and with the Advice of Our Councill to give Direction to Our Treasurer or his Deputie, that the Quitt-Rents be carefully and justly Levyed, and noe longer forbearance thereof, by reason or colour of such Occupacion or desertion as aforesaid; And you shall likewise require Our Treasurer or his Deputie to be carefull to enter upon all such Lands as lawfully Escheated to Us, and Authorise him to make new Grants of the said Escheated Lands, in such manner and with such limitation as shalbe directed by you and Our Councill.

6. Amongst other good workes Wee desire to Erect in that Our Colony of Virginia, Wee have a desire to erect such an Iron Worke, as may be in truth considerable, and above what a Private undertaking can goe through, and doe therefore, if we find encouragement thereto, resolve to undertake it Ourselfe, and in order thereunto Wee would have you debate the whole matter, and all that may conduce thereunto with Our Councill there, and upon a cleere State thereof, and upon a view that there is plenty of good Ore fitt for the same, you transmit your advice and opinion on how Wee may best undertake itt, what Wee must Transport from hence to that purpose, and all things that are necessary thereunto; And Wee shall thereupon provide as Wee shall thinke fitt.

7. You shall once every yeare Transmitt the true and full state of that Our Colony to Our Councill of Plantations here, with a particular Account of every Improvement you observed to be made by the Industry of the Planters, as well as of the direction of the Governor in the yeare past, what number of People have beene Transported thither that yeare, and what new Plantations they have entred upon, and what new Incouragement you desire from hence, that soe upon a representation made to Us by them, Wee may shew you by some New and Multiplyed Grace and favour, how much Wee take to heart, the good & benefit & advancement of that Our Colony, and Our good Subjects thereof.

Lastly. Wee having now upon your desire Granted a Commission of Oyer and Terminer[23] for the better Administration of Justice and punishment of Offences within that Our Colony, Wee do earnestly recommend to your care, and Wisdome and integritie, that Justice bee well and impartially Administred, and that Our good Subjects have noe cause of Complaint, And if you and Our Assembly shall find it requisite for the better execution thereof that some persons Learned in the Lawes be sent from hence, and shall provide competent Salaryes for them, Wee shall upon such Representation make choice of some fitt person for the Performance of that service.

Given att Our Court at Whitehall the 12th day of September, in the Fourteenth yeare of Our Reigne. 1662.

This is a true Copie of his Majesties Instructions then
Given to Sir William Berkeley – Governor of Virginia
H. Coventry [24]

A Copie written and carefully Examined from the Copie
Abovemencioned.
Samuel Wiseman

Document 9
13 November 1676

Additional Instructions to Our Trusty & Welbeloved Sir William Berkeley Knight, Our Governor of Our Colony of Virginia.

You shall besides the Former Instructions given you, when you were last in this Our Kingdome, Observe these Addicionall ones, and wherever there shall appeare anything of contrariety in them, these latter are to have the preference, and be observed by You.

23. "*court of oyer and terminer.*" Court established to try cases of treason and felony.
24 Sir Henry Coventry, (1619-1686), who signed the original, served as the king's secretary of state along with Joseph Williamson. No single department possessed responsibility for the king's dominions overseas. Instructions to the king's men in the colonies most commonly came from one of the two secretaries of state. The Lords of Trade and Plantations served in an advisory capacity, and in essence were little more than a standing committee of the Privy Council. For more on this, see G. E. Aylmer, *The Crown's Servants: Government and Civil Service Under Charles II, 1660-1685* (London: Oxford University Press, 2002), 53-54.

1. You shall be noe more obliged to call an Assembly once every Yeare; but onely once in two Yeares, unlesse some emergent occasion shall make it necessary, the Judging whereof Wee leave to your Discretion. Also whensoever the Assembly is called, Fourteene dayes shall be time prefixt for their Sitting, and noe longer, unless You find Good cause to continue itt beyond that tyme.

2. You shall take care that the Members of the Assembly be Elected onely by Free-holders,[25] as being more aggreable to the Custome of England, to which You are as nigh [26]as conveniently you can to conforme Your-selfe.

3. You shall Endeavour to make a good Peace with the Neighbour Indians, and in managing and concluding a Treaty with them, You shall make use of the assistance of the Commissioners Wee now send from hence to that Our Colony, whome You shall Receive and Treat with all due Respect, as Persons chosen by Us for their Loyaltie and Ability to Undertake and performe the **High Trust** Wee have reposed in them, with a **convenient Howse and Lodging.** You shall alsoe immediately upon their Arrival, make the Councill acquainted with it, as likewise with the contents of their Commission.

4. During these Troubles, You shall Exactly putt in Execution the Instruction, not to suffer any one to goe on board any Merchant Ship or other Vessells coming into any Port or Anchoring in any Roade of that Our Colony, without Your Certificate and Permission. And you shall have a speciall Care that neither Nathaniell Bacon in particular, nor any other of his Accomplices, bee suffered soe to doe.

5. Immediately Upon the Arrival of Our Said Commissioners, You shall call a new Assembly. The late Assembly to be by Your Authoritie dissolved, if it be not at the time of Your Receipt of These, And the New one to be Elected according to the Second of these additionall Instructions. But in the calling of Assembly, you shall avoid (as much as Our Affaires will permitt) the Convening of them in Court tymes.

---

25. *"freeholders."* An act passed by the House of Burgesses in 1670 allowed only free-holders and housekeepers to vote, in essence denying the franchise to Virginia's growing ranks of propertyless men. The Baconian Assembly in June of 1676 annulled the Franchise Act, granting the vote to all freemen, and not just property owners. See Hening, ed., *Statutes*, 2:280, 356-357.

26 *"nigh."* near, close.

6.   You shall Declare Voide and Null, all the Proceedings of the late Assembly; wherein the said **Nathaniel Bacon** and his Accomplices were Pardoned, and Force and Violence offered to the Assembly.

7.   And upon the Receipt of thse Instructions you shall immediately Summon the said **Nathaniel Bacon** to present himself in such place and manner, as You shall judge fitt, which when hee shall have done, you shall sieze him, and either make his Processe there, or send him on Ship-board, with the proofes relating to his Crimes, in order to his Transporting hither, for his Tryall, As You shall judge most convenient, according to his greater or lesser interest amongst the Generality of the People.[27]

8.   But if the said Nathaniel Bacon shall refuse to render himselfe, then the **Proclamacion** which you shall receive with these Instructions shall be immediately Proclaimed, and all wayes of Force and Designe used to surprize him. And to the end hee may not easily make his Escape, Wee have caused Our Letters to be directed to Our Most Deare Brother James Duke of Yorke or the Commander in Chiefe under him of New-Yorke,[28] as also to the Lord Baltimore, or the Commander in Chiefe under him in Mary-Land to seize the said Bacon, and returne him Prisoner to You, in case hee should retire to either of those Places.

9.   You shall reduce the Salary of the Assembly Members to such a moderate proporcion as may be noe greivance to the Country, And in the Regulacion hereof, You shall Advise with our aforesaid Commissioners.

10.   You shall according to your foresaid Instrucions Give once a Yeare an Account both to Our Councell of Trade and Plantacions, & likewise to the Commissioners or Farmers of Our Customes here of those severall things you are directed by the Fifth, Seventh and Eighth Articles.
Given att our Court at Whitehall the 13th day of November 1676, in the Eight and twentieth yeare of our Reigne.[29]

                                           C. R.

27. Bacon, of course, had died the preceding October.

28. James, Duke of York, the brother of the king, became proprietor of New York when the English conquered the province from the Dutch in 1664. James would rule England as James II from 1685 until 1688.

29. The commissioners received these instructions from the king two days later, on November 15. On November 19, they set sail for Virginia. The planning for the expedition had commenced much earlier. See Stephen Saunders Webb, *1676: The End of American Independence* (New York: Knopf, 1984), 199-209

Document 10
28 September 1676

A Letter Subscrib'd as followeth:
For Our very Loving Friends His Majesties Commissioners for the Affaires of Virginia

After our hearty commendations unto You. Whereas Wee did by our Letters of the Fourteenth of April last,[30] signifie to Sir William Berkeley, that it had pleased his Majestie to committ unto our Care the businesse of the forrein Plantations; and did therefore direct him to give us an account of all proceedings concerning that Colonie of **Virginia,** and more particularly touching the Act of Navigations and how the Rules and directions thereof were observed by him; As also that hee would send us Answers unto severall heads of **Inquiries** that relate unto the whole State and Condition of the Place.[31]

Wee doe therefore thinke it convenient upon this occasion of your going thither to direct, that Copies of all those Papers bee putt into Your hands, that soe if you finde noe progresse made upon them by Sir William Berkeley, You may concerne Your selves in joining with him to Expedite and Answer therein.

And soe wee bid you heartily Farewell. From the Court at Whitehall the Twenty eighth day of September, 1676.

Your very Loving Friends
Craven[32]
H. Coventry
J. Ernle[33]
Robert Southwell[34]

This is a true Copie examined by me,
Samuel Wiseman

---

30. See Document 11, below.
31. See Document 13, below.
32. William Craven, Earl of Craven, (1606-1697). Longtime supporter of Charles II, who returned with the king to England upon his restoration in 1660. Served on the Privy Council from 1666-1681.
33. Sir John Ernle served as chancellor and under-treasurer of the exchequer.
34. Robert Southwell, (1635-1702) was sworn to the king's Privy Council in 1664.

Document 11
14 April 1676

To Sir William Berkeley from the Committee of Trade[35]

After our heartie Commendations unto you.

His Majestie having in his Wisdome thought fitt to supersede the Commission by which His Council of Trade and Forrein Plantations lately acted, and reducing all the Businesse, of that nature, to its accustomed chanel of a Committee of His Privy Council. And his Majestie having more especially committed to a select number of the Board (whereof wee are) the Care and Management of things relating to His Plantations; Wee have therefore thought it convenient to give you advertisement thereof.

And because wee find not, among the Bookes and Papers of the late Council any further account of things under your Government, than what you represented in your Narrative of the 20th of June 1671,[36] but doe consider that the condition of Colonies is subject to many changes and alterations, Therfore it is that wee send you here annext the same heads of Inquiry which formerly you had and the addition of some other points, that you may with all convenient speede, returne us all transactions, and passages, since your former account, together with the present state and condition of that place; and inlarge Your Representation in the other particulars, which are also recommended unto you.

And soe not doubting of your care to advise us in these, and from time to time, in all other matters, that may conduce to His Majestes Service, and our better discharge of the Trust reposed in Us.

Wee bid you heartily farewell. From the Council Chamber at Whitehall, the 14th day of April, 1676.

Your Loving Friends,
G. Finch[37]
Anglesey[38]
Ormond[39]

35. A committee drawn up and comprised of members of the king's Privy Council to advise the Crown on colonial matters.

36. The "Narrative" in reality consists of a list of questions with Berkeley's answers, treating subjects such as the colony's political and judicial system; its state of military preparedness; its boundaries; its population; and the economic activities that occurred there. It is reprinted in Hening, ed., *Statutes*, 2: 511-517.

37. Member of the king's Privy Council and Committee of Trade and Plantations.

38. Arthur Annesley, First Earl of Anglesey (1614-1686). Sworn to the Privy Council on 1 June 1660. On 22 April 1673, he was rewarded for his loyalty with the office of Lord Privy Seal.

Carlisle[40]   Bridgewater[41]
Craven   H. Coventry
G. Carteret[42]
J. Williamson

A True Copie
Robert Southwell

For Our very loving Friend Sir
William Berkeley Knight, Captain General
& Governor in Chiefe of his Majesties Colony of
Virginia in America.

A True Copie
Samuel Wiseman

Document 12
14 April 1676

From the Committee of Trade, to Sir William Berkley

After our hearty commendations unto you. There hath been lately great complaints presented unto His Majestie about Omissions in Executing the Act of Navigation, made in the 12th, as alsoe of the Plantacion Act made in the 25th yeare of His Majesties Reigne, as if, by connivance or neglect there were permitted such a libertie of Trade in the Forrein Plantations, as will prove very pernicious unto this Kingdome.

Therefore, observing the great dangers & penalties in Law, which the Governors, and those that are intrusted, doe incurr, if the proof of any miscarriage of this nature, can be brought home, and charged upon them; and knowing withall, that if the Governors of the Plantations did, according to the provision of the

39. James Butler, Twelth Earl and First Duke of Ormonde, (1610-1688), returned to England with Charles II at the Restoration and was sworn to the Privy Council at that time.
40. Charles Howard, First Earl of Carlisle. Military officer in England who would later serve as Governor-General of Jamaica, 1678-1681. See Webb, *Governors-General*, 479.
41. John Egerton, Duke of Bridgewater.
42. Sir George Carteret (d. 1680), member of the Privy Council from the Restoration. One of the original proprietors of Carolina, Carteret also received from the duke of York a share in the colonization of New Jersey.

Law, send home Copies of Bonds, and Lists of Ships there laden, it would be of great avail to prevent the Frauds which are used in carrying the Plantation Commodities to other parts. Wee have thought it for his Majesties service, and for your owne security, to give you advertisement thereof. And the rather, because by a late account from the Commissioners of His Majesties Customs, Wee finde that the Bonds (which are to be returned twice every yeare) doe very sparingly come in; and that scarce any Lists of the Ships that lade within Your Government, the Commodities which are enumerated by Law, are sent over, which, with the Bonds, should bee returned once every yeare, at the least.

Therefore referring you, for the better Observation of what is Expected from You, to the said Lawes in generall, Wee yet thinke fitt to put you here in minde, that you are to take a strict care not to suffer any Ships to Trade, within that your Government, but such as are belonging to the people of England, or some of His Majesties English Plantations and Navigated according to Law. And that if any Vessell shall import into your Government any European Commodities, from any other place, but onely such as were actually laden and shipped in England (except such Commodities as are allowed by Law) that you cause seizure to be made of all such Ships and Vessels, and all the Commodities therein imported. You are alsoe to take care that Bonds, with sufficient surety, bee taken of all Masters of vessels to bring and unlade in some part of England, Wales, or Berwick,[43] and noe other place, all the enumerated Plantation Comodities they shall take on Board in the respective Plantations: Copies of which Bonds are to be returned twice every yeare at least, together with the Bonds, as by the Law is required. And that any of the said Bonds upon forfeiture thereof, bee put in suite, & prosecuted according to Law.

And soe not doubting of your care and punctual observance in this matter, which is of so high importance to his Majesties service, and so penal to you in the Omission whereof Wee are resolv'd to be very strict Inquisitors, and to exact from you a frequent & punctuall account, Wee bid you very heartily Farewell. From the Court at Whitehall the 14th day of April. 1676.

Your very Loving Friends
Finch. C.
Anglesey
Ormonde
Carlisle
Bridgewater
Craven

For our very loving friend
Sir William Berkley Knight Capt.
Generall & Governor in chiefe of his
Majesties colony of Virginia in America

---

43. Vital city in the north of England which during the Elizabethan period became "the major base of the crown's domestic, political police actions in the northern counties while it still sustained its ancient role as the anchor of the Scots Border defenses." See Webb, *Governors-General*, 7-9.

A true copie

Samuel Wiseman

G. Carteret
H. Coventry
J. Williamson
Robert Southwell

Document 13

Inquiries to bee sent to Sir William Berkeley Knight, Capt. General and Governor in chief of His Majesties Colony of Virginia.

1. **What** Councils, Assemblies, and Courts of Judicature are within Your Government, and of what nature and kind.
2. **What** Courts of Judicature relating to the Admiralty.
3. **Where** the Legislative and Executive Powers of Your Government are seated.
4. **What** Statutes, Lawes and Ordinances are now made and in force.
5. **What** number of Horse and Foote are within Your Government, whether they bee Trained Bands or Standing Forces,[44] how they are armed, divided, and Executed.
6. **What** Castles and Forts are within Your Government and how Scituated, as alsoe what stores and provisions they are furnished withall.
7. **What** number of Privateers or Pyrats doe frequent your Coast, what their Burthens are,[45] the number of their Men and Guns, and the Names of the Commanders.
8. **What** is the strength of your bordering Neighbours, whether Indians, or of any other Nation, by Sea and Land, what is the State and condition of their Trade and Comerce.
9. **What** Correspondence doe you keepe with your Neighbors.
10. **What** Armes, Ammunitions and Stores did you find upon the Place, or have beene sent unto You since, upon his Majesties accompt, when received, how imployed, and what part of them is remaining.
11. **What** Moneyes have been paid, or appointed to bee paid by his Majestie, or levyed within your Government for and towards the buying of

---

44. *"Trained Bands."* In 1661 the House of Burgesses ordered that each militia regiment raise three train bands. These units were expected to be "always ready in armes" and prepared to march "to the rescue of such distressed places or persons as he their Commander shall direct." Quoted in Shea, *Virginia Militia*, 174.
45. i.e., the size of their ships.

Armes, or making, or mainteining of any Fortifications and Castles, or for any other public uses; and how have the Moneyes beene Expended.

12.   **What** are the Boundaries, Longitude, Latitude and Contents of the Land within your Government, what number of Acres Patented, setled or unsetled, and how much is manurable Land.

13.   **What** are the Principal Townes and Places of Trade, and what manner of Buildings are most used in Your Colony, as to the strength and largenesse of them.

14.   **How** many Parishes, Precincts, or Divisions are within Your Government.

15.   **What** Rivers, Harbors & Roads are within your Government, and of what Depths and Soundings they are.

16.   **What** Commodities are there of the production, growth and Manufacture of your Plantation, and of what value yearely, either Exported, or consumed upon the Place, and particularly what is the present State of the Silke-Trade, what advantages or impediments doe attend it.[46] And what Materials are there already growing, or may be provided for Shipping, As alsoe what are the Commodities imported, and of what yearely value.

17.   **Whether** Salt Peter is, or may bee produced, within your Plantation, and if soe, in what quantity, and at what rates it may be deliver'd in England.

18.   **What** number of Merchants and Planters, English or Forreiners, Servants and Slaves, and how many of them are Men able to beare Armes.

19.   **What** number of English, Scotch, Irish, or Forreiners have, for these Seaven yeares last past, or any other space of time, come yearly to plant and inhabit within your Government. And alsoe what Blacks, or Slaves have been brought in within the said time, and at what rates.[47]

---

46. To raise silkworms and produce silk in Virginia had been a long-enduring dream of colonial and imperial officials. Little came of such efforts. See Philip Alexander Bruce, *Economic History of Virginia in the Seventeenth Century*, (New York: Peter Smith, 1935), 1: 240-243, 365-369, 396-400.

47 For studies of the enslavement of Africans in Virginia, see Winthrop Jordan, *White Over Black: American Attitudes Toward the Negro, 1550-1812* (Chapel Hill: University of North Carolina Press, 1968); Edmund S. Morgan, *American Slavery, American Freedom: The Ordeal of Colonial Virginia* (New York: Norton, 1975); and most recently, Anthony S. Parent, Jr., *Foul Means: The Formation of a Slave Society in Virginia, 1660-1740* (Chapel Hill: University of North Carolina Press, 2003). Wiseman's *Book of Record* reveals here that Virginians had not yet developed a full-fledged system of racial slavery; some blacks, at least, were free. The children produced from black-white sexual encounters, moreover, apparently were in some cases free. Morgan, in *American Slavery, American Freedom*, emphasizes that Bacon's Rebellion marked a critical point in the transition from white indentured servitude to African slavery.

20. **What** number of Whites, Blacks or Mulatto's have beene borne and Christned for these Seaven yeares last past, or any other space of time.

21. **What** number of Marriages, for Seaven yeares last past, or any other tyme.

22. **What** number of People have yearly Dyed within your Government for Seaven yeares past, or any other space of tyme.

23. **What** Estimat can you make touching the Estates of the severall degrees of Merchants and Planters within your Government; And how you may compute the wealth of the Colony in generall.

24. **What** number of Shipps, Sloops, or other Vessells doe Trade yearly to and from your Plantation, and of what Built and Burthen, and whether there be any belonging to the Country.

25. **What** Obstructions doe you find to the Improvement of the Trade and Navigation of the Plantations of your Government.

26. **What** advantages or improvements doe you observe that may be gained to Your Trade and Navigation.

27. **What** Rates and Duties are charged and payable upon any Goods Exported out of your Plantation, whether of your owne growth and manufacture or otherwise, as also upon Goods imported: And to what public ends or Uses are the same applyed.

28. **What** Revenue doth or may arise to His Majestie within Your Government, and of what Nature is it, by whome the same collected, and how Answered and Accompted to his Majestie.

29. **What** Perswasion in Religious matters is most prevalent; and among the Varieties which you are to Expresse, what proportion in numbers and qualitie of People the one holds to the other.

30. **What** course is taken for the instructing of the People in the Christian Religion, how many Churches and Ministers are there within your Government, and how many are yet wanting for the accommodation of your Colony. What provision is there made for the maintenance of them, as also for relieving poore, decayed and impotent persons. And whether you have any Beggers or Idle Vagabonds.

A True Copie

Robert Southwell

Vera Copia.
Samuel Wiseman

Document 14
October or November, 1676

A Forme of an Indictment for Rebellion by Leavying Warr

The Jurors for the Kings Majestie doe present, that A. B: of C. in the Countie of D. and other false Traytors against our said Soveraigne Lord King Charles the Second, by the grace of God of England, Scotland, France & Ireland, Defender of the Faith &c., Not having God before their eyes, nor considering their due Allegiance but being seduced by the instigation of the Devil, imagining and endeavouring Him the Kings Majestie their now supreme soveraigne Lord of the Royall estate, Government and Power of His Colony of Virginia, to disturbe, and the Government of the said Colony at their will and pleasure to change, By force of Armes (that is to say) with Guns commonly called Musquetts, Sclopis,[48] called Pistolls, with speares, swords and other Armes, aswell defensive as offensive, in warrlike manner armed & arraied on the   day of   in the 28th yeare of the Reigne of our said Lord the King; att the Towne of N: in Our County of D; their wicked designes to accomplish, themselves falsly, Rebelliously, and Trayterously, with a great Multitude of Traytors and Rebells, to the number of Five hundred Men, did rise convene and assemble all together, and a horrid Warr against our said Lord the King, did then and there in hostile manner, rebelliously and trayterously prepare, leavy, execute and perpetrate, against their due Allegiance, to the great danger of the subverting the royal Estate and Government of our now Lord the King, within His Colony of Virginia and against the Peace of Our said Lord the King, His Crowne and Dignitie; as also against the Forme of the Statute in like cases made and Provided.
Translated from the Foregoing Latine[49]

Samuel Wiseman.

Document 15
1 February 1677

An Inventory expressing what the severall particular Patents, under the Broad Seale, and Paper writings are, which Wee delivered to the hands of Sir William Berkley Knight His Majesties Governor of Virginia, as followeth (that is to say) Inprimis[50]

---

48. "*sclopis.*" A handgun.
49. Wiseman included copies of the indictment both in Latin and in English. I have omitted the Latin version.
50. "*inprimis.*" Also *imprimis*, a phrase used to introduce the first of a number of items, as in an inventory or will. *OED.*

1.   His Majesties Grant and Declaration in Favour of his Subjects Inhabiting in **Virginia**.[51]

2.   A Pardon granted unto the Governor and Assembly of His Majesties Plantation of Virginia, for passing of certaine Acts, being under a Force.[52]

3.   A Commission, Giving Power to the Governor of Virginia to Pardon Offences.[53]

        All these are under the Broad Seale.

4.   Additional Instructions to Sir William Berkley Knight Governor of Virginia, under the signet Royall and signe manuall.[54]

        Five hundred Printed Proclamations
        A forme of an Indictment[55]

I Sir William Berkley, His Majesties Governor of Virginia doe hereby acknowledge the Receipt of the severall things above specified with my owne hands from Sir John Berry Knight and Francis Moryson Esquire His Majesties Commissioners for the settling of Affaires of Virginia, the First day of February 1677, whereto I have Subscribed my hand for their discharge in this particular.

William Berkeley

51. See Document 3, above.
52. See Document 4, above.
53. See Document 5, above.
54. See Document 9, above.
55. See Document 14, above.

2 The Commissioners and Sir William Berkeley

Document 1
29 January 1677

A Letter from Sir John Berry to Sir William Berkeley, upon his First Arrival in Virginia.

Right Honorable,

These are to Advertize you, that I came to Anchor this Afternoone, and that there is on Board mee Col: Francis Moryson (joint Commissioner with mee and Col: Herbert Jeffreyes, by His Majesties Commission under the Great Seale of England for Settling the Grievances and other Affaires of Virginia) And that I have on board mee about Seaventy of His Majesties Soldiers Commanded at present by one Capt. Morris,[1] who are to bee forthwith putt on shore to receive orders from you; until the arrival of the rest of the Forces, which make up a Compleate Regiment of a thousand men under the Command of Colonell Herbert Jeffreyes, who hath also coming with him all kind of Provisions and Ammunition necessary for your Assistance in the carrying on the Warr against the Kings Enemies, and suppressing the Present Rebellion: all which were shipt[2] and readie to saile when I left England.

I also thinke fitt to acquaint you, that the King hath given mee full Power of Commanding all Merchants, Shipps and Seamen within the Rivers of Virginia, to bee ayding and assisting in His Majesties Service, to the suppressing and quieting the Disorders of the Country; And for what shott, powder, Greate Guns &c you shall stand in neede of the better carrying on of this His Majesties service. Upon your notice thereof I shall be readie to supply you with such stores as I can spare.

---

1. Captain Robert Morris, commander of the *Young Prince,* played a decisive role in bringing the rebellion to a close. He engaged in heavy combat against rebel forces from September of 1676 until January of 1677. The journal of his exploits during the rebellion is housed in the British Public Records Office, Letters and Papers Concerning American Plantations, 1 June 1676–7 October 1676, C.O. 1/37, 180-189, Virginia Colonial Records Project, Virginia Historical Society, Richmond, VA, [hereafter VCRP]. In 1679, the Privy Council awarded Morris £100 for his service to Crown and colony. See Privy Council Register, 1679, P.C. 2/67, 136 (VCRP).
2. i.e., aboard ships.

His Majesties Shipps now under my command are the *Bristoll* & *Deptford* Ketch; the *Rose* and *Dartmouth* Frigatts coming after with the rest of the Fleete of Merchant men and Forces.

Wee have severall other matters to impart to you, which cannot bee soe well imparted, but upon a personall Conference with you, which wee earnestly desire, and would be glad it might be here on Boarde (if the present State of your health will permit); or else that you will please to nominate unto us some such place of Meeting, as may seem agreeable to the Kings Honor, and your owne Conveniency.

Sir, I have noe more to add, but that when I left London your Ladie was well, and ready for her departure hither.

Col. Moryson writes not now, because hee knowes and suddainly Expects wee are to meete face to face, and soe gives you his most humble service, as doth

I, Your most Affectionate Friend and Servant,

John Berry

From on Board His Majesties Shipp Bristoll now riding at anchor in Kiccotan[3] in James River

The 29th day of January, 1676/7

Document 2
2 February 1677

INTERLOCUTORY HEADS of such matters, in Conference with Sir William Berkeley, Knight, His Majestyes Governour of Virginia, (as we conceiving) necessary for his Majesties Service.

Reade and communicated to him on Board the *Bristol* and afterwards delivered in writing at Greene Spring and by him promised to be answered.

Sa: Wiseman

1.   It is desired that you will be Pleased to take into your present and special care, to provide convenient Quarters and Dyett for His Majesties Soldiers already arrived to Your Assistance, and Quarters for those that are to come.

3. Kecoughtan was southeast of Hampton Creek on the James River, within the present day bounds of Hampton, Virginia.

2. For the Providing of Sloopes and other small Crafts, fitting to Land His Majesties said Soldiers, Provision, Ammunition, &c, for the use of the Colony.

3. That there be Convenient Storehouses for the Receipt and Safe-keeping of the Ammunition, and Provisions aforesaid.

4. Wee having delivered to you His Majesties Proclamations concerning Nathaniel Bacon and his Accomplices, that you please to act as to the Publishment thereof, as your Instructions require.

5. That you will be Pleased to Summon the respective County Courts, and then and there to tender and give the Othes of Allegiance and Supremacy as a test of their future Obedience and Loyaltie.

6. That you Please to call a new Assembly, and the Members of same bee soe Elected and Qualified, as his Majestyes Instructions doe in that case require and direct.

7. We conceive it very fitting, that there be a due Submission made by those of the Assembly, in the name and on the behalfe of the whole Countrey of Virginia, and an Humble and open Acknowledge of their Disobedience to His Majestie and His Government, whereby to render themselves more Capable of His Majesties Especial Grace and Mercy to bee Extended to them.

8. Whereas, His Majestie hath with greatest instance committed to our Care and utmost Endeavours the Procuring a Good and Just peace with the Neighbour Indians: and also wee ourselves being sufficiently sensible how much the Violation and want of such a Peace doth redound to his Majesties losse and detrement, His Customes and Revenues at Home arising out of this Colony; Wee doe therefore conceive, that it doth in a most Especiall manner concerne both you and us, earnestly to endeavour (by all wayes wee can) to effect such a good and firme Peace with the said Indians as shall (with the Peculiar Blessing of Almighty God on soe good and just a Worke) most conduce to His Majesties Honor and Interest, and also to the Profitt and Advantage of the whole People of Virginia; In all which wee doe most Heartily assure You that you shall find us ready to Assist you, with a Seale suitable to the Interprize, and the Instructions wee have received in this particular.

9. Wee having delivered us a Copie of His Majesties Instructions formerly Given You, bearing the date at Whitehall the twelfth day of September, in the fourteenth yeare of His Majesties Reigne,[4] Wee are to desire, and doe hereby Desire your distinct Answer to each respective head or Article thereof; how the same have beene by You observed from time to time, and wherein there hath been

4. i.e., 1663

any failer, and upon what groundes, and by whose neglect and wilfull default the same were; To all which wee pray Your full Answer in Writing; As also to certeine heads of Enquiry which you have formerly had, and whereof we have alsoe a Copie and are appointed to Enquire into.

10.   Lastly, Whereas the king hath willed us, in a particular manner, (among other matters), to inspect that Grievance of the Greate Salary paid the Members of the Assembly, and hath required us to bee Assistant to you in our advice concerning an immediate Redresse thereof: Wee conceive it Expedient in order thereunto, That there may an Act passe for a New Assembly to bee Elected and Called every two yeares, whereby to make those of the present Assembly more readie to Complie with his Majesties Commandes for Retrenching their former Salary. Whereas by reason of their Constant Sitting, they Receive onely, and pay not which this Alteration will well remedie, and make the Charge Equal by alternate Receipts and Payments, and soe remove the present pressure, which the People seeme so much concerned in.

Given under our hands the 2nd day of February, Anno 1676/7
From on Board His Majesties Shipp Bristoll

John Berry
Francis Moryson

Document 3
2 February 1677

A Letter from the Commissioners to His Majesties Principal Secretaries of State

Right Honorable,

Sir, That His Majestie may perceive wee imbrace all Opportunities, which may manifest our Care and Duty to informe His Majestie of the Condition of this Country soe farr as soe short a tyme will permit; Wee have dispatch'd this to acquaint your Honor, that after a tedious Passage of Tenne weekes and a day wee arrived within the Capes of Virginia, and pursuant to the tenour of our Instructions (immediately upon our Arrivall) sent to the Governour Sir William Berkeley, who upon notice thereof, was pleased to come on Board us: where we delivered him all the Proclamations, Broad Seales, Instructions and other Papers

that belong'd to him.[5] From whom we have this Account of the present posture
of Affaires. i. e. That the Rebell Bacon is dead, his Accomplices dispers'd, some
of the Ringleaders taken, tried and sentenced by a Councell of Warr, and about
twentie of them lately executed, and that the poore scatter'd Loyall partie of the
Country begin now to returne to their ruin'd homes, Bacon having totally Destroy'd and burnt downe to the Ground the City of James Towne and with his
owne hands sett Fire to the Church there, soe that the small number of soldiers
already arrived, by reason of these Devastations there, and in other parts of the
Countrey, are become quite destitute of Quarters, there being noe place fitt to
receive soe small a Body of Men, much lesse the number that are coming after;
Whereat the Governour, who did believe a single Frigatt (or two) would have
beene sufficient on this occasion, and professing never soe much as to have desired Soldiers, is much amus'd, and the whole People much startled and concerned, and many ready to desert their Plantations, and to retreat to other Parts,
which will force us to continue the Soldiers on Board till Col. Jeffreyes and the
rest arrive, rather than turne them loose on a naked shore, to subsist on the poore
Loyall partie, who scarse left wherewith to support themselves at present, such
has bin the miserable Consequences of these unhappie Disorders among them,
wherein as there is none has been a greater sufferer than the Governor, soe hath
there been noe one (under God) a more eminent or active Instrument in suppressing this Rebellion, and quieting the divisions and Disorders among the
people. And upon Conferrence with him wee find (to our great satisfaction) that
a good foundation is already laid of a Peace with the Neighbour Indians, and
that the Queene of Pamunckey is lately return'd to her usuall Place of Residence,[6] that also the Assembly is summon'd to meete on the Twentyeth day of
this Moneth at the Governours Howse at Green Spring in James River, which
the late Rebells have very much Ruin'd.

We are also preparing to summon in the respective counties of this Country
to declare to them the Occasion of our Coming and to cause them to bring in
their Grievances to us: in our Enquirie whereof, we can as yet find noe Appeare-
ance of any, save onely that of the Greate Salary paid the Members of Assembly, which wee doubt not but wee shall soone addresse.

Among other Discourses then had with the Gouvernour we find him very
much concerned about the Destribution of the Forfeited Estates and Possessions

---

5. In other words, Berry and Moryson delivered to Governor Berkeley all the items listed
in Document 15 of Chapter 1, above.
6. On the Queen of Pamunkey, see Martha W. McCartney, "Cockacoeske, Queen of Pamunkey: Diplomat and Suzeraine," in *Powhatan's Mantle: Indians in the Colonial
Southeast,* eds. Peter H. Wood, Gregory A. Waselkov, and M. Thomas Hatley (Lincoln:
University of Nebraska Press, 1989), 173-195; The principal Pamunkey village lay near
the mouth of the Pamunkey River. See Helen C. Rountree, *The Powhatan Indians of
Virginia: Their Traditional Culture* (Norman: University of Oklahoma Press, 1989), 11.

of such as have been concerned in this Rebellion, which hee would have to be disposed and given in Restitution to the Loyall Partie that have beene loosers by it: to which wee dare in noe wise give our Advice or Opinion, as being quite without our Instructions.

All we can say more is that (God assisting) in some short tyme wee may well Expect to see things soe settled, as shall best conduce both to his Majesties Honour and good liking, which wee will as earnestly endeavour, as wee desire. And by the present Prospect of things wee see noe cause to apprehend any occasion for a long stay in this Country, which should wee (for want of His Majesties Orders of Returning, which wee have not yet received) be forced to doe, till the Sickley Monethes of June July &c. it would not onely much endanger the falling downe and losse of the greatest part of the Seamen, but also Hazzard the spoiling the Kings Shipps by Wormes.

All which most Humbly, submitting to His Majesties Royal Consideration Wee humbly take leave of your Honour for the present, assuring you that His Majestie by all opportunityes shall not faile to receive a due account of our Proceedings from tyme to tyme. And thus with our Hearty Prayers for His Majestyes most happie Prosperity at Home and abroade, wee humbly remaine.

Sir. His Majesties Most Obedient Faithfull Subjects
and Your Honors Most Humble Servants,

John Berry
Francis Moryson

From on Board His Majesties Shippe Bristoll Riding att Kiccatan in James River in Virginia, February 2, 1676/7

The *Dartmouth* and *Deptford* Ketch are arrived, the former who had the convoy of those shipps that bring the soldiers, lost company with them neere the Westerne Islands.

The like letter (mutat. mutand.) & like date
sent to the Duke of Yorkes Secretary Sir
John Werden and then as followeth, viz.

In discourse with the Governor (when wee delivered him the Proclamations and other things) wee found by him, that in regard Bacon was deade, hee conceived it improper to publish the Kings Printed Proclamations, but discours'd framing another to be collected from that; wherein he intends to exempt about eight persons, not yett taken (besides what are already in Custodie) which are

the Chiefe of the Rebells.[7] Thus much wee thought it our Duty to informe His
Royall Hignesse by your Hand. Assuring you that his R. Highnesse, shall not
faile from time to receive such further Account from us of our Proceedings; as
becomes the Dutie of His Royall Highnesse's most Humble and Devoted Servants; and,

Sir,

Your Very Faithfull Friends and
Humble Servants

John Berry
Francis Moryson

Wee will not omit to lett his R. Highnesse know that the
Governour intends to try Bland (one of the Rebells in Custody)
by a Jury &c after the manner of the Lawes of England;[8]
those already executed having beene Tried and
Sentenced by a Councill of Warr.

P.S.

7. Governor Berkeley did not want to publish the king's printed proclamation, he said,
because it referred to men already dead or awaiting trial, and as such no longer was rele-
vant to conditions in Virginia. The best account of the sparring between the commissioners and the governor will appear in Warren Billing's forthcoming book, *Sir William
Berkeley: A Virginian's Biography* (Baton Rouge: Louisiana State University Press,
forthcoming), Chapter 14. I am indebted to Professor Billings for providing me with a
copy of the manuscript.
8. Berry here refers to Giles Bland, like Nathaniel Bacon a newcomer to the king's Old
Dominion. He had come to the colony to reclaim his father's plantation from two of
Governor Berkeley's closest associates, Thomas and Philip Ludwell, who had extorted
the land from the custody of one of Bland's elderly aunts. Bland challenged Philip Ludwell to a duel; when Ludwell failed to show, Bland pinned a note to the statehouse door
condemning him as a coward. Bland also served as a customs commissioner, and his ties
to the machinery of imperial enforcement provided him with the contacts necessary for
communicating Bacon's message to the king. Indeed, Bland provided the Crown with its
initial intelligence on the rebellion. Bland became one of the governor's harshest critics,
complaining to the Council of Trade and Plantations and the Secretaries of State that
Virginia faced the danger not only of Indian attack but of a corrupt and oppressive governor who had mismanaged colonial revenues. Bland was captured by Berkeley's naval
forces in August of 1676, and executed later. On Bland, see Stephen Saunders Webb,
1676: The End of American Independence (New York: Knopf, 1984), 50-56.

Sir,

The *Dartmouth* arrived here Yesterday, who informes mee, that he lost Company with the Fleete of Merchants Shipps nere the Westerne Islands in badd Weather.

By Capt. Temple I have received His Majestyes Instructions, by which I find one clause that I am to continue with his Majesties Shipps on this service until I receive further Orders from His Majestie, which I hope will come timely enough to remove us hence before the sickly Monethes of June, July &c.

I advised with Sr. William Berkeley, whether it were convenient to send away the *Deptford* Ketch with these Relations; hee gave me his Opinion that she ought to stay till the arrival of His Majestyes Forces and the Meeting of the Assembly. By a Ketch of London named the *Henrie and Joane*, Richard Simmons Master, bound for London, wee thought fitt to send away this Dispatch. This from

Sir, Your very Humble Servant

John Berry[9]

Document 4
6 February 1677

A Letter from the Governor to the Commissioners

My Most Honour'd Friends,

I was noe sooner landed at James Towne, but I sent Major Hone[10] to Col. Swanns[11] to provide Accommodation for the Right Honorable His Majesties

9. Berkeley, at about this time, sent his own letter home. It was edited and published by Wilcomb Washburn as "Sir William Berkeley's 'A History of our Miseries,'" *William and Mary Quarterly,* 3d ser., 14 (July 1957), 403-413. Washburn believes that Berkeley began writing the letter on February 1, when the commissioners first presented him with their orders. Berkeley had not asked for the commissioners' assistance, and complained that he could not possibly provide quarters and provisions for 1,000 soldiers in a country that had been ruined by rebellion. Berkeley felt aggrieved, and wrote to justify his conduct during the uprising.

10. Major Theophilus Hone had served as a burgess for James City County in 1666 and he served as sheriff of James City County in 1676. His house and its contents had been destroyed when Bacon burned Jamestown. See "The Sufferers in Bacon's Rebellion," *Virginia Magazine of History and Biography,* 5 (July 1897), 68. He died sometime around 1687.

11. Colonel Thomas Swann had been among the first to sign the orders issued by Bacon in August 1676, and was present with the rebels when they burned Jamestown in September. Berkeley thought him so guilty of treason that he explicitly excepted him from

Commissioners, hee sent mee noe letter backe, but Major Hone brought mee word this morning that hee shall bee Prowde of the Honour His Majesties Commissioners doe him in making use of his house for their Accomodation, and that they shall not want any thing hee can supply, which I believe wilbe in a plentifull manner, for his House and Grounds have not beene disturbed all this Warr.

I had Terrible Ague and Feavor all the day long coming up, but blessed be God I am now pretty well.

My Most Honour'd, I am
Your Most Humble Servant

William Berkeley

From by Bed at Greene Spring
Feb 6th, 1676/7

Document 5
Early February, 1677

To Mr. Watkins from His Majesties Commissioners[12]

The inclosed is a Copie of our Letter to the Secretarys of State which shewes you the reall Condicion wee found Virginia in at our Arrival, not only by the Governour's information, but alsoe by the Report of such of the Loyall partie we have yet discoursed with which (being soe short a tyme since our coming over, and the Multiplicitie of our present Affairs such) wee could not now conveniently impart Copies of our Letters to the Secretarys nor to all those Eminent and Honourable persons, wee are (upon our Gratitude and Devotions) Oblig'd to. Wee therefore desire that you will be pleased (with the soonest) to Communicate the contents of the Inclosed to the underwritten. Wherein we have omitted nothing conducible to our Affaires, or their Information. But onely the advice

the general pardon of 10 February 1677. Only two days earlier, however, Berkeley had asked Swann, whose plantation was not damaged during the rebellion, to house the commissioners. Swann agreed, and he succeeded in persuading the commissioners that he had done Bacon's bidding against his will, and that he was deserving of their trust. See Wilcomb Washburn, *The Governor and the Rebel: A History of Bacon's Rebellion*, (Chapel Hill: University of North Carolina Press, 1957), 102, 146; and C.O. 1/37, 133 (VCRP).
12. Thomas Watkins was one of four clerks in the Privy Seal Office, responsible for receiving documents from the Signet office and for preparing documents for the Great Seal, the royal seal that authenticated important documents from the king. See John Wroughton, *The Longman Companion to the Stuart Age, 1603-1714* (London: Longman, 1997), 137, 139.

wee gave the Governor not to suspend Acquainting the Trembling Countrey with his Majestyes Gracious Pardon, but forthwith to informe them therof before further matters were negotiated, whereof wee desire you to acquaint the Secretaries of State, as a matter omitted in ours to them; As alsoe that our Humble Duties to them, as well as to the abovementioned Honorable Persons shall be constantly Observed, and that wee are their Honors most Obedient servants and,

Sir. Your Very Affectionate Friends and Servants

John Berry
Francis Moryson

His Royall Hignesse
Prince Rupert
Lord Chancellor
Lord Archbishop of Canterbury
Duke of Ormond
Lord Arlington
Lord Ossory
Sir Thomas Chichely
Lords of the Committee of Trade and Plantations

Sir, Pray omit not to make knowne to the Honorable Secretaries of State that wee find by the Governours discourse, that in respect of Bacons Death, and the Quiett of the Country, hee supposes it improper to issue forth the Printed Proclamations, but intends to forme a Proclamation collected from that, wherein hee will exempt Eight Persons not yet in Custodie (besides what are already in hold) which are the Chiefe of the Rebells.

For His Majesties Especial Service, To Thomas Watkins, Esquire, at the Privy Seale Office.

Document 6
10 February 1677

A Letter to Mr. Watkins from Sir John Berry and Colonel Francis Moryson

Sir,
Wee thought necessary by this second Conveyance to Communicate to you, most humbly to impart to His Royale Highnesse, this following Advise.

That we have lately sett forth a Declaration to the People of Virginia in his Majestyes name timely to acquaint them with the Occasion of our Coming (whereof you have here a Copie) presented by them with aboundant satisfaction and heartie Expressions of Gratitude to his most Gracious Majestie, Affirming that they believed had Bacon beene now alive, and at the heade of his whole Partie, they would have readily and unanimously mett and embraced this His Majesties exceeding Grace and Favour, and Instantly have deserted, if not Destroy'd him with their owne hands.

But though Bacon bee now dead, and thereby the Faction weaken'd & fallen off, and soe much of His Majesties Proclamation as concern'd the taking of him become uselesse, yet for what remained materiall in it for the People to have knowne, wee could heartily have wish'd the timely Publishment of it. For certaine it is the Common sort of men here would have much sooner look'd on, and laid hold of the Kings Proclamation sent them in Print, than upon any written one the Governour can possibly devize to collect out of it, and the other Instruments of His Majesties Pardon, as he purposes (contrary to our Advise) to doe.

Sir, It may seeme strange, but 'tis most true by all handes; as also by the Governour's owne Report, that of about Fifteen thousand, there are not Five hundred untainted Persons in this Rebellion, and out of that small number but a few eminent Sufferers, as wee can heare of: Wee therefore conceive it well worthy of His Majesties Princely Care and Consultation, how the Retribution of the Forfeited shall goe to and be made the satisfaction of the Plunder'd Estates: for though the Governor is pleas'd to seize Estates of pretended Delinquents, tis without any legall Power soe to doe till first they be Convicted, much lesse to dispose of them afterwards at his owne uncontroulable pleasure: And although the Law seeme in itselfe a meanes of Redresse (in this Case) against the Rebellious partie, as Civil Trespassers, yet even here alsoe will arise soe insuperable a difficultie, that by reason of this soe generall a defection of the Country noe Jury wilbe found to give a faire or just Verdict. Besides, wee have Declared our Possitive Opinion, that as noe one can be a Delinquente before Conviction, soe none can bee now Convicted that were not taken actually such before his Majestyes Acts of Grace, from laying hold whereof there is noe waye to exclude any, that come in to imbrace the same under the Conditions thereby freely and graciously offered them; And as it was against our Advice, that any should bee excepted out of the Pardon, but what were exempted by the King himselfe, yet such was Sir William Berkeley's Contrarity to us, that perceiving the Patents and Proclamation seemingly to clash (in one Clause) about the Power Granted him by the former, of pardoning such as hee should thinke fitt and Convenient for His Majesties service, hee told us that hee would except about eight persons (without naming them) which wee advised him to nominate least the Comon feare, where the lott of this fatall exemption might fall, should putt the whole people of the Country in dread of their Lives, after his (already Hanging and intending to Hang upon this Rebellion, more than ever Suffer'd Death for the Horrid Murder of that late Glorious Martyr of Blessed Memorie.) And though wee rather commend than condemne what before hee might bee forced to doe (in furore Belli)[13] by a Martiall Power, considering how the face of Affaires then look'd. Yett now wee advised that the Lawes might returne to theire owne proper Channell and that all future Proceedings of his might bee by a Jury &c conceiving itt, both by His Majesties Instructions, and the forme of the Endictment (prepar'd to that end, and send him by us) to bee most agreeable to His Majestyes Royall Intentions.

Sir, It will be noe more than a bare skinning over a peace, if care be not had how to heale up matters firmly and effectually—in which the present constitution of the People is chiefely to bee Considered, whome wee find of soe sullen and obstinate a humour, that if not treated as befits their present Condition, with easy and timely methods of redresse, 'tis to be more than fear'd (as the common rumour Indicates) that they will either Abandon their Plantations, putt off their servants, and dispose of their Stocks, and away to other Parts; or else the most part of them will onely make Corne insteade of Tobacco and soe sullenly sit downe carelesse of what becomes of their owne Estates, or the Kings Customes. How dangerous would it then bee, if in soe unsettled a Juncture an unhappy Warr (which God divert) should breake out with any of our Neighbours, for a People so ill Qualified as to their Obedience and incouraged at soe remote a Distance from England to cast off the Yoke and Subjugate themselves to a Forreine Power, even this unhappie occasion of sending us hither does shew, and how greate the Difficulty, how heavy the Charge & Burden will then prove to reduce them backe to their Allegiance, or continue Forces here to constraine and awe soe stubborne a People to the Obedience of His Majesties Royall Power and Government, the Great Charge His Majestie is now att, too simply demonstrates.

Of these things though wee now foresee the Consequences yet can wee not tell how to propose, or what to say or act in them, having noe such latitude left us in our Instructions concerning them. But Must (as wee most humbly doe) submit and lay all at the feet of His most Sacred Majestie, His wise and Most Honorable Councill and take leave for this tyme of you by subscribing ourselves.

Honored Sir,

Your most humble servants

February 10th, 1676/7   John Berry
                                 Francis Moryson

---

13. *"in furore belli."* In the madness of war.

Sir,

The Governor has now upon second Thoughts issued forth this day the Kings Proclamation, and hath Excepted out of the same Eighteene persons, whose names nor crimes wee doe not yett know.

Vera Copia

Sa: Wiseman

This Letter (mutatis mutandis) was sent to Mr. Watkins, to Sir John Werden and the Secretarys of State, but that to Sir John Werden was remanded.

Document 7
6 February 1677

A Declaracion to his Majesties Loving Subjects of Virginia

In Pursuance of his Majestyes Royall Will and Pleasure and of the Power and Authority to us Granted by virtue of his Majestyes Letters Patents under the Greate Seale of England, thereby appointing us (by the names of Herbert Jeffreyes Esqr. Sir John Berry Knight and Francis Moryson Esqr.) his Majestyes Commissioners to Enquire into all such Grievances and Pressures, which any of you his Majestyes Subjects of Virginia have suffered or layne under or doo now suffer or lye under, and more especially such Grievances, as have occasioned these late Divisions, Distresses and Disorders among You. These we therefore in his Majestyes name and by his Royall Command to declare and make knowne unto you, that one Chiefe Cause of his Majestyes sending us his said Commissioners over to you, is that you may bee sensible that as his Majestye is, and ever wilbe severe in punishing such persons, as shall at any time willfully violate his Majestyes Lawes and Royall Authority, and shall dare and presume to abett and promote Tumults and Rebellions, soe on the other hand, you are to know, that his most Gracious Majesty will be noe lesse favourable and indulgent to the just complaints of his oppressed People, and as soone as informed of their Grievances and Pressures, to direct proportionable Redresse for them when knowne, and take such due resentment upon the Authors and Continuers of them, as the quality of the Offense shall require. **To The End** therefore, that you his good and loving Subjects may be the better incouraged thereunto, Wee his Majestyes Commisioners in his behalfe intrusted and Appointed, doe hereby invite and require you the Inhabitants of this his Majestyes said Colony, and every of you (without Excepting of any Person) freely and impartially to impart to us your and every on your Grievances or Pressures by you or any of you sustained, and more particularly, such as you consider to have beene the sure groundes and original occasion of these late Troubles and disorders among you; in all which you are Required to deale plainly openly and indifferently without any kind of feare or favour of or to any person or persons of what Degree, ranke or quality hee or they bee, that soe wee also with the same Candor and Sincerity may render our Report of the same to his most Gracious Majesty, and you yourselves thereby find the fruite of his Majestyes Royall favour and wisdome in a swift and speedy redresse of the same. Among which you are to avoid presenting to us any matters under the notion of Grievances, which in their nature, are not really and essentially soe: wee conceiving such matters onely proper for our Enquiry and his Majestyes Information as shall directly concern the State of the Government in generall, and in particular the persons of any of his Majestyes Ministers or Officers Executing the same in what relates to their respective Trusts and Places and wherein you know any of them faulty, oppressive, defective or exorbitant in their administration of the same. In pursuance whereof, although wee debar or Exempt noe persons whatsoever yet will wee redresse the same onely in Writing by and from the hands of loyall, sober, and credible persons of such County, to whome (not exceedeing tenne in number for such County), wee shall promise Convenient tyme and place of Examination and hearing, as wee shall hereafter see fitt, in the mean tyme by this notice allowing you fitt space of preparing in order thereunto. Or if you shall thinke it more for our and your owne Ease, that you draw up a faire duplicate in writing of your aforesaid Greivances, the one to be delivered to such Member of the Assembly as served for your County, and the other to us his Majestyes Commissioners aforesaid, the same being sealed up and directed to us wherever wee shall bee.[14] Given under our

14. For the county grievances, see Chapter 6, below. Upon their arrival in the colony, the commissioners had received unsigned grievances that they could view as "noe better then scandalous libels there being noe names nor proofes to justifye them." The commissioners returned them, and informed the burgesses of the procedures they would follow for receiving grievances from the counties. Each county should send their grievances "sealed up and directed to us, at our place of residence at Swanns Point in James river, under the hands of such as will be ready to prove, and make out to us each article therein upon their respective oaths, which any two of us his Majesties Commissioners, have full power to administer. Therefore, to the end that noe man may hereafter pretend ignorance, or want of information for the Right drawing of & presenting their grievances aforesaid, wee doe hereby declare, & Explaine to them that we will receive noe paper of grievance from the hands of any, but of such onely as are qualified according, as by our late declaration we have expressly (meaning those who shall best deserve his Majesties Royall pardon, and appear most worthy of this appointment, without diminuation to his Majesties honor). All which wee Leave to you their Burgesses to be the judges and Attestors of. And wee hereby appoint Mundayes, Wednesdayes, and Fridayes, for days of receiving and examination of grievances which wee desire may be forthwith made knowne to each Countie by you their Burgesses, that they may bring them accordingly." See the Commissioners to the House of Burgesses, 27 February 1676/7, in *Journals of the House of Burgesses of Virginia, 1659/60-1693*, ed. H. R. McIlwaine (Richmond: Virginia State Library, 1914), 94-95.

handes from on Board his Majesties Ship *Bristoll*. Riding in James River in Virginia the Sixte day of February. In the Nyne and twenty of years of the Reigne of our Soveraigne Lord Charles the Second by the Grace of God of England, Scotland, France and Ireland, King Defender of the Faith, etc. Anno. Dom. 1676/7

John Berry
Francis Moryson

To the High Sheriffe of
James City Countie for
the tyme being.

Sir

You are hereby Required to communicate the persuall and copies hereof to all persons desiring the same, after you shall have first read and published the samein your County Court and parish Churches, whereof you are not to faile, with the soonest and first opportunity for doing the same.

By Order of His Majesties Honorable Commissioners

Samuel Wiseman

Document 8
7 February 1677

A Warrant Signed by Sir William Berkeley

WHEREAS his Majesty hath been Pleased to Commissionate the honorable Col. Herbert Jeffreys Esqr. Sr. John Berry Knight and Col. Francis Moryson Esqr to make Enquiry after the Aggreivances of His Majestyes Subjects of Virginia, to rectifie the said Abuses administering Equity to every man without resepect of persons, and Report the same to his Majestie, this is therefore to will and Require you   Sheriff of   County, and every one of the resepected sheriffs of their severall Counties to call a County Court, and there to take a Report of the Inhabitants of the said County, what abuses and agrievances have beene done to them, by whome, and for that reason, without regard to the Qualities of any man in the said Colony, and such tyme as you shall receive orders from the aforesaid Commissioners and to take care to Obey such Commands and Instructions as you shall receive from tyme to tyme from them. Given under my hand this seven day of February, 1676

William Berkeley

Document 9
Early February, 1677

A Letter from Sir John Berry and Col. Moryson to Col. John Custis.[15]

Wee have thought it most fitt to make choice of yourselfe as a person on whose approved Loyaltie and Integrity wee may rely, in using your care to Communicate (with all possible speed) the inclosed Declaration to the hands of the Sheriffe of Accomac and Northampton to the Inhabitants of the same Countyes as directed. And to expresse to them how desireous we are (in regard of their remote distance from the place of meeting) to excuse and spare them as much as may bee. By acquainting them that wee shall not expect their Appearance, where the necessity of a personall proofe to any matter to be by them presented to us does not absolutely require it: And if their Grievances be comprehended in any of those generall ones of the Great Salary of the Assembly; Their too frequent Meeting and long sitting &c you may lett them know that wee can dispence with their Absence on these Accounts; Wee having with us his Majestyes Instructions & expresse Directions for Redresse thereof, or if there bee any other matter whereof there is noe neede [of] such proofe, it shall suffice that they instruct their Burgesses aright to Present them to us on their behalfe. Trusting the rest with our care and concernment, and resting assured of our sincerity and service, as you may that wee are

Sir, Your Affectionate Friends to serve you,

John Berry
Francis Moryson.

P.S.

15. John Custis (1630-1696), of Northampton County. Berkeley's headquarters on the Eastern Shore during the rebellion had been at Custis's plantation. See Washburn, *Governor and the Rebel*, 70.

Honest Jack,

It is much my satisfaction to find soe old a friend and Acquaintance under soe excellent a Character of a Prudent and Loyall person, which commends you most affectionately to mee, and assure yourselfe you shall not want one to make knowne to his Majesty your just merits,
in mee

Your very reall Friend
Francis Moryson

Document 10
Early February, 1677

The Commissioners to Captain Armsted[16] of Peancatanck in Gloster Countie with the like letter to Captain John Tiplady[17] in York County

Sir,
    To make you sensible how much wee study the Ease and Conveniency of the Country as farr as possibly we may; Wee hereby lett you, and them know, that in case their or your Grievances extend not to matters requiring Personall proofe, But onely those generall ones of the Greate Salary of the Members of the Assembly, Their too frequent meeting and long sitting; that Charge and trouble of attending as may bee spar'd, and their absence dispenced with; wee having by us (for our expresse Directions) His Majestyes Instructions in that behalfe, and can proceede to the Redresse thereof, without their appearance at our Meeting. And this much wee thought necessary for them to know, to prevent a needlesse trouble to the Country. For wee are their, and

Your, Very Loving Friends

John Berry
Francis Moryson[18]

16. Most likely the reference here is to John Armistead, a close supporter of Governor Berkeley who was a member of the James City County court and a captain in the county militia.
17. Captain John Tiplady held the rank of captain in the York County militia, and would continue to play a leading role in his county's affairs after Bacon's Rebellion. See *Virginia Magazine of History and Biography,* 1 (1894), 248 and 37 (1929), 163.
18. This particular letter was undated, but it likely was written sometime in February of 1676/7.

Sir,

You are desired to lett a Copie of this Letter passe from Sheriffe to Sheriffe.

A true Copie,
Samuel Wiseman.

Document 11
8 February 1677

To the Governour from Sir John Berry and Col. Moryson

Right Honorable,

Since you lately left us there are more Soldiers come in and more wee hourly Expect: Wherefore wee did resolve to Dispatch away Capt. Morris to you, to hasten the Preparacions for their Landing, and to survey (in order to it) the Ground allotted for their Station, that soe wee may receive a speedie account thereof, as also what care is taken for Providing fitt Magazines and Store Howses for the Kings Ammunition, Provision, &c. and good shelter for the Soldiers, which (with great instance) presses a ready contrivance; for that the Charge of maintaining them on Board is now at least Five Poundes a day to the Merchant, and as much more to the King (after their Arrival 14 dayes). And if the whole Complement of men doe arrive (as suddainly they may) before things are in a fitt posture to receive them, the Demurage wilbe little lesse than a hundered poundes per diem charge to his Majestie, all which wee pray you will consider.[19]

And, Sir, wee may not omit making knowne to you, that observing the generalitie of the People to looke very amazedly one upon another, att our and the Forces coming over for want of a right information of the true end and occasion of it (which those Printed Proclamations of the Kings would have well removed) Wee take leave to impart to your Honor, as our serious opinion, and most earnest desire, that the trembling people bee putt out of paine in this particular, especially in such a juncture as this, when Rumours and forg'd Reports obtaine soe fast upon them, and get the start of Truth (though back'd with authority), and (indeed) what can now stopp or restraine it, unless the timely publishing of His Majesties Royall Acts of Grace and Pardon, the defects whereof these soe early Consequences more and more convince us of the former necessitie of it.

And since to our (as well as your) Satisfaction noe materiall Greivance has yet beene soe much as whisper'd against you; how heartily were it to bee wished, that none might now at last arise, upon the winding up of all and even

---

19. On the forces sent to Virginia, see John Childs, *The Army of Charles II* (London: Routledge and Kegan Paul, 1976), 158-161.

while wee are here. Therefore, Sir, thinke it not lesse for your owne Honor and Interest, than it is for His Majestyes service, that wee advise you (like faithfull, well-meaning friends to you and good subjects to His Majestie) not to proceede soe as to give just occasion to Merchants and Traders to complaine that you obstruct or retarde their Trade, by causing mens Hogsheads to be mark'd with the Broad Arrow-head, as goods forfeited to the King, which cannot (in our opinion) be justified by any colour of Law, nor can any man be made liable to seizure as a delinquent before due Conviction, especially when the King has granted full Restitution of Estate &c by expresse words in the Proclamation and Pardon; Nor can wee conceive any Pretence to have prohibited Commerce or Trading by the Loyall or Neutrall party (but onely of the Ships to trade with those of the Rebellious side) for that were to make the Loyall party sufferers in a double sense, both by the oppression of the Rebells, and then by being thus debarr'd of Reaping all honest Advantages of their owne, which (as wee conceive), is hard Measure.

·   And as for the disposing of the Delinquents Estates in Restitution to the Loyall Sufferers, we also conceive that most fitt to bee referr'd to his most Gracious Majestyes Determination, and to secure the same onely (in the meane tyme) until his Royall Pleasure be knowe herein. And the Loyall Sufferers not debarr'd to bring their Actions at Law against the others as Trespassers though not as Delinquents.

Sir, Wee most earnestly desire you to consider hereof, and then act as your owne Judgement and Prudent knowledge shall direct you. Receiving this (as truly intended) no other than the serious Opinion and Advise of,

Your Very True Friends and Most Faithfull Servants,

John Berry
Francis Moryson

From on Board the *Bristoll*, now
at Newports Newes, the 8th day of
February, 1676/7

P.S.

Sir,

Wee pray your Answer in Writing, and that for the future our mutuall Conferrence may be also in writing, which we apprehend a much better way than by word of mouth, perceiving it a greater trouble to you and us; because by your

Defect of Hearing, which not onely denies Privacy, but lookes Angerly, by lowd and fierce Speaking.[20]

Dear Governour,

I am just now come to Col. Swanns, and beg your Excuse that I cannot (as yett) waite on you, by reason I feele myselfe under some Indisposition, which I would endeavour to remove now by taking Physick before much Businesse prevent mee, but be assured, Sir, I am neverthelesse,

Deare Sir,
Your most humble Servant

Francis Moryson.

Document 12
9 February 1677

From the Governour to Sir John Berry and Colonel Moryson

Right Honorable, and my Most Honour'd Friends,

I am yet very ill since I came up, but to the two Great Particulars that you write to mee of, I shall answer thus: That since your arrival I have not marked one Hogshead of Tobacco, nor intended to doe till I have His Majestyes Gracious Permission which I have write to the right Honorable Henry Coventry to obtaine for mee.

For the other matter of Providing Magazines for the Soldiers, Victualls and Ammunition, I hope you doe not thinke I am able to doe Impossibilityes: the Rebells left mee but one Oxe and six more I have borrowed (which is more than they are able to doe) to bring Woode and Victualls for two hundred men, which I have now in my Howse, and must feed them all, and God knowes the Rebells left me not one Graine of Corne, nor one Cow to feed mee. Colonel Moryson, I have bought six and thirty Oxen on my owne Creditt, and have bespoken Nyntey thousand Boards. When they come up, if there are Carpenters and Oxen or Horses to draw in the Tymber, ten Houses at least may bee built in a day; But who shall give Creditt to the Workemen? For God knowes I have not Five poundes in the world, nor for ought I know noe Creditt for more.

---

20. Berkeley was nearly deaf in 1676 and ailing quickly. To avoid the problem of a governor who could not hear, the commissioners opted instead to carry on all their correspondence with him in writing. On Berkeley's declining health and poor hearing, see Billings, *Sir William Berkeley*, Chapter 12.

Honour'd Gentlemen: I shall be glad that all our transactions bee in Writing as you desire, all which I will send to the Right Honorable the Secretaryes of State, and begin with these two letters of yours and mine. The Proclamations shalbee sent out tomorrow, with my Exceptions, which I have authority from His Sacred Majestie to make, and I thinke my Exceptions to bee necessary for His Majestyes Honour, and the future Peace of the Countrey, least too much lenity should incline the Rabble to a new Rebellion. Most Honor'd Friends, I am,

Your Most Humble Servant,

William Berkeley

February 9th, 1676/7

P. S.

If you send mee word, it is Lawfull for me to Presse Oxen, or Horses for His Majesties Services, having none of my owne, I will immediately doe it.

Document 13
11 February 1677

A Letter to the Governour from Colonel Moryson

Sir,
   Finding by Capt. Morris, that you Expected an Answer to your letter, which I could not imagine (ours being a joint one to you, and Sir John Berry absent) yet that it may not bee mistooke for a Disrespect, which I shall never bee Guilty of to You, I make this returne. That I cannot conceive of any thing in ours can give you the least distast (if rightly considered) since it is noe more than a friendly advice, at your owne Choise to reject or imbrace as your Reason shall direct you. Therefore, Sir, I shall beseech you to lay aside all unnecessary Jealouseyes, which (if Foster'd) may raise Groundes for true ones. Sir, I am very confident, we have hitherto given you noe cause for them, since both those letters which were first writt (which yourselfe saw) and those since, speake more in your Honour and Commendations, than perhaps your owne Modestie would lett you doe yourselfe; therefore I cannot but wonder at that Postscript in your Letter wherein you ask our Opinion, whither you may Presse Horses or Oxen for His Majesties Service, as though you had Power to act nothing because wee are here. Sir, wee have beene soe farr from lessening Your Power and Authoritie (which wee came to Vindicate) that upon all Applications to us, in what particu-

larly concernes not our Commission wee have still referr'd them to you, as His Majestyes Governour, without giving our opinion, or advice in it. Therefore wee shall desire you will not suffer your better reason to draw wrong inferences from our right meaning towards you, but believe I must first forfeit the name of an Honest man and a Gentleman, when I shall once offer any thing (with a salvo to His Majestyes service) that shall misbecome that Honour and Regard I bear your Character, besides the particular Friendshipp to your person, by which I am ever oblig'd to bee,

Sir,

Your most affectionate humble servant,

Francis Moryson

Swanns Pointe
Sonday February 11th
1676/7

Document 14
After 11 February, 1677

The Governour to Colonel Moryson

Dear Colonel,

I confesse I was troubled to be Admonished for that which was ever Practiced in all Nations, especially in our owne which has the best lawes in the world for securitie of the Subject. You know that Colonel Garrett (now Lord Garrett) went to my Lord of Northumberlands House and tooke away all his Horses for the Kings service, yet that Lord, though manifestly against the King, never bore Armes, nor was ever convicted, but this I have onely on Report.[21]

But when I waited on the King in the pursuite of Essex, the King gave order to seize the Houses, Goods, and Cattle of many that had declared against Him, and I was by when Sir Richard Greenvill tooke the House of my Lord Roberts, and out of it at least two thousand Poundes stirling in Plate, very Rich Hangings and much household stuffe yet that Lord was soe farr from being Convicted, that at the Kings Coming into England, hee was made Lord Private Seale, and I seised no Toll or Goods, but in the height of the Warr, but indeede shall doe it hereafter, for from divers honest men I heare that those that are Criminally Obnoxious, dayly and howerly conveigh away their Goods and Cattell, which can never bee Distinguished from their Goods to whome they are conveighed. Most

---

21. Berkeley found in the history of England's tumultuous civil war an excuse for his seizure of property from persons he judged to be rebel sympathizers.

Honoured Sir, I shall ever seeke and bee most Proude of your Friendship, and shall returne it with all possible care.

From my bed Expecting my Feavour,

> Your most Affectionate Friend and
> humble servant,
>
> William Berkeley

My Wife, who lay by mee last night, presents her service to you; God help us, nothing but vocall kindness pass'd betweene us.
(This Letter came by Capt. Morris Sonday night Feb: the Eleaventh).
(The same day came Col. Jeffreyes [with Sir John Berry] to Swanns Pointe).

Document 15
20 February 1677

Colonel Moryson to the Governour

Right Honorable,
    Though my fellow Commissioners be both absent,[22] yet I have taken the Freedome at the desire of the bearer to acquaint you (as hee informs mee) that divers people, who are enjoyned by his Majesties Proclamation to take the Oath and give Securitie for their future good Behavior, are render'd incapable (by their owne Defection) of procuring any of the Loyall partie to stand bound for them; which will make the maine part of the Kings Proclamation impracticable unlesse one may bee Security for the other (*alternis Vicubus*)[23] which (I conceive) cannot be by Bond to any Private Person, but to the King onely by way of Recognizance. Wherein I desire you will please to advise with the Assembly how to render this matter feasible, being an important pointe of the said Procla-

22. Moryson's fellow commissioners were engaged in equipping and overseeing the King's troops, who by this point had arrived in Virginia. See the postscript to Document 17, below.
23 "*alternis vicubus.*" Alternate place or location.

mation, which ought to bee most punctually performed; And Impossibilityes are not to bee Expected. This, (Sir), from

Your most affectionate Faithfull Servant,

Francis Moryson

20 February 1676/7

P. S.

Sir,

When a Speaker is chosen, and you are a House of Assembly, wee shall desire to bee acquainted therewith from your Honor. That you and they may receive from us an account of the occasion of the Kings sending us hither.

Document 16
21 February 1677

The Governor to Colonel Moryson

Right Honorable,

I have received your Letter by Captain Swanne, and shall doe as you Require mee, that is, I will consult with the Assembly, and not onely with them, but with the other Commissioners. I thank God I am soe perfectly well Recovered, that I hope to goe for England with the first Ship and am most heartily glad to heare that you are in perfect health. My wife presents her service to you, and I am,

Your most humble Servant

21 February 1676/7   William Berkeley

Document 17
23 February 1677

Colonel Moryson to the Governour

Right Honorable,

I received an Answer to myne by Captain Swanne, and must needs say I am a little Troubled to find you use this Expression (I shall doe as you Require mee)

which is a language I never use to my Equalls much lesse to a person of your Honorable Character: therefore it must needs bee a mistake in the reading (not in the writing) of mine, of which I keepe a Copie by mee. Sir, I conceive I have the Libertie without my fellow Commissioners being by, to write any thing that imports His Majestyes present service, by way of advice, where you have your owne latitude left you, to act as you shalbe best advis'd. Sir, as to the Title of Right Honorable, I conceive it in noe Capacity belongs to mee; but shall desire I may doe His Majestie Service under the true Title that's due to mee and noe otherwise. I desire therefore I may not now bee mistaken when I tell you I am,

23 February 1676/7   Your Most Humble Servant

                                                     Francis Moryson

Sir,
    My Fellow Commissioners are not yet return'd from Placing the Kings Stores, when they doe, wee shall write to the Assembly of the Occasion of our Coming.

Document 18
24 February 1677

The Governour to Colonel Moryson

Most Honour'd Sir:
    I thinke all His Majestyes Commissioners of soe High a Qualitie are Right Honourable, and soe I write and style Col. Jeffreyes and Sir John Berry, who have not yett taken it Ill, neither doe I whil'st I am the Kings Governour.
    For the word *Require*, truly I know not whether it were *Desire*, or not.
    The Burgresses are not yett halfe mett, the weather having kept backe all the Northern Burgesses, and those of Accomack, to my great Charge and Trouble.
    Col. Moryson (my Friend), I would faine have you think mee Yours, and there shall be nothing wanting in mee to lett you know I am soe,

                                        Your most humble servant

                                                William Berkeley

24 February 1676/7

Document 19
13 February 1677

His Majesties' Commissioners to the Governour

Sir,

Being informed of the seizure of severall Peoples goods, &c in this Country, and that the same is by your owne Servants; which, although we will not believe to be soe much as by your knowledge or Connivance: Yett because such actions (sheltering under your name and Power) may too severely reflect upon your Honour, Justice, and Experience, Wee could not but Advertize you hereof, and withal to Desire that if any such unwarrantable Practices have beene, you will please to stopp & redresse the same; or else if the same be by your owne Privity and Directions, that then you will reflect with how ill a Face a Grievance of this nature will looke at home, when wee shall be forced to Report to His Majesty that these things are acted and done by your Power, without soe much as any legall Warrant or Officer appointed by you to execute the same.

Sir, Certainly this must bee soe necessary a Caution and Advise to you, that it must needes deserve your serious consideration, and Reforming for the future, and not to take amisse this our Concernment in the Peoples Grievances, which makes us hereby acquaint you with our Contrariety to such Proceedings, wherein wee conceive you have neither Law, Right, nor His Majestyes Royall Will to support you. Wee might therefore leave itt at your owne door and remaine,

Sir

13 February 1676/7   Your Affectionate, Faithfull
Friends and Humble Servants,

Herbert Jeffreys
John Berry
Francis Moryson

P. S.

This worthy Gentleman, (the bearer hereof) can cleere the Particulars of this Information to you.[24]

---

24. The gentleman in question was Captain John Tongue, a man of long military experience and close association with the Earl of Carlisle. Tongue served on Jeffrey's staff as quartermaster and provost marshal of the battalion. See Stephen Saunders Webb, *The*

Document 20
13 February 1677

The Governour to His Majesties' Commissioners

Right Honourable,

I give you many humble Thanks for Your Friendly Adminicion in soe weighty an Affaire. But truly it is without and beyond my knowledge if any such thing has beene done, and those that have done it (when complained of) shalbe Punished. True it is, that almost all my Neighbours have had considerable shares of my Goodes, and they have beene willing to spare mee some Corne and Hoggs, in lieu of what they stole from mee, and is yett visible in their Houses. Add to this that I keepe at least Thirty Prisoners in my house, and mainteine a Guard of Fifty to secure them, and this I have done this Moneth, on the Charity and Benevolence of some Charitable People, who know I had not one Cow, nor one Graine of Corne left mee. When the Assembly shall remove these Prisoners and their Guard, I doubt not but I shall have Creditt enough to feed my owne Poore Family

My most honour'd Friends, you will highly oblige me if you send this my Answer to the Secretaryes of State.

13 February 1676/7   Your most humble Servant

William Berkeley

Md.[25]

On Monday Morning (Feb. 12) the Commissioners went over to Greene Spring to Sir William Berkeleyes where they found the Councill with him, and Col. Jeffreyes Commission &c being then and there read: It was Put by Sir William Berkeley to his Councill, whither hee was immediately to resigne up the Government to Col. Jeffrys, or noe? Whose result was in the Negative, and that hee had this Latitude left him (by the word *Conveniency*) to take his owne Convenient tyme of Departure hence.

Whereupon it was further laid before the Councill, maturely to Consider, whither the word Conveniency, shalbe meant in respect to his Majesties immediate service, or Sir William Berkeleys own Private Convenience.

Governors-General: The English Army and the Definition of Empire, 1569-1681 (Chapel Hill: University of North Carolina Press, 1979), 136, 350-510.
25. A memorandum inserted by Wiseman.

Document 21
12 February 1677

From the Councill of State of Virginia (Subscribed as followeth)
To the Right honorable Herbert Jeffreys, Esq., His Majestyes Lieutenant Governour of Virginia

Right Honorable,

Having Diligently read over his most Sacred Majestyes Commission under his Majesties' Broad Seale of England, being thus indorsed [A Commission Requiring Sir William Berkeley's Returne to England, and Appointing Herbert Jeffreys Lieutenant Governour in his Absence] Wee Conceive your Honour to be by the same Commission Constituted & Appointed Lieutenant Governor of Virginia, and that upon the Absence of the Right Honorable Sir William Berkeley, his Majesties' Governour from Virginia. You are (as his Majesties Lieutenant Governour) to Execute and performe all Jurisdictions Powers and Authorityes belonging to the Office of Governour of the said Plantacion and Colony. And shall be most ready, upon the said Governours Departure from Virginia, to obey, assist and advise you, according to his Majestyes Command being,

February 12, 1676/7

Right Honorable
Your most humble servants,

Nathaniel Bacon[26]
Thomas Ballard[27]

26. Colonel Nathaniel Bacon the Elder, a member of Governor Berkeley's Council and a cousin of the rebel. The elder Bacon was 56 years old when the rebellion began. He earlier had aided his young cousin after the rebel Bacon arrived in Virginia in 1674. He provided the younger Bacon with contacts that allowed him to purchase his plantation at "Curles," forty miles upstream from Jamestown, and additional undeveloped lands farther to the west. Through the elder Bacon's efforts, Governor Berkeley appointed the younger Bacon to his council in March of 1675. Despite his young cousin's ingratitude, the elder Bacon never wavered in his loyalty to the governor. See Webb, *1676*, 28.

27. Thomas Ballard (1630-1679), first became a member of the governor's council in 1670. Though he issued orders during the rebellion permitting Bacon to impress supplies for the rebel expedition against the Indians, Governor Berkeley forgave him, his "Mary Magdalene." He would remain loyal to the governor and, after Berkeley's ouster by the commissioners, would oppose Jeffreys, Moryson, and Berry. Jeffreys considered Ballard "a fellow of a turbulent, mutinous spirit," and he dismissed him from the Council on 11 June 1677. See Letters and Papers Concerning American Plantations, 20 April–22 June 1677, C.O. 1/40, 32, 225-226 (VCRP); Webb, *1676*, 125; and William Glover Stanard and Mary Newton Stanard, *The Colonial Virginia Register* (Baltimore: The Genealogical Publishing Company, 1965), 39.

John Bridger[28]
James Bray[29]

This was all the answer they would give in this affaire, although Col. Jeffreyes and the other Commissioners press'd them to consider and expound the word *Conveniency* upon which Sir William Berkeley clung, taking the latitude of the word to serve his owne turne, private interest, and advantage.

Document 22
13 February 1677

From the Councill of State, to the Commissioners
Right Honorable,

Because wee would not occasion any stop to the Barge Sir Jon Berry was pleased to promise this morning for receiving our Opinions upon His Most Sacred Majestyes Commission to the honourable Colonel Jeffreyes wee finished that the last night, that with the Commission it selfe, which hee was pleased to leave with us, it might bee expeditiously return'd to you. And with them wee fully resolved to have waited upon you ourselves to present that due respect and service, which belongs to His Majestyes Honourable Commissioners: But Gentlemen the weather hath unfortunately prevented that visit, and will wee hope bee our reasonable Excuse. Wee shall always demonstrate a readynesse to expresse our resolution of serving you in our joint or severall Qualifications;

28. Joseph Bridger (1628-1686), from "Whitemarsh" in Isle of Wight County. First named to the governor's council in 1670. Bacon and the rebels singled Bridger out for particularly harsh treatment. Bridger fled to Maryland, but when he returned after Bacon's death, he found his plantation destroyed and his herds of livestock carried off. In December of 1676 he took command of militia forces loyal to the governor. Transported by Captain Robert Morris's fleet, Bridger led attacks on Bacon's followers in the James River, and plundered the properties of Governor Berkeley's opponents as he did so. See Stanard and Stanard, *Colonial Virginia Register*, 39; Webb, *1676*, 96.
29. James Bray (d. 1691), like Bridger and Ballard, was appointed to the governor's council in 1670. He actively supported the governor during the rebellion. It was at his home that the rebel William Drummond was executed on 20 January 1677. See Washburn, *Governor and the Rebel*, 75.

wherein Colonel Bridger (whome wee desired to deliver this) concurs, and wee doe assure you that we are.

Right Honorable,

Feb 13th 1676/7

Feb 13th 1676/7   Your most Humble Servants,
Nathaniel Bacon
Thomas Ballard
James Bray

Document 23
14 February 1677

Colonel Jeffreys to Sir William Berkeley

Sir,

Since yourself and the Councill have been pleased to passe your conjunct opinion, that his Majestyes Commission granted mee does not take Place, until after you shall have left and gone out of this Country; I doe therefore hereby apply to you (as a matter that highly imports His Majestyes present service) that speedily as the urgency of the occasion requires, I may know your expresse determination of what Provision is to bee made ready for the necessary Reception of his Majestyes Forces under my Command, as to Carts, and Store Houses for the Ammunition, Provision and other things appertaining to the Traine of Artillery. All which, if not effectually performed out of hand the Demurage will inevitably fall upon His Majesty. Which your care (not mine) can alone Prevent, to which I commit it and remaine,

14 February, 1676/7   Sir,

Your most Humble Servant,

Herbert Jeffreys

Document 24
14 February 1677

To the Right Honorable Henry Coventry, His Majesties Secretary of State

Right Honorable,

Since our last Letters to Your Honor of the 3rd Instant, wee have onely this to acquaint His Majestie.

That the rest of the Fleete is lately Arrived, Whereupon wee all three mett at our Quarters at Swanns Pointe against James Towne, and immediately went over together to Sir William Berkeleys House at Green Spring where wee found the Councill with him, where having open'd and read to him and them His Majestyes Royall Commission concerning the present Government here, upon some Clause therein (that Sir. William Berkeley should continue Governour till his Death or Departure out of this Colony) hee putt it to his Councill to resolve him what their Opinion was, whither thereby he was Required presently to Resigne up the Government or noe? Whose Result was in the Negative, and Sir William Berkeley left at large to [interpret][30] his owne Conveniency, the expresse words of the Commission.

Whereupon wee laid before him and the Councill advisedly to consider whither the word *conveniency*, should bee taken in respect to His Majesties service and Pleasure, or onely his owne private Conveniency, which is at present before them to consider of.

As to His Majesties Commission of Oyer and Terminer, directed to Sir William Berkeley (as then Governour) it beares *Teste Jurimo Sexto dis 9bris*[31] which date is subsequent to the Secretary of States Letter, and soe has wrought this effect, to cause the Councill to give this their Result. That by virtue thereof he was continued in (not recall'd from) the Government, which neither the Letters of State, nor his Majestyes particular Instructions (which are quite thwarted and frustrated by itt) can yett possibly evince the contrary hereof to them.

Sir, We here send you Copies of such Letters as have pass'd betweene the Governor and us, by which you will find with how great Difficultyes wee have been surrounded, to dispose of these soldiers now arrived, wherein, though we have taken all possible care to Prevent any Demurage from falling on His Majestie, yett very much still remaines undone for the complete harbouring the men, and well landing and securing the Ammunicion, Trayne of artillery, Provisions, Stores, &c. about all which extraordinary has beene our care and concernment, By reason wee find the whole Countrey soe ruin'd and dessolate a Place, and not a House left in all James Towne to shelter them, and the Clime proving soe severely sharpe, the ground cover'd ore with deepe Snow and Ice, that it (almost) impossible for men to subsist on shore, such is the forlorne and harbourlesse Condicion wee here find Places in at present.

---

30. The brackets appear in Wiseman's original.
31. *"Teste Jurimo Sexto dis 9bris."* In legal witness, the 26th of November.

Sir, This is all the present unsettlednesse of things will lett us informe Your Honour of, at this tyme, however wee thought necessary His Majesty might know thus much from His Majestyes most dutyfull and Loyall Subjects, and,

Swanns Pointe

February 14th, 1676/7

Sir, Your Honors most Humble
Devoted Servants,

Herbert Jeffreys
John Berry
Francis Moryson

Document 25
27 February 1677

To Mr. Thomas Watkins from His Majestyes Commissioners

Sir,

When you shall have received our Pacquet, wherein wee desired you to Communicate the Secretaryes of State Letters to the severall Ministers we have mentioned to you, Wee (upon second thoughts) doe desire you will deliver Secretary Coventryes Letter (whose Province Virginia is) in the first Place, and to advise with his Honour, how much of the Contents of our Dispatch may fitly be communicated to those Ministers which it is desired to be imparted to.

Wee have noe more to advise you, but that the Assembly here are begun to sitt, and that wee have prepared a Letter to the Assembly, to acquaint them with the cause and end of our Coming Which even they shall have received and Answered wee will send both by the next Conveyance. This is all from,

From our Residence at
Swanns Pointe against
James City, February 27,
1676/7

Sir,
Your Affectionate Friends and Servants

Herbert Jeffreys
John Berry
Francis Moryson

Document 26
27 February 1677

A Letter to the Grand Assembly

To the Right Honourable the Governor
The Honourable the Councill
and the Right Worthy the Speaker
of the House of Burgesses,
Now Assembled at Green Spring
This to be Communicated to the whole Assembly
From his Majestyes Commissioners for the
Affaires of Virginia,

Most honour'd Gentlemen

Wee doe most heartily Congratulate this your happy Convention and re-turne to your late interrupted Freedome and Libertyes from the Force, Fury, and constraint of the late Wicked & ruinous Rebellion among you, which the hand of Heaven itself (in soe generall a Defection) hath defeated and confounded, and most mercifully restor'd your former Peace (to a good degree) without the Aid or Assistance of these Forces, by his Majesty (at his Great expence) most gra-ciously design'd and sent over to your Reliefe and Succour. Beseeching Almighty God of His infinite wisdome to direct, Councill and assist you now at this your meeting, in all your Debates and Consultations, that they may Centre in the Glory of God, the honour of his most Sacred Majestie, and the happy Restauration, Publique Good and long-lasting welfare and Resettlement of this so miserably shatter'd and lacerated Colony: that thereby you may deservedly Atchieve to yourselves the name and memorable Reputation of the **Healing Assembly**. And that you may the more truly be stiled soe, wee hope and desire you will be very heedfull (both for his Majestyes Satisfaction, your owne and our Information) thoroughly to inspect and search fully into the depths, and yet hidden roote & sourse of this late Rebellious Distemper, that hath broke forth and beene so contagious and spreading over the whole Country; which when rightly understood and made knowne will best direct and indicate to his Majestyes Royall wisdome and your owne discretions what apt and wholesome Lawes may bee most properly apply'd, not onely to prevent the like evil Consequences for the future, but also soe effectually to stanch and heale the fresh and bleeding Woundes these unnaturall Warrs and Rebellions have caused among you; that there may bee as few and small scars & markes remane, as you in your prudent care and tendernesse can possibly bring them to; which cannot be better effected (as wee conceive) than by well and advisedly weighing and consulting the present distemper'd Condicion & constitution of the generall Body of the People, and by treating them accordingly.

As for what is incumbent for us to Declare, and concern ourselves in, Wee doe most heartily assure you, That according to His Majestyes Royall Commission granted to us under the Greate Seale of England and his Majestyes Instructions therewith given us, wee shall (pursuant to the Power thence derived) most readily assist, Promote and Advice you to the utmost of our Understandings and Abilityes: And shall conclude ourselves most happie to returne home to his Majestie Straight with those Burdens, wherewith you have at any tyme beene oppressed and Groaned under (the Particulars whereof are yet unknowne to His Majestie) which have thus Disturbed that Peace and Tranquility, which his good subjects here have soe long Enjoyed under His Majesties most happy Government, and which (by reason of the greate and remote distance from the usuall Place of his Royall Residence) you could not soe easily make knowne to him, as other his Majestyes Subjects who live at a neer distance may. And therefore his Majesties Royall Care and Concernment for you hath beene such, as to send us (his Commissioners) purposely over to you to the end his Majestie may be by us thoroughly informed of your respective Grievances that have caused the Distractions aforesaid, which be they few or many, great or lesse, shall be received and most sincerely Reported and Represented by us to his most gracious Majestie, who out of his Royall Pitie and Compassion has beene pleased to Promise you a fitt and speedie Redresse thereof, as to his Royall Wisdome shall seeme meete.

And since it hath Pleased his most sacred Majestie of his owne mere motion (as a matter noe lesse Pleasing to God, than emergent to his Majesties Service) to commend to our and your Care and Endeavours the Procuring a Peace with the Neighbour Indians, wee will in noe wise be wanting with all Earnestnesse to presse you to a speedy Prosecution hereof, and that you will joine your utmost endeavours with ours that it may be a truly good and just Peace (since such a one is like to be most secure and lasting) and that you will Please to call to mind how much you all owe to the Equitable Policy and Prudence of the Right honourable Governour (here present) next under God, for your Preservation, and being here at this day, First by his successful Conquest, next by his just and wise Peace formerly made with the Indians, the Breach and Violation whereof having beene still accompanied with soe ill Consequences, as well to Yourselves in Generall by interrupting the Freedome & debarring you the Benefit of your owne Trade and Labours, as also the Greate Detrement and losse which thereby redounds to his Majestie in his Royall Revenues and Customes in England.[32]

And for that inconsiderate sort of men, who soe rashly & causelessly Cry up a Warr with, and seeme to wish and ayme at an utter Extirpation of the Indians (and are yet the first that Complaine and Murmer at the Charge and Taxes that on any just occasion attends such a Warr) wee would wish such to lay their han-

---

32. For Berkeley's Indian policies prior to the Rebellion, see Michael Leroy Oberg, *Dominion and Civility: English Imperialism and Native America, 1585-1685* (Ithaca, NY: Cornell University Press, 1999), Chapter 5.

des on their hearts, and seriously Consider with themselves, Whither it be not a base Ingratitude, a namelesse Prodigie of Infatuation and mere madnesse in such men as would make a Breach with or strive to destroy and Extirpate those Amicable Indians (who are soe far from hurting them or us), That wee must justly Confesse they are the best Guards to secure us on the Frontiers from the Incursions and suddaine Assaults of those other more Barbarous Indians of the Continent, who never can be brought to keepe a Peace with us, But will still continue our most Implacable & Mortall Enemies; And the more their daylie Murders and Depredations are upon us, the more earnestly it inforces this Argument for a Peace with the Frontier Indians.

Therefore wee would feigne endeavour to Persuade these unreasonable sort of men to consider and understand theire owne security and interest, and to sitt downe satisfied that they can quietly enjoy soe large and faire a portion of their Possessions as now they doe, enough (and more than they either will or can Cultivate to Profitt); and not still seeke to deprive them of more out of a mere Itch of Luxury, rather than any reall Lack of it. Which shames us, and makes us become a Reproach and a Byword to these more Moral Heathens.

To conclude this Particular, wee shall most Earnestly Exhort you and them, as you may justly hope and Expect the Blessing of Almighty God (who is a lover of Peace and Justice) and that God should Prosper this poore Country, and your present Consultations that you endeavour to gaine and preserve a good and just Peace and Correspondence with your Indian Neighbours, That they may not hold up their handes, and cry out against you, nor call you unjust and perfidious, least God in his owne Divine Justice should againe make them Spectators of our Punishment, and lett them (as he but lately did) looke on While like men devoyd of reason, Religion, Loyaltie, or Humanitie, wee were murdering, Burning, Plundering, and Ruining one another, without remorse or Consideration.

Gentlemen,

There is another thing, which wee must also Recommend to your Consideration (viz.) the Reducing the Great *Salary* of the Members of the Assembly to such moderate rates, as may render them lesse Grievous and Burdensome to the Country. And this wee cannot but earnestly offer to you, for that his Majestie hath been Pleased to shew himselfe soe signally concerned therein as appears both by his Royall Proclamation to you, and his Private Instructions to us.

In order to an immediate Redresse whereof, wee offer you our joint Opinion as followeth.

First,   That an Act of Assembly may passe for the future calling of a new
           Assembly to be elected every two yeares under the Qualification which
           the Right Honourable the Governour can Declare to you from his Majesties late Instructions sent him over by us, whereby to make those of
           the present Assembly more ready to comply with his Majestyes Royall

Commands for Retrenching their former Salary. Whereas by reason of their constant sitting, they Receive onely and Pay not, which this alteracion will well remedy, and make the Charge & Expence equall by alternate Receipts and Payments, and consequently alleviate the Present Pressure, which the People seeme soe much concerned in.

2ly. Wee are of Opinion that for the future noe Salary bee paid, received or continued for any Member of Assembly for any longar tyme than hee or they shall there personally sitt, and shall cease during the Travelling time of their coming and Returning to and from the said Assembly.

3ly. That from henceforth there be noe Account or Reckoning demanded, paide, or allowed for Liquors dranke by any Member of Assembly at Committees here.

4ly. That every Chairman of the severall Committees of Assembly doe for time to come, draw up their owne Reports themselves, whereby to save the Country that great Charge of Clerks, purposely imploy'd and paid for writing the same; some having (as wee are informed) 4000£ of Tobacco for scarse Twenty lines Writing.

5ly. That the People of the several Countyes for which you serve as Burgesses may noe longer Complaine of the largenesse of your Salaryes, nor yourselves of the Lessening and Retrenching of the same. Wee also commend to your present care and Regulation the abatement of Excessive and unreasonable Rates set by Ordinary Keepers upon all sorts of Liquours, especially in and about James City at Assembly times, which seemes to us the true reason, that the Members of the Assembly cannot find their Accounts or be content with a reasonable Salary because of such excessive Rates and Prices which the ordinary Keepers doe arbitrarily and at their owne Pleasure and Libertie impose upon Liquors and the People.

For Remedy of which Exorbitant abuse, wee desire you will please speedily to consider of Providing such good Acts and Lawes as may best reforme and redresse the same, which we conceive must bee done by bringing downe the great Prices and Rates of Liquours and other things and sitting such reasonable and moderate Rates on the same, as the Retaillers may afford them for with fitt gaines. And that this Law (soe to be made) may be the more strictly inforced and observed, we also desire you will lay such a Penalty or forfeiture upon the willful Transgressours thereof, as may keepe them within the just boundes and Limitts to be sett and prescribed them, Which wee are of Opinion will be best effected by transmuting that Odious name of Informer, into that more Genuine one of calling such men Conservators of the Law.

This course being taken the Burgesses will easily apprehend that this will be soe far from being a Diminuation of their Salary that it will rather prove an Augmentation of it; For it is still as ample as before, when this lesser Allowance, shall more than suffice and serve to the same end as the Larger did, by Lowering the said Extravagant rates, which wasted and expended their former Salaryes.

As to such other *Grievances* as are of Publique Concernment (as fast as they shall come to our knowledge and Examination) wee shall prepare to transmit them home to his Majesty for his Royall Redresse.

And for all others that relate onely to Private Interest of Party and Partie, wee shall returne such to you of the Assembly to Consider of (as improper for our Inspection) and leave them to the Remedy of your Lawes already Provided, and hereafter to be made for their just Reliefe therein.

Wee shall wind up all, in this one Heartie wish, That you may soe Unite, accord and Proceed in all your arduous Enterprizes and endeavours (tending to the Peace & Resettlement of this Distressed Country) that you may putt a timely stopp to his Majesties Resolves of sending a far greater force over than what is already arrived to effect what your owne readie Conformity and Dutifull Obedience to his Royall will and pleasure may (and ought) to doe without it, and can alone Prevaile for the Recalling Home the Soldiers that are now here, which his most Sacred Majestie shall find by your due and Humble Submission, most sincere Repentance, and our true Report of the Quiet and Peaceable Posture of Affairs here, that there is noe more need for his Rigour and Justice, but of his Royall Grace and Favour towards you.

Wee can only add, that wee are upon all Occasions most readie to manifest ourselves for our Royall Masters, and this his Country's Service.

Most honor'd Friends,

Your Most Faithfull
Humble Servants

From our Place of   Herbert Jeffreys
Residence at Swanns Pointe   John Berry
In James River this 27th day   Francis Moryson
Of February, Anno 1676/7 in the
29th yeare of his Majesties Reigne
(whome God long Preserve)

Document 27
13 March 1677

By His Majesties' Commissioners for the Affaires of Virginia
March 13th, 1676/7

Whereas in our late Generall Letter to the Governor and Assembly wee have recommended two things, both of them very important to the Peace and Settlement of this Country, i. e. the Renewing a Peace with the Neighbour Indians, and the Redresse of the Great Salary paid to the Members of the Assembly, in both which wee have his Majesties Instructions Especially to concerne ourselves; and for the First the present Governour is particularly ordered to demand our Assistance in the Management and Concluding of a Treaty with the said Indians; Which though wee have Declared by our said Letter to the said Assembly his Majesties desire of a Peace with the said Indians, yet for that the sole Power of Peace & Warr are onely inherent to his Majesties Royall Prerogative. It is therefore to be understood, that this part of the letter, relating to the Peace, is not before you of the Councill and Assembly to Judge and determine whither or noe it be fitt or necessary, but onely to offer your best Judgements & Opinion as to what meanes and methods shall most easily, safely and honorably conduce thereto, and no further are you to concerne yourselves in this matter, for it is peculiarly in his Majestyes Governor and is neither in the Councill nor Assembly any further than is aforesaid.

As to that of the Salary of the Assembly Members, his Majesties Instructions are peremptory in that particular. You shall reduce the same to such a moderate proportion as may be noe Grievances to the Country. And for the Regulation thereof the Governour shall have our best advise whenever demanded of us.

Therefore this and the foregoing Article wee desire to recommend by you particularly to the Governor as appertaining solely to his Province. And if hee shall not have space of time sufficient to pursue and effect this part of his Majesties Royall Instructions, wee shall then offer them to the Governour that shall succeed him, to act therein as his Majesties Instructions doe impower and direct him.

Signed,

By Order of his Majesties Honourable
Commissioners

Document 28
6 March 1677

The Commissioners to the Governor

Right Honorable,
Wee finding not onely by former Complaints, But by the Petitions this day before us (and herewith sent you) that severall illegal seizures have beene made of the Goodes and Estates of his Majestyes Subjects without any due Conviction or Attainder, whereof wee have not been sparing by Letter more than once to advertise you, protesting against any such unwarrantable Practices, and espe-

cially for that there is noe Pretence, or Colour for such kind of Proceedings, But rather (on the contrary) of Restitution to them, and that for these Reasons, as wee conceive, First, since the Pardon granted to Yourselfe and the Assembly is grounded upon the acting under a Force, the same or like Circumstances causing others of his Majestyes Subjects to act contrary to their consciences and allegiance, equally entitles them alsoe to the same Benefitt, there being the same groundes and reason on both sides. Next for that Stat. of 1.R.3.c.3[33] is against Seisures before Conviction & Attainder. And Lastly, for that his Majestyes Proclamation of Pardon forgives not onely the Rebellion &c. But all Punishments and forfeitures by reason of the same, besides the latternesse of the date.

Sir, Wee have this once more (for all) delivered you our sense herein which wee leave you to consider, and speedily as you may to get yourselfe cleere of, that noe more Clamours of this kind may surround us here, nor pursue you home to England, obstruct your or our Proceedures for the Peace of this Country, and give new (if not just) occasions for more Disturbances among the People finding themselves thus abridg'd of the Benefitt of his Majesties Royall Proclamation, which they most of all looke and lay hold on, as coming immediately from the King himselfe, and finding his Royal Favours soe Gracious, generall & diffusive. Sir, wee shall neede say noe more, if you Please but to Consider of this much, as from,

Your most Faithfull, Humble Servants

Swanns Pointe   Herbert Jeffreys
March 6th, 1676/7   John Berry
                                                 Francis Moryson

Document 29
7 March 1677

Sir William Berkeley's Answer to the foregoing Letter

Right Honorable,

I have received your letter with some Wonder; for you tell me noe mans Estate is to be seised for Treason without Conviction, which I know is contrary to all the Practice of all the Kingdomes in Christendome, But for this I do Appeale to the King and his Councill and his learned Judges of the Law. Besides

---

33. The statute in question, enacted by parliament under Richard III in 1483, prevented the attempts of "eny persone [to] take or sease the goodes of eny persone arrested [for suspecion of felonie] afore that same persone so arrested and imprisoned be convycte or attaint of suche felonye according to the Lawe." *The Statutes of the Realm*, 11 vols. (London: The London Institution, 1816), 2: 479.

this, I was by when the king seised the Estates of many that were in Rebellion against him without Conviction. Soe that Againe I say that I appeale to the King and his Councill, and I desire you to take a list of what I have seised. But for Alexander Walker[34] the Case is much different for hee voluntarily offer'd it, as you shall have the Oath of a Councellour and another Gentleman. Ad to this, that I have seised nothing since the Kings Commissioners came in, and what is seised amounts not to the Thirtyeith part of my lost Estate. This letter will shewto the King and his Judges that they have *Consitentem Reum*[35] if I have acted as a Criminal, and therefore to them doe I appeale.

March 7th, 1676/7

Your Most Humble Servant,

William Berkeley

P. S.

Right Honorable,

I have taken an Authentique Copie of this Letter I send you, and shall doe you the right to give the King and his Councill all your Admonitory Letters to mee.

Document 30
21 March 1677

The Commissioners to the Governor

Right Honourable,

Wee having (soe far as his Majesties service did at that time require and permitt) complied with the Commission of Oyer and Terminer, that the Country might well take notice wee came not in the least to countenance but to try and condemne Criminalls. And having since received from you a short letter, desiring our further sitting on the same occasion, wee doe in returne, assure you that wee can in noe wise comply therewith, as else wee would, without detrement & neglect of some more immediate service of his Majesties which takes up (at present) our whole time & attendance and therefore held ourselves Excus'd (as we trust you also will) at this tyme, because wee well know (also) that the maine

---

34. Alexander Walker's tobacco, 23 hogsheads in all, was seized by Governor Berkeley, according to the testimony of the London merchant Major Robert Bristow, dated 26 February 1678/9. See Letters and Papers Concerning American Plantations, 5 February 1678/9–19 December 1679, C.O. 1/43, 35ro (VCRP).

35. "*Consitentem Reum.*" To proceed no further against the accused.

reason of his Majesties making soe small a Quorum was to the intent that his Majesties other important Services might not upon this account be diverted or retarded.

Sir, wee must againe desire you to be mindfull of those soe emergent matters, that have thus long layne before you and are yet unanswered, which are innumerated to you by a Paper of ours intitled Interlocutory heades &c[36] and also lately reinstanc'd by another Paper sent you by Col. Bacon. Since (Sir) it is more than tyme that wee had your Answer in Writing; and that you will be pleased to make it your present care that a particular account in writing (relating to his Majesties Revenue) may be by you fully and faithfully made out of all seizures, Composicions, Amerciaments[37], Fines and Forfeitures which (by the late Rebellion) devolved to the Crowne, and belongs to us to Enquire into and transmit home to the Right honorable the Lord High Treasurer of England (without any diminuation, concealment or Embezzlement) since the first seising thereof of all Criminals impeached, convicted, sentenced and Executed for their actuall Treason and Rebellion as well as before as since our Arrival in Virginia, whereof a very strict account wilbe Exacted of you at your returne to England. All which being incumbent on us to acquaint you with, and on yourselfe to answer, wee could in noe wise bee guilty of an omission of this high nature, and importance to his Majesties Royall Interest. And soe not doubting of your just care herein, wee remaine

Swanns Point   Your most humble servants
March 21 1676/7

                                      Herbert Jeffreys
                                      John Berry
                                      Francis Moryson

          Noe answer was Returned to this Letter, nor did Sir William Berkeley write any more letters to the Commissioners after this till upon the occasion of the Postillion[38] a little before his departure.

Memorandum: The Commissioners seeing Sir William Berkeley would not comply with the contents of the foregoing Letter, caused mee to draw up a Commission to Lt. Col George Jordan[39] and Major Theophilus Hone to impower

---

36. See Chapter 1, Document 10.

37. *Amerciaments.* A punishment or penalty left to the "mercy" of the inflicter (OED).

38. *Postillion.* One who rides a post horse, a swift messenger (OED).

39. Jordan, a member of the House of Burgesses for Surry County under Berkeley who had not been elected to the June Assembly of 1676. The commissioners requested that he and Hone "make an enquiry into all forfeitures, carrying away of goods and cattle in the counties of James River, New Kent, and York." C.O. 1/40, 121 (VCRP).

them to Enquire into the Estates and Forfeitures which devolved to the Crowne during the late Rebellion &c. which they did, and have given an account of the same in writing under their hands.

Samuel Wiseman

Document 31
22 March 1677

The Commissioners to Mr. Watkins

Sir, Wee are upon preparing our intended Dispatch for England by Captain Grantham[40] the next weeke, But by the present opportunity of a ship called the *Lady Francis* of Virginia (John Allen Commander) just now readie to saile, wee would not omitt giving you this generall Advice, That the face of things is much amended since our Arrival and we hope by degrees this poore Country will recover its former Peace and Prosperity. There is a generall Submission of the whole Country, and a joyfull resentment[41] of his gracious Majestieties most Royall favour and Compassion shewn them. Sir, the tyme will not now admitt of particulars, soe wee much be feigne to referr ourselves to the account that is suddainly to follow, which is as large as the present Condition of Affairs here will let us write, and thus much you may acquaint the honorable Secretary Coventry.

Your Affectionate Friends and Servants,

22 March 1676/7

Herbert Jeffreys
John Berry
Francis Moryson

40. Captain Thomas Grantham, commander of the *Concord* of London, the most powerful ship in Virginia waters. He was respected by the Duke of York but also was a tobacco planter acquainted with the leaders of the rebellion. He arrived in the York River in November of 1676, a month after Bacon's death, and served as an intermediary between the rebels and the supporters of Governor Berkeley. In January, he negotiated with Bacon's successor, Joseph Ingram, for the surrender of 800 rebels at West Point. One of Berkeley's closest supporters, William Sherwood, concluded that Grantham had played a major role in ending the rebellion, and that had he not interposed, "the whole Country had been laid in Ashes." See Webb, *1676*, 119-124.
41. In the seventeenth century, "resentment" occasionally could be defined as "a gratefull appreciation or acknowledgement . . . a feeling of expression of gratitude" (OED).

Document 32
27 March 1677

A Letter from the Commissioners to Mr. Secretary Coventry

Right Honorable,

Sir. Although the present Condition of Affairs here bee such, as will not permitt us to give his Majestie soe ample an account of our Proceedings as wee could desire, yet wee still hold ourselves bound to make all Oportunityes a meanes to expresse our Duty and observance to your Honour, and shall let you know that as soone as the Assembly was mett, a Speaker chosen and they were a full house, wee laid before them by a general Letter, the whole Businesse of our coming over, but they having now satt a whole Moneth have not yett proceeded soe far, as to Answer that our joint Letter. Wee have also taken all occasions both Publique and Private to possesse the People of this Colony as well of his Majesties Severity and Justice, as of his most Royall Clemency and Indulgence towards fitt & proper Objects for either. And for the first, wee have satt together on the Commission of Oyer & Terminer both at the Tryall and Condemnation of Seaven or Eight of the most notorious Criminalls, and gave advice to have them Executed in their owne severall Counties, whereby to convince this Country that wee are come to condemne and Punish, and not to Countenance or bolster out their Rebellions, nor have we beene wanting on the other hande by all meanes to make them rightly apprehensive of his Majesties most transcendant Royall acts of favour and Indulgency to his oppressed and Seduced Subjects, which also hath had its due effects on them and been generally received with suitable Impressions of Joy and most Loyall, hearty Expressions of humble Gratitude for his Majesties soe surpassing Grace & Goodnesse extended towards them, and Princely care of them at a tyme when they had soe far forfeited all his Royall Favours. And, Sir, wee must needes say that had not his Majesties Royall Proclamation and other acts of Mercy and Pardon taken its timely effect, wee had in all likelihood found things farr worse than now (God be prais'd) they are, if not a new Disturbance kindled and broke out, great as the former, and more insuperable, for soe generall was the guilt of the Country, and the innocent Partie soe few, that nothing but a Pardon soe Royall and Diffusive could extend to the making up soe wide a Breach made by Rebellion & disobedience, soe that Bacons death was not enough to frustrate and stifle this Proclamation, or suspend the Publishment of it, soe long as Lawrance,[42] a Colonell & grand Accomplice

---

42. Richard Lawrence, an Oxford-educated burgess from Jamestown. Along with William Drummond, Lawrence was one of Bacon's strongest supporters. He despised Berkeley and his circle of supporters. His exclusion from the provisions of Governor Berkeley's pardon is included in Letters and Papers Concerning American Plantations, 4 January–19 March 1676/7, C.O. 1/39, 64-65 (VCRP). An account of his estate, nearly

of Bacons, a most stubborne resolved & desperate Rebell (with others fitt to head a new faction) is yett out. Besides how should the People (perhaps) have understood the Conditions or termes of his Majesties gracious Pardon, without his Royall Proclamation had told them. And thereafter for that Sir William Berkeley might else at his owne Pleasure have imposed upon the ignorant his owne termes and conditions as neverthelesse he has endeavoured to doe (as wee conceive) contrary and in wrong to his Majesties Royall intent, interest, and meaning, and against reason, law, and justice.

Sir, If wee have beene mistaken & deceived in our former Character of Sir William Berkeley, it may bee imputed to our too easy Credulity at first being overpersuaded by his own Protestations and calling God to Witnesse and us to be strict Inquisitors of his Actions, when there was noe Body by who could contradict him, which hath since appeared much contrary to his first Professions, and our late account, whereof wee have not beene sparing to tax him home as our Letters to him will manifest, and if the reports of credible persons may be believed not in the least unjustly or untrue. And sir to speake yet more plainly, wee thinke it impossible for us to take a right and thorough Prospect into the matters whereof wee are required to acquaint ourselves & you, or that ever things should be put into that Peaceable posture and happy composure desired and by us endeavoured while Sir Wm. B. continues Governour upon the Place, for until the awe of this stay be removed from the People, wee can never thoroughly search and penetrate into the bottome of Businesses, for 'tis his onely artifice to perswade the People that Col. Jeffreys is but his Deputie and that hee shall the next yeare returne Governor againe.

As for the generall Grievances wee are sent hither to Enquire into, Report & Redresse (by what wee can hitherto see) they are like to come within a very narrow Compasse, That of the great Salary being now at this tyme under the Assemblyes Consultation and Redresse. The maine Grievances are chiefely concerning Fort-Money, and other Publique accompts and Leavyes of the Colony, proper also for the Inspection and Redresse of the Assembly, soe that had not Sir William Berkeley by studdyed Evasions of his, interrupted and diverted the course of our Proceedings, but have gone hand in hand with us for the Kings interest wee verily believe (ere this Tyme) wee should have fully received and examined all the Grievances, satisfied the People, Concluded the Indian Peace, and in sum fulfilled our whole Instructions and beene ready (upon Orders) to returne home, and soe have saved his Majestie considerable part of this weighty charge hee here continues at, on this occasion.

And, Sir, wee having by Letter upon Letter as well as by word time after time protested against Sir William Berkeley's illegall and arbitrary proceedings, as to seizures of Estates of persons not Convicted of any crime, since the surren-

illegible, is in the Proceedings and Reports of the Commissioners for Enquiring into Virginian Affairs and Settling Virginian Grievances, C.O. 5/1371, 247ro (VCRP).

der at West Pointe, and upon our arrival here, he (as often as wee urged the illegality of such his Practices in tyme of Peace) is still pleased to reply with a story of something done in the Heighth of the late Civill Warrs of England Asserting it is the Law of all Nations, then hee Appeals herein to His Majestie, his Councill, and the learned Judges at Law, and againe that hee has writ home to your Honours selfe in this behalfe. Nor could we decline this our concernment being almost every day pursued with Petitions and Complaints of things of this nature, as first his sitting the Broad Arrow heade upon severall Hogsheads of Tobacco, and afterwards putting his owne private marke of **W** upon them; And having found all our private friendly monicions in vaine, wee made noe difficultie to declare our opinion in open court, that the Country might perceive wee did not combine with or connive at such unwarranted Practices. Which when hee saw we could not be drawne to consent to & palliate, he then said hee would propose a middle way, and instead of taking such Forfeitures, lay Fines upon Criminalls, and this way said hee will Justifie, and have it recorded here in Court, which hee has not onely begun to put in Practice, but (as wee have since heard) hath compounded severall Treasons &c for Hoggsheads of Tobacco, Cattell &c. Sir, Wee Beseech your Honour that this candid Relation of ours may not bee mistaken at home, as if there were any feuds or differences betweene us and the Governour, for both with him, and betwixt ourselves wee have still endeavoured to mainteine a faire and even Correspondence, as his and our mutuall letters will manifest.

And therefore to make noe more disputes or cavills on this score wee have wound up all in one short Letter of ours to him since his peremptory appeale home, to desire of him an exact account of all such seizures, Composicions, Fines and Forfeitures which devolve to the Crowne to send or carry home to my Lord Treasurer to whose Province it appertaines.

The Goale is now almost cleere, the Governour having condemn'd some and Pardoned and transported others. Whereupon Query: What forfeitures belong to his Majestie upon Transportation, &c.

Another thing we have to acquaint your Honor with is, That upon the Tryall of the Rebells before us, one of the Prisoners at Barr publickly Produced and Pleaded in open Court a Copie of the Kings Private Additional Instructions to Sir William Berkeley writ out at large, at which wee were greatly surprised, and demanding of the Prisoner how he came by them, Hee would not declare, the Governour (in Court) calling God to Witnesse that hee had never lett them goe out of his owne hands or Trunke, which he againe affirm'd at his owne Table when the same day wee dined with him and the Councill, but said Mr. Povey[43]

---

43. Thomas Povey, a long-serving imperial bureaucrat with powerful commercial interests, maintained close ties to Giles Bland's father. In August of 1676, Povey received copies of Bacon's proclamations, along with a request from Bland that he use his influence to present the rebels' grievances to the king. Povey did so. See Webb, *1676,* 153,

had sent over a Transcript of them from England, and by his great Interest procured it out of Mr. Secretary Coventry's Office.[44] But upon our further Enquiry wee are well satisfied that they came from noe other hand than his owne, hee having dispersed Copyes of them, signed by Beverly[45] Clerke of the Assembly and others, soe that they are become Common all over the Country, especially pernicious to his Majestyes Interest at this tyme to have the Common Rabble and disaffected party observe those articles of the Kings Private Instructions, which take their measures by Bacons greater or lesser Interest among the People here.

Sir, since our coming hither, there hath beene with us the Nottoway, Nancymond, Appamatuck & Pamunckey Indians, their Kings, Queene and Great Men to signifie theire readynesse to enter into a firme League of Peace with the English,[46] which wee hope a short tyme will produce. Onley the Suskahannocks and Doeggs (two remote Nations) have lately cutt off some English families at Rappahannock, of which great Complaints are made in those Parts.

It will not now be long before the Assembly Rise, upon which we intend to send home the *Deptford* Ketch, with a more ample account of our Proceedings, which we could not possibly doe sooner, and in the meane tyme this cursory

204; On Povey's career in imperial administration, see Webb, *Governors-General*, 154-157, 195, 199, 213-214, 313.

44. The defendant in question was Giles Bland. Bland went on trial in February of 1676/7 before a court that included Governor Berkeley, the two Ludwells, and the royal commissioners. Bland surprised the commissioners at this trial, reading from a copy of the governor's instructions that had been signed by Robert Beverley, a favorite of the governor. The commissioners could draw only one conclusion: Berkeley had made public his instructions, and the discretionary powers contained therein, in order to cow the public, and to reveal "that the policy of the crown varied with the degree of popular resistance to it." Bland's gambit embarrassed the governor, but it did not save his life. The commissioners would not allow Bland to escape condemnation for his part in the rebellion. Hoping that somehow Bland's execution would be stayed on appeal, they joined Berkeley and the Ludwells in condemning him to death. On 24 March 1677, Bland was hanged. He became the last of Governor Berkeley's victims. See Webb, *1676*, 151-154.

45. Robert Beverly, a loyal supporter of Governor Berkeley. He led the counterattacks the governor ordered against the rebels in October of 1676. His rough band of sailors captured Thomas Hansford in November. Beverly aggressively plundered the estates of the governor's opponents, and in some cases the estates of those wishing to remain neutral. The commissioners struggled to control Beverly after the rebellion, with little success. See Webb, *1676*, 104-105; Washburn, *Governor and the Rebel*, 125.

46. The peace treaty is included in Chapter 3, below. The commissioners revealed to Secretary Coventry that they had met with the leaders of several Powhatan chiefdoms, allies of the colony since their defeat in 1646, upon whom Bacon had fallen during the rebellion. On the resolution of Virginia's troubles with the Susquehannocks and Doegs, a resolution largely effected through the efforts of New York's governor Sir Edmund Andros, see Webb, *1676*, 374-378 and Oberg, *Dominion and Civility*, 212-216.

one, and the Papers herewith sent will prepare your Honor thereunto. Sir, Wee remaine,

Your Honors most Humble Servants,

Swanns Pointe   Herbert Jeffreys
James River   John Berry
27 March 1677   Francis Moryson

Sent with this Letter,

Queries for the Learned Councill at Law to Resolve

1. Whether a Person, dying before Conviction, his Estate to be Forfeited to the King, and if soe, and by what course it becomes Lyable when there is none to answer?
2. Whither Persons Condemned, Sentenced and Executed by Martiall Law and not by a Legall Jury of twelve men, be forfeited?
3. Whether any seizure be legally Executed, before Conviction or attainder and especially if Goods Cattle &c may be carryed off the Ground?
4. Whether by Law the Estates of Banished or Transported persons be Lyable to seizure & Forfeiture?
Wee humbly desire a solution to these Queries (by the next) signed by an authentique hand for Law.

Document 33
27 March 1677

From the Commissioners to Mr. Secretary Coventry

Right Honorable,

Sir, Considering with ourselves the present State of this Poore Country, which is truly much more miserable than either was at first Reported or could be expected, by reason of the generall depredations & Ruines here by the late Rebells, and especially by the Burning of James Citie, neere which wee reside, there not being any House within lesse than foure or five miles of us.

And that seeing the occasion of our Coming and present Residence here invites from all Parts of this Country a constant resort of People to us upon Publique Businesse, wee cannot possibly decline (in common humanity) entertaining them at our owne Table, for which wee have noe allowance from home, nor have wee had the value of an Egg presented us here, where the rates of Provisions are as deare as at Gravesend, Deale or Dover, Peoples stocks being soe generally wasted & destroyed by these plundering Rebells; and many tymes by reason of Badd weather, and frequent Northwest Windes men cannot safely crosse the Rivers to returne home, soe that wee are forced to keepe them here, to our noe small Expence and Charge. Now, Sir, wee doe most humbly desire that considering how great Charge wee were att in attendance before wee obtain'd our Dispatch from Court, and afterwards for our owne Provisions at Sea, as also the Qualifications wee are under, and the necessity of doing what is before mencione, Besids the keeping up the Honour of His Majesties Great Seale, whereby wee must needes sink low in our owne Estates and Fortunes which will be severely felt in our Familyes at home, That therefore your honor wilbe pleased to lay this our Pressure under his Majesties most gracious Consideration, that after his accustomed Princely Benignity, Honor and Goodnesse, his Majestie will be pleased that a Lymitted Salary may not include an unlymitted stay and expence.

All which most humbly leaving to your Honor to prostrate before his Majesty, wee remaine,

Swanns Point
27 March 1677

Sir, Your Honors most humble servants

Herbert Jeffreys
John Berry
Francis Moryson

Document 34
27 March 1677

From the Commissioners to Mr. Secretary Williamson

Right Honorable

Sir, In humble Complyance with the Duty which wee all owe to Your Honor, wee shall hereby render You our Opinion & Account of the present Condition of this late miserable Country of Virginia, as followeth.

That the Peoples ready Submission and returne to their Obedience has bin as generall as their late Disloyall Revolt to that Grand Rebell Bacon and his Adherents; and indeede had the Governour beene as openhanded to extend his Majesties Royall Acts of Mercy and Pardon, as hee first expressed himself sensible of the Benefitt and necessity of his owne, it had ere this tyme had the happy effect to have quieted and compos'd the mindes of the whole Country, who have (for the most part) the same pretence of Claime to his Majesties Royall Remission as himselfe and the Assembly, since they have bin severally constrained under the like force to act as they did against their Allegiance & Consciences, which rather shews his Politique, selfish partiality than equitable Prudence and Comisseration thoroughly to heale himselfe before hee car'd to stanch the bleeding gashes of this woefully lacerated Country. In spight of Law, and contrary to his Majesties most gracious acts of Forgivenesse and Restitution, making and treating men as Delinquents before any due Conviction or attainder, by seising their Estates, Cattle, Servants & carrying off their Tobacco, and afterwards altering it to his own Private marke **W** calling this securing it to the Kings use.

Sir, many and grievous have beene the Complaints of Marchants and Factors here for having their Trade retarded, their owners Goodes seised in their handes, and themselves made culpable for what is within the benefit of his Majesties Acts of Mercy and Restitution. The Merchants Ships having beene made Goales of Rebells and Refugees for the Loyal (obsconding) Partie, who devoured their Sea-Provisions, which should carry them home to England, having noe Regard or recompence given them therefore, the Governour not soe much as promoting them in their freight homewards bound; some mens Estates being taken away for the indiscrete tattle of their wives here, while some of them were about their Lawfull Affairs in England. [47]

And wee have still observed here that those who stile themselves the Loyall Party are the onely chiefe Disturbers and Obstructers of the Peace and Settlement of this calamitous Country, by aggravating former offences, to the exasperating the Peccant[48] party, soe that now nothing but a generall Penall act of Oblivion can serve to make up these Breaches, and reconcile the Rancors and bitter Animosityes among them, the seeds for future Discontents and disturbances; the Neutral (we cannot say) Loyall Party complaining of too much lenity of ours towards the Criminal, when as wee ourselves have satt at the Tryall and condemning of seaven or Eight persons, And when the dictates of others fears Councelled & Caution'd the not sending them to dye without a strong Guard to attend them, wee gave advice against it, that the Country might not have cause to thinke or say that wee were afraid of any Rescue or Tumults on this occasion, and that wee might hereby make Tryall of the Temper of the People, which proved very Peaceable and Submissive. One Arnold, a horrible, resolv'd Rebell & Traytor, Wee advised to have hang'd in chains in his owne County, to bee a more remarkable Example than the rest, because his Crimes were more horrid and heinous, saying that (twas well knowne) hee had noe kindnesse for Kings, and that they had noe Right but what they gott by Conquest and the Sword, and hee that could by Force of the Sword deprive them thereof had as good and just a Title to it as the King himselfe, And that if the King should deny him right (or what in himselfe hee thought such) hee would make noe more to sheath his Sword in his Heart or Bowells then of his owne mortall Enemyes. For which and other Treasonable words and Actions hee is accordingly Executed; this Country not being capable of Executing the sentence peculiar to Traytors according to

---

47. Both of the instances mentioned here could apply to the case of Thomas Grindon. See his petition in Chapter 7, below.

48. *Peccant.* That which has committed a fault or is at fault or guilty (OED).

the Lawes and Custome of England, though they were all sentenced according to the Judgement pronounced in cases of High Treason.[49]

Sir, Wee have now noe reason to feare a New Mutiny, but rather if this Rigid Prosecution be continued, it may be a meanes partly to depopulate this Country, and (without Banishment) cause many to desert this Plantation, which the Assembly themselves are now at length soe sensible of, that they have made it their vote and Addresse to the Governour to forbeare, and stop his hand from all further Sanguinary Punishments, since noe one that is brought to Tryall, but brings with him Guilt & Circumstances sufficient to Condemne, noe Body knowing by this course when or where it will end, or on whome it may last fall: To which wee are informed hee has (with some difficulty) beene prevailed on to give his consent, and soe hath dismiss'd the Juryes & Witnesses that attended the Court on this occasion, since when (wee are told) hee has found out a new way, of Fining some for their Treasons & Rebellion, and condemned others to Banishment into England &c.

Sir, Wee hope this Briefe account of the state and present posture of Affairs here will suffice at this time, and that the hast of this Dispatch (not permitting us to dilate on further particulars) will Excuse us to Your Honour, But by Mr. Watkins our Correspondent you willreceive what is here wanting from,

Swanns Pointe   Your most Humble Servants
27 March 1677

                                         Herbert Jeffreys
                                         John Berry
                                         Francis Moryson

Document 35
27 March 1677

From the Commissioners to Mr. Watkins

Sir,

Wee have writt twice to you with our Two Former Dispatches and by the second sent you a Duplicate to the Secretary &c. wee doe now send you Secretary Coventry's Letter with Papers and Proofs of some Particulars, desiring that

---

49. The commissioners especially despised Anthony Arnold, a man who repeatedly and publicly expressed his anti-monarchical views, in addition to leading forces in Bacon's army. The commissioners wanted Arnold hanged, drawn, and quartered, but a lack of skilled executioners made that impossible. Instead, the commissioners ordered Arnold suspended from the gallows in chains to die a slow death and decay in front of any Virginians who shared his views. On Arnold, see Webb, *1676*, 35, 150.

you will inforce the heads of those Proofs as occasion offers, that you doe also attend my Lord Treasurer with Walkers Papers and Mrs. Grindons.[50]

That you please to assure the severall honorable persons you attend that it is our onely aime and endeavour to give his Majestie the most acceptable account that this his Majesties Colony is in a Peaceable Quiet Condicion, which is his Majesties maine Interest at present, and that all that obstructs it is the Governours abiding upon the Place and the Frynesse of those that call themselves the Loyall partie which are not many, and among them not twenty eminent Sufferers in Estate, yet most of them soe rapacious, implacable, highly valuing & vaunting themselves for their Passive valour, swell'd to such huffing Insolence at their owne nothing to be prais'd or bragg'd of, that they but help to exasperate the other Party, and blow the Cole of Strife & discord afresh among the People by violent accusations and bitter recriminations, in which wee believe they take a larger freedome & priviledge under the Protection of these forces, which perhaps alone prevents the breaking forth of a fresh flame of Mutiny. Most Importunately have they also solicited our constant sitting to Try and Condemne the Guilty Party (which indeed is little lesse than the whole Country) after wee had soe farr comply'd herein as we thought was requisite to shew our open discountenance to Rebellion, refusing any further to concerne ourselves not onley because it would have obstructed His Majestyes more emergent service, but for that wee found the Governour for filling the Goale as fast as we were able to emptie it of Prisoners. Sir, from these hints you will discover the necessity of Passing a Generall Act of Oblivion here, which we doubt the Governour and this Assembly will not doe without his Majestie had strictly Enjoyned it to be done as in England.

The Generall Grievances are soe few and Triviall, that if the Governour and his Party would leave off their depredations, and Answer to those Matters hee by his Majestie is Instructed and by us desired to doe, Wee can see noe urgent occasion to stay a fortnight longer upon the Place: But his contrariety and aversion is such, that it begets new Troubles, and obstructs the smooth course of our Proceedings. For though his owne as well as our Instructions bespeak our advice and Assistance for Retrenching the great Salary of the Assembly, yet has he never soe much as once sought us in it, least perhapps hee might thereby disoblige and thwart his owne ends & interest in the Assembly by such abatement of their Salary. Whereupon wee have been forced againe and againe to urge the necessity of fulfilling this article, as being peremptorily order'd by the King himselfe, and that otherwise wee ourselves were resolved to proceede to see it Effected.

But now that also is effected, and the Salary reduced to 120. £ per diem, which is the very lowest allowance the Burgesses can support their charge at.

---

50. Both petitioned the commissioners for relief from the exactions made by Berkeley's followers. Their grievances are included in Chapter 7, below.

Sir, there is this thing (among the rest) to be considered, in reference to Seisures, that when the Governour shall have carryed off & taken to himselfe, the Estates of Tobacco, Cattle, Servants &c as hee does (which are the stock upon the Place) of what value or consideration the bare Acres can be of to his Majestie.

These things, we pray you, as you find the face of things who are upon the Place, to presse and lay home in our behalfe, especially the Inspection of the Letters betweene us and the Governour, And having first Communicated to Mr. Secretary Coventry what is in your Judgement necessary, to take his opinion of what he thinks proper to impart to other Ministers of State you are by us desired to attend in this behalfe. And if any of the present Ministers (at our departure from England) should happen to be deade, removed, or altered to apply to those in their Places, and after you have beene with the Honorable Secretary to attend to the Duke of York[51] with this Advice.

Finally, Wee desire that what wee shall from time to time by Letters informe or report home may have that credence from our Patrons as is due to the Character wee remaine under; that Loose extravagant Reports & Storyes may not take up that roome or find that Reception which is chiefely due to our Letters. Sir, wee are

March 27th

Your very affectionate
Friendes & Servants,

Herbert Jeffreys
John Berry
Francis Moryson

Document 36
27 March 1677

The Commissioners to the Lord High Treasurer[52]

Sir,

Your Honour will receive herewith a Transcript of a joint Letter of ours to Sir William Berkeley together with his Answer and the Copies of some Peti-

---

51. James, Duke of York, the brother of Charles II. For his career as imperial administrator, see Webb, *1676*, 415-416; Idem., *Governors-General*, 95-96, 101, 112-113, 136-137, 214, 228-229, 233-234, 347-359.
52. Sir Thomas Osborne, Earl of Danby, served as Lord Treasurer from 1673 until 1679. A close adviser to the king, he presided over the royal revenues. On Danby's career in imperial administration, see Webb, *1676*, 179-180, 192-196.

tions, relating to his Majesties Revenue, which being properly within Your Lordships Province and Cognizance, Wee thought it our Duty to Advertize You of, most humbly referring Your Lordship for further Satisfaction to certaine other Letters which Mr. Watkins our Correspondent will attend and Communicate to your Lordship, which is all at present, But most humbly to assure your Honor wee are,

March 27th 1677

From Swans Pointe   Your Lordships most Humble
James River   and most Devoted Servants

                                                Herbert Jeffreyes
                                                John Berry
                                                Francis Moryson

Document 37
5 April 1677

The Commissioners to Mr. Secretary Coventry

Right Honorable,
    Our last Paquet to your Honor was very lately by Captain Grantham, Commander of the Ship *Concord* of London, and now we intend, within a few dayes, to send away the *Deptford* Ketch (our Final Dispatch) for on Tuesday last the Assembly concluded, and wee onely waite an account of the whole of their Proceedings which the Speaker has promised us. They have given Sir William Berkeley five hundred poundes, But wee find nothing done on his part in Order to a Peace with the Indians, which the present dangerous condition of the Country and their soe late Murders & Depredations committed makes more than ever necessary.
    Sir William Berkeley gives us noe account of his late Seizures Fines and Forfeitures as we desired and himself at first Promised us, nor has hee yet sought us in any one particular of his or our Instructions, or Answer'd any Article of them, But now insists on seeing our Private Power by our Instructions, which wee declined shewing; finding him soe Criticall and Captious[53] at all advantages to himselfe, that wee are sure that would rather more and more retarde than expedite the Kings Businesse about which wee are come hither, and should soone be able with ease to accomplish, were hee (the onely Impediment) removed hence; for both his Councill, and generally the whole Assembly and People, are and have beene soe over aw'd & Byass'd by him, that it is also im-

---

53. *Captious.* Disposed to find fault with others (OED).

possible to expect that account from them either, which our Commission and Instructions require, some Countys not daring to bring in their Grievances to this day with that Freedome wee have invited them (and they are else ready to doe) before Sir William Berkeley be gone hence, for which he has frequently prefixt his Tymes, But is still as backward as at first for ought wee perceive; And wee feare at last Col. Jeffreys must be forced to send him home, before those Mists hee by all Artifices casts before us can bee soe clear'd, as that wee may come to a plaine & open Prospect of things, which most of the Country as well as ourselves wish for, and not without good cause doe wee desire it for then one Fortnights tyme will probably show us more than all his tyme has done, and bring the whole Businesse to that passe, as that wee may [have] nothing more to Expect than his Majestyes Orders to returne home.

But, Sir, a maine Businesse of this Letter by Captain Robert Morris is to give your Honour an Account of his very eminent Services & Sufferings here, and he not having had that recompence and regard due to his deserts, wee therefore desire his Majesty be acquainted herewith, and that hee and two or three more Masters of Shipps have beene more serviceable to his Majestie and this Country than all those together, who vaunt themselves worthy persons, having lost to a considerable sum himself, but much beene a Receptacle to the Loyall Partie, but to the Rebells a Prison. Sir, wee having done Captain Morris this Right in speaking this true and short account of his services, wee doubt not but your Honor will doe him also the Justice to Present the same on his Behalf to his most Gracious Majestie, This Being all at this tyme from,

Swanns Point Your most humble & Obedient Servants
April 5th 1677

John Berry
Francis Moryson

At the writing hereof, Col. Jeffreys was absent, at the Camp at Middle Plantation with his Officers.

Document 38
13 April 1677

From the Commissioners to Mr. Secretary Coventry

Right Honorable,

By the Advice of Sir William Berkeley, the stay of the Ketch has beene retarded to this tyme of the Assembly's Rising in Expectation of receiving and sending home a full account of their Proceedings, Acts and Lawes, but hither to wee are without any; and soe have Dispatcht her for England with this advice onely, that Sir William Berkeley intends to imbarque for England the 20th instant in the Shipp *Rebecca*, Captain Larrimore Commander, and carrys home his owne Answers with him to the Articles of Inquiry, and our Interlocutory heads, to which wee desired and hee long since promised an Answer but now utterly refuses to give us any at all.

When hee shall have left this Country (and not before) wee expect a short tyme will shew boldly those things which now but cautiously peepe forth, and to find proofes upon Oath of all his Transactions, to second all wee have sent, or shall send or bring home, notwithstanding hee (to leave an awe upon the People) has done all that he can to persuade them, that hee shall certainly returne Governour againe a few moneths hence, Besides hee keepes such a Brow upon his Councill & the Assembly, that what ever hee approves, or dislikes, proposes, or perswades is onely done & comply'd with, soe that wee cannot informe ourselves of the state of the Militia we are Instructed to Enquire into, nor of the Publick accompts & Imposicions of on the Country, for the awe and restraint hee has upon them who should informe in these & other particulars; Degrading and preferring Officers after his owne dislike or favour, merely as his owne Private By-ends (not His Majesties interest & service) inclines him; For instance, advancing one Hill to the chair of President of Charles Citie County, and to be an eminent officer in the Militia, who is not onely a most notorious Coward, But a most insolent, turbulent fellow, and the only Grievance and hated person of that Countie, which may serve for a Specimen what the rest of his Creatures are.[54]

Sir, Though not onely his Royall Highnesse did assure Col. Jeffreys and Col. Morison that the two Patents prejudiciall to this Country should be called in and vacated without any Charge to them, and also my Lord Culpepper himselfe had told Col. Moryson that the Duke of Yorke had likewise layd his Commands on him not to stir in quest of his Patent, yet notwithstanding hee has since impower'd one Lieutentant Hoblyn, an officer belonging to the Regiment here, to

---

54. Bacon's followers detested Colonel Edward Hill, a close associate of the governor. He was, according to the members of the June Assembly, one of "the greatest instruments and occasion of raiseing, promoteing and stirring up the late differences and misunderstandings that have happened between the Honourable Governour and his majesties good and loyall subjects" in Charles City County. It was Hill, Bacon's followers remembered, who hounded planters for the "illegal and unjust burthensome taxes which for divers yeares last past by the art and skill and cunning" of Hill and his cronies "were for theire private ends and gaine imposed and raised." See William Waller Hening, ed., *The Statutes at Large: Being a Collection of All the Laws from the First Session of the Legislature in the Year 1619*, 2nd ed., vol 2 (Richmond, VA: R. & W. & G. Bartow, 1823), 364-365. His home sacked by Bacon's forces, Hill took his pound of flesh after the rebellion, joining with the governor in the plunder of Berkeley's enemies. After Berkeley's departure, he would oppose the efforts of the commissioners to limit the autonomy of the colony. See Washburn, *Governor and the Rebel*, 84-85, 134.

revive and uphold the same, which had it not beene timely found out and prevented by the lucky Discovery of Captain Middleton, & prudent care of Col. Jeffreys, it might have beene of dangerous consequence at such a tyme as this, after the Assembly had Risen all satisfied in that our Assurance to them, and written their most humble Thanks for it. But wee believe the Officer might know nothing of the Dukes Promise & Commands, or of his Majesties Royall intentions in his affaire.[55]

Having nothing more of moment to incert in this Letter to Your Honour, wee referr you to the worthy Captain Middleton, that brings this Dispatch, and to our Correspondent Mr.Watkins for what they may further informe You, and so include in all humble Duty,

Your (Honors)

Swanns Point   Most Humble and most Obedient
April 13th 1677   Servants

Herbert Jeffreys
John Berry
Francis Moryson

55. In 1649, Charles II granted to several of his loyal supporters the peninsula that lay between the Potomac and Rappahannock rivers, known in Virginia as the Northern Neck. Settlers in Virginia may not have known about these grants, or they may not have cared, for large numbers of English settlers began moving into the region after 1650. Soon they began to patent the lands. The holders of these patents worried when Charles II was restored to the throne, for the king had asked Governor Berkeley to provide assistance to a number of investors who had leased the lands granted in 1649 from the original beneficiaries of the king's largesse. Berkeley, in 1663, sent Francis Moryson, his lieutenant governor at the time, to England to try and persuade the King to revoke the grant, which already had thrown land titles in the colony into confusion. Moryson failed in 1663, but in 1669 Berkeley acquired from the king a recognition of all patents issued by the governor prior to 1661. This was a start, but Charles II had done nothing for those who had moved into the rapidly growing region since the Restoration.

Berkeley recognized the threat the king's capricious generosity posed for the colony's future, so he asked the House of Burgesses to raise taxes to provide the funds to buy out the Northern Neck proprietors. Only after sending an agent to England did the Virginians learn that the king had granted the remainder of the colony's public lands to Lord Thomas Culpeper and Henry, Earl of Arlington, for a period of 31 years. An additional agent was sent to help negotiate a revocation of both grants, and to secure a colonial charter that might prevent further wayward grants by the king. The tax bill amounted to 100 pounds of tobacco for each tithable in the colony. See Edmund S. Morgan, *American Slavery, American Freedom: The Ordeal of Colonial Virginia* (New York: Norton, 1975), 244-246.

Document 39
13 April 1677

The Commissioners to Mr. Secretary Williamson

Right Honorable,

Though this Dispatch imports little of concernment worthy Your Inspection, Yet in humble Conformity to that just Regard & Duty which becomes us in our respective Obligacions to your Honour, wee would not pretermit writing to lett you know, that the Assembly here is now lately risen, from whome wee were Promised & Expected to have had an ample Account of their whole Proceedings, But they are return'd home without transferring to us that satisfaction. Wee can therefore onely for the present refer you to Mr. Watkins, who will waite on Your Honor from us, and Promise a further account of such matters as shall hereafter occurr, and at this tyme, conclude and remaine,[56]

Your honors most Humble and Obedient
Servants

From Swanns Pt.
James River   Herbert Jeffreys
April 13th 1677   John Berry
                                               Francis Moryson

Document 40
3 February 1677

A Warrant Signed by Sir William Berkeley which Should have bin att the Beginninge of the Booke

Whereas his Majestie hath bin pleas'd to Commissionate the Honorable Sir Herbet Jeffreys, Esq., Sir John Berry, Knight and Francis Moryson Esq to make inquiry after the aggrievances of his Majesties Subjects of Virginia to rectifie the

---

56. The legislation enacted by the Assembly of February 1677 is included in Hening, ed., *Statutes,* 2: 366-406. The Assembly passed an Act of Indemnity that pardoned all treasons committed since 1676 (which, arguably, the assembly had no power to do). It punished Bacon's followers, provided relief for "such loyall persons who have suffered losse by the late rebells, and repealed the acts of Bacon's June Assembly of 1676, some of which were subsequently modified and enacted. See also Morgan, *American Slavery, American Freedom,* 275-276.

said abuses, administeringe equity to every man without respect of persons, and to report the same to His Majestie, this is therefore to will and require you, Sheriff of   County and everyone of the respective sheriffs of their severall counties, to call a County Court, and there to take a report of the Inhabitants of the said Countie, what abuses and grievances have bin done to them, by whome and for what reason, without regard to the quality of any man in the said Collony, att such time as you shall receive orders from the Commissioners, and to take care to obey such commands and Instructions as you shall receive from time to time from them. Given under my hand this 3d daye of February, 1676/7

William Berkeley

Document 41
No date given

The Names and Short Characters of those that have bin Executed for Rebellion: Sentenc'd to death by a Councill of Warr Taken and transcribed from Sir William Berkeley's own hand

First one Johnson, a stirrer up of the people to rebellion butt noe fighter.

2ly.   Farlow, one of Cromwells Souldiers verry active in this rebellion, taken with forthy men, coming to surprise me at Accomac.

3ly.   One Carver, a valiant, stout Sea man, taken miraculously who came with Bland with equall Commission and two hundred men to take me; and some few Gentlemen assisted me with the help of two hundred souldiers.

4ly   One Wilford an Interpreter that frightnened the Queen of Pamunkey from the land that she had granted her by the Assembly, a month after the Peace was concluded with her.[57]

5ly.   One Hansford, a valiant stout man, & and a most resolved Rebell.

All these att Accomack

57. Cockacoeske, the Queen of the Pamunkeys, apparently did not need an English interpreter. She spoke English. She used one, nonetheless, to distance herself from the English. The Peace of 1677, included in Chapter 3 of this volume, which the commissioners negotiated with the Pamunkeys and other tributary Indians within Virginia, reflects the great concern local Indians felt about the damage that corrupt interpreters could do. See Charles M. Andrews, ed., *Narratives of the Insurrections, 1675-1690* (New York: Charles Scribner's Sons, 1915), 14-15; Helen C. Rountree, *Pocahontas's People: The Powhatan Indians of Virginia Through Four Centuries* (Norman: University of Oklahoma Press, 1990), 94.

Att Yorke whilst I laye there:

> One Young commissioned by Generall Monke long before he declared for the King.[58]

2ly One Page, a Carpenter formerly my servant, butt now for his violence used against the Loyall party made a colonel.

3ly One Ha that shott to death a valiant Loyall person.[59]

4ly. One Hall, a Clerke of a County, butt more useful to the Rebells than forty armed men, who dyed Penitent, confessinge his Rebellion against the King & his Ingratitude to me.

Att the Middle Plantation

> One William Drummond, a Scotch man that wee all suppose was the originall cause of this rebellion, with a common Frenchman that had been very bloody.[60]
>
>> Condemned att my House and Executed when Bacon's Army laye before James Town:
>>
>> One Colonell Crews, Bacons Parrasite, and Trumpett, that continually went about the Country extollinge all Bacons actions & justifyinge the Rebellion.
>>
>> 2ly One Cookson twice taken in Rebellion
>>
>> 3ly One Digby, from a servant made a Captaine.

58. Captain Thomas Young had served in England under General George Monck (1608-1670) during the Interregnum. In Virginia, he had obeyed the order of council member Thomas Ballard to collect men and supplies for Bacon's march against the Indians. See Webb, *1676*, 125. On Monck's role in the Restoration of the Stuarts to the throne, see Webb, *Governors-General*, 57-63, 225-226.

59. Berkeley left a blank space after the first two letters in this rebel's name.

60. William Drummond, who long had opposed an administration of the colony's government that he considered thoroughly corrupt, was one of Bacon's most prominent supporters. Bacon had met with Drummond just before the rebel leader was first captured in June of 1676. Berkeley's forces captured Drummond on 14 January 1677, in New Kent County. He was hanged at the home of James Bray on the twentieth. See Webb, *1676*, 26 and Washburn, *Governor and the Rebel*, 51. On Sarah Drummond's attempts to protect her interests before the Crown, see Wilcomb E. Washburn, "The Humble Petition of Sarah Drummond," *William and Mary Quarterly*, 3d ser., 13 (July 1956), 354-378.

Document 42
27 March 1677

From Colonel Morrison to Mr. Cooke

Sir,

I confess I am a letter in your debt, and now paye it with a short one for the business incumbent on us will admit of noe other, especially I hope you will have the Perusall of the Secretarys and Mr. Watkins his letter, to which I am forced to referr you. I shall therefore speake nothinge of what is mentioned in either, but only give you a general prospect of things, etc. Thatt wee doubt not butt matters will be shortly composed to his Majesties Satisfaction, which is the Peace and Quiett of this poor Country, if Sir William Berkeley would please butt with freedom to permit his Majesties acts of Grace to pass, as his Majestie royally intended him, and not to limit them only to sutch persons as himselfe in his own private favour and interest approves worthy.

Sir, I have two things to trouble you with which are to lett the Honorable Secretary Coventry know how I have managed that affaire he was pleased to leave to me, to acquaint the Country with his Royall Highness' promise, that the two Patents shall be taken in and vacated, without any charge to the Country, which I have not only made knowne to the Assembly, butt allso Severall other Gentlemen in their particular persons; and by his Royall Higness will receive their most humble thanks by letter suitable to so gratious and Princely an obligation, which I thinke the handsomess waye to putt the Duke in mind to see itt effectually done.

In the next place to give Mr. Secretary my Humble thanks for Joyninge one with soe worthy and Generous persons as my fellow Commissionars are; Gentlemen who have noe farther end nor aime than his Majesties Honor and interest, and are soe excellently qualified for the imployment in which they serve: for this I must in public saye of Coll. Jeffreys, that a fitter person could not have bin found out, or sent hither to have quell the Rebellion, had Bacon still been alive and his party in arms, nor one more capable to quell and preserve the peace in the place he is likely to govern. As for Sir John Berry, there was never a person of more unbiased principle, prudent conduct or unwearied industry in the King's service. For my selfe, I shall make this humble solemne Protestation: that neither in my quality of an agent nor under the Character I am now in for this Country, did I ever offer any thing in the sincerity of my heart I thought not conducible to His Majesties Service & interest. Therefore, Sir, if through any Inadvertancy or humane frailty of mine I shall be soe unhappy to lapse into any errors, I hope itt may bee construed an error of Judgement and not of Will.

On the other hand, if any of my honest aimes and actions shall happily extend to any thinge like merritt, I shall desire noe more than humbly to offer it up under the place name of duty only; and account my selfe sufficiently happy if itt may butt truly deserve that name; nor shall I ever presume to have itt recommended soe to my Royall Master, before that humble person, Mr Coventry, shall be pleased to thinke just and fittinge to doe itt on my behalfe.

I shall saye nothing of the straitness of my salary and my own fortune, more than what he already knows, and is in our joint letter to his Honor, and I thinke itt a kind of Injury to praye him or you to remember mee least itt confess as it t'were a distrust in me; Butt if I were not afraid to breake the Bounds of that Humble modesty which become the meanes of my desert, I should desire you more than Cursorily to consider what I have before hinted, and if occasion presents to exert Mr. Coventry to apply his interest to our joint letter, which I take to be somewhat particularly my concerne, least I goe a looser out of this service and worse than when I came into itt. Sir, I know not whither I be made of the Right stuff for a Courtier, yett I cannot say I am of the best fashion, if truth and Honesty be that, for as I have not hitherto, soe I never shall weare any disguise on my actions, for I know Sincerity to be a plaine and impolite thinge, & the less trick'd the better.

Sir, I have not, but might saye somethinge of my old age for others to consider, that a yeare of my life is to me more than tenn yeares in a younger person, and how hard itt is to be kept att this wide distance from the comforte of a wife and Children, that noe one loves better; Butt sir, your own age will serve to explaine the truth of whatt I saye, better than I expect others will consider. Wee have desired Mr. Watkins to communicate all Paper of ours to Mr. Secretary Coventry, before they be delivered to the persons he is directed to since this is his Honors particular province, which wee shall never by any act of ours lessen or infringe. I beseech you, sir, present mine and my fellow Commissioners humble Service to that truly Honorable person and assure him that noe person livinge has a healthier Honor and Regard towards him, nor noe one shall upon all occasions owne those unmerited obligations on me than my selfe, which is all I saye butt that I am, Sir,

Swanns Point, 27 March, 1677   Your truly affectionate Servant,
                                                      Francis Morryson

Document 43
25 March 1677

From Colonel Morrison to the Lady Berkeley[61]

Most Honour'd Madam,

There is one Jones, a poore, condemned person, whose ignorance chiefly led him from his allegiance, and whose loyalty first brought him here for a Refuge, bearinge in his body many markes of a Loyall Souldier and Subject to the late Kinge of blessed memory, and by his further Character given me by Captain Bird and Colonel Farrar, I doe not find he was a bloody malitious Rebell, but one merely seduced into that fatall snare, by the artifice of others, and return'd to his obedience upon the Governor's Indemnity.[62] In short, Madam, there appears more prevalent arguments for mercy than Justice on his side, his offense beinge not by farr soe hainious and Criminall as the rest. Haveinge satisfied your Lady ship with much truly of this person, I doubt not Madam, butt that your own Mercifull and tender bosome will move you to intercede with the Governor in behalf of this poore unfortunate wretch. In which I doe hartily joyne my request.

Madam, I am not ashamed to appear att any time in a Plea of Mercy, nor can I be now doubtfull of my cause, intrustinge itt to the hands of soe fitt, soe good an advocate as your Ladyshipp.

Madam,

Swanns Point, 25 March 1677   Your Most Humble Servant
                                     Francis Moryson

---

61. Frances Culpeper Berkeley, a cousin to Lord Culpeper and the wife of the governor (who also happened to have been one of the original proprietors of Carolina) was an extraordinarily assertive woman, who countered politically the Commissioners' attempts to bring the colony under more effective imperial control. She was at the center of the Green Spring faction and she continued, even after the death of her husband, to oppose the commissioners' efforts to curb provincial autonomy. Her contempt for the commissioners was, indeed, readily apparent. She replaced, after all, the commissioners' postilion with the Green Spring executioner, a grave insult. See Webb, *1676*, 5, 8.

62. Jones, in short, had fought with Royalist forces in the English Civil War, and he suffered for his loyalty after the Puritans defeated Charles I. After Jones was wounded and captured, his Puritan opponents sold him into servitude in Virginia. He survived his term of service, and ultimately established himself as a tobacco planter along the James River. He joined Bacon, apparently, because the rebel leader promised to eradicate the Indian enemy that threatened exposed settlements like his own. William Byrd and Colonel John Farrar, both commanders of Bacon's forces during the rebellion, pleaded for Jones's life and persuaded Moryson to intercede on Jones' behalf. See Webb, *1676*, 154-155.

Document 44
25 March 1677

The Lady Berkeley to Colonel Moryson

Sir,

If I am att all acquainted with my hart I should with more easiness of mind have worne the Canvasse Linnen the Rebells said they would make me glad of, than have had this fatall occasion for my intercedinge for mercy; Butt in this perticuler of Jones, there needs only your opinion in the case to make the Governor consent to itt, and you maye please to assure his friends he shall be pardoned, Mercy being as inherent in him as itt is in, Sir,

March 25th 1677   Your most Humble Servant,

                                                         F. Berkeley

Document 45
9 April 1677

From the Commissioners to Mr. Watkins

Sir, You will herewith receive a coppy of a commission from Sir William Berkeley to Sir Henry Chicheley,[63] which is desired to be by your self communicated with the severall letters to the Honorable Secretary Coventry, Sir Thomas Chichley and Alderman Jefferys; and represented to them of a manifest intrenchment upon the Power and authority immediately derived from his Majestie himselfe. Upon the conclusion of the Assembly and att their own request wee sent Mr. Wiseman to write their letters of Submission to his Majestie, and thanks to his Royall Highness and Lord Arlinton;[64] with all desiringe and promised duplicates of them to send or bring home themselves. Butt it seems they are thought too submissive for William Berkeley and the Councill to owne or subscribe, and soe will be allter'd by them and sent home by Sir William with their own Panegricks on him, however we shall send coppies of ours allso by the *Deptford* Ketch which will shortly sail home. Butt, Sir, the occasion of this is on behalfe of Captain John Consett[65] bearer hereof who havinge with a few other

63. Berkeley's deputy governor.
64. Henry Bennet, the first Earl of Arlington, received the grant to all of Virginia's public lands, along with Lord Culpeper, in 1674. See Morgan, *American Slavery, American Freedom,* 244-246.
65. John Consett commanded the *Mary* of London. He arrived in Virginia in November of 1676, and he aided Governor Berkeley in the mop-up fighting that followed Bacon's

masters of shipps here been a most eminent and signall sufferer upon his owner's score and more active and serviceable towards reducinge the late Rebells than those that assume to themselves the name of the Loyall Party, and brag soe highly of their great deeds and mighty manhood, without any regard or compensation of his services or Sufferings, haveinge also with the hazard of his life and fortune, and with his own hands, slaine Groves, one of the cheifest of the Rebells, except Bacon the Grand Rebell, that therefore his just deserts may not want their due commendation, wee desire that you will please to represent this much to the Honorable Secretary Coventry, that soe his Majestie maye not be Ignorant of a Person of his worth which wee trust you will not be wantinge in, and soe in hast wee Remaine,

Your most affectionate Friends and Servants,

Swanns Point April 9th, 1677

Herbert Jefferys
Francis Moryson

P.S.

Sir,

It is the desire of Col. Jeffreys and my selfe that you doe as occasion presents to confer with Alderman Jeffreys and sometimes to dine with him, and particularly to Impart a Coppy of the Commission to him. Butt above all I beg of you for Jesus Christ's sake to endeavour for my returne home, for the time draws nigh that you must expect noe more State letters home, "for this Country will make us all fools and shortly bring us to Cudy: Cuddy!"[66] Praye, Sir, endeavor through my Lord Arlinton to make the trifling present of two Redd Birds I have sent acceptable to the Honorable Lady Duchess of Essen his Lordshipps' Daughter. You will have many applications made you by our recommendations of suffering persons in the late Rebellion, whome I praye assist with your best care and interest.

death. In combat near Isle of Wight County on Christmas Day, Consett shot and killed William Groves, the commander of rebel forces in the area. Charles II appreciated his efforts, and the Privy Council granted him an award for his efforts. See Webb, *1676*, 95, 97, 103; Order of the Privy Council, 19 March 1678/9, Entry Book of Letters, Commissions, Instructions, Charters, Warrants, Patents and Grants Concerning Virginia, and Especially the Rebellion of Nathaniel Bacon there, and the Governorships of Berkeley and Culpeper and Lt. Governor Jeffreys, C.O. 5/1355, 273-275 (VCRP).

66. The source of the quotation is obscure. Moryson could have been referring to Cuddy, a buffoon in Thomas Dekker's novel, *The Witch of Edmonton* (1621). The Oxford English Dictionary suggests that the word "Cuddy" applied to a foolish or asinine person.

Your Affectionate Friend and Servant,
Francis Morryson

Signed by the order of the Honorable
Col. Jefferys and Col. Morryson

Document 46
14 April 1677

Colonel Morryson to the Lord Culpepper[67]

Right Honorable,

Sir, I must needs confess myselfe somewhat surprised to find your Lord-shipp was now for prosecutinge and settinge on foot againe the Business of the Patents, notwithstanding I left your lordship soe well satisfied in myselfe, with your acquiescence in his Royall Highness pleasure and Commands. And not only I butt Coll Jefferys also havinge both of us as Instructed told the Country that the duke of York was gratiously pleased to promise the callinge in and va-catinge these Grants that were soe prejudiciall to this Collony, without any charge to them, and certainly your Lordshipp cannot forgett, that when I had last the Honor to see your Lordshipp at my Lord Treasurers, you were then pleased yourselfe to saye his Royall Highnesse had layd his Commands on you to acqui-esce in this Perticuler, nor that wee are against his Majesties Royall compensa-tion to the Proprietors, for wee thinke it noe less just than reasonable. Therefore, I hope your Lordshipp will not mistake this civill memorial of mine, In which I and my fellow Commissioners are forced to write to the Honorable Secretary of State, as well as to acquaint your Lordshipp with the Country's most grateful Resentment of this Royall favour; and that upon the Assemblys risinge they were all highly satisfied in this Perticuler and ordered their Generall Letters of thanks on behalfe of the whole Collony. Now how pernicious this Revival would have prov'd upon itt and what a new Storme of troubles itt might have raised, you Cannot butt be sensible: Therefore, I trust your Lordshipp will con-ceive itt not to your own Honor and Satisfaction than this poor Countrys ease and Benifitt to enjoy the effects of soe Royall a favour, that soe whenever your Lordshipp shall assume the Government, you maye find this Country in a Peaceable and Prosperous condition to your hands. Sir for this farther perticuler

---

67. Thomas, Lord Culpeper, a long-serving imperial administrator who, earlier, had re-ceived a grant from the Crown to the colony's public lands. The Duke of York, later James II, opposed grants of this sort, which in his view weakened royal power in the colonies. For Culpeper's avaricious determination to profit from his colonial posts, see Webb, *Governors-General*, 112-122, 338-340.

the worthy Gentleman Captain Middleton who is now come from England will informe your Lordshipp to whose account I shall write you and at this time excuse myselfe and remaine,

> Your Lordshipps most Humble Servant,
> Francis Morryson

Swanns Point, April 14th 1677

Document 47
14 April 1677

The Commissioners to Mr. Watkins

Sir,

That you maye be the better able to Judge of the state of affaires here, & the reality of our former relations, wee shall advise you that you confer with the worthy Captaine Middleton who has had a generall Knowledge of occurances duringe his stay here upon the place. And that he and our selves maye allso understand the present state of things att home in England, wee referr him and our selves to your best and speediest information more particularly in the busyness of the Patents. Wee leave you to Captain Middleton's relation, who verry fortunately and prudently discovered first to us the Lord Culpepper's design of setting them on foot again after his Royall Highnesses Command and his own professions to the contrary. Had not Col. Jeffreys timely stopt, itt must needs rais'd new distrusts and dissatisfactions in the people here, and have called the verity and Reputation of our Report to them in Question. Wee have sent you a Coppy of a letter to my Lord on this occasion; wee also send you duplicates of the Assembly's letters of thanks together with their own requests to us to spare them Mr. Wiseman to attend the howse of Burgesses for Penninge them, which he did by their directions, and to their then satisfaction. Butt itt seems there that since some dislike by others of beinge worded too submissively and plainely Confessory. Sir, wee have noe more to saye att present butt remaine,

> Your very Affectionate Friends and Servants,

> Herbert Jefferys
> John Berry
> Francis Moryson

By the Deptford Ketch, April 14th 1677

Document 48
21 April 1677

Colonel Moryson to the Governor

Right Honorable,

Wee intend to waite on you tomorrow beinge Sunday, to take our farwell leave of you before you goe hence, and that I might offer nothing in discourse to make you uneasy, I have therefore before hand writt this, as a matter very necessary for you to know and me to informe, though before I say anythinge you cannot be ignorant of the Perticulars, that Colonel Jefferys and my selfe haveinge satisfied most of the Members of Assembly of his Royall Highness Gratious Promise to them, that the two Patents wee soe laboured to overthrow should be recalled without puttinge the Country to a penny charge. This Royall favour enjoyed us by his Royall Highness to requaint the Country with right as itt truly merited soe high a sense of gratitude in the Howse of Burgesses, that they resolved upon a letter of thankes as wee find by the assemblys orders; and the speaker left and Intrusted to Signe itt after they were dissolved. But in stead of that, I heare here there is another letter contrived than what was att first intended and concluded on, where in the only motive of the letter the matter of thanks is omitted &c.

Therefore I desire to be well Informed before I write home, and that you will please to send us a Coppie as wee have sent coppies of ours, as Mr. Wiseman Penn'd when att the Assembly's request to our correspondent in England, and also written to his Royall Highness's Secretary; or else I must send the very orders of Assembly and my owne former Instructions (as Agent) signed by your own hand, which last referred us as agents to that application in this affaire as I believe you will now unwillingly own.

Praye, Sir, Remember you have twice Superseded these Patents, and what a Charge itt has bin to this poor Country, and now itt maye be had at soe easy a price as thankes, doe butt thinke how it will be taken both here and in England, that you only are the obstructer of this good and Royall Act, especially when two soe near Relations as yours and your Lady are concerned. Sir, I shall expect your Answer which with a coppie of this very letter you shall send to the Duke of Yorke, for I would not now, as I never yett did or ever shall doe, willingly disserve you, nor would I injure my selfe in beinge silent in a matter of this Moment, Butt could much rather wish an Expedient might be found out to Prevent both since I am,

April 21 1677   Your most Humble Servant,

                                       Francis Moryson

Document 49
23 April 1677

The Commissioners to the Governour

Sir,

Wee all thinke the Civill complement wee paid as due to the Honour of your Character had deserved a better returne than what you have made us, to Turne us off by the coach and the Common hangman Postillion; which is an affront not only to the Reverence due to his Majesties great Seale, but to us in our Private persons as Gentlemen.[68] Sir, wee are resolved to make his Majestie himselfe a Judge in this high Indignitie offered to us his Majesties Commissioners, which you as well know us to be, as wee believe you did the Postillion to be the Hangman, whome wee Cannot imagine to be a Meniall Servant of the Governour of Virginia, butt that he was purposely sent for as a Retainer to Performe

the Ceremonys of yesterdaye, when wee deserved to have bin noe otherwise treated by you than as becomes

April 23 1677,   Your Humble servants,
                                          Herbert Jefferys
                                          John Berry
                                          Francis Moryson

Document 50
23 April 1677

The Governour to the Commissioners

Right Honorable,

It is the will and pleasure of my great and gratious God, to whose will & pleasure I must Submitt, that I should be accused of many things I am not guilty of, but of this perticuler of the Postillion, if itt be lawfull to compare Glorious Celestiall Bodies with vile dust and ashes, I am as Innocent in this as the Blessed

---

68. Obviously the commissioners' final meeting with the governor had not at all gone according to plan. Intending to pay the departing governor a courtesy call, one of the commissioners recognized that the province's executioner served as the postilion, a great insult indeed. Governor Berkeley's response, in Document 50, reflects the extent to which Berkeley felt himself treated unjustly in a colony he had served for so great a portion of his life.

Angells themselves; butt though God suffers me to be accused, he has in his mercy left me a great Example to Comfort me; for he Suffered his only glorious sonn to be accused of what he was not guilty of, and our late bless'd King Charles the first was brought to his death by accusations he was not in the least manner guilty of, and you Cannot be angry that this last great misfortune as I am sorry for itt; though itt were in me a Sinn of Insuperable Ignorance; for I never saw the fellows fall but once before, and did not Know he was in my howse. Butt I have sent the Negro to you to be Racked, tortured or whipped till he confess how this dire misfortune happened, and I hope this will give you Satisfaction, if not I hope to find more mercy which by King and the King of Kings who I trust will never be angry for faults of reall Ignorance. Right Honorable, I am

April 23 1677   Your most Humble Servant,

                                                      William Berkeley

Document 51
25 April 1677

The Governor to Colonel Moryson

Coll. Moryson,

I give many and harty thankes for the tobacco and waters you sent me, but am soe distracted with this late dire misfortune that I scarce know what I doe or say, for though I am as Innocent as anyone in the extremity of the world, yett I cannot butt thinke God was angry with me when this dire misfortune happened; for I all ways thought that if I carelessly threw a stone over a howse and killed a friends child, I was att that tyme out of the favour of God, and of this nature was this late dire accident, for I know not the man nor can doe yett if I see him with two men of his age. I have sent the Negro and desire you to examine him to the Quick, Butt as I said before, noe man can be more troubled, and sorry for this Horrid misadventure, and am ready to give all possible Satisfaction for itt.

April 25 77   Your most Humble Servant,

                                                      William Berkeley

Document 52
25 April 1677

Colonel Moryson to the Governour

Right Honorable,

Sir, I have too much charity of anyone, as to believe those high and solemn protests of yours, and that it was noe more possible that you should intend than that ever wee could deserve soe great an indignity to be thrown on us; But Sir John Berry being absent when the letters came to our hands wee cannot now give our joint answer to itt yett wee believe itt will take the like charitable Impression on him also as itt hath done on us.

Sir, I shall intreat you to take my last letter into your Second thoughts, soe as seriously to consider its weighty contents, which maye give your selfe and me much Satisfaction, for otherwise I must be feigne to write home on purpose to his Royall Highness whome it soe highly conerns as well as my selfe; Thatt my own Perticuler trust and Integrity maye be cleare in the Representation of this affaire committed to me and afterward reiterated to Colonell Jeffreys, which I have done with all the Candor and Sincerity I on my part possibly could. Therefore, good Sir, take once more my former letter in your hands and thinke itt worthy of a full and Perticuler Reply which is as earnestly expected as deserved by

April 25 1677   Your most Humble Servant,
                                 Francis Moryson

Sir, I hope the waters I sent you will give you great reliefe, and I assure you itt did me in as great a weakness, butt least perhaps itt may prove too strong in quantity for your Stomach my Lady maye please to take a small dram of itt to judge of the strength and Proportion fitt for yourselfe to take.

Sir, if there is anything putt into the Assemblys letters to ingage his Royall Highness in any Particulars which were in our former Instructions of Agency and then distastefull to him, I know itt will be soe now, and therefore must protest against them.

Document 53
October, 1676

A Letter Written to Sir William Jones, the Kings Attorney Generall prefatory to the present state of Affairs in Virginia in October 1676 by Francis Morryson, Esqr.[69]

69. This document is not placed in Wiseman's book in chronological order. It was written by Moryson from England, before his appointment as commissioner. In it, Moryson-

Most Honor'd Sir

It is soe farr from my opinion, that it is any wayes necessarie for a Commission to issue from anie to exercise Martiall law in Virginia, that I conceive itt the most destructive means can be used to attaine the ends intended by itt. And this I conceive must be either for the carrying on of the warr against the Indians, or for quellinge the mutiny amongst the English. If for the first who ever rightly considers the distance of Virginia from England, the great difficulties of the Continent to those unacquainted with the Ground, the distemper of the Clime to Bodies not inur'd to itt, the nature of the Enimy and manner of fight, must rationally conclude with me that the warr must be managed by the Inhabitants there and not by forces sent from home, and the most of the warr on their side must be defensive; Soe that I believe there will need noe Commission sent for Martiall Law to force men to defend themselves. First, Honor'd sir, his Majestie can send noe person over goes as near away as the Merchante does, but shall stand by his Majestie in ten pounds for his meer transportation; This, sir, is a considerable Number and loss will come to a Considerable Sum; Butt suppose his Majestie values not such a sum in respect of the Peace itt may bring to his Countrie, yett I shall desire to be satisfied by any that knows the place what shall be done with the forces when they come here[?] There are noe Towns to quarter them in; The Plantations are remote from one another, the howses built and furnished accordinge to their families; Soe that five hundred men must be lodg'd in three hundred howses, and these att great distances. Next in case of sicknesses the first yeare for few Escape, who shall looke too or provide for those men, or where shall they have pay to provide for themselves[?] His Majestie has no Exchecquer there nor can they staye to have their Pay from hence. Must they not then if they be stronger force itt from the Inhabitants and instead of a help be an insupportable burden to the people, or if weaker must they not in all probability starve[?] Butt I will admit all these inconviences, and many more that I can offer, if that any will please to show me the least good or advantage his Majestie can reap by these. First the Country wants noe men to fight if the enemy will appear, and if they will not who can find them in their Coverts, and if soe what signifies a Supply from hence[?] Whoever is acquainted with the Indians waye of fighting must acknowledge itt is only by way of Surprize, soe that all our offensive warr is butt a huntinge of them as wolves and not fighting with them as men. We may feele them once a week and not see them once a yeare, they will burne a lone howse or two tonight, and be forty miles off tomorrow. And therefore the present Governor most discretely and with a success answerable managed a former warr greater by farr than this for then he had fewer English to lead and more

recommends the course of action that he felt a royal commission should take. On Moryson's earlier experience in England, see Webb, *Governors-General,* 322-340.

Indians to oppose him, and they commanded by a warr Capteine, then he who conquered from Mexico thither.

The waye Sir William Berkeley tooke then and what they must use now, they act prudently, was to send out small parties in July and August to burne the Indians Corne that bordered on our frontiers, and to secure the Howses and men from the Suddaine assauits of the Indians. He strengthened the weake families on the frontiers by joyninge two or three families together, and to Palasaded the Howses about with Punctions.[70] By these two wayes in a short time he soe disabled the Enimy that he forc'd him to beg and sue for Peace, which they had and strictly observed, until this unhappy breach which I feare was occasioned by our own fault: Wee petitioned not then for any Commission for Martiall Law, and yett in all that warr was never known that any refused to goe against the Enimy, or in the least disputed the Command of their Superior officer. Butt itt may be objected there is more need now, since there is a mutiny of the English, and the people refractorily refused to march with the Governor against the Rebells.

I Grant all this and from itt make this Inferrence:

That the defection is greater than is owned here, or else itt is not to be imagined how itt should come to pass, that amongst soe many thousands of reputed honest men there should not a thousand be found to fight five hundred inconsiderable fellows by which itt is evident to me that the Major part of the body of the Country is distempered and itt is to be feared if Martiall Law be sent in and not a Power sufficient to back itt which is impossible for his Majestie to doe from hence, itt may make many more declare themselves, for all will have a jealousie that has guilt, that itt is to Punish them. Butt if the Governor wanted it then, I wonder he writt not for itt now, butt without question if he had had such a Commission, he would not then have used itt, lest instead of making men goe against Bacon itt would have carried the rest to him. Butt he had a power then and exactly drawn, as if his Majesties Advocate Generall had pen'd it, for all places will naturally have as much of it as they need in time of Warr. For Martiall Law, as I take it butt a Branch of the Law of Nature by whose Impulse wee are commanded to defend ourselves, and if opposed by multitudes, then to resort to multitudes to defend us where reason dictates such rules to be observed both by them that Commanded and obey.

Soe that the question will not be now, as I suppose whither Virginia shall have martiall law butt whither or noe from hence: If the law be from the Assembly there it is butt temporary, and ceases when they thinke fitt, butt if thatt Keen sword bee drawn by his Majesties Commissioners here, they must resort hither, for none butt his Majestie can sheath itt for that the distance beinge soe great many maye wrongfully suffer if itt should happen to be putt in a rash hand, nor is his Majestie Infallible in his choice, he maye be deceived as well in his Gov-

---

70. Suggestions of this sort had been made before in Virginia. See Oberg, *Dominion and Civility*, 73–78, 176–180.

ernor as his Grants, and then the people will be in a miserable condicion, all there beinge Souldiers and none exempt from that Tryall.

Honored Sir, though this defection att this distance has an ugly aspect, yett the face of things would soon be changed, if his Majestie would be pleased to send in two or more discrete Commissioners into the Country, to inquire into their Grievances, and faithfully to report them, for Grievances undoubtedly they might have, or else tis impossible that a Country of soe signall a loyaltie should in soe short a time shew more of disloyaltie than any part of his Majesties Dominions. Butt I am confident if this course be taken by his Majestie and he pleased to promise redress of all such grievances as shall apear soe to him, and a Generall Pardon to all that shall laye down armes and come in, the heads of the Rebells excepted, his Majestie will quickly find they will returne to their old obedience, and leave those miserable Wretches to his Majesties Mercy or Justice. Butt if the People shall still be stubborne and not returne to their obedience upon his Majesties Acts of Grace, then in my opinion noe better waye can be thought on to reduce them then whatt was found practicall in the time of the late usurpation, by sending two small frigatts to prohibit trade, since whatt did itt then, may, naye must necessarily doe itt now, there beinge the same Causes and reasons for itt.

And for whatt concerns the Governor as itt is impossible, butt he must have contracted some Odium in soe long a time of Government, yett I am confident the Grievances they can justly lay to his charge will goe in a little room, therefore I shall desire that the Commissioners may be ordered if any complaints be brought against him, that they early desire his own answer to present to his Majestie; that one great Seale maye not arraigne another.

Sir, I should ask your Pardon for the length of this letter, though I thinke the weightiness of the matter may excuse itt, for itt is impossible in a few words to give a clear prospect of things soe remote, for really I feare there will be wrong measures taken though I should say much more, butt it is the last paper I shall write in this agency, and shall Conclude itt with a Protestation, that I have never offered any thing to any Minister of State, butt whatt I thought necessary for his Majesties Service.

> Sir, I am,
> Your most Humble Servant,
>
> Francis Moryson

Document 54
Late Summer, 1677

A Perticular Account how wee your Majesties Commissioners for the affaires of Virginia have observed & complied with the Severall Articles of our Instructions, which with all lowliness wee here laye before your Majestie as a faithfull Demonstration of our most humble obedience, and our Conformity to your Royall Commands Thereby Given us.[71]

1. Instruction:
    You shall with the first convenience Embarque your selves upon our good ship the *Bristoll* and with what speed you can, wind and weather permittinge, Transport yourselves to our said Collony of Virginia.

1. Answer:
    Havinge received the Instructions at Whitehall on Wensdaye night the 15th day of November, 1676, wee went awaye to Portsmouth next morning before daye breake; and from thence embarqued on board your Majesties ship *Bristoll*, and on Sundaye the 19th daye of November wee sett saile for Virginia.

2. Instruction:
    Beinge arrived there you shall in the first place take all the convenient wayes you can of Informinge yourselves truly and thoroughly of the State of Affairs in that our Collony; and as often as you shall Judge itt necessary make use of those Powers allowed you in our Commission given you.

2. Answer:
    Beinge arrived there January 29th 1676/7 after a tedious passage of tenn weeks & one daye, wee immediately dispatched advice thereof to Sir William Berkeley; who came on board us the first of February, and gave us an account of the condition of your Majesties said Collony; wee also tooke all other Convenient wayes wee could to Informe our selves, the best and trulyest of the present state of affaires there; as well by those of the Councill, as by such other persons as were able to give us any account thereof.

3. Instruction:
    You shall be assistant to our Lieutentant Governor or Commander inchiefe there with your council and advice, whensoever he shall demand itt, & particularly in that affaire of Renewinge a Peace with the Neighbour Indians, in which wee doe particularly order him to demand your assistance.

3. Answer:
    Wee have offered our advice and assistance to Sir William Berkeley with most earnest professions of our Service whensoever he should demand it, particularly in that affaire of Renewinge a Peace with the Neighbour Indians, in which your Majestie did especially order him to aske our advice and

---

71. In Wiseman's original, the king's instructions and the commissioners' reply were presented in parallel vertical columns. For readability, I have included the king's instruction, and the commissioners' response in a horizontal fashion.

assistance. Butt he tooke noe notice att all of itt, or ever consulted us in that affaire, or made the least step himselfe towards itt whilst hee stayed on the Place, soe that upon his departure for England wee took itt in hand ourselves, and sent to the Queen of Pamunkey who not only came in her selfe but brought in severall scattered nations of Indians who were afterwards reduced under her Subjection as anciently they had bin. And finally wee were not only assistant to the Governor with our best advice to the Government that now is in concludinge a good & Honorable Peace with the Indians but were ourselves Personally Present att the Ceremony, and signinge the same att the Congress att Middle Plantation.

4.   Instruction:
     You shall have delivered to you a Coppy of our Instructions given to Sir William Berkeley, our then Governor of the Collony att our first cominge to the Exercise of our Royall authority in England & you shall informe yourselves how those Instructions have bin pursued and wherein there hath bin any failer, & upon what grounds and upon whose neglect and Willful fault.

4.   Answer:
     Wee have endeavoured by the best meanes wee could to find how those instructions given to Sir William Berkeley, upon your Majesties first comminge to the Exercise of your Royall authority in England have bin pursued, Butt havinge applied ourselves to the Councill and others most likely to Informe us of those particulars, wee could not attaine to any satisfaction therein; nor would the Governor himselfe give any answer concerninge them, altho wee had, among other things, therein mentioned our Interlocutory heads and earnestly Importuned the same of him.

5.   Instruction:
     You shall informe yourselves of all grievances in Generall butt particularly of that which the people seem soe much concerned in, the great sallary paid to the members of the Assembly; and you shall be assistant with your advice to our Lieutentant Governor in causinge an immediate redress of itt.

5.   Answer:
     Wee are fully informed of all grievances in generall, having enquired into and taken the complaints of the Respective Counties in Virginia in writing att large & particularly that of the great Sallary paid to the Members of Assembly; In which wee offered our advice and assistance to the Governor for an immediate Redress thereof and a Retrenchment therein to a degree soe low, as Burgesses can support their ordinary Expence att, & they effected by our joint letter to the Assembly.

6. Instruction:

You shall take all opportunitys you can to possess our subjects of that Collony, that as wee are and ever will be severe in punishinge such as shall willfully violate our laws and Royall authority and shall presume to encourage and abett Tumults & Rebellions: Soe shall wee be noe less Indulgent to the just complaints of our opressed people, and as soon as Inform'd of their grievances direct proportionable redresse for them, and take such resentment upon the authors and Continuers of them as the quality of the offence shall require: And this you maye lett them know was the chiefe cause of our Sendinge you thither.

6. Answer:

Wee have taken all opertunities both private & publick to possess the people of Virginia, as well of your Majesties just Severity, as of your Royall Indulgency and mercy, towards objects merittinge of either, and this wee have done most fully and satisfactorily by that declaration of ours wherein wee recited the express words of this very article of your Majesties Instructions; and by sittinge ourselves at the Tryall of the Criminalls & condemnation of the cheife, upon your Majesties Commission of oyer and Terminer.

7. Instruction:

You shall make particular acquaintance with those of our Councill there, and that not only in generall as a Councill, butt Seperately and in their perticular persons both in order to a clearer and more impartiall information of yourselves of affaires in Generall and likewise to render yourselves more capable of Informinge us of the Capacity and Dispositions of those that Compose the Councill, and how far fitted and qualified for such a trust.

7. Answer:

Wee have had a generall & separate acquaintance with those of your Majesties Councill of Virginia, and find them for the most part Honest men, and as to their qualification for such a trust, of the best that can be had in that Country where there is soe Small a choice, but as to their disposition somewhat rash and implacable towards the late Peccant Party, tho some of themselves are not wholly Innocent or excusable in their own actings Especially Ballard who was both a taker & giver of Bacons oath & a known abettor of the late Rebellion, yet for all this in Sir William Berkeleys favour, while Coll. Swann, another of the Councill, and of those made soe by the great Seale, who had noe greate crime butt only takinge that oath of Bacons against his will, stands Suspended by the Councill.

8. Instruction:

You shall likewise make a particular enquiry into the militia of that Country, the quality, disposition & capacity of the officers, soe that at your Returne or sooner wee may have from you a thorough Information of the Strength and allso of the Defects of that Government.

8.   Answer:
Wee have not bin wantinge to make particular enquiry by the Assembly, who were less able to give an account of the condition of the militia, & of the quality, capacity and disposition of the officers. Butt the members themselves, beinge most of them officers, and by your Majesties Royall Patent of Pardon forgiven their late faults and defections answered in these words: "That it Could not now in fairness be required of them"; But the Governor hath taken care in this Perticular, that your Majestie maye have a full and Impartiall account as the sunne now stands after the Regulatinge and Reformminge the Military Commands.

9.   Instruction:
The like enquiry you shall make into the Laws of the Place, which you are to returne as a Coppy to be Inspected here, togeather with your Remarks upon them, and which and why you thinke inconvenient and fitt to be altered or abrogated.

9.   Answer:
Wee found upon enquiry made into the Laws of Virginia that there were many of them wantinge to the Printed booke which wee Could not then have written coppies of, or time soe deliberately to Inspect or consider them as to make our Serious remarks on them. Before wee found it a worke not to be well done, and which wee dare not presume to take in hande, without the advice of your Majesties learned Councill in the Law: Butt have brought home with us such acts as were made by the last assembly att Green Spring beinge promised by the Secretary to have the Rest of the Laws that are wantinge Returned us by the next shipps.

10.   Instruction:
You shall upon all occasions give unto us or to one of our Principall Secretarys of State an account of all your Proceedings and of the Condition of affaires there: Given att our Court at Whitehall the 9th daye of November 1676.

10.   Answer:
We have not bin Remiss upon all occasions in givinge frequent accounts of all our Proceedings, and the Condition of affairs in Virginia to your Majesties Principall Secretary of State, and have allso drawn up a full Narrative of the whole;[72] togeather with a Breviary from that with a further account of the late and present Estate of that your Majesties Collony and our most

72. See Chapter 4, below.

humble opinions for the firme settlement of the place thereof for the future. All which with the lawes of the Assembly wee laye before your Majesties Royall and most mature Judgement according to the duty of

> Your Majesties most humbly devoted,
> most faithfull & most obedient
> Subjects and Servants,
>
> John Berry
> Francis Moryson

3 The Treaty of Middle Plantation

Articles of Peace betweene the most Mighty Prince, and our Dread Soveraigne Lord Charles the Second by the Grace of God King of Great Britaine, France and Ireland, Defender of the Faith, &c. And the severall Indian Kings and Queens &c. Assenters and Subscribers hereunto, Made and Concluded at the Camp at Middle Plantation the nine and twentieth day of May, (1677), being the day of the most happy Birth and Restauration of our said Soveraigne Lord, and in the nine and twentieth yeare of his Majesties Reigne, By the Right Honorable Herbert Jefferies Esquire, Governor and Captain Generall of his Majesties Colony of Virginia.[1]

Present

The Honorable Sir John Berry Knight
Francis Moryson Esquire
His Majesties Commissioners Appointed Under the Great Seale of England, for the Affaires of Virginia

and

The Honorable Councill of State of the said Colony

Whereas his Most Sacred Majestie hath of his owne Royall Grace and meer Motion, Intrusted to my Care and Endeavours the Renewing, Management, & Concluding a good Peace with the Neighbour Indians, In order whereunto (with the advice and Assistance of the Honorable Sir John Berry, Knight, & Francis Moryson Esquire) I have caused to be drawne up these ensuing Articles & Overtures for the firme Grounding & sure establishment of a good and just peace with the said Indians, and that itt may bee a secure & lasting one (founded upon the strong Pillars of Reciprocal Justice) by confirming to them their Just Rights, & by Redresse of their wrongs & Injuries that soe the great God (who is a God of peace, & Lover of Justice) may uphold & prosper this our mutuall League & Amity, It is hereby concluded, consented to and mutually Agreed, as followeth;

---

1. The treaty was published in London after Berry and Moryson returned home. See *Articles of Peace Between the Most Serene and Mighty Prince, Charles II . . . and the Severall Indian Kings and Queens, &c.* (London: John Bill, 1677).

First. That the Respective Indian Kings and Queens doe from henceforth acknowledge to have their immediate Dependency on, and owne all subjection to, the great King of England, our now dread Soveraigne, his Heirs and Successors, when they pay their Tribute to the Right Honorable His Majesties Governour for the tyme being.

2. That thereupon the said Indian Kings and Queens and their Subjects shall hold their Lands, & have the same confirmed to them & their Posterity by Patent under the seale of this His Majesties Colony, without any fee, Gratuity or Reward for the same, in such sort and in as free & firme manner as others his Majesties Subjects have and enjoy their Lands and Possessions, Paying yearly for & in lieu of a Quitt Rent or acknowledgement for the same onely three Indian Arrowes.[2]

3. That all Indians who are in Amity with us and have not land sufficient to plant upon, bee (upon Information) forthwith provided for, & land laid out & confirmed to them as aforesaid, never to be disturbed therein, or taken from them, soe long as they owne, keep, & maintayne their due obedience & subjection to his Majestie, His Governour and Government, & amity & friendship towards the English.

4. Whereas by the Mutuall discontents, Complaints, Jealousyes & fears of English and Indians, occasioned by the violent Intrusions of divers English into their Lands, forcing the Indians by way of Revenge to kill the Cattle & Hogs of the English, whereby offence & Injurys being given and done on both sides, the peace of this his Majesties Colony hath been much disturbed & the late unhappy Rebellion by this meanes (in a great measure) begun & fomented which hath involved this Country into soe much Ruine and Misery; For prevention of which Injuryes and Consequences (as much as possibly wee may) for tyme to come; Itt is hereby Concluded & established that noe English shall seat or plant nearer than three miles of any Indian Town, and whosoever hath made or shall make any Incroachment upon their Lands shall bee removed from thence & proceeded against as by the former peace made when the Honorable Colonel Francis Moryson was Governour, and the Act of Assembly grounded thereupon is provided & Enacted.

5. That the said Indians bee well secured & defended in their persons, goods and propertyes against all hurts & Injuryes of the English, and that upon any breach or violation hereof, that the aggrieved Indians doe

---

2. *quitrent.* A small rent paid by a freeholder in lieu of services which might be required of him.

in the first place repaire and addresse themselves to the Governour, acquainting him therewith (without rashly & suddainly betaking them selves to any hostile course for Satisfaction), who will inflict such punishment on the wilfull Infringers hereof, as the Lawes of England or this Country permit, and as if such hurt or Injury had been done to any English man, which is but just & reasonable, they owning themselves to bee under the Allegiance of his most Sacred Majesty.

6.   That noe Indian King or Queene bee imprisoned without a speciall Warrant from his Majesties Governour & two of the Councill, & that noe other Indian be Imprisoned without a Warrant from a Justice of Peace, upon sufficient cause of Commitment.[3]

7.   That the said Indians have and enjoy their wonted Conveniencyes of Oystering, fishing, & gathering Tuckahoe, Curtenemons, Wild Oats, Rushes, Puckoone[4], or any thing else (for their naturall support) not usefull to the English, upon the English Dividends. Always provided they first repaire to some public Magistrate of good repute, & informe him of their number & business, who shall not refuse them a Certificate upon this or any other Lawfull occasion, soe that they make due returne thereof when they come backe, & go directly home about their businesse, without wearing or carrying any manner of weapon, or Lodging under any English mans dwelling house one Night.

8.   That noe forreigne Indian bee suffered to come to any English Plantation without a friendly Neighbour Indian in his Company, with such Certificate as aforesaid, & noe Indian King is to refuse to send a safe conduct with the foreigner, upon any lawfull occasion of his Coming

---

3. In this and the preceding article, the commissioners were clearly trying to relieve the pressure placed upon Indian lands by the English frontier population. These settlers treated Indians badly at times, provoking native retaliation and contributing directly to the outbreak of the rebellion. See Michael Leroy Oberg, *Dominion and Civility: English Imperialism and Native America, 1585-1685* (Ithaca, NY: Cornell University Press, 1999), 174-216.

4. Curtenemons were the seeds or berries of the arrow arum, a starchy food found in marshes, valued by the Indians but not used by the English. Curtenemons could be eaten all year, but were best in the spring. Tuckahoe was the plant's roots. See Helen Rountree, *Pocahontas's People: The Powhatan Indians of Virginia Through Four Centuries* (Norman: University of Oklahoma Press, 1990), 101; Helen C. Rountree, "A Guide to the Late Woodland Indians' Use of Ecological Zones in the Chesapeake Region" (unpublished paper, 1995), 9-10. I am indebted to Professor Rountree for providing me with a copy of her paper.

in, & that noe Indian doe paint or disguise themselves when they come in.[5]

9.   That all Indian Kings and Queenes, (Tributary to the English), having notice of any march of strange Indians neare the English Quarters or Plantations, doe forthwith repaire to some of the next Officers of the Militia & acquaint him of their Nation, Number & Designe, & which way they bend their Course.

10. That (if necessary) a Convenient Partie bee presently sent out by the next Colonell of the Militia to aid, strengthen, & joine with our friendly Indians, against any forreigne attempt, Incursion, or depredation upon the Indian Towns.

11. That every Indian fitt to bear Arms of the Neighbouring Nations in peace with us have such Quantity of Powder & Shott allotted them, as the Right Honorable the Governour shall thinke sufficient on any occasion, and that such numbers of them bee ready to goe out with our forces upon any March against the Enemy, & to receive such pay for their good services as shall bee thought fitt.

12. That each Indian King & Queene have equal power to Governe their owne people & none to have greater power than other, Except the Queene of Pamunkey, to whom several scattered Nations doe now againe owne their ancient Subjection, and are agreed to come in, & plant themselves under her Power & Government, who with her are also hereby included into this present League & treaty of peace, & are to keep & observe the same towards the said Queene in all things as her Subjects, as well as towards the English.[6]

5. The English feared still the strength of the Doegs and Susquehannocks on the frontier, as well as that of the Iroquois raiders who preyed upon them. See Matthew Lawson Rhoades, "Assarigoa's Line: Anglo-Iroquoian Relations and the Definition of the Virginia Frontier, 1677-1774" (PhD diss., Syracuse University, 2000).

6. The 1677 treaty reflects the tremendous skills of Cockacoeske as an intercultural diplomat. The Queen of Pamunkey, she came to lead the Powhatan Indians of Virginia in 1656. She seems to have believed that her people's best hope for the future lay in reestablishing the unity of Powhatan's chiefdom, which decades of warfare and white settlement on Indian lands had eroded. The commissioners in this article in effect recognized the preeminent position of the Pamunkeys in the Powhatan chiefdom, and Cockacoeske's right to oversee the former Powhatan tributaries. See Martha W. McCartney, "Cockacoeske, Queen of Pamunkey: Diplomat and Suzeraine," in *Powhatan's Mantle: Indians in the Colonial Southeast,* eds. Peter H. Wood, Gregory A. Waselkov, and M. Thomas Hatley (Lincoln: University of Nebraska Press, 1989), 179.

13.   That noe person whatsoever shall entertaine or keepe any Neighbouring
         Indian as servant or otherwise, but by Lycense of the Governour, and to
         bee upon Obligation answerable for all Injuryes & damages by
         him or them happening to bee done to any English.

14.   That noe English harbour or Entertaine any Vagrant or Runaway Indian
         but convey him home by way of Passe from Justice to Justice to his
         owne Towne under penalty of paying soe much per day for harbouring
         him, as by the Law for entertaining of Runaways is Recoverable.

15.   That noe Indian (of those in amity with us) shall serve for any longer
         time then English of the same ages should serve by act of Assembly, &
         shall not bee sold as slaves.[7]

16.   That every Indian King & Queene in the Month of March every yeare,
         with some of their great men tender their Obedience to the Right Hon-
         ourable his Majesties Governour at the place of his Residence wherever
         it shall bee, & then & there pay the accustomed tribute of Twenty Bea-
         ver Skins to the Governour, & alsoe their Quitt Rent aforesaid, in ac-
         knowledgement, that they hold their Crownes & Lands of the great
         King of England.

17.   That due Care bee had & taken that those Indian kings & queens, their
         great men & Attendants that come on any publique businesse to the
         Right Honourable the Governour, Councill or Assembly, may bee ac-
         commodated with Provisions, & House-Roome at the publique Charge,
         & that noe English Subject, shall abuse, revile, hurt or wrong them at
         any time in word or deed.

18.   That upon any Discord or breach of peace happening to arise between
         any of the Indians in amity with the English, upon the first appearance
         and beginning thereof, & before they enter into any open acts of hos-
         tility or war one against another, they shall repaire to his Majesties
         Governour, By whose Justice & Wisdome itt is concluded, such differ-
         ence shall bee made up & decided, & to whose finall determination the
         said Indians shall submit and conforme themselves.

7. For studies of Indian slavery in the southern colonies, see Alan Gallay, *The Indian
Slave Trade: The Rise of the English Empire in the American South, 1670-1717* (New
Haven, CT: Yale University Press, 2003); and J. Leitch Wright, *The Only Land They
Knew: The Tragic Story of the American Indians in the Old South* (New York: The Free
Press, 1981), 248-278.

19.   That for the preventing the frequent Mischiefs & Mistakes occasioned by the unfaithfull & Corrupt Interpreters, & for the more safety, satisfaction, & advantage both of the English & Indians, that there bee one of each Nation, of our Neighbouring Indians that already can speake, or may become capable of speaking English admitted (together with those of the English) to bee their owne Interpreters.[8]

20.   That the severall Indians concluded in this peace doe forthwith restore to the respective English   Parents & owners all such Children, Servants, & horses which they have at any time taken from them, & are now remaining with them the said Indians, or which they can make discovery of.

21.   That the trade with the said Indians bee continued, Limitted, restrained, or laid open as shall make best for the peace & Quiett of the Country; Upon which Affair the Governour will consult with the Council and Assembly, and conclude thereon at their next meeting.[9]

8. The commissioners knew of the story of an interpreter named Wilford, whom Governor Berkeley executed for his role in the rebellion. Wilford, apparently as hungry for Indian land as many of his fellow English frontiersmen, exploited a law passed by the Baconian Assembly that allowed settlers to appropriate abandoned Indian lands. He told Cockacoeske that unless she fled from the lands the Berkeleyan Assembly earlier had granted her, she would be killed. See McCartney, "Cockacoeske," 176.

9. The published version concludes with the following memorandum, dated 29 May 1677: "That this Instrument of Peace being Read and Expounded to the several *Indian* Kings and Queens then present (at the Court at *Middle Plantation*) by Interpreters Sworn truly to perform the same, the said *Indian* Kings and Queens Signed and delivered the Articles to the Honourable Governour upon their Knees, and received that other part, Signed and Delivered on behalf of the Kings Majesty, in the same posture of kneeling, of their own accords kissing the Paper as they Transferred it from hand to hand to each other, until every one had done the like Mark of Reverence to it, in sign of a most free and joyfull acceptance of this Peace concluded with them. At the same time *Pericuhtah* King of the *Appomatucks* being then present, did earnestly desire to be admitted to the Signing this Peace with the rest; but he being suspected, and Complained of to have Committed by himself or Subjects some Murthers of His Majesties Subjects of *England*, was not admitted or included into this League at this time, nor is to partake of the benefit of this Peace, before he shall have cleared himself of this Guilt imputed to him, and Committed since His Majesties Commissioners came into *Virginia*, as they were credibly informed: Which Exemption gave the English general satisfaction, to find there was so just Inquisition made of the Bloud of their Slaughtered Brethren.

                                                            John Berry
                                                            Francis Moryson.

The Signe of the Queen of
Pamunkey on behalfe of
Herselfe & the severall Indians under
Her Subjection

The Sign of the Queene of Waonoke

The signe of the
King of the Nottoways

The Sign of the King of the Nancymond Indians

The Sign of Captain John West.
sonne to the Queen
of Pamunkey

Convenit cum Originali
Test. Tho. Ludwell, Secretary

4   The Commissioners' Narrative

A Narrative of the Rise, Progresse and Cessation of the late Rebellion in
Virginia
By his Majesties Commissioners[1]

In all due observance of his most sacred Majesties commands wee have imployed our best endeavours to informe ourselves (for his Royal Satisffaction) by
the most knowing, credible and indifferent Persons in Virginia of the true state
of affairs in that his Majestyes Colony, and of such other matters as occasioned
the late unhappy Divisions, Distractions, and Disorders among the People there;
which as farr as wee can possible collect from a strict Inquiry, observation, examination and the most probable impartial Reports by us made and received
during our stay upon the place, seems to take its originall Rise as followeth, viz:

Few or none had bin the Damages sustained by the English from the Indians, other than occasionally had happen'd sometimes upon private quarrels and
provocations, until in July, 1675, certain Doegs and Susquehanock Indians on
Maryland side,[2] stealing some Hoggs from the English at Potomake on the Virginia shore (as the River divides the same), were pursued by the English in a
boate, beaten or kill'd and the hoggs retaken from them; whereupon the Indians
repairing to their owne Towne, report it to their Superiors, and how that one

1. Two original copies of the commissioners' "Narrative" exist, one in Wiseman's *Book
of Record* at the Pepys Library at Magdalene College, and another in the Colonial Office
Papers at the British Public Records Office in Kew, England (Proceedings and Reports of
the Commissioners for Enquiring Into Virginia Affairs and Settling Virginian Grievances, C.O. 5/1371). The narrative has been reprinted in the *Virginia Magazine of History and Biography*, 4 (1896), 119-154 and in Charles M. Andrews, ed., *Narratives of
the Insurrections, 1675-1690* (New York: Charles Scribner's Sons, 1915), 99-141. Andrews used the version in the Public Record Office.
2. On the Susquehannocks, see Michael Leroy Oberg, *Dominion and Civility: English
Imperialism and Native America, 1585-1685* (Ithaca, NY: Cornell University Press,
1999), 195-198; Francis Jennings, "Glory, Death and Transfiguration: The Susquehannock Indians in the Seventeenth Century," *Proceedings of the American Philosophical
Society*, 112 (1968), 25-26; Barry Kent, *Susquehanna's Indians* (Harrisburg: Pennsylvania Historical and Museum Commission, 1984), 38-39; Elizabeth Tooker, "The De-
mise of the Susquehannocks: A Seventeenth-Century Mystery," *Pennsylvania Archae-
ologist*, 54 (1984), 1-10.

Mathewes[3] (whose hoggs they had taken) had before abused and cheated them, in not paying them for such Indian trucke as he had formerly bought of them, and that they took his hogs for Satisfaction. Upon this (to be reveng'd on Mathews) a warr Captain with some Indians came over to Potomake and killed two of Mathewes his servants, and came also a second time and kill'd his sonne.

It happened hereupon that Major George Brent and Col. George Mason pursued some of the same Indians into Maryland, and marching directly up to the Indian Towne with a Party of 30 Virginians came to a certaine House and there killed an Indian King and 10 of his men upon the place; the rest of the Indians fled for their lives.[4]

On this occasion the Governor of Maryland writes a Letter to Sir Wm. Berkeley, complayning of this rash action and intrusion of the Virginians on his Province without his leave or knowledge, the Indians and them being at that time in Peace.

By what authority Brent and Mason went over into Maryland and kill'd those Indians is an Article of Inquiry in the Rappahannock Grievances[5] and the supposed originall cause of the many murders that ensued in that county as themselves complaine.

The Indians persisting to Revenge themselves Inforted in Maryland and now began to be bold and formidable to the English who Besieged them;[6] their Boldness and daring Behavior of late tymes and their promptnesse to Fire arms, being (indeed) wonderfull, over what they seem'd formerly indued with, which doubtlesse was of some advantage extraordinary to them considering their Small Body, the Virginians and Marylanders that Besieged them being said to make a neer a thousand men. The siege held 7 weekes, during which tyme the English lost 50 men, besides some Horses which the Indians tooke, and serv'd themselves to subsist on. But Provisions growing very scarce with them during this siege the Indians sent out 5 greate men to Treate of Peace, who were not Permitted to return to the Fort, but being kept Prisoners Some tyme were at last murdered by the English.[7]

---

3. Thomas Mathew, a planter who lived in the Northern Neck of Virginia, long had maintained a tense relationship with area Indians. See Oberg, *Dominion and Civility*, 198-199; "Mathew's Narrative," in *Narratives of the Insurrections, 1675-1690*, ed. Charles M. Andrews (New York: Charles Scribner's Sons, 1915), 17-20.

4. For other accounts of this incident, see "Mathew's Narrative," 18-20.

5. See below, Chapter 6.

6. On the Susquehannocks' fortress, and how they came to occupy it, see Oberg, *Dominion and Civility*, 195; Stephen Saunders Webb, *1676: The End of American Independence* (New York: Knopf, 1984), 4.

7. The event is described in Oberg, *Dominion and Civility*, 199. See also "The History of Bacon's and Ingram's Rebellion," in *Narratives of the Insurrections*, ed. Andrews, 47-48.

Att length (whether through negligence or cowardize) the Indians made their escape through the English, with all their wives, children and goods of value, wounding and killing some at their sally and going off.

After which the English returninge as Report sayeth, the Marylanders composed a Peace with the Salvages, and soe diverted the warr from themselves.

As yett the Generall Peace and Government of Virginia continued undisturbed only some Ignorant People grumbled att the sixty pounds of Tobacco per pole, that necessary Tax raised att two payments to take off the Patents granted to the Lord Arlington and Culpepper.[8]

Butt about the Beginninge of January 1675/6 a party of those abused Susquahanocks in Revenge of the Maryland business came suddainly down upon the weak Plantations att the heade of Rapahanock and Potomaque and killed att one time thirty six persons and then Immediately as their Custome is, ran off into the Woods.

Noe sooner was this Intelligence brought to the Governour but he immediately called a Court and ordered a competent force of horse and foot to pursue the Murderers under the Comand of Sir Henry Chicheley and some other Gentlemen of the County of Rappahannock, giving them full Power by Commission to make Peace or Warr. But the men being ready to march out upon this Service the Governour on a suddaine recalls this commission, Causes the men to be disbanded, and without any effectual course being taken for present Preservation, referrs all to the next assembly; in the meantime leaving the Poore Inhabitants under continual and deadly feares and terrors of their Lives. In soe much that in the upper Parts of the Parish of Citternbourne in Rappahannock, w'ch consisted of Seaventy one Plantations, on the 24th of January 1675-6, by the 10th of Febr following was reduced to eleven what with those that ran away into the heart of the country, and such as stay'd and were cutt off by the Enimy.

The assembly mett to consult for the Safety and defence of the Country ag't Incursions and destructions of the Indians, dayly Comitted upon the Inhabitants of Virginia, there having beene within the space of about 12 months before neer three hundred Christian persons murder'd by the Indians Enemy.

Whatt care the Assembly tooke to prevent these massacres was onely to build Forts at the heads of each River and on the Frontiers and confines of the country, for erecting of which and maintaining Guards on them a heavie leavy was laid by act of Assembly on the People; throughout the country universally disliked before the name of that Imposture Bacon was heard of,[9] as being a mat-

---

8. Andrews' version of this sentence continues with the phrase "and the Earl of St. Albans and Lord Berkly etc." The poll tax referred to here was levied by the Berkeleyan assembly to send agents to England to negotiate a nullification of the patents issued to several of the king's favorites in 1669 and 1672.

9. In other words, the Virginia colonists detested the heavy taxation required to finance the construction of the fortifications before any word was heard of Bacon's intended

ter from which was expected great charge and little or noe security to the Inhabitants, the Scituation of the Virginian Plantation being invironed with thick woods, swamps and other covert, by the help of which the enemy might at their Pleasure make their approaches undiscover'd on the most secure of their habitations, as they have often done not onely on the Frontiers but in the very heart and centre of the country, their sculking nature being apt to use these advantages.

The Murders, Rapines and outrages of the Indians became soe much the more Barbarous, fierce and frequent, by how much more they perceived the Public Preparations of the English against them, Prosecuting their mischiefs upon the extreme Plantations thereby forcing many to desert them to their Ruines, and destroying those that adventur'd to stay behind.

The unsatisfied People finding themselves still liable to the Indian Crueltyes, and the cryes of their wives and children growing grievous and intolerable to them, gave out in Speeches that they were resolved to Plant tobacco rather than pay the Tax for maintaining of Forts, and that the erecting of them was a great Grievance, Juggle and cheat, and of noe more use or service to them than another Plantation with men att itt, and that itt was meerly a designe of the Grandees to engrosse all their Tobacco into their owne hands.

Thus the Sense of this oppression and the dread of the common approaching calamity made the giddy-headed multitude madd, and precipitated them upon that rash overture of Running out upon the Indians themselves, at their owne voluntary charge and hazard of their Lives and Fortunes, onely they first by Petition humbly craved leave or commission to be ledd by any commander or Commanders as the Governor should please to appoint over them to be their Chieftaine or Generall. But instead of Granting this Petition the Governour by proclamation under great Penalty forbadd the like Petitioninge for the future: This made the people jealous that the Governour for the Lucre of the Beaver and otter trade, &c., with the Indians (they complaine) hee privately gave comission to some of his Friendes to truck with them, and that those persons furnished the Indians with Powder, Shott, &c., soe that they were better provided than his Majesties Subjects.

The People of Charles City County, near Marchants Hope, beinge denyed a Commission by the Governor, although he was truly informed as by a letter of his to his majestie' he confesseth of Several formidable Bodies of Indians comminge down on the heads of James River within fifty or sixty miles of the English Plantations, and knew not where the Storme would light, they begin to beat up drums for Volunteers to goe out against the Indians and soe continued Sundry dayes drawing into armes, the Magistrates being either soe remise or of the

rebellion. Virginia planters already confronted an enormous tax burden. See Edmund S. Morgan, *American Slavery, American Freedom: The Ordeal of Colonial Virginia*, (New York: Norton, 1975), 245-247, 253-254.

Same faction, that they suffered this disaster without contradiction or endeavouring to prevent soe dangerous a beginninge and goeinge on.

The Rout being gott togeather, now wanted nor waited for nothinge butt one to head and lead them on their designe:

It soe happened that one Nathaniell Bacon, Junior, a person whose lost and desperate fortunes had thrown him into thatt remote part of the world about fourteen months before, and framed him fitt for such a purpose, as by the Sequell will appeare, which maye make of him a short Character, noe impertinent digression:

Hee was a Person whose Erratique fortune had carryed and shewn him many forraigne Parts, and of noe obscure family. Uppon his first comminge to Virginia he was made one of the Councill, the reason of the advancement on a suddaine beinge best known to the Governour, which Honor made him the more Considerable in the eye of the vulgar, and gave some advantage to his Pernicious designs.

Hee was said to be about fower or five and thirty yeares of age, indifferent tall butt Slender, black haired and of an ominous pensive melancolly aspect, of a Pestilent and prevalent Logicall discourse tendinge to Atheisme in most Companyes, not given to much talke, or to make suddaine replyes, of a most Imperious and dangerous hidden pride of heart, dispisinge the wisest of his Neighbours for their Ignorance, and very ambitious and Arrogant, butt all those things laye hid in him, till after he was a Councillor, and until he became Powerfull and Popular.

Now this man being in company with one Crews,[10] Isham,[11] and Bird, who growing to a height of Drinking and makinge the Sadness of the times there Discourse, and the fear they all lived in, because of the Susquahanocks who had settled a little above the Falls of James River, and committed many murders upon them, among whom Bacon's overseer happen'd to be one, Crews and the rest persuaded Mr. Bacon to goe over and see the Souldiers on the other side James River and to take a quantity of Rum with them to give the men to drinke, which they did, and as Crews &c had before laid the Plott with the Souldiers; they all att once in the field shouted and cryed out a Bacon! a Bacon! a Bacon, which takinge fire with his ambition and spirit of faction and Popularity easily prevailed on him to resolve to head them: His friends endeavourringe to fix him the faster to his Resolves by telling him that they would allso goe along with

10. Captain James Crews of Henrico County was one of Bacon's best friends, who had persuaded him to take a leading role in the rebellion. According to Andrews, he was hanged on 24 January 1677, above Bacon's siege-works outside Jamestown. See Andrews, ed., *Narratives*, 110n; and Webb, *1676*, 99.

11. Henry Isham, Jr., returned to England after the rebellion, in which he apparently played no role. His plantation, called Doggams, was located in Charles City County. He died in 1679. See Andrews, *Narratives*, 110n.

him, to take Revenge upon the Indians, & drinke damnation to their Soules to be true to him, and if he could not obtaine a Commission, they would assist him aswell and asmuch as if he had one, so which Bacon agreed.

This forwardness of Bacon greatly cheer'd and animated the people who looked upon him as the only Patron of the Country & Preserver of their lives and fortunes: for he pretended and boasted what great service he would doe for the Country in destroyinge the common Enimy, securinge their lives and Estates, removeinge their Pressures and enlarginge their Liberties, and such like faire frauds he subtily and Secrettly insinuated by his owne Instruments over all the Country, which seduced the vulgar and most ignorant People to beleeve (two thirds of each County beinge of that sort, soe that their whole hearts & hopes were sett now upon Bacon. Next he charges the Governour as negligent & wicked, treacherous and Incapable; the Laws and Taxes as unjust and Pressive and urges up an absolute necessity of Redresse.

Thus Bacon encourag'd the Tumult, and as the unquiet crowd follow and adhere to him, he Listeth them as they come in upon a large Paper, writing their name Circular wise, that their Ring Leaders might not be found out.

Havinge conjur'd them in to this Circle, givinge them Brandy to wind up the Charme, & enjoyn'd them by an oath to stick fast together, and to him, and the oath beinge administered he went and infected New Kent, a County ripe for Rebellion.

Bacon havinge gott about 300 men togeather in armes, Prepared to goe out forth against the Indians; the Governour and his Friends endeavour to divert his designes butt Cannot.

He proclaimes Bacon and his followers Rebells and Mutineers for goinge forth against the Indians without a Commission: And gettinge a company of Gentlemen togeather the Governor marches up to the falls of James River, to pursue and take Bacon or to seize him att his Returne, Butt all in vaine for Bacon had gott over the River with his forces and hasteninge away into the woods, went directly and fell upon the Indians, and Killed some of them that were our best friends of Indians and had fought against the Susquahanoks Enemys to the English.[12]

The Governour havinge issued forth a Proclamation importinge noe commerce with the Reputed Indian Enimys, besides the clogs and conditions which were putt on the Garrrisons placed or to be placed in the New Erected forts, enjoyning them not to make any attempt upon the Indians until they should first

12. This would have occurred in May of 1676. The rebel apparently hoped that the governor would ultimately recognize the value of the work he did for the colony. On May 2, Bacon wrote to the Governor and asked him not to believe evil reports spread of his intentions. "I am just now goeing out," Bacon wrote, "to seeke a more agreeable destiny than you are pleased to designe mee." Bacon quoted in Morgan, *American Slavery, American Freedom,* 259.

give the Governor account thereof and receive orders from them therein, Putt many to a stand, made the People expostulate and saye, how shall wee know our enimyes from our friends, are not the Indians all of a Colour, and if wee must not defend our selves before they oppose us, they maye take their usuall advantage of Surprize and soe destroye us ere wee are capable of makinge any resistance, Soe that after all that charge in Erectinge of forts, after all the Trouble of the Congress of our forces, after all this toyle and diligence used in discovering the Ennimy, who are seldome to be dealt with butt in their own waye of Surprize, the very point of Execution was to be determined by a person residinge in all likely hood att least a hundred miles distant from the place of action, to the loss of opertunities and utter discouragement of the Souldiers and our Selves. Besides, of whatt security was these forts like to be when the Indians cutt of & destroy'd divers People within a Smale distance of the forts and some of the very Souldiers in them and they not daringe to stir out to relieve any that were in danger & distresse, themselves being scarce secure upon the Place they were Posted on.

Nor would the people understand any distinction of friendly Indians and Indian Enimies, for att that time itt was Impossible to distinguish one nation from another, they being deformed with Paint of many Colors, and att best say they who is hee that can doe it for there was never any open or free Trade among us that we might know them, butt the whole trade Monopoliz'd by the Governour and Grandees.

Soe the Common cry and vogue of the vulgar was awaye with these Forts, awaye with these distractions, wee will have warr with all Indians, which come not in with their Armes, and give Hostages for their fidellity, and to ayd against all others. Wee will spare none, and if wee must be hang'd for Rebells, for killinge those that will destroye us, lett them hang us, wee will venture that rather then lye att the Mercy of a Barbarous Enimye and be Murdered as wee are.

Thus went the ruder Sort raginge and exclaiminge against the Indians, expressing the Callamity that befell New England by them.[13] While the Governour was in the upper Partes to waite Bacons returne the people below began to draw into armes and to declare against the forts.

Hee to appease the Commotion of the people leaves off that designe and comes Immediately back to his own Howse, and caused att his returne the Surrey and other forts to be forthwith dismantled, and dissolvinge the Assembly

---

13. The commissioners here refer to King Philip's War, which began in Plymouth Plantation in the summer of 1675 and rapidly spread throughout the New England colonies. For treatments of the war, see Oberg, *Dominion and Civility*, Chapter 4; James D. Drake, *King Philip's War: Civil War in New England, 1675-1676* (Amherst: University of Massachusetts Press, 1999); Douglas Edward Leach, *Flintlock and Tomahawk: New England in King Philip's War* (New York: Macmillan, 1958), and Eric B. Schultz and Michael J. Tougias, *King Philip's War: The History and Legacy of America's Forgotten Conflict* (Woodstock, VT: The Countryman Press, 1999).

that enacted them, gave the Country a free new Election, which new Assembly were to be for the Settlement of the then distracted condition of Virginia.[14]

Att this new Election (such was the Prevalency of Bacon's Party), that they chose instead of freeholders, freemen, that had butt lately crept out of the condition of servants (which were never before Elgible)[15] for their Burgesses and such as were Eminent Abettors to Bacon; and for faction and Ignorance fitt Representatives of those that chose them. Att the same time Bacon, beinge come back from his Indian March; with a thousand braginge lyes to the credulous, Silly people, of what feats he had performed,was chosen a Burgess by the Inhabitants of the County of Henrico, as was also Crews for the same Countie.

The Assembly beinge mett Bacon comes down in a sloop to James Town, but the people beinge very fond of him, would not trust his person with out a guard, fearinge some violence should be offered him by the Governour, for whatt he had already acted against his will and soe sent forty armed men along in the sloop with Bacon.

Coming somewhat nearer to Town than Swanns Point dropt anckor, and sent as tis said on shore to the Governor to know if he might in safety come on shore, and sitt as a Member: what answer was Returned wee have not heard, only what the Governor caused him to be given from the great Gunns, that fired att the sloop from the Town Fort soe that havinge gott his sloop out of Gun shott, he lay higher up the River, and in the night time with a Part of his men ventured on shore, and havinge had some conference, att Lawrence his Howse, with Lawrence and Drummond, came of again undiscovered.

Severall Propositions were made and Severall boats sent off to apprehend him, butt could effect nothinge: Bacon endeavours to make his escape up the River. In this juncture of time Captain Thomas Gardner master of the Shipp *Adam and Eve* beinge att Town,[16] haveinge an order from the Governour to pursue and seize him Immediately gott on board his ship and as Bacon returned up the River commanded his sloop in by firinge att him from on board, and soe

14. Berkeley dissolved the assembly on 7 March 1676. See *Narratives*, ed. Andrews, 113n.
15. Technically, the commissioners are incorrect on this count. A law passed by the House of Burgesses in 1670 deprived Freemen of the right to vote and limited the franchise to the owners of property, whether Freeholders or Housekeepers. For a discussion of the tightening restrictions on the former servants in the decades preceding Bacon's Rebellion, see Morgan, *American Slavery, American Freedom*, 196-270.
16. Gardner served Berkeley well, and played a critical role in pursuing Bacon, but the assembly, friendly to the rebel, fined him £70 for seizing Bacon and, in effect, "for violating the privilidge of a Burgess." Charles II would later award him £567 for his assistance in crushing the rebellion. See Webb, *1676*, 103; and H. R. McIlwaine, ed., *Journals of the House of Burgesses of Virginia, 1659/60-1693* (Richmond: Virginia State Library, 1914), 66.

tooke him and all his men Prisoners and brought them awaye to the Governour at Town.[17]

Bacon beinge delivered up Prisoner to the Governor by Captain Gardner, the Governour liftinge up his hands and eyes said in the hearinge of many people, "Now I behold the greatest Rebell that ever was in Virginia," who with a dejected look made noe reply till after a short pause. The Governor asked Bacon these words, "Sir, doe you continue to be a Gentleman, and maye I take your word, if soe you are at liberty upon your own Parrol."

Bacon feignes a most deep sense of shame and sorrow for his guilt & expresses the greatest kind of obligation to Gratitude toward the Governor imaginable.

And to make itt look the more reall and Sincere, drew up an humble Submission and acknowledgement, of his soe late crimes and disobedience, Imploringe thereby the Governors Pardon and favour: Which Bacon beinge in readiness to present, on his comminge before the Governor, he told the Councill then sittinge, "Now you shall see a most Penitent Sinner."

Whereupon Bacon in a very humble manner and with many low Bowinges of his Body approacht the Governor, and on his Knee gave up his Parasiticall paper into the Governors hands & soe withdrew himselfe. After a short while he was sent for in againe and had his Pardon confirm'd unto him: Is restored into favour, and readmitted into the Councill to the wonder of all men.[18]

Now Captain Gardner instead of a reward for the Service he performed in taking and bringinge away Bacon Prisoner, was suffered to be fined seaventy pounds damage for seizinge him and the sloop, although Captain Gardner had discharged himselfe of her, the said sloop beinge afterwards by a storme drove on shore and lost.

However soe powerfull (it seems) was Bacon's interest in this new Assembly, that he procured a publique order to pass against Gardner for the payment of the 70 £ where upon he threw Gardner into goale till he found security for his Inlargment.[19]

---

17. The assembly gathered on June 5. Though Bacon had been elected as a burgess from Henrico County, he did not dare openly challenge Berkeley's proclamation. Bacon did sneak into Jamestown to confer with his supporters on the evening of the sixth, and Gardner captured him the next morning. See Wilcomb E. Washburn, *The Governor and the Rebel: A History of Bacon's Rebellion* (Chapel Hill: University of North Carolina Press, 1957), 51-52; Webb, *1676*, 32.

18. Governor Berkeley knew that perhaps 2,000 heavily taxed, well-armed followers of Bacon had entered the capital to rescue their leader. For this reason, he pardoned Bacon on June 10 and restored him to his seat on the council. See William Sherwood to [?], 28 June 1676, Letters and Papers Concerning American Plantations, 1 June 1676–7 October 1676, C.O. 1/37, 40 (VCRP); Oberg, *Dominion and Civility*, 203.

19. "It is a wonder Sir Wm. Berkeley (being then in Towne) did not protect or preserve a Person he had imploy'd in so signal a service." (Marginal note in Wiseman's original).

The late news of Bacons beinge taken prisoner beinge spread over all the Country soe alarmed the people of the upper parts of James River and those of New Kent, that they resolved to release him per force, and as they saye were decendinge to Towne in armes to secure his Inlargement.

Butt when they understood that the Governor had not only set him free but readmitted him into the Councill, with promise allso of a Commission to be given him to goe out against the Indians, the people were soe well pacified for the present, as that every man with great Gladness return'd to his own home.

Bacon attendinge att Town for a commission, which the Governor is said to have promised him, and being delayed or putt off, was secretly whispered by some of his friends that those delays would endanger his life, and that if speedily he endeavoured not to prevent it there was a conspiracy to murder him on such a night. Upon which hee privately leaves to Town. Now whether this were a raised rumour of Bacons or a reall truth wee Cannot determine; butt beinge raised after Bacon was gone wee suppose itt false.

Hee no sooner was Come to the upper parts of James River but the Impatient people run to him to aske how affaires stood, exclaiminge more and more against the Indians, and desired to know if he had gott a Commission, and understandinge he had or could not obtaine any, they began to sett upp their throats in one common Kry of caths and curses, and cryd out aloud that they would either have a Commission for Bacon that they might serve under his conduct, or else they would pull down the Town, or doe worse to some if they had itt not, and if Bacon would goe butt with them they would get him a Commission.

Thus the Raginge Tumult came down to Towne (sitting the Assembly) & Bacon att the head of them havinge entered the Town he seizes and secures the Principal places and avenues, setts sentinels and sends forth scouts, soe that noe place could be more securely guarded. Havinge soe done he draws up all his men in Armes against the State howse, where the Governor, Councill and Burgesses were then Assembled and Sittinge: and send unto the Assembly to know whither they would now grant him a Commission, which sir William Berkeley utterly refused and risinge from his Chaire of Judicature came down to Bacon and told him to his face and before all his men that he was a Rebell and a Traytor &c and should have noe Commission, and uncoveringe his naked bosom before him, required that some of his men might shoot him before ever he would be drawn to signe or Consent to a Commission for such a Rebell or Bacon. "Noe," said the Governor, "lett us first try and end the difference singly between our selves," and offered to measure swords with him. All the answer Bacon gave the Governor was: "Sir, I came not, nor intend to hurt a hair of your Honors head and for your Sword your Honor maye please to putt itt up; it shall rust in the scabbard before ever I shall desire to draw itt. I come for a Commission against the Heathen who daily Inhumanely Murder us and spill our Bretherens blood & noe care is taken to prevent itt;" addinge, "God damne his blood, I

came for a Commission and a Comission I will have, before I goe," and turninge
to his Souldiers said "make ready and present," which they all did.

Some of the Burgesses looking out the window and seeinge the Souldiers in
that posture of firinge cryed out to them, "for God's sake hold up your hands,
and forbear a little and you shall have what you please." Much hurryinge, solicitation and Importunity is used on all sides to the Governor to Grant Bacon a
Commission.[20]

Att last the Governor consents, a comission is drawn up & sent him, he dislikes itt, they praye him to draw or direct one himselfe, and the Governor should
signe itt, whereupon Bacon draws up the Contents of a Commission according
to his owne mind, and Returns itt to the Clerke to prepare one by, which is done,
liked and Received.[21]

After the Governor had signed the Principall Commission to Bacon he is
allso pleased to signe 30 commissions more (Blanke) for officers that were to
serve under him. Butt Bacon findinge occasion for more, sent to Sir William
Berkeley to signe others also who said he had signed enough already, and bid
him signe the rest himselfe if he would.

The Assembly allso pass orders to raise or Press a thousand men, & to raise
Provisions &c. for this intended service against the Indians, wherein severall of
the Councill and Assembly members were concerned and acted in the Promot-
inge of this designe encouraging others to list themselves into Bacons service,
and particularly one Ballard who endeavoured to perswade some (who scrupled
the Legality of Bacon's Commission) that itt was fairly and freely granted by
Governor, Councill and Burgesses, this Ballard beinge one of the Councill, and
of those that both tooke and administered Bacon's oath.[22]

There was allso an Act of Indempnity passed to Bacon and his Party who
committed the force on the Assembly, and a Publike letter of Applause & approbation of Bacons loyalty and actions writt to the King and signed by the
Governour and Assembly, which upon the breakinge up of this session were sent
abroad and read amongst the Ignorant people who believed thereby that all was
well, & nothinge comminge forth of a long time to quash, contradict or disown
this Commission, Indempnity, Letters, &c granted to Bacon; Butt on the con-

20. This took place on the 24 June 1676.
21. "Thus as itt seemes to be Bacons force upon the Assembly, soee itt appears to be the
Assemblys force upon the Governour, which might have bin prevented, had he att a word
dissolved them, seeing it was apparent that they had more regard at that time to Bacons
Honour than to the Kings or his Governors Honour." (Marginal note in Wiseman's
original).
22. The individual referred to is Colonel Thomas Ballard of Jamestown. According to
Andrews, Ballard "seems to have been particularly influential in persuading the people to
take Bacon's 'unlawfull' oath of August 3." Apparently, Ballard did not suffer for his
disloyalty. He served as a member of the council again in 1677, and became Speaker of
the House of Burgesses in 1680 and 1684. See *Narratives*, ed. Andrews, 117n.

trary other Commission of the Governors own signinge, and sealed with the Publicke seale of the Collony comminge to them, they were the more easily induced to swallow down soe faire a Baite, not seeinge Rebellion att the end of itt, and most men grew ambitious of the service, as thinkinge itt both safe and for the Publike good, as haveinge the Approbation of the Governor and assembly; att least there yett appeared nothinge to the Contrary, nor of a good while after.

Severall volunteers and Reformadoes came in to list themselves under Bacon, and many were prest into this service, till att last haveinge his complement of men, and all things else beinge in a Readiness, accordinge as the Assembly had provided for this expedition.

A Generall Rendezvous is appointed by Bacon att the falls of James River[23] where all things beinge well appointed for the March, Bacon makes a Speech to his men, assuringe them all of his Loyallty to his Prince, declaringe to them thatt his designe was noe other than meerly to serve his King and Country. And to clear all Suspition of the Contrary, if any were amongst them by what had bin by him already acted or Proclaimed against him, as allso if what might be said about the procuringe his commission, he urges to them the reasons that induced itt, the necessity of that time that compelled him, the negligence & coldnesse of others that heated him, and the cryes of his Bretherens blood that alarm'd and awakened him to this Publike Revenge, usinge what motives he could to raise up the Spiritts of his men. And finally before them all he tooke the oath of Allegiance and Supremacy willinge his souldiers allso to doe the like,[24] which haveinge freely comply'd with, he drew up an oath of fidellity to himselfe, which he as their head and Generall required them to take. Itt comprehended these following contents or heads:[25]

Thatt they should not conceale any Plott or conspiracy of hurt against his Person butt immediately reveale the same to him or such others by whome he might come to the Knowledge of itt.

Thatt if any harme or damage was intended towards any of his men whether by Surprisall or the like or any conference used or counsel kept about the same to discover itt.

That noe commerce or correspondence should be had with the heathen, and if any known to discover itt.

Thatt noe news or information should be sent out least himselfe or army by such intelligence should be indangered either in Repute or other wise.

All Councills, Plotts and conspiracys known of the Heathen to discover them &c.

---

23. "July 15th." (Marginal Note in Wiseman's Original).
24. "Bacon takes the oath of Allegiance and Supremacy and enjoins the souldiers to doe the like." (marginal note in Wiseman's original).
25. "An Oath of Bacons taken by his souldiers." (Marginal note in Wiseman's original.)

Just now (even on the verry night before their goinge out on the Intended march against the Indians) a messenger comes Post from Gloster County bringing Intelligence to Bacon, that the Governor was there, endeaveringe to raise forces to come and Surprize him and his men, & that he was Resolved by force to take his Extorted Commission away from him, for that the whole county had Petitioned against him as a Rebell and a Traytor, &c.[26]

This amusinge message was noe sooner brought to Bacon butt Immediately he causes the drums to beat and Trumpetts to sound for calling his men togeather, to whom he spake after this manner:

Gentlemen & Fellow Souldiers

The Newes just now brought me maye not a little startle you as well as my selfe. Butt seeinge it is not altogeather unexpected, wee maye the better beare itt & provide our remedies.

The Governor is now in Gloster County endeavouringe to raise forces against us, havinge declared us Rebells and Traytors: if true, crimes indeed too great for Pardon, our Consciences herein are the best witnesses, and theirs soe conscious, as like cowards, therefore they will not have the courage to face us. It is Revenge that Hurrys them on without Regard to the peoples safety, and had rather wee should be murdered and our Ghosts sent to our slaughtered Countrymen, by their actings, then wee live to hinder them of their interest with the Heathen, and preserve the remaininge part of our fellow Subjects from their Cruelties. Now then wee must be forced to turne our Swords to our own defence, or expose our selves to their Mercyes, or fortune of the woods, whilst his Majesties Country here lyes in blood and wastinge, like a candell att both ends.

How incapable wee maye be made if wee should proceed through sicknesse, want of provisions, slaughters, wounds, loss or more, none of us is void of the sense hereof.

Therefore while wee are sound att heart, unwearied and not receiving damage by the fate of Warr, lett us descend to know the Reasons why such proceedings are used against us. That those whom they have raised for their defense, to preserve them against the fury of the Heathen, they should thus seeke to destroye, and to Betraye our lives whom they raised to preserve theirs. If ever

---

26. Late in July, Berkeley received a petition from the residents of Gloucester County, who complained that Bacon and his men had commandeered their horses and weapons. Berkeley, misreading the county's mood, granted them the right to resist Bacon. The governor failed dismally in his attempt to raise forces in the county, however, when the recruits realized that Berkeley intended to march them out against Bacon rather than the Indians. Without further support from the Gloucester men, Berkeley fled across the Chesapeake Bay to the Eastern Shore. See the "Humble Petition of the County of Gloster," and "The Governor's Answere to that Petition, in "The Aspinwall Papers," *Collections of the Massachusetts Historical Society*, 4th ser., 9 (1871), 181-183.

such treachery was herd of, such wickedness and Inhumanity and call all the former ages to witnesse and if any that they suffered in like nature, as wee are like by the Sword and Ruins of warr. But they are damn'd Cowards, and you shall see that they will not dare to meet us in the field to try the Justness of our case, and soe wee will down to them, &c.

To which they all cry'd *Amen Amen,* wee are all ready and will rather dye in the field, then be hang'd like Rouges or Perrish in the woods, exposed to the favours of the Mercyless Indians, &c.

How unhappy, unsuccessful and how fatal this Avocation prov'd, the consequence will but too plainly shew.

For Bacon (then the hopes of the People) was just upon the point of marchinge out, and nothinge could have call'd him back, or turned the Sword of a Civill warr into the heart & Bowells of the Country but soe ill tym'd a Project as this Proved. And although it is asserted by some, that att this time there was a paper publikely read to the People that the Governor design'd only to raise a partie to goe out against the Indians and not against Bacon, offeringe not only their Estates, butt a solemn oath to bind and confirme this Pretention to the People. Yett this did noe feats with the People, or tooke any other Impression on them, save only that it still more confirmed that Bacons cause was not only as good as the Governors (when their Pretensions were now equally against the Indians), but allso that the Commission granted him was faire and Legall, seeinge he protested not to prosecute or goe against him for itt.[27] Now in vaine the Governor attempts raisinge a force against Bacon, and although the Industry and endeavours he used to effect it was great, yett att this Juncture itt was impossible.[28] For Bacon at this time was so much the hopes and darling of the people, that the Governors interest prov'd but weake, and his friends soe verry few, that he grew sick of the Essaye, and with very griefe & sadnesse of spirit for soe bad success (as is said) fainted away on horseback in the field. And hearinge of Bacons being on his march to Gloster, he was feigne to fly thence to Accomack,[29] leavinge now the seate of the Government liable to the Usurpation of that Rebell, who had then allso the Militia of the Country in his hands, to Inforce his own arbitrary Impositions on the People, as he afterwards did at his Comminge

27. "The Indian warr recoiles upon the Country in an intestine Rebellion." (Marginal comment in Wiseman's original).
28. "By this it is plaine that the Governor was putt upon this Successless Essaye by the few contrivors of Gloster, for had itt bin the address of the whole County as pretended they would doubt not all have owned itt and stood by the Governor and not soe basely have abandoned him and his cause, butt there was not one Subscriber for this Petition." (Marginal comment in Wiseman's Original).
29. "Part of the Collony of Virginia disjoined 7 leaugs." (Marginal comment in Wiseman's original).

to Gloster. [30] Where being arrived with his forces he finds the Governor fled, (and without more adoe), the field his own; soe leading his men to Middle Plantation, the very heart and Centre of the Country, he there for some time quarters them. Then issues forth Proclamation inviting the Gentlemen of Virginia to come in and consult with him for the Present settlement of that his Majesties distracted Collony, to preserve its future peace, and advance the effectuall prosecutinge of the Indian Warr. [31]

Severall Gentlemen on appearinge on this Summons of Bacons att Middle Plantation mett him att one Capt: Thorp's, [32] where under a great guard were severall persons confined. After a long debate pro and con, a mischievous writinge was drawen up and produced by Bacon, unto which (the doors of the Howse beinge fast locked on them) many by threats & force and feare were faigne to subscribe. The tenor of the oath is as follows: [33]

1.   You are to oppose whatt forces shall be sent out of England by his Majestie against me till such time I have acquainted the Kinge with the state of this Country & have had an answer.

2.   You shall sweare that whatt the Governor and Councill have acted is Illegall & destructive to the Country, and whatt I have done is accordinge to the Laws of England.

30. "Bacon comes down to Gloster." (Marginal comment in Wiseman's original).

31. Bacon's proclamation was issued "in the name of the People" from Middle Plantation. In it, the rebel condemned Berkeley for "greate and unjust taxes" that bought no security; for monopolizing the Indian trade through his licensing practices; and for having "protected, favoured, & Imboldened the Indians agt. His Majesties loyall subjects, never contriveing, requiring, or appointeing any due or proper meanes of satisfaction for their many Invasions, Robbories, & murthers committed upon us." Bacon denounced as well the recall of Chicheley's force from its Indian targets, "when we might with ease have destroyed them" For these crimes, Bacon condemned Berkeley and his supporters "as Traytors to the King & Country."

His "Manifesto" appeared shortly thereafter, in which he declared his followers' "open & manifest Aversion of all, not onely the Foreign but the protected & Darling Indians" of which he was "informed is Rebellion of a deep dye." C.O. 1/37, 128, 179 (VCRP).

32. Captain Otho Thorp, an apolitical planter from York County. Thorp suffered greatly during the rebellion. His petition, in which he complained of his heavy losses, was referred by the Privy Council to the Committee for Trade and Plantations on 22 December 1677. see Privy Council Register, P.C. 2/66, 205, 212-213 (VCRP), and Chapter 7, below.

33. "The oath that Bacon administered to the People." (Marginal notation in Wiseman's original).

3.   You shall swear from your hearts that my Commission is Lawfull and Legally obtained.

4.   You shall swear not to divulge what you shall heare att any time spoken against me.

5.   You shall keep my Secretts and not discover them to any person.

Copy's of this oath are sent to all or most of the Countyes of Virginia, and by the magistrates and others of the respective precincts administered to the people, which none or very few for feare or force durst or did refuse.

To perfect all att once and to make all Secure which soe long as the Governor was att Liberty they thought could not be.[34] Butt that he would still seek meanes whereby to regaine his place and authority, and not to be soe basely extruded that high trust lawfully residinge in him. They take Captain Larrimores ship by Surprize, man her with two hundred men & guns to goe to Accomack and seize the Governor, pretendinge to send him home prisoner to his Majestie for to receive Tryall of his demerits towards his Majesties Subjects of Virginia and for the likely loss of that Collony for want of due and timely care for the preservation of itt against the daily Incursions and Encroachments of the native Salvages, who had destroy'd and laid wast the Plantations, and cutt of many of the families of the English &c.

The command of which charge was Committed to one Carver, a valiant stout seaman, and Gyles Bland, both since executed, only Mr. Bacon puttinge more confidence in Carver had chiefly instructed Carver on this designe, by a Private Commission which Bland knew not of but supposed they had both equall Power.[35]

Things thus agitated Bacon reassumes his first designes of marchinge out against the Indians, imprisoninge some before he went out;[36] others he had of a long continuance in hold, who in the begininge thought and tryd to divert his designes. Other some he subtly brought over to his side; and such whose liberty if left behinde he jealously suspected might raise a party against him in his absence he tooke along with him.

---

34. "A ship & souldiers sent to seize the Governour at Accomack." (Marginal notation in Wiseman's original).
35. See below, footnote 46.
36. "Bacon's Second march against the Indians." (Marginal notation in Wiseman's original. Wiseman is unclear in this sentence. Bacon imprisoned some of his colonial opponents before he began his march.

Bacon goes up againe to the falls of James River where he bestirs himselfe lustily in order to a speedy march against the Indians in prosecution of his first pretentions which were against the Occanechees[37] & Susquahanoks.

From the falls of James River he marches over to the freshes of Yorke to pursue the Pamunkey Indians whose propinquity and neighborhood to the English & conversing among them was a pretended reason to render the Rebells Suspitious of them, as beinge acquainted, and knowinge both the manners, custometes, & nature of our people, & the strength, situation and advantages of the Country, and soe capable of doeinge hurt and Damage to the English. Although it was well known to the whole Country that the Queen of Pamunkey and her people had never att any time betray'd or injured the English. But among the vulgar itt Matters not whether they be friends or foes soe they be Indians.[38]

Bacon beinge here mett with all the Northern forces from Patomack, Rapahaonock and those parts under the Command of Coll. Brent, they joyne together, and marchinge to the highest plantations seated upon Yorke River, were there detained by a day or two's Raine, and for fear of want of provision, Bacon addresses himselfe to the Army and speakes to them after this manner: That he feared the badness of the weather which was like to continue, would much hinder their expectation of meetinge with the Enimy soe soon as otherwise they might the weather beinge good which would cause a second loss not to be helped or prevented att present, which he feared would be in the want of Provisions, To help which in time and to lett them all know for the future he would order butt allowances; soe that beinge not farr out of the reach of the settled Plantations, all those he gave free leave to returne, the heat of whose courage and Resolutions for the suppressinge of the Heathen and Revenge the blood of their friends and acquaintances they had shed, were not above and more than the particular regard and care they had for theire Belly. Bidding them draw forth if any such were, And begone, for I am sure (said he) "where there shall be occasion for such to fight I shall find them the worst of Cowards, servinge for number and not for service, and starve my best men who would bear the Brunt of all, and dishearten others of halfe mettall from freely Engaginge" &c, amongst which only three withdrew, soe they were disarmed and sent in.

The bad weather abatinge, he proceeds on his march, and in a short time falls into a Path of the Indians which led to a maine one, which made him Imagine himselfe to be near their maine camp; but by the Scouts sent out for discovery, he found nothinge more yet than a continued large path and woods which made them breake the order of marchinge & for expedition and conveniency to march att randome. Soe continuinge all along, till this path brought them to a

---

37. On the Occaneechees, see H. Trawick Ward and R. P. Stephen Davis, "The Archaeology of the Historic Occaneechi Indians," *Southern Indian Studies*, 36-37 (1988), 1-128.
38. This sort of hostility towards friendly Indians manifested itself during King Philip's War in New England as well. See Oberg, *Dominion and Civility,* 170-173.

Point, on each side whereof and before it was a Swamp, upon which point the Pamunkey Indians had severall Cabbins.

Some Indian scouts were sent out before for discovery which were 10 Indians for the service of Bacons army, whoe beinge espied by the contrary party of Indians, they lett them come up soe nigh, as to fire at them which gave the Alarum to the English, who ridinge down in great disorder and hast to the Point beinge about halfe a mile distance off the Indians tooke to the verry edge of the Swamp, which proved soe mirrey that Bacon and his men were presently att a *ne plus ultra.*[39] Soe that the mighty deal that was done att this time was, only the takinge of a little Indian child and the Killinge of an Indian Woman.

Itt chanced that the Queen of Pamunkey with severall of her principall Indians and others were not farr off when this onset happened, and had notice of Bacons approach on her Track, of which her own Scouts had made discovery to her, who leavinge behinde her all her Goods and Indian Corne Vessels &c., and as much as she could to decline all occasion of offendinge the English, whome she ever soe much loved and reverenced, privately obscured from them, charginge her own Indians that if they found the English coming upon them that they should neither fire Gun nor draw an arrow upon them.

It soe happened in this straglinge pursuit that they lighted on an old Indian Woman that was the Queens Nurse, whom they tooke prisoner, and hoped she would be their guide to find out those Indians that fled, butt instead of leadinge that waye she lead them quite contrary, soe that followinge her the remainder of that and almost another daye, perceivinge themselves mislead by her and little likelihood of meetinge with them; Bacon gave Command to his Souldiers to knock her on the head which they did and left her dead on the waye.

This marchinge after this att Randome, yet hopinge and ayminge still to find them out, at last meet with an Indian path againe, which led them to the maine Swamp where Severall Nations of the Indians laye encamped, and striking through straight of one of them fell upon them; where the first thatt was taken was a young woman belonginge to the Nanzaticoe Indians halfe starved, and soe not able to escape.[40] The maine of them fled, and upon Search made after them, they discovered and killed two or three Indian men and as many women.

39. *"ne plus ultra."* The highest point attainable or attained. The commissioners here make the first reference to Indian scouts assisting Bacon. Bacon and his men chased the Pamunkeys into the heart of the Dragon Swamp, located between the Piankatank and Mattaponi Rivers in New Kent County.
40. The Nanzatico Indians originally lived on lands at the head of Portobacco Bay in Caroline County, Maryland. By the late 1660s they had relocated to the Northern Neck, where they suffered from close contact with pushy frontier settlers. In 1669 they had 50 bowmen, in 1702 they had 30, and by 1704 they were encircled and marginalized. The Nanzatico town at the time of Bacon's Rebellion likely was occupied by Indians from several Northern Neck and Potomac Valley Indian tribes. See Helen C. Rountree, *The*

The time of the meetinge of the new Assembly (called Bacon's Assembly) now drawing nigh, he thought itt expedient to give the starv'd and languishinge expectations of the people a little reliefe, and sends some on purpose to give them an account of the Proceedings, and the hopes they had of destroyinge the Heathen, and that he would be with them with all possible speed.

Now had Bacons high Pretences rais'd the peoples hopes to the highest pitch, and att the same time putt him on a necessity of doeinge somethinge before he returned which might not alltogeather fall short of his own vantinge. Butt being hitherto disappointed, his army, tyred, Murmuringe, Impatient, hunger starv'd, dissatisfied, he gives libertie to as many as would to returne in which the foot he had ordered to March in before him, givinge them two dayes provisions to reach if they could the English Plantations; those that were dismissed, beinge the Northerne forces commanded by Coll. Brent, the whole beinge nigh fower hundred men, with the rest he moves on hunting and beatinge the woods and Swamps up and down, att last he meets with an openinge of a tract upon high land, which he follows soe long that almost all the Provisions were spent, and forced to come to quarter allowances, and having led them far into the woods, he makes a short halt and speaks thus to them.

Gentlemen[41]

The Indifatigable pains which hitherto wee have taken doth abundantly require better success than hitherto wee have mett with. Butt there is nothinge soe hard butt by Labour and industry maye be overcome, which makes me not without hope of obtaininge my desires against the heathen in meetinge with them to quitt Scores for all their Barbarous Cruelties done us. I had rather my Carcase should lye rottinge in the woods, and Never see English Mans face againe in Virginia, than miss of doinge that service the Country expects from me, and I vowed to performe against these heathen, which should I returne not successful in some Manner to damnifie and affright them, wee should have them as much animated as the English discouraged, and my adversaries to insult and reflect on me; that my defence of the Country is but pretended and not Reall, and as they already say I have other designes and make this but my Pretence and cloke. Butt that all shall see how devoted I am to itt consideringe the great charge the Country is att in settinge me forth and the hopes & expectations they have in me. All you Gentlemen that Intend to abide with me must if need be eate chinkapins[42] and horseflesh before he returns. Which resolve I have taken,

Powhatan Indians of Virginia: Their Traditional Culture (Norman: University of Oklahoma Press, 1989), 12, 95, 120-121.

41. "A speech of Bacons when he was out on the Indian March, upon sending on some of his sick & tyred Souldiers before him." (Marginal notation in Wiseman's Original).

42. The dwarf chestnut. See Andrews, *Narratives*, 126n.

therefore desire none butt those which will soe freely adventure, the other to Returne in, and for the Better knowledge of them I will separate my Camp some distance from them Bound home.

Which done and the next morning by an hour and halfe of the sun, the one Marchinge on towards the Plantations, the other on the Indian designe, they were not three hours seperated before the Rebell Bacon falls upon the Pamunkey Indians who laye encampted beyond a smale branch of a Swamp or run of water, haveinge a Swamp on the right hand and a smale swamp or Run on the left of them, between which was a fine piece of Champion land, butt full of thickets, smalle oake, saplings, Chinkapin bushes and grape vines, which the Indians made their Covert.[43] As the onset was given they did not att all oppose butt fled, beinge followed by Bacon and his forces, Killinge and taking them Prisoners, and looking for the Plunder of the field, which was Indian Matts, Basketts, matchcotes, parcels of Wampampeag[44] and Roanoke, which is their money in Baggs, skins, furrs, pieces of Linnen broadcloth and divers sorts of English goods which the Queen had much value for; 45 captives all which upon sound of Trumpett was brought tegeather and delivered in by Bacon; the plunder and captives estimated noe lesse worth than 6 or 700 the goods beinge three or fower horse loads.

The Good Queeen of Pamunkey duringe this attaque to save her life betooke her selfe to flight with only one little Indian Boye of about ten yeare old along with her, and when she was once cominge back with designe to throw herselfe upon the Mercy of the English, she happen'd to meet with a dead Indian woman lyinge in the waye beinge one of her own Nation, which struck such terror in the Queen, that fearinge their cruelty by that gastley example, she went on her first intended way into the wild woods, where she was lost and missinge from her own people fourteen dayes, all that time beinge sustained alive only by gnawinge sometimes upon the leg of a Terrapin which the little boye found in the woods, and brought her when she was ready to dye for food and of a great while had not provisions for her support; butt noe necessity could incline her to adheare to Bacons overtures.[45]

While Bacon continued out upon this Indian March & Enterprize, the Governor had the good fortune to retake Larrimores Shipp from the Rebells, with

---

43. "Bacon falls upon the Pamunkey Indians." (Marginal notation in Wiseman's original).

44. Wampumpeag, or *wampum.* Indian currency, means of exchange, and signifier of status, manufactured from shell beads. For wampum, see Rountree, *Powhatan Indians,* 71-73.

45 For the story of Cockacoeske, see Martha W. McCartney, "Cockacoeske, Queen of Pamunkey: Diplomat and Suzeraine," in *Powhatan's Mantle: Indians in the Colonial Southeast,* ed. Peter H. Wood, Gregory A. Waselkov, and M. Thomas Hatley (Lincoln: University of Nebraska Press, 1989), 177-180.

which they designed to seize the Governor and Carry him prisoner to England, the manner of this reprisal was thus: Carver, with a Party of men beinge gonn on shore to treat with the Governor att Accomack, before which Larrimores shipp laye (the command whereof Carver had usurped) and leavinge only Bland on board with a number of men to which the Seamen of the shipp were not inferior. Larrimore sends a letter to the Governor to acquaint him how things stood on board; and that if he could send him off a Party of Gentlemen in Boats, he would enter them all att the Gunroom Ports, where havinge already secured the Enimys arms, he doubted not butt to Surprize the men and retake the ship.

The Governor privately ordered of a Party of his own under the Command of Coll. Philip Ludwell, while he capitulated with Carver in dilatory manner to give his own party time to gett on board, which they did, all things succeeding answerable to their designe. Bland beinge taken togeather with the Rest of the Rebells. Soon after Carver partinge with the Governor rows on board; they permit the Boat to come soe near, as that they might fire directly down upon her, and soe they allso commanded Carver on board & secured him; when he saw this Surprize he storm'd; tore his haire of and curst & exclaim'd at the cowardice and negligence of Bland, that had betrayed and lost all their designes.[46]

The Governor having regained this ship goes on board & in Company with the ship *Adam and Eve,* Capt. Gardner commander 16 or 17 sloopes with about 600 men in armes goes up to James Town wich he fortifies as well as he Could, and againe proclaimes Bacon and his Party Rebells and Traytors, threateninge them with the utmost Severity of Law.

Upon this Bacon calls his few men togeather, which upon a Muster made a little after the last skirmish with the Indians, with Baggatiers[47] and all, were but 136 tyred men, and told them how the Governor intended to proceed against him and them. But this rather animated and provoked new Courage in them then any wise daunted them, soe that among other cheerfull expressions they cryed out they would stand by him their Generall to the Last. Hee hearinge such harty expressions from Tyred Souldiers, who Imbraced his service and refused the Plunder he now offered them, was highly pleas'd and said to them:

46. Berkeley suspected a trap, for he heard that Larrimore had helped Bacon. Philip Ludwell persuaded the governor that he had little choice. Together, Larrimore and Ludwell took the ship on 2 September 1676. Berkeley ordered Carver hung three days later. See Washburn, *Governor and the Rebel,* 77-78; Webb, *1676,* 54-57.
47. Andrews suggests that the term might be a synonym for "Baggage Carrier." See Andrews, *Narratives,* 129n.

Gentlemen & fellow Souldiers[48]

How I am Transported with gladness to find you thus unanimous, Bold and daringe, brave and valiant. You have the victory before you fight, the conquest before Battle. I know you Can and dare fight, while they lye in their Place of Refuge; and dare not soe much as appear in the field before you. Your Hardiness shall invite all the Country along as wee march to come in and second you. The Indians wee beare along with us shall be as soe many motives to cause reliefe to be brought from every hand to you. The Ignominy of their actions cannot butt soe much reflect upon their Spiritts, as they will have noe courage to fight you. I know you have the Prayers and well wishes of all the People in Virginia while the other are loaded with their curses.

Bacon in most incensed manner Threatens to be revenged on the Governour and his party, swearinge his Souldiers to give noe quarters and professinge to scorne to take any themselves, and soe in great fury marches on towards James Town only haltinge a while about new Kent to gaine some fresh forces and sendinge to the upper parts of James River for whatt they could assist them with.[49]

Havinge increased his number to about 300 in all he proceeds directly to Towne, as he marches the people on the high wayes comminge forth prayinge his happiness and Railinge against the Governor and his Party, and seeing the Indian Captives which they led along as in a shew of Triumph, gave him many thanks for his Care & endeavours for their preservatione, bringinge him forth fruit and victuals for his Souldiers, the women telling him if he wanted assistance they would come themselves after him.

Intelligence cominge to Bacon that the Governor had good in Town a 1000 man force well armed and resolute, "I shall see that," saith hee, "for I am now goinge to try them." Beinge told that there was a Party of Horse of the Governors about 60 scountinge out to observe his motion, he smilingly answered hee feared them not cominge soe neare him as to Know how he did.

Butt he nott heedlesse of all Reports, nor in himselfe too shure of their Cowardise, draws up his men in Green Spring Old Fields, hee tells them that if ever they will fight they will doe itt now, before saith hee "I march up to their workes, havinge all the advantages of ground, places, retreats, their men fresh and unwearied, and not whatt advantages saith Bacon to us soe few and weake and tyred. Butt I speake not this to discourage you butt to acquaint you as you

48. "A Speech of Bacons to his Souldiers goinge to James Towne against the Governour." (Marginal notation in Wiseman's original).
49. According to Andrews, Bacon marched his forces from New Kent County down the Chickahominy River to Green Spring, where Berkeley's house stood. From thence, Bacon and his men marched on to Jamestown. See Andrews, *Narratives*, 129n.

shall find whatt advantages they will lose and neglect, which" sayes he "if they had the Courage to maintaine, that which they declare against us as Rebells, Traytors &c their allegiance would be butt faintly defended to lett us take that which they might command. Come on, my hearts of Gold, hee that dyes in the field lyes in the bedd of Honour."[50]

In the eveninge Bacon and his Small tyred body of men, his forlorne Marchinge some distance before, comes into Paspahayes old fields,[51] & advancinge on horseback himselfe on the Sandy Beach before the Town, commands the Trumpett to sound, fires his Carbyne, dismounts, surveys the ground and orders a French worke to be cast up.[52]

All this night is spent in fallinge of trees, cuttinge of Bushes and throwinge up of earth, that by the help of the moon light they had made their French before daye, although they had but two axes and two spades in all to performe this work with.

About daye breake next morninge six of Bacons Souldiers ran up to the Pallasades of the Town, and fired Briskly upon the guard, retreatinge safely without any damage.

Att first as is reported the Governor gave Command that not a gun should be fired against Bacon or his Party upon paine of death, pretendinge to be loath to spill blood, and much more to be the Beginner of itt, supposinge the Rebells would hardly be soe audacious as to fire a gun against him; but that Bacon would rather have sent to him and sought his reconciliation, soe that some waye or other might have bin found out for the preventinge a Warr, to which the Governor is said to have shewn some inclination upon the account of the service Bacon had performed as he heard against the Indian Enimys, and that he had brought severall Indian prisoners along with him, and especially for that there were severall Ignorant people that were deluded and drawn into Bacons Party, and thought of noe other designe than the Indian Warr only & soe knew not what they did.

Butt Bacon pretendinge distrust of the Governor was so farr from all thoughts of a Treaty that he animates his men against it, tellinge them that he knew the party to be as Perfidious as Cowardly, and that there was noe trust to be reposed in such, who thinke itt noe treachery by any ways to suppress them, and for his Tendernesse of shedding blood which the Governor pretends, and preventinge a warr sayes Bacon "there are some here, that know itt to be noe longer since than last weeke; that he himselfe commanded to be fired against us

---

50. "September 13th, 1676: The siege of James Town. Note: Bacon's men had marched that day betwixt 30 & 40 miles to come to James Town." (Marginal notation in Wiseman's original).

51. The Paspahegh homeland stood west of the mouth of Chickahominy Creek in James City County. See Rountree, *Powhatan Indians*, 11.

52. Some kind of enfilade, presumably.

by boats which the Governor sent up and downe to places where the Country's provisions was kept for Maintenance of the Indian Warr, to fetch them awaye to support a war amongst our selves, and wounded some of us which was done by Sorrell, which were against the designe of convertinge these stores to soe contrary use and intention of whatt they were raised for by the People.[53]

Bacon moveinge down towards the Towne and the shipps beinge brought before the Sandy beach the better to annoye the Ennimy in case of any attempt of theirs to storme the Pallasadoes, upon a signall given from the town the shipps fire their great Gunns, and att the same time they lett fly their small shott from the Pallasadoes. Butt that small sconce that Bacon had caused to be made in the night of Trees, Brush and earth under which they lay soe defended them that the shotte did them noe damage att all, and was returned back as fast from this little fortress. In the heat of this firing Bacon commands a party of his men to make every one of his Faggott and putt itt before his Breast, and come and laye them in order on Top of the French on the outsides, and att the end, to enlarge and make good the fortification, which they did, and orders more spades to be gott to help make itt yet more defensible, and the better to observe their motion ordered a constant sentinel in the dayetime on top of a brick chimney hard by to discover from thence how the men in Town mounted and dismounted, posted and reposted, drew on and off, what number they were and how they moved.

Hitherto there happened noe other action than fireinge great and smale shott att distances. Butt by their moveinge and drawings up about Town Bacon understood they intended a Sally and accordingly prepares to Receive them, drawinge up his men to the most advantageous Places he could, and now expected them, but they were observed to draw off againe for some time, and was resolved to enter the Town with them as they retreated, as Bacon expected & foretold they would doe. In this posture of Expectation Bacons forces continued an hour till the watchman gave notice that they were drawn off against in Town, soe upon this Bacons forces did soe too.

Noe sooner[54] were they all on the Rebells side gone off and squandered, butt all on a suddaine a Sally is made by the Governors Party, yett in this great hurry and disorder on t'other side, they soe received them that they forced them to retreat in as much confusion as they found them to the shame of their Brag-

---

53. Captain Robert Sorrell did not survive the rebellion. His wife, Rebecca, petitioned the House of Burgesses for relief. She had lost her husband, and her property had been plundered by the rebels. The Burgesses voted to allow her "out of the publique Levye, foure thousand pounds of tobacco & Caske, and what of her Goods can be founde be returned to her." See McIlwaine, ed., *Journal of the House of Burgesses,* 70. Wiseman included at this point in his narrative a marginal notation reading: "The Provisions raised by acte of Assembly to supply the Indian Warr is by the Governors Party forceably taken awaye to maintaine a civill warr against the givers of itt."
54. "September 16." (Marginal notation in Wiseman's original).

ginge pretences of valour & Resolution att their undertakinge this attaque, and of the cause they defended, who yet call themselves the Loyall party, and yet before their Governor, and now begin to importune him to quit the Town. Butt wee cannot give a Better account, not yet a truer, soe farr as we are informed of this action than what this letter of Bacon's relates:

Captain William Cookson   From the Camp att Sandy Beach
Captain Edward Skewon[55]   September 17th, 1676[56]

Before wee drew up to James Towne a party of theirs fled before us with all hast for Feare: with a small party of horse (beinge dark in the eveninge), wee rode up to the point att Sandy beach and sounded a defiance which they answered, after which with some difficulty for want of Materialls wee intrenched our selves for the night & men with a great deale of Bravery ran up to their works and fired briskly and retreated without loss. The next morninge our men without the workes gave them some Braves and contempts to try their Mettle; upon which they fired their great guns with smale shott to clear their workes; butt our men recovered the workes, and wee are now intrenched very secure both from the shipps and Town.

Yesterdaye they made a sally with horse and foot in the van, the forlorne being made up of such men as they had compelled to serve; they came up with a narrow front, and pressinge very close upon one anothers shoulders, that the forlorne might be their shelter, our men received them soe warmly that they retired in great disorder, throwinge down their armes left upon the Bay; as allso their drum and dead men; two of which our men brought into our Trenches and buried with severall of their armes. This day wee shewed them our Indian Captives upon the workes. The people come in from all parts most bravely, and we are informed that great multitudes of men are up for us in Isle of Wight and Nancymond, and only expect orders as allso the South side of the River over against us in great numbers. They shew themselves such Pitifull cowards, [so] contemptable as you would admire them. It is said that Hubert Farrell[57] is shott in the Belly, Hartwell[58] in the Legg, Smith in the head, Mathewes with others,

---

55. Little more is known about Skewon than what is included in this document. Cookson was executed by Berkeley's supporters. See Andrews, ed., *Narratives*, 133n. For the trial of Cookson before Berkeley and his council, see H. R. McIlwaine, ed., *Minutes of the Council and General Court of Colonial Virginia*, 2nd ed., (Richmond: Virginia State Library, 1979), 454.

56. "Bacon's Letter from the Campe." (Marginal notation in Wiseman's original).

57. A member of Berkeley's party who Bacon denounced in his declaration against the government. He survived his wounds and led forces after the rebels. See Andrews, ed., *Narratives*, 133-134n.

58. Bacon here refers to William Hartwell, who with force and viciousness helped crush the rebellion later that fall. Ibid., 134n. Evidence of Hartwell's plundering of Governor

as yet wee have noe certaine account. They took a solemne oath when they Sall-eyed out either to Rout us, or never Returne; But you know how they use to keepe them: I believe the Shipps are weary of their Bargaine finding their shotts all inconsiderable. This is our present Intelligence; be sure to take care of the Upper Parts against the Pyrats, and bid the men be courageous for that all the country is bravely resolute. I had almost forgot to tell you that Chamberlaine[59] out of a Bravado came with a Sloope, and lay under our workes, and with abundance of vaunting and railing expressions, threatned great things, but finding it too warme was feigne to take his Boate and leave his Sloope; Wee guesse hee was wounded by his ceasing to Baule beinge much jeer'd by our men which you know hee is not us'd to doe. Be sure you Incourage the Souldiers in that upper parts, and lett them know whatt a Pittifull Enimy wee have to deale with. Wee have just now two great guns come for our Battery, which they are much a fraid of as I am Informed. This is the most of our present news; of other Passages by the Messenger you maye be informed.

Your Reall Friend
Nath: Bacon.

After this Successlesse Sally the courages and numbers of the Governors party abated much, and Bacons men thereby became more bold and daringe; in soe much that Bacon could scarce keep them from immediately fallinge to storme and enter the Town, butt he being as wary as they rash, perswaded them from the attempt, biddinge them keep their courage untill such time as he found occasion and opportunity to make use of them, tellinge them he doubted not to take the Town without loss of a man; & that one of their lives was of more value to him then the whole world. Havinge planted his great guns, he takes the wives and female relations of such Gentlemen as were now in the Governors service against him (whome he had caused to be brought to the workes) and places them in the face of his Enimy as Bulworks for their Battery, by which Policy he promised himself and doubtless had a good advantage, yett had the Governors party by much the odds in number besides the advantage of time & place. Butt soe great was their Cowardize & Baseness of the generality of Sir William Berkeleys party; beinge most of them men intent only upon plunder, or compelled and

Berkeley's opponents can be found in the petitions of Thomas Bubby, Richard Clarke, and John Dean, all of James City County, Letters and Papers Concerning American Plantations, 20 April–22 June 1677, CO 1/40, 2-5, 7 (VCRP), as well as the petitions of Thomas Glover, Andrew Goedion, and many others, in CO 1/40, 10-17, 19-27, 29 (VCRP). See, as well, Chapter 7, below.

59. According to Philip Alexander Bruce, in his *Institutional History of Virginia in the Seventeenth Century* (New York: G. P. Putnam's Sons, 1910), 1: 507, Thomas Chamberlaine of Henrico, whose house Bacon's men sacked, was "cursed with a passionate temper that brooked neither opposition nor restraint."

hired into his service; that of all att last there was only some 20 Gentlemen willinge to stand by him, the rest whome the hopes or promise of plunder brought thither, being now in hast all to be gonn to secure what they had gott; Soe that Sir William Berkeley himselfe who undoubtedly would rather have dyed, on the place, then thus deserted itt, what with importunate and resistlesse solicitations, of all was att last over perswaded, nay hurried awaye against his own will to Accomack, and forced to leave the Town to the Mercy of the Enimye. Soe fearfull of Discovery they are, that for secrecy they imbarque and weigh anchor in the night and silently fall downe the River, thus flyinge from the face of an Enimy that during this siege which lasted one whole weeke, lay exposed to much more hardship, want & inaccommodation than themselves, besides the fatigue of a long march att their first coming to Towne, for this very service was supposed to be the Death of Bacon, who by lying in a wett Season in his Trenches before Towne contracted the Disease whereof hee not long after dyed. Bacon havinge early Intelligence of the Governor and his Party quitting the Town the night before, enters it without any opposition; and soldier like considering of what importance a Place of that Refuge was, and might againe bee to the Governor and his Party, instantly resolves to laye itt levell with the Ground, and the same night he became possessed of itt sett fire to Town, Church and Statehouse, wherein were the Country's Records, which Drummond had privately convey'd thense and preserved from Burninge. The towne consisted of 12 new Brick houses, besides a considerable number of Frame houses with brick chimneys, all which will not be rebuilt as is computed for fifteen hundred thousand weight of tobacco. Now those who had soe lately deserted itt, as they rid a little below in the River in the shipps and sloops to their shame and regret beheld by night the flames of the Town, which they soe basely forsakinge, had made a Sacrifice to ruine. Bacon goes next down to Green Spring, and duringe his stay thereabouts draws up a protest or oath against the Governor and his Party, which is said to be Imposed on the people, and taken by about 600 at once in Gloster County, and allso forced upon others in severall parts of the Country & is as followeth:

Bacon's Oath of Fidelity

Whereas Sir William Berkeley Knight late Governor of Virginia hath in a most Barbarous and abominable manner exposed and betrayed our lives, and for greedinesse of sordid gaine did defer our just defence and hinder all the Loyall endeavours of his Majesties faithfull subjects; and further when the Country did raise a sufficient force for the effectual proceeding against the Indian Enemy, he did, contrary to all Equity and Justice and the tenors of his commission, endeavour to oppose the said Forces by himself and the Assembly sett forth: of which attemts being severall tymes defeated by the Peoples abhorrence of soe Bloody a design he left the country in a small vessel, it being unknown to all People to what parts of the world he did repair, and whereas our army upon his departure betaking themselves to the care of the Frontiers did march out against the Indians and obtain soe great a victory, as hath in a manner finished all the disaster and almost Resettled the country in a happy Peace, yet notwithstanding Sir William Berkeley with Forces raised in Accomack, did invade the country with acts of hostility, with all intentions to persecute the said Army with these aforesaid reasons, as also having betray'd his Trust to the King by flying from his seate of Judicature, and acting wholly contrary to his commission, We protest against him unanimously as a Traytor and most pernitious Enemy to the Publick, and further we sweare that in all places of his Majestyes Colony of Virginia wee will oppose and prosecute him with all our Endeavours by all acts of hostility as occasion shall present, and further whereas Plotting and wishing in his heart a totall Ruine and Destruction of this Poore colony he hath Endeavoured to set the heart of our Soveraigne against us by fals Information and Lyes, requesting Forces of his Majestie wherewith to compel and subdue us, hindering, interecepting, and preventing all our Remonstrances for Peace, which might have gone home in our Justification, as also hindering our sending home of agents in the Peoples behalf which was the most humble and earnest request of the People at first.[60] We doe further declare and sweare that wee think it absolutely consisting with our allegiance and Loyalty to treat with and discourse with the said Forces and commissioners with all submission to his Majesty. But otherwise if it shall soe prove that notwithstanding all intreaties and offers wee shall make, they shall offer to land by Force, in our owne Defense to fly together as in a common calamity and jointly with the present army now under the command of General Bacon, to stand or fall in the Defense of him and the country in soe just a cause, and in all places to oppose their Proceedings (onely untill such time as his Majesty by our agents shall fully understand the miserable case of the country, and the Justice of our Proceedings). Which most just request if they shall refuse and by force endeavour to enter the Country, wee are resolv'd to uphold the Country as long as we can and never to absent and joyne with any such army whatever, and lastly in case of utmost extremity rather than submit to any soe miserable a slavery (when none can longer defend ourselves, our lives and Liberties) to acquit the Colony rather than submit to soe unheard of Injustice, and this wee all sweare in the presence of Almighty God as unfeignedly and freely as ever wee desire of him for happiness to come.

By the Generall

---

60. On 3 June 1676, Berkeley wrote to Secretary of State Henry Coventry, to ask that a replacement be sent to govern the colony. "I am not able to support my selfe at this Age six months longer," Berkeley wrote, "and thereof on my Knees I beg his sacred majesty would send a more Vigorous Governour." See Berkeley to Coventry, 3 June 1676, in *The Old Dominion in the Seventeenth-Century: A Documentary History of Virginia, 1606-1689*, ed. Warren M. Billings (Chapel Hill: University of North Carolina Press, 1975), 272.

The Governor and his forces being gonn, Bacon orders the shore to be guarded all along to observe their motion and as they moved to follow them and prevent them from landinge or having any provisions sent on board them. Bacon now begins to shew a more merciless and absolute authority than formerly plunderinge and Imprisoninge many, & condemninge some by Power of Martiall Law: Butt among all made only one Exemplary: (to witt) one James Wilkenson that had fled from his Colours with one Mr. Clough Minister of James Town[61] was condemned to dye butt the first onely was executed, which as a souldier wee look on to be more an act of his Policy than cruelty, to prevent and awe others from disserting hum, wee not observing him to have bin Bloodely inclined in the whole progresse of this Rebellion.[62] Intercession beinge made for Mr. Clough, Captaine Hawkins, and Major West,[63] Bacon proposed to accept of Carver, Bland & Farloe[64] in exchange for them, butt it was not accepted, neverthelesse none of the first three were put to death by Bacon. Now Bacon findinge that his Souldiers Insolenceys growinge soe great and intolerable to the people of whome they made noe due distinction, and findinge their actings to reflect on himselfe, he did not only betake himselfe to a strict discipline over his men, butt allso to more moderate courses himself, releasing some Prisoners, pardoning others that were condemned, and callinge those to account against whom any complaints came for seizures or Plundering their Estates without his order or knowledge.

This Prosperous Rebell, now concludinge the daye his own, marcheth with his army into Gloster County intendinge to visit all the Northerne parts of Virginia to understand the state of them, and to settle affaires after his own measures, in which wee are informed he proposed this method:

1.   One committee for Settlinge the South side of James River, and enquiringe into the spoiles that had bin committed there.

2.   Another Committee to be allwayes with the Army, to inquire into the cause of all seizures & to give orders for doeinge the same, and to regulate the rudeness, disorder, spoile and wast of the Souldiers, as they had formerly committed.

61. The Reverend John Clough was an active supporter of Sir William Berkeley. See Andrews, ed., *Narratives*, 138n.

62. "One shott to death by Bacon for flyinge from his Colours." (Marginal notation in Wiseman's original).

63. Thomas Hawkins, Jr., lived in Rappahannock County. Captain John West hailed from New Kent. See Andrews, ed., *Narratives*, 138n.

64. George Farlow, who had fought in England for Cromwell, was, according to Berkeley, "very active in this rebellion, and taken with forty men coming to surprise me at Accomack." See Andrews, ed., *Narratives*, 138n.

3.   And another Committed to be appointed only for the management and proceding of the Indian Warr, & givinge dispatches for affairs relatinge to itt.

Butt before he could arrive att the Perfection of his designes, which none but the eye of Omniscience could penetrate, providence did that which noe other hand durst or at least did doe, and cutt him off.

He lay sick att one Mr. Pates in Gloster County of the Bloody flux and as Mr. Pate himselfe affirms accompanied by a Lousey Disease, soe that Swarmes of Vermine that bred in his Body, he could not destroy butt by throwinge his shirts into the fire as often as he shifted himselfe. He dyed very much dissatisfied in mind, enquiring ever and anon after the arrival of the frigatts and forces from England, & askinge if his guards were strong about the house.

After Bacon's death one Joseph Ingram tooke up his Command, a man more spruce and finical than wise or valiant,[65] being butt a stranger in Virginia, and came over butt the yeare before this Rebellion; under whose conduct the faction began to fall into severall parties and opinions which gave Sir William Berkeleys party opertunity by these diversions to surprise the Rebells in small bodies as they sculked up and down the Country.[66] Butt the maine service that was done for reducinge the Rebells to their obedience was done by the Seamen and Commanders of shipps then ridinge in the Rivers, especially the Generall Surrender at West point of those headed by Ingram, and Walklate, which was managed and concluded by Captain Grantham to the disgust of those Gentlemen of the Governors Party, because Sir William Berkeley had not made them concerned in soe considerable a piece of service.[67]

After Ingram had submitted to the Governor, who then lay on board Martyns ship in Yorke River, Lawrence that notorious Rebell fled, who was the first man that sett fire to James Towne by Burninge his own house;[68] some others

---

65. Andrews omitted this phrase from his version. The word "spruce," as used in the seventeenth century, implied "neat," while "finical" meant "over-nice or particular, affectedly fastidious, excessively punctilious or precise" (OED).

66. "The Assembly observing the late Rebellion to be sett on foot by newcomers, have now enacted that noe man shall receive advancement tillhe has bin 3 years in Virginia, Bacon beinge preferred to a Councillorship att his verry first coming over." (Marginal notation in Wiseman's original).

67. If Ingram did succeed Bacon as leader of the rebellion, Walklett likely became his second in command. We know surprisingly little about Ingram. Prior to his surrender, Ingram's forces had attempted to capture men loyal to Governor Berkeley. Historian Stephen Saunders Webb argues, in fact, that Ingram's army was more formidable than the commissioners recognized: it did not break up after Bacon's death, but rather went into winter quarters as was typical of seventeenth-century armies. See Webb, *1676*, 84.

68. Richard Lawrence, an Oxford-educated burgess based at Jamestown, detested Berkeley and the governor's circle, men he considered *nouveaux riches*, who did not deserve

were taken prisoners after they had layd down their arms, and the rest went home in Peace. Soe that about the 16 of January 1676/7, the whole Country had submitted to the Governor, and the two and twentieth he came home to House att Green Spring and had issued out new writs of Summons for the conveninge a free assembly att his own House, the Statehouse being ruined with the Rest of James Town.

The Particulars of this foregoing Narrative being what wee could collect or observe from the most credible disinterested persons, most authentique papers, Records, Reports, and the publique grievances of the respective Countyes of Virginia; wee have with all Integrity of mind and the best ofour understandings, without favour or Partiallity, selected and sett down what wee thought most consonant to Truth & reality, & on the other hand rejected whatever wee found or suspected to be false or improbable: And doe here according to his Majesties Royall Commands and our own duties, most humbly leave itt to his Majesties most prudent Consideration and Judgement.

Document 2

A true and faithfull account in what condition wee found your Majesties Collony of Virginia: Of our transactions duringe our stay there, and how wee left itt; Togeather with our most humble opinion, what means will best Conduce to the firme groundinge and securinge the future peace thereof.

Upon our 1st arrival within the Capes of Virginia, January 29 1676/7, we had advice of the death of that grand Rebell Nathaniel Bacon; his Burninge James Town, & of the Governors his returne to his house at green springe. The same daye wee dispatched letters to Sir William Berkeley to advertise him of our arrival & such other perticulers as were necessary for his Knowledge; upon receipt whereof the Governor was pleased to come on board the *Bristoll* then ridinge in Kequetan in James River where wee read him our own Commission & did him the severall instruments under the great seale and privy Signett, to-

the lofty positions that they held. His commitment to the rebellion is evidenced by his decision to torch his own house when the rebels fled from the capital. See Webb, *1676*, 7, 26, 64. An account of Lawrence's estate is in the Proceedings and Reports of the Commissioners for Enquiring into Virginian Affairs and Settling Virginian Grievances, 1677, CO 5/1371, 247ro (VCRP). For a scholarly view that emphasizes the importance of men like Lawrence in Bacon's Rebellion, see Bernard W. Bailyn, "Politics and Social Structure in Virginia," reprinted in *Colonial America: Essays in Politics and Social Development,* eds. Stanley N. Katz, John M. Murrin and Douglas Greenberg, 4th ed. (New York: McGraw-Hill, 1993). For a refutation of Bailyn's thesis, see Jon Kukla, "Order and Chaos in Early America: Political and Social Stability in Pre-Restoration Virginia," *American Historical Review,* 90 (April 1985), 275-298.

geather with the Printed proclamations, inquiries, & former instructions, as allso certaine interlocutory heads in writinge; which wee had prepared in order to your Majesties Immediate Service, for the landinge and quarteringe the Souldiers, and preventinge any demurrage to your Majestie as allso to desire, an answer and account of such other matters as appertained to our enquiry. Upon further conference with him wee understood that he had executed severall persons for the late rebellion by power of Martiall law, and gave us a list of their names; but wee resolved for the future to desist from that course, and to lett the laws run againe in their old Channell; Pleadinge a necessity before of tryinge and condemninge by Martiall Law; for that he doubted whether a Legall jury would have found them guilty; of the contrary of which he was afterwards sufficiently convinced when he saw upon the Tryalls held upon your Majesties Commission of Oyer and Terminer, that there was not a Prisoner that came to the Barr, but what was brought in guilty by the Jury. Att first wee found the people under a Generall consternation, by reason the number of the unconcerned in the late defection were very soe few, which in our sense served to urge a kind of necessity of openinge to them your Majesties Royall act of Grace and forgiveness, when the whole body of a Country lay tremblinge and in panic in this perticuler, & many for feare ready to forsake their habitations, & not at such a time to stifle and conceal them from the people; & further because severall Gentlemen of Virginia, had seen and brought your Majesties proclamation printed in England, soe that wee could not conceive amiss for the Governor to publish them to your people. He told us he would draw and publish a proclamation of his own with such exceptions as he had latitude to make; which he said att first should not exceed 8 persons. After we had opened our own commission for hearinge and examininge grievances wee found the people generally complaininge & petitioninge against illegal seizures of their estates, before and without any warrant, Tryall, Charge or conviction; & severall that came in and submitted themselves upon the governors proclamation of pardon and Indemptnity; that they were Imprisoned afterwards, & their estates wholly taken from them or large fines and compositions paid for them. For soe it was that seeinge none did escape beinge found guilty, condemned and hanged that putt themselves upon Tryall, there happened to be soe much of guilt or fear in most men, that there was not a man but would much rather acquiess to have any fine imposed upon him, before he would venture to sand by his Tryall, soe that at last this was the question to criminalls, will you stand your Tryall or be fined & sentenced as the court shall thinke fitt, which latter was for the foresaid reasons laid hold on by all, and a fine laid arbitrary wise without a Jury or Power by your Majesties Instructions, or other Royall instruments, but quite contrary of restitution with Pardon, for soe wee observed of words to run, and were not wantinge to tell Sir William Berkeley, as well publickly as by letter, that wee humbly conceived this course contrary to your Majesties royall intentions and that your Majestie had either pardoned all things or nothinge of penalty and punishment and that there was noe medium. Wee also observed some of the Loyall party that satt on the bench with us at the Courte to be soe fierce and fierry in impeachinge, accusinge, revilinge the prisoners at the Barr with that inveteracy as if they had bin the worst of the witnesses rather than Justices of the Commission; both accusinge & undermininge at the same time. This severe way of proceeding beinge represented to the Assembly they voted an address to the Governor that he would desist from any further sanguinary punishment for none could tell when and where it would terminate, soe the Governor was prevailed on to hold his hand after the hanginge of 23, eight of which wee sate att the tryall & condemnation of and advised that they should be executed in their own countryside with small guards to try the temper of the people which proved all peaceable. In the whole course of the proceedings wee have avoided to receive any complaints of publike grievances, butt by and under the hands of the most credible, sober and loyall persons of each county; with caution that they did not doe itt in any mutinous manner & without any mixture of their old leaders, but in each sort as might become dutifull subjects and sober rationall men to present. Whereas wee did upon the dayly complaints of divers of your Majesties Subjects by severall letters presented to Sir William Berkeley that itt was a most apparent contradiction to the common course of the Laws of England to seize or dispose of any mans estate before a lawfull Tryall and conviction of the crime and shew'd him the opinion of the learned Lord Cook positively against itt; whereof he tooke little caution or notice, butt writ us word that he appealed to Your Majestie and most Honorable Privy Councill, & the learned Judges of the Law. Soe wee desired him that all estates forfeited or conceived to be forfeited of any person as well as such as without any tryall have died in actuall rebellion, as of those that have already suffered death might be fairly inventoried and appraised after the just value at the time of seizure, good security given for the preservation of Your Majesties right in the said forfeitures, untill Your Majesties Royall pleasure should be Knowen in such cases. And Sir William Berkeleys appeale answered, which he not doeinge, we Impowered certaine persons under oath to enquire into & report to us the true number, value and nature of such forfeited estates, dispossessinge none in whose custody they were, but only Taking to your Majesties use in the mean time; which bonds were delivered to Secretary Ludwell and are 15 in number, and the first precedent of this nature was made by Sir William Berkeley himselfe by grantinge the petition of the widow Bacon to enjoy the Estate of her late Husband under the conditions before specified, to which he desired and had our convenient assent.[69] And for other estates seized by the Governors party as

69. In other words, Berkeley asked the commissioners to approve his grant to Elizabeth Bacon, the rebel leader's wife. Elizabeth Bacon is an interesting woman. She traveled to Virginia with her husband in 1674, a man she married in opposition to her father's wishes. She was disinherited and disowned, and her letters home reflect the loneliness and isolation that could characterize life on the early American frontier. For her views of

by severall petitions was to us suggested, and by oaths approved doe apear, wee allso made one Generall rule or order, that such persons in whose hands any such goods, Cattles, slaves or servants were, should give a true Inventory & security for the same till your Majestie shall be graciously pleased to determine concerninge the restitution thereof accordinge as your Majestie and your most wise Judgement shall soe cause. And wee were then and still are of opinion, with all humble satisfaction to your Majesties Royall will and pleasure, that such estates, goods & things as were plundered or forceably seized during the late rebellion and especially since the layinge down of armes att West point from or by either party should be restored on both sides, if the same were to be found in specie:[70] and also declared that the fininge of people without any Tryall, Jury or conviction as delinquents, and of some without summons or hearinge was and is in our opinion against the Law, and that it looked like partiality and Injustice to fine others while Ingram, Walklett, & Langston had free and full pardon from the governor without any fine or other punishment: Who made full restitution of what they had plundered as well from the Indians as of English; the Indian plunder excepted which Sir William Berkeley called his though taken by the Rebell Walklett, and had given him againe for his good services. As to the retrenchinge the great Sallary paid to the members of the assembly upon our especiall Instance in a publike letter of ours to the Governor, Councill and Burgesses, and reinstance afterwards; they have reduced to as low a proportion as itt could possibly be brought to for the members to support their ordinary charge att. Butt also that most important affaire of the Indian Peace, the breach and want whereof had soe apparently involved that Collony into such misery, daily dred, heavy taxes, & occasioned such generall dissatisfaction among your Majesties Subjects, and was the ground of the Rebellion itselfe. Sir William Berkeley nor the Assembly made not the least stopp afterwards nor progresse in itt, although wee had soe earnestly recommended & pressed the necessity of itt, by our Publike letter at the meeting of the Assembly, and reinstance afterwards, as also your Majesties by your own private instructions requiringe his endeavours with our assistances therein, which seeinge he had not done upon his departure the Honorable Herbert Jeffreys your Majesties now Governor with our best advice and assistance hath soe effected and performed, as not only the neighbour Indians that then signed to the peace, are highly pleased and satisfied with it, But the equality and justice of itt arrivinge to the knowledge of other remote Indians, and lately our implacable and most treacherous enemyes, they allso of their own accord come in and expressed themselves very desirous and foreward to be included in the same leaug and amity. Butt the Governor being sick a further time was prefixt for meeting on this occasion. Lastly, wee shall lett your Majestie

frontier life, see her letter to her sister, Egerton MSS 2395, folio 550, British Library, London, (VCRP) and Oberg, *Dominion and Civility,* 174-176.

70. *Specie.* Real money, as opposed to paper, in actual coin (OED).

know in what condition wee left your Majesties collony of Virginia as so the
peace & resettlement of itt wee humbly conceive it to be secure and duringe &
that this good peace with the Indians, which wee trust allso is like to be a long
and lastinge one will not a little conduce thereto; the people of Virginia from the
great charge they formerly underwent & damage sustained by reason of a warr
with the Indians, beinge now made sensible how much peace with them is their
safe security and Interest. As to the condition wee left the army therein, truly it
was but bad, for at the cominge awaye the daye before we sailed, the Commis-
sary Mr. Needler[71] beinge on board us told us that in Captain Middleton's company there was about 150 such men & the officers all sick and that the like number of sick were in every other company, and that their provisions were soe far
spent that had they bin able to march they must of necessity have bin quartered
att large in the Country. The like calamity attended your Majesties seamen, reducing them to the strange degree of weakness by the violence and various
manner of seizinge them that it is almost impossible to express: Soe that we had
scarce men to get up our ankers, and not above six weeks provisions left us, and
the Country not able to supply us havinge consulted the ablest most discreet
Gentlemen of Virginia in order to it, who all agreed it was impossible to it as
your Majesties service required, & soe noe body would undertake itt. As to any
fear of likelihood of future commotions or insurrections, there is not the least
ground or appearance, butt perhaps of some petty breaches of the peace among
the disagreeing parties that maye happen by reason of recriminations & mutuall
aggravations frequently used on both sides: for preventions whereof and securinge a good a firme peace for the future in that your Majesties collony, wee shall
with all Humility lay down our best opinions and judgements as followeth: 1st:
That a generall Penal act of oblivion by your Majesties command prescribed and
drawn here[72] and sent over to the Governor and Assembly of Virginia and they
enjoyned to pass & publish the same which of themselves they will never doe.
2^{ly}: That a good fort beinge orderd to be built at James Town the ancient and
most convenient place for one, as allso for the state howse where the brick
worke may be yet serviceable that your Majestie will be pleased to order that
ordering of both there, though by a single supernumerary vote of last assembly
they were for removinge the Town and State howse elsewhere; That your Majestie will please that a certaine number of the seasoned souldiers may remain in
Garrison there for maintayninge whereof without being a charge to your Majestie or a burdeninge to the people; wee most humbly propose that the quitt rents
of the Colonies which is of small account to your Majestie and comes not to
your exchecquer, maye goe and in use to the end and purpose proposed, as allso
that your Majestie would be pleased to order the Assembly to lay such an Impo-

71. Thomas Needler, part of Jeffrey's headquarters staff, who served as deputy paymas-
ter.
72. By the summer of 1677 Berry and Moryson had returned to England.

sition on liquors imported there, as in your Majesties Island of Barbados is raised & imploy'd for the like and which will both build a fort and maintaine the Souldiers therein:[73] 3[ly]: That for the future the Virginia shipps goe in fleets every yeare accompanied with one of his Majesties frigatts, untill such time as the peace of the Collony be soe firmly grounded as not to be shaken: 4[ly]: Thatt the act of attainder past by the last assembly be by your Majesties command repealed and taken of to all those that are not excepted in your Majesties proclamation, and such as are yet out in Rebellion & fled from Justice, which act had not bin made nor consented to, but that the Governor refused also to pass an act called an act of oblivion which in effect is little more than by name one. 5[ly]: That the Independent plantations of Carolina and Maryland, beinge att present very prejudiciall, will in time prove utterly destructive to your Majesties interest & Government in Virginia, therefore wee most humbly proposed that with a Salve[74] to the right of the Honorable proprietors, the Jurisdictions & Power of Government maye soe reside in your Majestie that they maye be readily obedient to all order, rule & process of Your Majestie and most Honorable Councill, else your Majestie will not only find you have given away soe much land, but soe many Subjects also, and the next Generation there will not know or own the Royall Power; if their writs, tryalls, and process be permitted to continue as they now are, in the names of the Proprietors, and their oaths of fealty without any Salve of allegiance to your Majestie and it is dayly how that not only men's Servants, butt allso Runaway Rouges and Rebells fly to Carolina on the Southward as their common Subterfuge and lurkinge place; and when wee remanded some of the late Rebells by letters could not have them sent back to us.[75]

Wee should not have presumed to present this to your Majestie did wee not confidently believe in our humble opinion and judgements that what wee have informed or most humbly propounded to your Majestie is true, & for the Peace and happy settlement and advantage of your Majesties Collony of Virginia,

---

73. The commissioners here refer to the 4.5% duty the colonial assembly imposed on all "dead" commodities exported from the island of Barbados. Sugar, the most lucrative West Indian export, was not considered alive. In return for this grant of revenue from the assembly, Charles II pledged that all funds raised would remain in the island to pay for its administration and defense.

74. *Salve.* An act or agent intended to heal (OED).

75. On the early history of Carolina, see Peter H. Wood, *Black Majority: Negroes in Colonial South Carolina from 1670 through The Stono Rebellion*, (New York: Knopf, 1974); Converse D. Clowse, *Economic Beginnings in Colonial South Carolina, 1670-1730* (Columbia: University of South Carolina Press, 1971); James H. Merrell, *The Indians' New World: The Catawbas and Their Neighbors from European Contact through the Era of Removal* (Chapel Hill: University of North Carolina Press, 1989); M. Eugene Siemans, *Colonial South Carolina: A Political History, 1663-1763* (Chapel Hill: University of North Carolina Press, 1966).

which as it has bin the unwearied endeavours, is the hearty prayers and desires
of

July 20th 1677   Your Majesties most dutifull, faithfull
                                            Subjects and Servants

                                            John Berry
                                            Francis Morison

Document 3

A Review, Breviary, & Conclusion drawne from the foregoing Narrative, being
a summary Account of the late Rebellion in Virginia

The First occasions of the late Commotion among his Majesties distressed
Subjects of Virgina was meerly upon the account of selfe preservation against
the Indians who committed frequent Murders & almost daily Incursion, & depredations on the Inhabitants of that Colony.

> The slow & Dilatory proceedings to provide for the public
> safety.
>
> The great & heavy Imposition of Fort Money, & the little or
> noe defence or use they proved of to the Country
> against the Indians.
>
> The Pressure of the Patent money, a necessary (but grievous)
> tax, considering the generall poverty of the Country,
> which tax might have been made much more easy to
> them if but a few persons would have followed Mr.
> Secretary Ludwell's Example, who freely offered to
> lend the Country 500£ for three years without
> Interest.

To which may be added the suddaine disbanding of the force raised against
the Indians, under the command of Sir Henry Chicheley, Lieutenant Generall of
Virginia, being just ready to march out & disarme the Neighboring Indians.
The Refusing to grant a Commission for the Raising of new forces against
the Indians under the Command of such Generall as the Governor should bee
pleased to appoint, earnestly petitioning & freely proffering themselves to you at
their own charge.

This gave occasion to the unquiet, impatient Crowd to follow & cry up Bacon whose forwardness to head them encouraged them to choose him their Generall.

April ulti. 1676: In about twenty dayes after the beating up of Drums for Volunteers, Bacon gains a considerable party and begins his March against the Indians without any Commission.

The Governour and his friends endeavour to divert his designes but cannot. Hee proclaimes Bacon & his followers mutineers & Rebells for going against the Indians without a Commission.

Followes him with a party of Gentlemen to the falls of James River to seize him. Returnes without effecting any thing.

In the Governours absence, the People below draw into armes, and declare against forts, as a most intolerable Pressure and of noe use at all to them.

May 18th:The forts are ordered to be dismantled, & the Assembly is dissolved, that enacted them, & all to appease the rage of the People, & still their Clamours against the government.
A new Election of Burgesses being gone forth, the dissatisfied party choose freemen (not officeholders) that were never before Eligible for their Burgesses, packing up a party for their owne turne, & and at the same time choose Bacon and Crewes Burgesses for Henrico County.

June 4th: at the meeting of this new Assembly Bacon comes downe to James Towne in a sloop, & armed men in her, is shott att from the Towne fort, & forced to fly up the River.

June 7th: Is pursued & taken Prisoner by Captain Thomas Gardner & delivered up to the Governour.

9th: Bacon is pardoned by the Governour & sett at large on his own Parole.

11th: Bacon is reinvested & sitts againe in the Counsell of Virginia (& as credible Report sayes) was promised a Commission to goe out against the Indians.
For which Commission Bacon waites some time in Towne, but perceiving himselfe delayed, or disappointed, departs privately without one.
Informs the people hee cannot obtaine a Commission.

This enrages the people, whereupon they offer Bacon to goe downe to Towne along with him themselves, & if they cannot gaine him a Commission by faire meanes, to Compell one by force.

They accordingly come and surprise James City, surround the state house, the Assembly sitting, rage, threaten, storme and cry out for a Commission for Bacon, which upon the earnest importunity & solicitation both of the Counsell & Assembly, was at length obtained of the Governour, as alsoe an Act of Indempnity was passed to Bacon & his Party, for Committing this force, & a high Applausive Letter writt in favour of Bacon his designes & proceedings to the Kings Majestie signed by the Governour, Counsell, & Assembly and Copies thereof dispersed abroad among the seduced people, alsoe several blanck Commissions were given to Bacon to appoint officers under him, signed with the Governors owne hand, & sealed with the publicke seale of the Colony.

Now since itt was as easy & more safe & Honorable for the Governor at a word to have dissolved the Assembly, itt could much have been wished, that the Counsell in stead of importuning the Governor to grant Bacon a Commission had rather advised him to dissolve that Assembly (as afterwards was done) and so to have prevented the force and its consequences.

But since they did not, itt is much to bee wondered att, that none of the Councill should see a necessity to disowne the force by Publick Proclamation or Declaration timely to undeceive the People, which they were soe far from doing that one of the Governors Bosome Counsellors (Ballard by name) assured some who were pressed to goe out with Bacon & doubted of the legality of his Commission, that it was freely Granted by the Governour, Councill and Assembly.

July 15th: A Generall Rendezvous is appointed by Bacon at the head of James River, the Provisions sent up for this Expedition, by order of Assembly & the new raised forces now ready to march against the Indians. But news coming to Bacon & his Party of the Glocester Petition, contrived by a few & unknown to the Generality of that County, yet granted to all Counteys though never petitioned for, or one of a thousand ever heard or knew of itt, was the Ruine of the whole Colony, in Causing the Indian designe to recoyle in a Civil war upon the Colony.

For when Bacon (then the hopes of the people) was thus upon the very point of marching out the Governor strove to raise men against him, which in that Juncture of time was not to bee done, which forces Sir William Berkeley to leave the Government, when the militia was intrusted in the hands of the Rebell Bacon, who at his Coming downe to Gloster, finds the Governor fled to Accomack, soe that the Governour being gone, itt was hard for the Soldiers to have their Colours, under which they were placed by the lawfull magistrates, by whome they were first pressed into this service & Provision, armes, & Ammunition, provided them by the Assembly.

> Note: It is said by some that there was a paper publickly read to the people, that the Governor designed onely to raise a party to goe out against the Indians, & not against Bacon, & offered their estates, & an oath to bind this pretention to the people.

Aug. 3rd:The Governour gone, Bacon summons in the Country, to meet him at Middle Plantation where hee propounds the settlement of the distracted Condition of affairs on which the Government was left, the Prevention of future Commotions, & the effectual prosecution of the Indian War, and (having many persons of Eminence in Virginia under a strict Guard, and the doors fast locked upon them), forces them to subscribe & take an Oath, which hee had caused to bee drawne up & appoints Commissioners for the severall Countyes, to administer the same to others, soe that very few escaped taking or giving this Oath of Bacons.

Captain Larrimar's ship is seised on by Mr. Giles Bland & a party of Bacons men, who carry her to Acomacke designing to seise the Governour & carry him home Prisoner on board her to England, to answer their charge against him before his Majesty, the command of which service for the surprisall of Sir William Berkeley & the intended agency in England was Committed to, & undertaken by Bland, (since tryed and executed near Bacon's works by James Town by power of the Commission of Oyer and Terminer) who with the ship & men in her was retaken by the advice of Captain Larramore, who sent to the Governour to send off a party of Gentlemen in boats, whom hee would enter on board him at the Gun Ports, which the Governour did, & and with this party commanded by Colonel Philip Ludwell, Bland and his party was surprised in the absence of one Carver, a stout Rebell & able Mariner who had usurped the Command of the Ship from Larimore, which Carver was taken Prisoner at his returne on board, having been with a party on shoare, to treat with the Governour & was Executed before our arrival in Virginia.

About the latter end of August: Bacon resumes his first designes against the Indians, & againemarches to the falls of James River from prosecuting whereof, hee had the pretence of Gloster petition that at first had diverted him, and brought him & his forces downe into the very Bowells of the Country, which in truth was the Original, Rise and Occasion of a civil war in Virginia.

After a tiresome quest of the Indians amongst the Woods, Wilds & Swamps, with by hunger, hardship, sickness, nor success, & the fatigue of a fruitless march Bacons party is dwindled into a very inconsiderable body of men, whome with much adoe hee kept together, encouraging them to patience under these disappointments, in himselfe eager & impatient of atchieving somewhat to answer his owne vaunting pretences, & the peoples fond affiance[76] & expectations in him, before the Assembly (of his own Convening) mett, which was now nigh at hand.

At length Bacon findes out, destroyes, & takes many Pamunkey Indians with much valuable Indian & English Trucke, which Indians were a friendly Nation, but the Vulgar looke upon all Indians alike, & (they being all of a Colour) make noe distinction between Enemyes & friends.

The skirmish being over, Bacon musters his men, who (with the Baggateers) were found in all but 136 men.

September 7th:   In this Intervall of time, having retaken Larrimores ship, the Governour returnes to James Towne, from Acomacke, in Company with the ship *Adam & Eve*, Captain Gardiner Commander, with 16 or 17 Sloops, & about 600 men in Armes.

Bacon and his party are againe proclaimed Rebells, & Traytors & threatened with the utmost severity of Law.

Upon this Bacon calls his few men together, & telling them how the Governour had proceeded makes this an Argument to encourage them (though tyred) to advance to James Towne, against the Governour, which they did, by the way making up their small number about 300 men, leaving along with them their Indian Captives, in a show of Tryumph, & thereby to gaine the affection & applauses of the people as they came in.

Bacon coming before the Towne, rydes up very neare itt sounds a defiance & fires, dismounts, surveys the Ground, causes a Trench worke to be cast up composed of felled trees, earth and bush. This was built at night by moonlight.

Next morne about day breake a small party of Bacons run up to the Palasadoes, & fire briskly upon the Guard, retreating without any damage.

---

76. *Affiance.* Pledging of faith; promise; the act of confiding (OED).

September 15:   A sally is made by those of James Towne, with great pretence of Resolution but little reall valour, & lesse successe, the forlorne fallinge off, being followed by the rest as if they had fled, as now in good earnest they all did, leaving both their dead & their drum behind them on the place.

17th: Bacon gets great Guns, & places them on his workes, which indeed commanded the Sloopes, but (though it terrified) could not annoy the Towne.

18:    Now though the Governor & his party had by much the advantage of the Enemy both in time, place, & number, yet the Cowardice & Baseness of the generality of Sir William Berkeley's party (who were more intent onely upon Plunder, by promise of which hee drew them on with him, & to secure which they made grounds at last to leave him) was such that of all there was onely some 20 Gentlemen willing to stay by him, & at last onely Sir William Berkeley himselfe, who undoubtedly would rather have dyed on the place, then have diserted itt, had hee not been over persuaded to itt, & hurried away to Accomacke against his Will.

And such is their fear of discovery, that for secrecy they imbarque & weigh Anchor in the Night, & silently fall downe the River, thus flying from the face of a languishing Enemy, that had for a weeks space lay exposed to much more hardship, want, & inaccommodation than themselves, for this very service was supposed to bee the death of Bacon, who contracted the disease whereof hee dyed by lying in a very wett season in the Trenches before the Towne.

19:    Bacon having early Intelligence next morning of their having thus quitted the Towne, enters it without the least opposition, & considering of what importance a place of that Refuge was, or might bee to the Governor & his party, immediately resolves to lay itt all in Ashes, & the same night setts fire to the Towne, Church, & Statehouse, which they themselves which had soe lately & basely deserted beheld to their shame & regret, as they rode in the ships & sloops a little below in the River, & the same night arrived two ships in Virgina, Prynne and Morris Commanders.[77]

77. Nicholas Prynne, master of the *Richard and Elizabeth*. Along with Captain Morris, he raided rebel positions throughout the winter. (See Washburn, *Governor and the Rebel*, 84, 86, and Webb, *1676*, 91-92). Prynne's petition for payment from the Crown for his services was granted. See Entry Book of Letters, Commissions, Instructions, Charters,

October 26:   Bacon having layen some time sicke of a blood flux, dyes at
                   one Mr. Pates house in Glocester County.

     After his death the Rebell party was headed by Lawrence, Ingram &
Walklett and much spoile & rapine done, & little or no considerable
service done on the other side to hinder or subdue them, but onely what
was done by the Seamen, which caused Sir William Berkeley to see a
necessity to offer Ingram & Walklett termes, to deliver up West point
with the plunder they had taken, the Governor remaining then on board
ship in Yorke, from whence hee wrote severall Complementall letters
to Walklett.

     Groves, the chiefest Rebell on the south side of James River, was shot
dead by Captain Consett & all his Guard, with Drum, Colours, &
Ammunition taken.[78] Alsoe about the same time the greatest part of
James River declared for the Governor.

     Captain Grantham is entrusted by the Governor to manage the treaty at
West point, & to receive the Countryes Armes & Colours with the
plunder; all which hee effectually performed to the ample satisfaction
of Sir William Berkeley, & the peace of the Colony, But to the disgust
of divers Loyall Gentlemen of the Country, because themselves were
not concerned in soe Considerable a Piece of service.

     In fine, what signall services were done as to the suppressing this
Rebellion must bee justly attributed to the incessant toyle, Courage, &
good successe of those few Sea Captaines, Morris, Consett, Grantham,
Prynne, & Gardiner, who merit this due Commendation, & the more
because the Country have bin ungratefull to them, in not mentioning
them.[79]

January 22:   His Majesties Colony being thus put into this happy posture of
                   peace, the Governour returns to his owne Howse at Green Spring,
                   which the Rebells had much spoyled & plundered in his Absence, &

Warrants, Patents and Grants Concerning Virginia, and Especially the Rebellion of Nathaniel Bacon There and the Governorships of Berkeley and Culpeper and Lt. Governor
Jeffreys, 1675-1682, C.O. 5/1355, 273-275 (VCRP).

78. "From Grantham's Letter to Walklate, 26 November 1676," (Marginal Notation in
Wiseman's Original).

79. For more on the commissioners' respect for the English sea captains who helped
bring the rebellion under control, see Chapter 7, below.

prefixt the 20th of the ensuing Month for the Convening of a new Assembly there, for the Settlement of the distracted affairs of this Colony.

Thus having given a briefe and impartiall account of the Rise, progresse, & Cessation of the late troubles in Virginia, with some few Reflections thereupon, Wee shall conclude this present Narrative with the time of the Governours returne to Green Spring, which was not above a weeke before our arrival, and for what relates to the Condition wee found & left his Majesties Colony in, and such other matters, whereof his most sacred Majestie expect or Command an account, Wee are in all humble Obedience ready to Remonstrate, who are his Majesties most Dutifull Loyall Subjects.

5 *The Commissioners' Resolve*

Document 1

A Commission of Oyer and Terminer for the Plantation of Virginia[1]

Charles the Second by the grace of God of England, Scotland France & Ireland King Defender of the faith &c., To our trusty and well beloved Sir William Berkeley, Knight, Governor of the Colony or Plantation of Virginia for the time beinge: To Herbert Jefferys, Esquire, deputy Governor of our Colony or Plantation aforesaid, and to the deputy Governor of the same Collony of Plantation for the time beinge; to the Commanders in chiefe of our forces within our Colony or Plantation aforesaid for the time beinge; To Sir Henry Chicheley Knight; Sir John Berry, Knight; Thomas Ludwell Esquire, Secretary of our Colony or Plantation aforesaid[2]; Colonel Francis Morrison; Colonel Abram Wood[3]; Colonel Nathaniel Bacon the Elder; Colonel Nicholas Spencer[4]; Colonel Philip Ludwell; Colonel William Cole[5]; Major Leigh[6]; and Captain Ralph Wormley[7]

1. An earlier commission of Oyer and Terminer, dated 16 November 1676 and written in Latin, and granted by the Crown to the same individuals listed in this document, is included in Wiseman's original.
2. Thomas Ludwell, a member of the governor's council, who sailed to England in 1674 at Berkeley's urging to join in the colony's efforts to secure a revocation of the enormous grants of land Charles II had made to some of his favorites. He was appointed secretary of state for the colony on 4 September 1676. See the Patent Roll of Charles II, C 66/3186 (VCRP).
3. Abraham Wood had joined the governor's council in 1657/8 and remained a part of that body at least until 1671. A resident of Henrico County, he was ill over the course of 1676 and apparently took little part in the rebellion. He died at some point between 1681 and 1686.
4. Nicholas Spencer first appears in the records as a member of the Governor's council in 1671. Born in England, he died in Virginia on 23 September 1689. He would succeed Thomas Ludwell as the colony's secretary of state. His appointment is at Patent Roll, 31 Charles II, Part 6, 1679, C 66/3213 (VCRP). See also William Glover Stanard and Mary Newton Stanard, *The Colonial Virginia Register* (Baltimore: The Genealogical Publishing Company, 1965), 40.
5. Bacon denounced specifically "Colonell Coales Assertion" in his "Manifesto." Cole, Bacon asserted, had told the inhabitants of New Kent County that the Pamunkey Indians were "our friends, and that we ought to defend them with our blood." This claim did not play well with the county's inhabitants, who concluded from it that the governor cared more about Indians than he did about frontier settlers. See Wilcomb E. Washburn, *The*

Salutinge: **Know Yee** that wee have assigned you or any two or more of you; of whome our Governor or deputy Governor or Commander in chiefe of our forces within our Collony or Plantation aforesaid for the time beinge wee will to be one: Our Justices to enquire by the oath of honest and lawfull men within our Colony or plantation of Virginia or by other waye, manners, or means which you shall be best able to Know, as well within and without the Libertyes by whome the truth of things may the better be known of all manner of treasons, misprisions of Treasons, Insurrections, Rebellions, Murders, Manslaughters, felonys, Burglaries, Rapes of Women, unlawfull Assemblys or Conventicles, Spreadinge abroad of words; coadjuvacation Conferacys facte or Allegations, Trespasses, Riots, Routs, Retentions, Escapes, Contempts, falsehoods, Negligencys, Concealments, Detentions, Exchanges, Deceipts and other offences and Injuries whatsoever. And allso the accessoryes in the same within our Colony or Plantation aforesaid; as well within as without the Liberties, by whomsoever howsoever had done, perpetrated or committed, and by when or by whome, to whome, when, how, and after what manner. And of other the Articles & circumstances premised, and any waye concerninge the premises or any or either of them. And the same Treasons and other the Premisses to hear and determine after the Laws and Customes of our Colony or Plantation aforesaid and as near as maye be according to the Laws and Statutes of the Realme of England: And therefore wee Command you that att certaine dayes and places which you or any two or more of you (of whome the Governor or deputy Governor or Commander in chiefe of our Army or Forces within the Colony or Plantation aforesaid for the time beinge wee will to be one) to this purpose shall diligently provide to make Inquiry upon the Premises, & that all and singular the premises that you hear & determine & to doe and fulfill in forme aforesaid, What thereof doth belong to Justice according to the Laws & Constitution of the Colony or Plantation aforesaid, and as near as may be after the Laws and Statutes of our Kingdome of England, savinge to us the Amerciments and other things thereof to us belonginge. Wee therefore Command by the virtues of the presents all our Sheriffs & other officers and Ministers to whome these things belongs within the Collony or

Governor and the Rebel: A History of Bacon's Rebellion (Chapel Hill: University of North Carolina Press, 1957), 34. Cole was born in Virginia in 1638. He died there on 4 March 1694. See Stanard and Stanard, *Colonial Virginia Register*, 40.

6. Wiseman left a blank space for Leigh's given name, which he evidently did not know at the time this commission was copied. Major Richard Lee was born in Virginia in 1647, and died on 12 March 1714. The king viewed him as a man loyal and full of integrity, a man of great service to the Crown. See Stanard, *Colonial Virginia Register*, 40 and Letters and Papers Concerning American Plantations, 7 March 1675–30 May 1676, C.O. 1/36, 56 (VCRP).

7. Captain Wormeley, a member of the council, collected customs along the Rappahannock River. See Audit Office-Accounts, Various-Customs, Receipts, America, 1677–1787, A.O. 3/305, 1280 (VCRP).

Plantation aforesaid that att certaine dayes and places, which you or two or more of you (of whome our Governor or deputy Governor or Commander in Chiefe of our Army or forces within our Colony or Plantation aforesaid for the time beinge wee will to be one) to doe cause and come before you or any two of you (as is aforesaid) such and soe many honest and Lawfull men of the Colony or Plantation aforesaid by whome the Truth of the matter in the Premisses; maye be the Better Known and inquired into. In Testimony wherof wee have made these our Letters Pattents. Wittness ours Selfe att Westminster the 6 daye of November in the 29th yeare of our Reigne.[8]

Document 2

Notes and Other Documents Chronicling the Activities and Concerns of the Commissioners

Met Sunday 25th February, 1676/7

That itt is the Concurrent opinion of the right Honorable Commissioners that the people complayning soe farr forth as his Majesties proclamation enjoynes, as to the oath & submission such as are the most innocent and unconcerned in the late rebellion, shall & may be security for the others and the others for them: Alternis Vicibis which they conceive must be the right meaninge of his Majesties proclamation, since there is else an impossibility of rendringe that Important point practicable.

Concurrent.
Samuel Wiseman

Colonel Morison, Sunday February 25th

That the Proclamation is in force for this reason: first though Bacon be reported dead, yet for that some of his accomplices are out in Rebellion att this daye, & such that are capable to procure and head a new party, if not some of the old faction who are not yet well qualified as to their obedience: 2[ly]: As to the Summons to Bacon in the first place the Colonel conceives that the maine intent of that was noe more than to see if he would render himselfe, and to save the King that price sett upon his head: 3[ly] That the Power of Pardons granted only to Sir William Berkeley, is that the people might not be deprived of the present benefit of the Kings pardon which was peculiar to his power by Patent, and if he had bin dead before the receipt of that Commission, Colonel Jefferys was noe wise capable of actinge by that Power only peculiar & expresse to the Governor,

8. 6 November 1676.

and it therefore follows that Colonel Jefferys must have made use of the Kings proclamation to convey his Majesties Mercy to the people, which bears a subsequent date, & is more effectual as wee conceive for the people to lay hold on, by beinge the last which in Law has always the Preference, and is of more availe, for that the same pardon is derived Immediately from the King himselfe which is better than from the Governor to them.

Concurrent.

February 26

The query being putt by Sir John Berry whither havinge seized a parcel of goods of one Drummond, lately executed for his rebellion, & soe become forfeit to the Kinge from on board the Ship *Francis* of London, Captain John Warner, Commander.

The Commissioners are of opinion that they being *bona pitura,*[9] Sir John maye dispose of the same to the best advantage, and to be accountable to the King and his Ministry.

That it is also their assent that Captain Warner maye have a third claret and a quarter caske of Brandy, att the first penny cost in England for his care in preserving the said goods and his readiness to discover and render the same to the Kings use.

Samuel Wiseman

February 26th

It is not meet that Colonel Jeffereys should goe to the Assembly before they or some members from them shall first have bin with the Commissioners at their Rendezvous, they havinge bin before to attend the Governor and his Councill, and havinge a letter in readiness to deliver first to them to acquaint the Assembly with the occasion of their comminge over hither.

Concurrent
Samuel Wiseman

February 27th, 1676/7

It was then declared by the Honorable Commissioners that although the maine intent of their comminge was and is to make up the rents of the divided Country and draw them into one peace, that though the Governor or any two of the Commissioners of Oyer and Terminer have power of themselves of sittinge upon the Business of that Commission, yet they the said Commissioners doe intend to sitt with them uppon the said Commission to show that they doe noe wise countenance or approve of any of their late disloyall actions.

Concurrent
Samuel Wiseman.

---

9. "*bona pitura.*" Probably *bona peritura,* perishable goods.

1st March, 1676/7

That Colonel Moryson is of opinion that such as shall slight or contemne the Kings pardon are in noe wise worthy to reape the benefitt of itt, but on the contrary that they be apprehended and that if any such evidence be brought against them or shall make them liable to the Law that they shall be proceeded against accordingly.

And in case their Crimes or misdemeanors shall not amount to paine of death, yet that such other corporall Punishment be inflicted on them by Imprisonment or otherwise as the Assembly shall judge most accordinge to their just demerits & offenses upon hearinge & Examination.

> Concurrent
> Samuel Wiseman

The Same Day

That Colonel Moryson is of opinion, that seeinge divers of the notorious accomplices in this late Rebellion doe yet stubbornly and contemptuously stand out and doe not submit & conforme themselves to the Kings Royall Injunctions as by his Proclamation is made Known: that if they returne not to their obedience within the time therein limited, he or they shall utterly lose and be excluded the benefit thereof, and be proceeded against as Rebells and Stubborn Traytors, and contemners both of his Majesties Mercy and Justice.

> Concurrent
> Samuel Wiseman

They beinge read heard and fully considered by the right Honorable Herbert Jefferys Esquire and Sir John Berry Knight they did concur in the said opinion, and if rather for that Colonel Moryson did lay before them this late president: That Scroop, one of the Regicides,[10] not being executed in the Act of Parliament, was yet for speaking slightly & unsubmissively of what he was charged to Sir Richard Brown, in bare discourse and not as a Magistrate, was afterward excepted, Tried and executed. And therefore the said Commissioners that this their concurrent opinion maye not only be published but entered on record.

3 March, 1676/7

Colonel Moryson is of opinion that seeinge his Majestie by his Royall Pardon granted to the Governor and Assembly of Virginia for passinge certaine acts beinge under a force, and for that the said pardon granted them is grounded upon these words: "All which they the said Governor & Assembly were for fear of their lives and by the terrour of the said threats and violence compelled to pass

---

10. Moryson here referred to Adrian Scroope, one of the nine Regicides who suffered death for their role in the execution of Charles I. See C. V. Wedgewood, *A Coffin for King Charles: The Trial and Execution of Charles I* (New York: Macmillan, 1964), 211.

&c." That seeinge also divers others of his Majesties Subjects out of the like feare and force upon them have bin prevailed on to act contrary to their duty, conscience and allegiance. That since there is the same colour and reason that such of his Majesties Subjects as are able to make out that they were constrained under the like circumstances; that they be not debarred of the benefit of his Majesties Acts of Mercy and Pardon, under the condicions by his Majesties proclamation enjoyned them.

Sir John Berry agrees hereto.

Samuel Wiseman.

5th March 1676/7

That whereas uppon the complaint of severall Persons this daye that upon the taking up of great quantities of land by particular persons from 5 to 20 thousand acres, & their settinge such dear rates upon this land to others to purchase, which poor men are not only unable to purchase but unwilling to become Tenants upon a continent, is a apparent cause of the straggling of the people, and enlarginge and wideninge the Bounds, which they nor wee are in noe wise able to defend. We therefore thinke the best expedient is as well for our security against the Indians, as an equall adjustment of the Taxes to the poor people: that every 100 acres of land above a thousand that any one possesses which is enough and more than any one will Manure, shall be by the Assembly taxed equall to a Tythable, which beinge first layd before the Assembly to reduce to this proportion if they by reason of their own possessione, shall not be brought to consent hereto, that the same be represented to his Majestie to reduce and redress.[11]

March 7th 1676/7

The Commissioners are of opinion that such goods, cattle or other things whatsoever that have bin plundered or forceably taken from or by either party

11. The idea of substituting a tax on land for tax on polls had been suggested by Governor Berkeley in the 1660s. Giles Bland, in his complaints to the king about Berkeley's misgovernment, also recommended a land tax. The commissioners also favored a land tax. If large landholdings were taxed, the logic went, the engrossers might give up their unused acres, thus increasing the land available for purchase by aspiring planters. Despite the potential a land tax offered to relieve social tensions in the colony and reduce the amount of pressure planters placed on Indian lands, the king never acted on these recommendations. See Edmund S. Morgan, *American Slavery, American Freedom: The Ordeal of Colonial Virginia* (New York: Norton, 1975), 278-279.

duringe the late Rebellion, and since the layinge down of Arms, shall be restored on each side if the same can be found in Specie and in beinge.

Concurrent:
Samuel Wiseman

March 10

Colonel Moryson is of opinion not to mediate, intermeddle, Counsell or be any wise concern'd in the repreivinge &c of any of the Criminalls, condemned & sentenced for their treason and rebellion against his Majestie, but that the same be whole left to the Breast &c of the Governor as chiefe Judge of the Court of Justice to act therein as he shall thinke fitt or see cause.

March 10

Colonel Moryson enters his opinion as follows: "That seeinge it is part of the Royall Prerogative inherent to the Crown to make peace or warr, as is apparent by that Article of the Instructions to his Governor of this Collony of Virginia &c which enjoynes him only to take and use their advice and assistance in procuringe and concluding a Peace with the Neighbour Indians: I conceive it not proper or necessary to consult or advice with the Assembly or any other in order thereto, further than shall conduce to the means and methods, of attuninge the Same; most for his Majesties Honor & interest & not otherwise: for the matter as to the Assembly is not whither a Peace shall be but how it shall be for the conveniency of the King and Country."

Concurrent
Samuel Wiseman

March 11th, 1676/7

That seeinge the Power and Prerogative of Peace and Warr is only inherent to the Crown & that all Plunder taken by rebells against the King is direct Roberry; therefore they especially ought to restore againe what they have unlawfully taken from the Loyall parties and be glad they escape. Soe on the other hand such of the Loyall Partie as have seized any of the goods, chattels, or estates of the disloyall party which the King by his Proclamation and other acts of Pardon has given them restitution of, and disclaimed his own Royall right, ought by like parity of reason and Justice to be restored back to the Rebellious partie, if the same be yet in Specie, or otherwise that part of his Majesties Royal pleasure is unperformed.

March 14

Whereas sundry of the Servants, and other persons of desperate fortunes within this his Majesties Colony of Virginia during the time of the late Rebellion have deserted their masters and run into Rebellion upon the Invitation and encouragement of libertie, and have bin heinous actors & upholders of the same;

and that for the future upon any such unhappy occasion which God prevent, noe such opportunity maye be open to entertaine any such Rouges and Rebells: It is the concurrant opinion of his Majesties Commissioners that every such Servant as shall hereafter desert his masters service and betake him selfe to Arms, or be any waye an ayder or abettor of Rebellion against his Majestie and other offences not requiringe death, May by an act of Assembly to be made in that behalfe be compelled not only to serve out the remainder of his time to his Master or owners but be forced to serve as a public Servant and Slave of the Colony for the Space of Seaven years after the Expiration of his Servitude to his said master or owners, which beinge not consonant with the former laws & customes of this Collony maye be a fitt provision in the case aforesaid and that the law maye also extend to other inferiour and despicable persons that shall be guilty of the Crimes aforesaid.

Concurrent
Samuel Wiseman

March 15

The Commissioners are of opinion that seeinge his Majesties Pardon and proclamation are soe generall and diffusive, and therefore such limitations as the governor by the power peculiar to himselfe, shall see just cause to impeach and except any person for Rebellion, who shall be soe notorious, and the circumstances of his crimes such as shall bring him in danger of correction and loss of life & estate: That (de futuro)[12] such person shall give an Inventory of his Personall Estate & security not to embarrass or wast the same except for the support of life and that the same togeather with his nature and process of his Crimes and offenses be transmitted home to his Majestie for himselfe to explaine his owne Royall acts of Mercy.

This was read to the Governor
Concurrent
Samuel Wiseman

March 15

This daye the Prisoners formerly tryed and found guilty were brought to the Barr to receive sentence of death for their Treason and Rebellion, which the Governor pronounced accordingly. After which Joseph Ingram came into and pleaded and humbly beg'd the benefit of his Majesties Pardon havinge before performed his Majesties Royall Injunctions declared by the Proclamation, readinge his submission upon his Knees in open court which the Court granted. Afterwards several others desired by petition to the Governor's Court to receive the Benefitt of the Kings Pardon; came to the Barr of the Court, i.e. Scar-

---

12. In the future.

brough,[13] Seaton,[14] Wheeler[15] and Knowles.[16] Here upon a fierce debate arise in open Court, first moved by the Governor, concerninge Restitution of the Estates of these persons and other offenders of the like nature, which the Governor would have all seized and forfeited.

To which Colonel Morrison stood up in Court, and asked the Governor what was their crimes to which the Governor reply'd Treason and Rebellion and beinge in actuall armes, mentioning all the aggravations of their offenses that he could then thinke on which his Counsell seconding this with much sharpness.

Whereupon Colonel Morrison asked the Governor how came these men here at liberty to which Sir William Berkeley said they are out upon Baile. "Sir," said Colonel Morrison, "by your favour I conceive the Law allowinge noe such liberty as Baile in such cases," to which the Governor answered that it does for Rebellion.

Sir William Berkeley asserted further that he would justifie his proceedings, and as to that of Seizure, said that itt was against the law of nations to deny itt. Whereupon Sir John Berry read the clause of Restitution in the words of the Kings Proclamation to the Court and urged the necessity of observinge that clause, for without it, it was impossible to putt the Country into that Posture of Peace, which his Majestie aimed att & intended. Colonel Morrison argued to the same effect, and used this expression with reiterated earnestness to the Governor: "Sir, the King has either pardoned all or has pardoned nothinge, and whome he has pardoned for life he has pardoned for Estate, for there is noe medium." To which the Governor returned, "Sirs, I doe declare then that a fine shall be inflicted on all offenders, and this is my opinion which I will owne and I will have it recorded in court and justifie it.

Then the Commissioners unanimously said to me, "Praye enter itt as our opinion that noe such thing ought to be; for itt directly cutts off & contradicts the very express words of his Majesties Pardon, which are a Record to Justifie our protest against such proceedings for none but such as are out of the Capacity of layinge claime to this clause of the Pardon can forfeit any thing or be liable to any further fine, punishment or forfeitures."

---

13. Captain Charles Scarburgh had been specifically excluded from Berkeley's pardon of 10 February 1677. See *Letters and Papers Concerning American Plantations,* 4 January-19 March 1676/7, C.O. 1/39, 64-65 (VCRP).

14. George Seaton lost property to the value of £150 to Governor Berkeley's raiders. His appeal to the commissioners is included in Chapter 7, below.

15. I have not been able to identify Wheeler.

16. Lands Knowles, a planter from Gloucester County who had played no role in the rebellion, suffered the destruction of his plantation at the hands of Robert Beverley. Knowles' petitions for relief are included in Chapter 7, below.

Memorandum: upon the Governors afferminge that one of the Criminalls att the Barr stood out till the very last untill Bacon was dead; which said he was not certainly known then, nay it is a question, said he, if he be yet dead.

Test: Samuel Wiseman

March 18

Colonel Morrison and Sir John Berry moved:

That the Howse of Burgesses doe more for an act of oblivion to settle the Country in Peace, and if the upper house will not assent and confirme the same, it will be to your Honor and reputation to have moved the makinge & enacting such a Law. Then they moved the Business of Jones his wounds received in the Kings Service, he comminge in upon the Governors indemptnity &c. and that Major Burely was desired by Colonel Jefferyes as Commander in chiefe of his Majesties forces, to move the Governor to looke upon him as an object of pity and mercy, but not to present it as that the Commissioners concern or intermeddled with the matter of Pardon that noe mistake maye be made in the Matter.

March 29

I was sent over to waite on the Governor with a letter to the Governor, and with all to acquaint his Honor that the Commissioners desired him to hasten his reply to those particulars intimated by the Interlocutory heads: The Governor told me then within a fortnight or 18 dayes at farthest he would be goeinge for England, and that he should not give his answer to the matters required till he had a sight of their Commission & instructions impoweringe them thereto under his Majesties or the Secretarys of States hand: And that he had never stil'd Colonel Jefferys deputy Governor, but if that the sheriff had done soe, he thought himselfe Innocent; and that he was a foole and a Knave that had done it for he never saw itt. That he should have the himsmith[17] requir'd for his Majesties service if hee pleased to send for him. That the persons that had bin abusive to the Government should be sent for and Punished.

I waited on the Assembly and presented Colonel Jefferyes commission under the great Seale, with the Kings letter to Sir William Berkeley, and Sir Phillip Lloyd's certificate of the Colonels oath as Governor, which they prayed me to be left to the Inspection of the House.

And thereupon three of the Members were sent from the Howse of Burgesses to know the Governors pleasure, if he did grant his assent to the readinge them which he did, and ordered 4 of his Councill to attend the House and hear itt read.

Declared not fitt that the Governor be present at the hearinge itt read.

Samuel Wiseman.

---

17. "*himsmith.*" the meaning of this word is obscure. It is not included in the OED.

I received the Commission and they tooke time to
Consider of an answer.

Aprill 3rd 1677

Mr. John Tresham, Sheriff of Westmoreland County, declares that upon his
readinge formerly the Governors Proclamation the people of the County said
they were made under a hedge[18] & none of his. Butt upon the Readinge of the
Kings Majesties Royall Proclamation, printed and sent over, He told the people
that this was noe hedge proclamation but his Majesties (which beinge now a
factious people) did yet embrace and gladly receive the same as a most gratious
Proclamation, & thereupon were induced to take the oath of allegiance upon his
Instance; beinge before all depart away dissatisfied without takinge any further
notice of itt.

Samuel Wiseman

To the truth of this declaration I doe subscribe my hand this 3rd of Aprill, 1677.
John Tresham, Sheriff of Westmoreland County

Aprill 13

Whereas by his Majesties Royall Instructions under the Privatt Signett and
signe manuall given at Whitehall the 16th November 1676, it is by the second
Article of the same directed as follows: "To Thomas Needler, Esquire deputy pay
master of the forces: Secondly you are in such manner as our said Commissioners shall advise, to goe along with the said Trunke on ship board, and to take the
same into your Custody duringe the voyage; & after landinge in Virginia in such
manner as our said Commissioners shall appoint," which Commissioners are
termed before our Commissioners for the Civil Government of Virginia. His
Majesties Honorable Commissioners are concurrent in their opinion & appointment for sendinge of his Majesties chest of money for the present service in Virginia from on board the *Deptford* Ketch to be deposited att Mr. Pages Howse in
the Middle Plantation as beinge near the maine Guard of Souldiers.

Samuel Wiseman

April the 20th

Colonel Moryson enters his Opinion that its against the liberty of the Subject to be Imprisoned without warrant and the Crime expressed therein: and not
to be imprisoned without the Governors Knowledge or warrant sent:

---

18. "*hedge.*" as used in this sense implies a barrier.

Aprill 20th

Sir John Berry is of opinion that the Governors warrant is Sufficient to Imprison any man that had bin actually in Rebellion, till they could Come legally to their Tryall or Pardon

Samuel Wiseman

Aprill 23:

This daye William Hartwell captaine of the Governors guard came before the Commissioners but the Commissioners beinge absent noe hearinge; but when he was asked by the Commissioners by what power he did imprison severall persons, he answered he had noe warrant butt the Governors Bare word, and nothinge to produce under hand and seale, he produced a warrant from a Councill of warr for takinge away provisions for the Guard without any limitation or quality or Kind of provision; or nomination of persons, soe that he was att large to plunder, whome he pleased, and if enjoyned to give any account, which account beinge by the Commissioners demanded he had nothinge to show.

The main objections in the Petition against him is for takeinge people prisoners without warrant, and makeinge composition with the Rebells att his own pleasure which beinge not yett paid therefore are not seizable in the sense of the order which was for a Present supply of the Governors guard in time of warr.

On Board the Bristoll: July 16, 1677[19]

Colonel Custis whither Sir John by his Commission is bound to staye here or not.

Resp: That is not the Question the Councill said it does not concern them:

Sir John asked if the Country is able to furnish the Kings ships with victuals and provisions, and who will undertake itt: And particularly Bisquett.

Sir John asked the question of the Captaines whatt provisions they have: Answer: They will give itt under their hands they had little enough to serve them to England.

Againe the Query is who shall provide provisions.

Colonel Bridger said he cannot ride safely on the road for fear of Rebells: "I can raise men enough if I knew where to find them."

Sir John Answers:

"Tell me where the Rebells you speake of are and I will send 300 men to shore to subdue them:" Againe Sir John thinkes fitt to continue, "Where is the provisions and who shall find them?"

19. A meeting between Sir John Berry, Francis Moryson and the members of Governor Berkeley's council.

Sir John Askes, "is there any Rebellion in the Country if you explaine that there is actually rebellion here at this time; if there, or that you feare any give us itt under all your hands that you desire me to staye here upon that account, and I will staye as long as the keele of the ship will hold:" Colonel Cole said "I feare none."

Colonel Bridger sayes that before the winter he fears that the Country will be in a worse condition than ever itt was if the fleet leaves us; "Pray God I maye be found a man mistaken; I was never soe in what is past: It is strange that Bacon could command & had biskett of the Country and the Kings shipps should want itt."

Colonel Bacon:[20] "Butt it proved bad att the falls and he had new made . . ." Colonel Moryson: "Fears and Rumours of Rebellion maye continue here this 20 yeares & where the Kings shipps must waite on your Lodgings and as long as there is a prating Knave in the Country."

Colonel Bridger sayes that "the Souldiers said Hang the Governor & God damn those Counsellors:"

Colonel Moryson: "If the ships must staye to awe the Souldiers; & if soe they ought to paye the charges."[21]

Colonel Custis sayes he "will be hanged if ever there be any mutiny att all give me but the power on the Eastern shore formerly:"

Sir John Berry: "Make knowne your fears; tis not enough to saye soe barely and not make itt out."

Colonel Bridger: "Itt is my opinion Virginia is now in a worse condition than before."

The query of victualinge prest againe.

Secretary Ludwell: "A question of this nature not to be answered presently. I would give 20 £ the shipps but staye for I fear their goinge away maye prove an Encouragement to the Rebellion."

Colonel Bridger: One of our Counties is able to furnish the fleet."

Q: Whither the Kings 3 frigatts now here can be provided with bread and other provisions and if itt can be soe who they conceive will undertake itt att the Kings price, which is about 7d per daye; bread meat and drinke 3000 pounds of bread per weeke; The Secretary stands to the first opinion he has given in writinge: Colonel Custis the like in writinge: Sir Henry Chichley conceives the country can provide itt, but knows not who will undertake itt: Colonel Bacon says that he cannot undertake itt nor knowes none will; and soe the same Effects say of all the rest.

Colonel Moryson sayes, "Praye enter my opinion: that it is not practicable to be done in this Country and especially att this time of the yeare."

20. Colonel Nathaniel Bacon, Sr.

21. In other words, if the troops had to remain in Virginia to preserve order, the costs of doing so should not be borne by the King or his commissioners.

Colonel Cole: "Itt is a thing soe difficult that it is not to be done, nor noe man will undertake itt, this is my Judgement."

Document 3

An Answer to the Enquries of the Right Honorable the Lords Commissioners for forraigne Plantations

To the Governor of Virginia

1: Whatt councells, Assemblys and Courts of Judicature are with in the Government and of what Nature and Kind?

Ans: There is a Governor and sixteen Councellors who have from his Sacred Majestie a Commission of oyer and Terminer, who judge and determine all causes that are above 15£ sterling: for what is under there are particular courts in every countie which are 20 in number; every year att least the Assembly is called, before whom he apeales, and this Assembly is composed of two Burgesses out of every countie: these laye the necessary taxes; the necessity of the Warr with the Indians and other Exigencies required.

2: Whatt Courts of Judicature are with your Government: relatinge to the Admiralltie?

Ans: In twenty eight years there hath never bin one prize brought into the countrie, soe that there is noe need of a particular court for that concern.

3: Where the Legislative power and Executive power of your Government are sealed?

Ans: In the Governor, Councill, & Assembly & officers substituted by them:

4: Whatt statutes Laws and ordinances are now made and in force?

Ans: The Secretary of the Country every yeare sends to the Lord Chancellor, or to one of the Principall Secretarys, what laws are yearly made, which for the most part concerne only our own private exigencies, far contrary to the laws of England; wee never did nor dare make any only this; that noe saile of lands is good and legall unless with in three months after the conveyance itt be recorded in the Generall Court or county Court.

5: Whatt number of horse and foot are with in your Government; or whether they be trained bands of standinge forces?

Ans: All our free men are bound to be trained every month in their particular counties, where wee suppose and doe not much mistake in the calculation, are near eight thousand horse; there are more butt it is soe chargeable for the poor people, as wee are to exercise them.

6:     Whatt Castles and forts are with in your Government, and how scituated, as allso what provisions they are furnished withal?

Ans: There are five forts in the Country, two in James River, and one in the three other Rivers of Yorke, Rapahanock & Patamack; but God knows wee have neither skill nor abilitie to make or maintaine them for there is not as far as my inquiry can reach ever one Ingineer in the Countrie; Soe that wee are att a continuall charge to repair unskillful and inartificall buildings of that nature; there is not above thirty great and serviceable guns, this wee yearly supply with powder and shott as farr as our utmost abilitie will permit:

7:     What number of Privateers doe frequent the coasts and neighboringe Seas, what theire burthen are; the number of their men and guns, the names of their Commanders?

Ans: None to our Knowledge since the last dutch warr.[22]

8:     What is the Strength of your borderinge neighbours be they Indians or others by Sea & land; What correspondence doe you keep with your neighbours?

Ans: Wee have noe Europeans seated near to us than St. Christophers[23] or Mexico that wee know of except some few French that are beyond New England: The Indians our Neighbours are absolutely subjected soe that there is noe fear of them, as for correspondence wee have none with any European Strangers, nor is there a Possibilitie, to have it with our own nation further than our trafique concerns.

9:     Whatt armes Ammunition and stores did you find upon the place, or have bin sent unto you since upon his Majesties accompt; when received, how imployed, what part is there remaininge and where?

Ans: When I came into the country I found one only ruinated fort, with eight great guns most unserviceable, and all dismounted but fower, scituated

22. The last Dutch War ended in 1674. On the history of Anglo-Dutch warfare, see C. R. Boxer, *The Anglo-Dutch Wars of the Seventeenth Century, 1652-1674,* (Palo Alto, CA: Pendragon House, 1974); J. R. Jones, *The Anglo-Dutch Wars of the Seventeenth Century,* (London: Longman, 1996).
23. West Indian Island colony founded by the English in 1624, which the French also occupied. Surely the geographic reckoning here was a bit off, as the French had settled in the St. Lawrence River Valley and the Spanish retained their outpost at St. Augustine. Both Berkeley and the commissioners, of course, were well aware of the neighboring English colonies.

in a most unhealthful place, and where if an Enimy Knew the Sounding he cold Keep out of danger of the best gunnes in Europe; his Majestie in the time of the dutch warr sent us thirty great gunns most of which wee lost in the ship that Brought them; before or since wee never had one great or small gunn sent us since my comminge hither, nor I believe in twenty years before; All that have bin sent by his Sacred Majestie are still in the Country with a few more wee lately brought.

10: What moneys have bin payd or appointed to be pay'd by his Majestie or levied with in your Government; for and towards the buyinge of Armes or makinge or maintaininge of any fortifications, or Castles, and how have the said moneys bin expended?

Ans: Besides those gunns I mentioned, wee never had any monies of his Majestie towards the buyinge of ammunition or buildinge of forts: what moneys can be spared out of the publique revenues Wee yearely lay out in ammunition.

11: What are the Boundaries & Contents of your land within your Government?

Ans: As for the Boundaries of our land itt once Contained tenn degrees in latitude butt now it hath pleased his Majestie to confine us to halfe a degree: Knowingly I speake this Pray God it maye be for his Majesties service butt I much feare the contrary.

12: What Commodities are there of the production, Growth & Manufacture of your Plantaton, & particularly what materials are there already growinge, or maye be produced for shippinge in the same?

Ans: Commodities of the growth of our countrie wee never had any butt tobacco; which is in harvest soe considerable that it yields his Majestie a great revenue, but of late wee begin to make silke, and soe many mulberry trees are planted and plantinge that if we had skillful men from Naples and Sicilie to teach us the art of makinge it Perfectly; in less then halfe an age, wee should make as much silke in one yeare as England did yearely expend threescore years since, butt now we hear tis grown to a greater Excess, and more common and vulgar usage;[24] now for shippinge wee have admirable masts and very good oakes, but for Iron oare I dare not saye there is sufficient to keep one Iron mill goinge for seaven yeares.

---

24. In other words, Berkeley believes with proper instruction, the Virginians could produce silk equal in value to all that consumed in England over the past six decades.

13:      Whither Saltpeeter is or maye be produced within your Plantation, and if soe att what rates may itt be delivered in England?

Ans: Saltpeeter wee know of none in this Country

14:      What Rivers, harbors & Roads are there in and about your Plantation and Government and of what depth and soundings are they?

Ans: Rivers wee have fower as I named before all able Safely & securely to bear and harbour a thousand ships of the greatest burden.

15:      What number of Planters, Servants and Slaves & how many parishes are there in your Plantation?

Ans: Wee suppose and I am very sure wee doe not much miscount that there is in Virginia above forty thousand persons men women and children, of which there are two thousand black slaves, six thousand Christian Servants for a short time the rest are borne in the Countrie or have Come into settle or seate in betteringe their condition in a growinge Countrie

16:      Whatt number of English, Scotch or Irish have for these Seaven yeares last past come yearely to plant and inhabit within your Government: as allso what blacks or slaves have bin brought in within the said time?

Ans: Yearely wee Suppose there comes in of servants about fifteen hundred, of which most are English, few Scotch & fewer Irish and not above two or three shippes of Negroes in seaven yeares.

17:      What number of people have yearely died with your Plantation and Government for these seaven yeares last past both white and black?

Ans: All new Plantations for a yeare or two are unhealthy till they are thoroughly cleared of wood butt unless wee had a particular Register office for the denotinge all that died, I cannot give a particular account neare to this querry; only this I can say, that there is not one of ten unseasoned hands (as wee soe arme them) that die now, whereas heretofore not one in five escaped the first yeare

18:      What number of Shipp doe trade yearely to and from your Plantation, & of what burden they are?

Ans: English shipps near Eighty come out of England and Ireland every yeare for tobacco; few New England ketches, but of our own wee never had yett more than two at one time and those not more than twenty tonns burthen

19:      Whatt obstructions doe you find to the improvement of the trade and Navigation of your Plantation within your Government?

Ans: Mighty and destructive by that seveer act of Parliament which excludes us from haveinge any commerce with any nation in Europe butt our own;[25] soe that we cannot add to our plantation any commodities that groeth out of itt as olive trees cotton or vines, besides this wee cannot procure any skillfull men for one hopefull Commoditie: Silke, for itt is not lawfull for us to Carrye a pipe stave or a bushel of corne to any place in Europe, out of the Kings dominions, if they were for his Perticuler Service or the good of his Subjects wee should not repugne what ever our Sufferings are for itt: Butt on my soule it is contrary for both, and this is the Cause why noe small or great vessels are built here, for wee are most obedient to all the Laws, whils the New England men breake through, & men trade to any place that their Interest leads them to.[26]

20:       What advantage and Improvement doe you observe that may be gained to your trade & navigation?
Ans: None unless wee have liberty to transport our pipe staves, timber and Corne to other places besides the Kings Dominions

21:       What rates and duties are charged and payable upon any goods exported out of the plantation, whither of your own growth or manufacture or otherwise as allso upon goods Imported?
Ans: Noe goods either exported or imported paye any the least duties here, only two shillings the pound on tobacco exported which is to defraye all publike charges, and this yeare wee could not get an account of more than 15 thousand pounds, out of which the King allows me a

25. Berkeley here refers to the Navigation Acts, first passed by Parliament during the Interregnum and reenacted in 1660 upon Charles's restoration to the throne. The Navigation Acts required that English ships dominate trade with the English colonists. To be defined as an "English" craft, the ship had to have been built within the empire, be owned by an English subject, and employ a crew three-quarters English. Certain "enumerated" items, principally sugar and tobacco, could be shipped only to England, were the Crown could collect a customs duty on them. The Navigation Acts were intended to ensure that colonial wealth enriched the empire.

26. The New England merchants had developed a strategy for evading the Navigation Acts. They carried Virginia tobacco to Boston or New York, and then claimed that they had met the requirements of the legislation by taking the tobacco to an English port before shipping it elsewhere. Virginians resented these practices, even if most of the tobacco shipped by the New Englanders went directly to England. See Morgan, *American Slavery, American Freedom,* 277. The Crown, meanwhile, had no shortage of evidence suggesting the disobedience of the Puritans. For a discussion of these charges, see Michael Leroy Oberg, *Dominion and Civility: English Imperialism and Native America, 1585-1685* (Ithaca, NY: Cornell University Press, 1999), 113-114, 134-136.

thousand yearely with which I must maintaine the port of my place, and an hundred interveninge charges that cannot be putt to publique account, and I cann knowingly affirme that there is noe Government of tenn yeares settlement butt has thrice as much allowed him but I am supported by my hopes that his gratious Majestie will one daye Consider me:

22:     What revenues doe or may arise to his Majestie within your Govern ment & of what nature is it, & by whome is the same Collected & how answered and accounted to his Majestie?

Ans: There is noe revenue arisinge to his Majestie but out of the quittrents and they he hath given awaye to a deservinge Servant, Colonel Henry Norwood:[27]

23:     Whatt course is there taken about the Instructinge the people within your Government in the Christian Religion, & what provision is there made for payinge of your Ministers?

Ans: The same course that is taken in England out of towns, every man accordinge to his abilitie instructinge his children; wee have forty-eight Parishes; and our Ministers are well pay'd & by my consent should be better, if they would praye oftner and preach less, but of all other commodities soe of this the worst is sent us, & wee had few that wee could boast on since the persecution in Cromwells livery drove divers worthy men hither, butt I thanke god there is noe free schooles nor printinge & I hope wee shall not have those hundred yeares, for learninge has brought disobedience and heresie and Sects into the world, & printing has divulged them, & libels against the best Govern-ment: Godd keep us from both.

A true copy. Sworn by John Hartwell

Document 4

Questions Proposed by his Majestie and Councill, to Which I returne this Humble plane and true answer:[28]

---

27. During the rebellion, Norwood served as the colony's treasurer, responsible for over-seeing its finances and revenues. A close friend of the governor's, his report on affairs in the colony confirmed in English eyes the charges brought forth by Giles Bland and others that Berkeley had badly mismanaged affairs in the colony. See Webb, *1676*, 50, 204.
28. Nothing in Wiseman's original suggests who composed the answers to these ques-tions, but it is almost certain that one of the three commissioners is responsible. The re-

Ques: Whither the site of the country is fitt for horses service, and whither if it be, horses may not be brought from Maryland to serve in Virginia?

Ans: The country is one continued wood, swamps and coverts in every two miles goinge, for horses Virginia has soe many, they are become a grievance by breakinge the peoples fences and destroyinge their Corne, soe that there is noe need of them from other Places were they of use there:

Ques: Whither Bacon has not possessed himselfe of those horses?

Ans: That it is Impossible for many of them are wild, and all run in the woods, there beinge noe Inclosures to keep them otherwise.

Ques: What provision the Country affords, and how this to be provided there for a thousand men to be sent from hence?

Ans: The provision for the ordinary sorts of people in winter is only mash, the Corne of the Country beat in a morter and boiled; the bread is made of some corne, but with difficulty by reason of the scarcity of mills, and of this mean provision there cannot be expected plenty this yeare by reason Bacons horses live upon itt; that has made none, & severall parts of the Rivers deserted that used to make provisions of itt, soe that itt will be hazardous for his Majesties forces to depend of itt, least they starve themselves & friends; naye in time of peace this is not allways plentifull; for Tobacco beinge the money of the Country, with which they buy everything they want, they plant soe much of this and soe little of Corne, that the Assembly was forc'd to make a law with a great Penalty that each man should plant and tend two aikers of Corne, soe that as (I humbly conceive) there is noe dependinge on provisions there.[29] The diet of the better sort is somethinge better which is poultry & hoggs, and what deare and foules their servants can kill them in the woods. In the Summer the Servants have milke and once or twice a weeke beefe which then have flesh on their backs. The drinke both in winter and summer for the Generall is water, the masters & mistresses of some families have beer and ale, butt this is not common.

Ques: How Bacon and his forces live, and why his Majesties forces should not subsist by the same waye?

spondent is clearly familiar with Virginia, and given that the questions appear to have been written before the commissioners departed from England, Francis Moryson seems like the most likely candidate. Governor Berkeley, as the answer to the penultimate question indicates, was not the author.

29. For the history of attempts to regulate tobacco production in the Old Dominion, see Morgan, *American Slavery, American Freedom*, 95-96, 109, 134-135, 186-195, 284-287.

Ans: Bacon has noe opposition butt quarters his men att large as amongst
         frends; his Majesties men will be looked upon by that party as Enimies,
         & therefore must keep close togeather, butt when an opposite power
         appears, itt is to be feared they will soon starve one another.

Ques: Whither Bacon have not possest himselfe of the most & best planta-
         tions the Country?
Ans: I believe that he has since noe party appears in Armes against him, and
         those that follow him thinke that he acts by his Majesties Power,
         haveinge a Comission from the Governour

Ques: Whither there be not more Servants then masters, and whither Bacon
         has not nor will proclaime freedome to them?
Ans: I answer he hath not taken that Corse yet of proclaiminge freedome to
         Servants, & when he doth, I verily believe itt will in a short time ruine
         him, since by itt he will make all masters his Enimies, and I cannot
         thinke the Generallity of Servants will Expect freedome on those
         tearmes, to live a life of wood Kerns,[30] which is the best they can
         propose to themselves.

                    I desire the truth of these particulars maye be thoroughly
                    inquired into of any that has bin there; which will excuse the
                    presumption of this paper which is noe waye to change the
                    measures his Majestie has taken; but that a due provision
                    maye be made for itt.

---

30. *Kerns.* Lightly armed Irish foot soldiers and, according to the OED, "one of the
poorer class among the 'wild Irish.'"

6 *The Counties' Grievances*

The Answers, Most Humble Report, Opinion & Remarks of us his Majesties Commissioners appointed to inquire into the Grievances of his Majesties Plantation of Virginia.[1]

James City County Grievances

1. The imposition of 2s. per pound of tobacco is complained of that the same is misemployed contrary to the first grant, & noe account thereof given to the Country how the same is disposed of; They desire that the said impost maye be employed as at first intended and to have an annual account thereof give to the Assembly &c: and wee find the like Complaints in the grievances of these followinge Counties, (viz.)

	6:	Rapahanock
	5:	Citternbourn parish in the same County
Article	6:	Surrey
	6:	New Kent
	3:	Stafford

Ans. The two shillings imposed by the act of Assembly upon every pound of tobacco exported out of the Colony beinge confirmed by his Majestie is the only support of the Government: & is for the use and good of the Collony; to be disposed of according to his Majesties Royall Instructions; accounts whereof are yearely transfer'd to the Right Honourable his Majesties Principall Secretary of State, & theire own Assembly, by which it maye bee seen how the same is imployed & disposed of:[2]

---

1. In Wiseman's original, the county grievances and the commissioners' response to those grievances appeared in parallel columns. For ease of readability and for the purposes of appearance, I have presented them horizontally, with the particular grievance immediately followed by the commissioners' specific response to that grievance.
2. The duty on tobacco, first enacted in 1662, provided support for the colonial government and, the House of Burgesses hoped, would cause "men to produce other usefull and benefitiall commodities." The duty was paid on each hogshead of tobacco exported from the colony, and the assembly appointed collectors for "the severall rivers and places in Virginia for the receiving of the said two shillings per hogshead." The 1662 act permitted planters to pay the duty in goods. A 1670 revision of the act, however, required that the duty "could be paid only in money or good bills of exchange well secured." See Wil-

2.   The money paid yearely for fort duties they complaine of as not beinge not truly accounted for nor imployed to the use intended by Act of Assembly; and that there is noe place of defence in the Country sufficient to defend or secure his Majesties Subjects against any forreigne Invasion and this is not only the Complaint of this County alone but of the Counties of:[3]

Surrey
Stafford
5.   Rapahanock

Ans.   Wee are well assured of the truth of this complaint, & doe know that the forts erected could be of no use, endurance, or defense being built & made up of mudd and dirt: Yett were they of great expence to the people who paid Exclusively for buildinge them and as to the account desired of the great sums leavyed and paid upon this occasion wee thought itt Just for the Assembly to Examine and report the same; & accordingly recommended the doinge thereof which wee conceive is done to their full satisfaction.

3.   They present as a grievance the Indians paintinge and disfiguringe themselves; they desire that upon a peace made with them that Bounds and Badges of separation and distinction be sett and appointed them; and that a restraint be putt upon Indian traders.

Ans.   This is answered by a particular article in the Indian peace; against their paintinge & disguisinge themselves, bounds are allso sett them; and wee Could have wisht that Badges could then have bin; or still might be provided as formerly for distinction amongst the Indians: As to the trade with them wee most humbly propose that

---

liam Waller Hening, ed., *The Statutes at Large; Being a Collection of All the Laws from the First Session of the Legislature in the Year 1619,* 2nd ed., vol 2 (Richmond: R. & W. & G. Bartow, 1823), 132-133, 176-177, 283. The Burgesses in 1662 declared that a hogshead should have the following dimensions: "forty-three inches in length and the head twenty-six inches wide, with the bulge proportionable." Ibid., 2: 125.

3. Periodically the House of Burgesses had enacted levies to support the construction of forts. They had done so in 1665, 1667 and again in 1672, though the 1672 measure was directed less toward new construction than for repairing shoddy workmanship on the earlier forts. Berkeley's decision to raise a levy in 1676 to build and man additional forts awakened the anger of a frontier population that already felt itself defenseless in the face of Indian attack. The frontier population questioned the efficacy of the governor's tactics, and believed that the forts would only enrich the men upon whose land they would be built. See Hening, ed., *Statutes at Large,* 2: 220, 257-258, 294 and 326-328.

the same to laye open att two or more prefixt times of the yeare att appointed Marts, and clerks appointed to take and give just accounts of what stores of powder, shott & armes are disposed of from time to time; and this wee have Considered and provided for; and left by the Articles of Peace with the Indians to the Consideration of the Governor to determine of att the meetinge of the next Assembly.[4]

4.   They present as a maine cause of the late rebellion & civill commotions in Virginia the slow prosecution of the Indian warr and the tax of 60 lbs of tobacco per poll,[5] and they praye an account of the reason and benefitt occurringe of the said Tax.

Ans: Wee have in our Narrative set forth the causes of the late troubles in that collony to have proceded from the slow prosecution made against the common Indian Enemy; as allso the tax of 60 lbs per poll; and have answered the query of this article by acquaintinge the assembly with his Majesties Regall Care and most gratious promise to redress this grievance complained of: by callinge the Right Honorable Proprietors to relinquish and render up their respective rights by Patents without any charge to the Country; for purchasinge in of which Patent the said tax was leavyed; soe that wee suppose the money raised upon account is or will be reimbursed to the Publick: The Assembly haveinge charged bills of Exchange upon their treasurers chosen in this behalfe for payment of itt:

5.   They present as a grievance the often meetinge of the assemblys &c: and desire their proceedings may be after the laws of England & allso that there maye be a Mittigation of Burgesses Expenses and Charges:

Ans: The frequent meetinge of the assembly is already regulated; and the manner of their proceedings prescribed by his Majestie to be as near as maye be to the laws of England and the great Sallary of the

4. For the history of Indian trade regulation, see Michael Leroy Oberg, *Dominion and Civility: English Imperialism and Native America, 1585-1685* (Ithaca, NY: Cornell University Press, 1999), 188-189.

5. Support for government and the funds required to support ministers and build and maintain churches came from poll taxes, imposed by the county courts on every "tithable," defined as any male over the age of 15 years and any woman engaged in tobacco production. Masters paid for each of their servants. See Edmund S. Morgan, *American Slavery, American Freedom: The Ordeal of Colonial Virginia* (New York: Norton, 1975), 209.

Members of Assembly is allso reduced to as low a degree as itt possibly can be brought to, and all this affected accordinge to his gratious Majesties Royall Instructions laid on us for doeing thereof by our advice and assistance.[6]

6.   They pray that for their own preservation they maye have libertie to keep gunnes & ammunition, & to have their armes restored which were taken from them.

Ans. The restraint upon persons to Keep armes was only duringe the time of the late rebellion but now every man may enjoye his former liberty and freedome to keep armes &c: and wee are humbly of opinion that restitution is fitt to be made to the right owners of such armes as have bin taken from them by those in whose hands they can be found: their firearms beinge to the meaner sort not only their preservation but a meanes to help them to subsistence by Killinge of game in the woods: & serve also to destroye Wolves and vermine which infest the Plantations.[7]

7.   They complaine of great fees taken by clerks and sheriffs and desire a Regulation and that the clerks of county courts maye be by the Countie courts elected and appointed, and that Sheriffs maye continue in their office but one yeare and noe more:

Ans. The fees of Courts are or maye be regulated by act of Assembly; and as so the electinge of Clerks of county Courts; itt has bin all

6. The point is worth making that the House of Burgesses met usually no more than once a year, and when they did so their sessions lasted no more than two weeks. Clearly, taxpayers in the Old Dominion did not see the value of the House of Burgesses as a governing institution. For a discussion of this issue, see Martin H. Quitt, *The Virginia House of Burgesses, 1660-1706: The Social, Educational and Economic Bases of Political Power* (New York: Garland, 1989), 280.

7. Wolves were viewed as a significant threat to the health of colonial society, and the burgesses frequently sponsored efforts to eradicate them. In 1661 the burgesses voted to pay local Indians 200 pounds of tobacco for each wolf killed. In October of 1666, they revised the 1661 statute, because in "some fronteer counties the number of wolves killed and brought in by the Indians . . . have very much inhanced the taxes of the said Countie." See Hening, ed., *Statutes at Large*, 2: 87, 236. In October of 1669, however, "since it is evident that the inhabitants of this country doe receive dayly damage by wolves, and noe fitt way . . . yet found for the destruction or diminishing of them," the burgesses declared that "the Indian tributaries be enjoyned and assessed to bring in a certaine number annually." See Hening, ed., *Statutes at Large*, 2: 274-275 for the act and the numbers of heads Indians in the several counties were expected to bring in.

wayes Customary for these courts to present their clerks to the Secretary & he to admit and confirme them & for the Continuance of Sheriffs in that office above one yeare; is not only contrary to the laws butt present practice under the new Governor.

8.   They present as a grievance the exempting of severall persons by act of assembly from Payinge Taxes; and pray a Remedy under some few exemptions thereby mentioned and the same is allso desired by:

7 Rapahanock

Ans.   This the last Assembly have remedied and left the Councill liable to paye leavyes & publick Taxes which before they were free from; in Respect of their Beinge of the Councill to his Majesties Governor of Virginia.

9.   Whereas Severall Indian slaves were taken in the late Indian warr, began and prosecuted att the publick common charge of the whole Country and are att present in the hands of private persons; they pray that the same Indians maye be disposed to a publick use and profitt[8]

Ans.   The Indian Captives beinge most of them belonginge to the Queen of Pamunkey & other friendly nations, wee humbly conceive it will be most for his Majesties Honor that upon the Peace lately Concluded: the said Indians maye be restored to them, in whose hands soever they now are or shall be.[9]

10.   They propose the raisinge of their public taxes maye be by a land tax accordinge to the Estate of the Inhabitants of that his Majesties Collony.

Ans.   This waye were to be as much wished as desired by them butt tis a thing impracticable there: Butt this in our humble opinion would be a thing both fitt and reasonable: that all Persons who shall ingross a greater quantity than a thousand acres of land in that Collony which is much more than any man can cultivate to profit,

8. By the 1660s at least, some Indians served as slaves for life in Virginia. See Oberg, *Dominion and Civility*, 194-195.
9. For the commissioners' opposition to Indian slavery, see Articles 13, 14 and 15 of the 1677 Middle Plantation Treaty, in Chapter 3, above.

should paye after the rate of a tythable for every hundred acres Supernumerary to the thousand, butt this beinge never to be admitted or liked of by those great Ingrossers of land there; if done it maye bee effected by his Majesties immediate Commands from hence; And wee must needs Conclude that this unlimited liberty of takinge up Such vast tractes of land, is an apparent cause of the many mischiefes and great Inconveniences that have and doe attend that his Majesties Collony; by hinderinge the vicinity of neighborhood buildinge of Towne and villages or makeinge up any ready force to oppose the Enemy, because of the Straglinge, remote distances of Plantations each fromother, for want of land to seat themselves nearer togeather; which beinge taken up before is not to be had butt by longe Tenants to the first ingrossers which noe man Cares to be; butt thinke itt hard to be a Tenant upon a Continent.[10]

Rapahanock County

1.   The first thinge they complaine of is this: the want of able pious orthodox minsters and the due administration of divine Ordinances; to have bin a maine cause of the Miseries and seveer judgements that have fallen upon that land & desire to be supplied of these wants from England.

Ans.   Wee have made Known to them the pious Care and Concernment of the Right Reverend Father in God Henry, Lord Bishop of London, to provide for them in this Perticular of the ministry to whose province itt appertains as beinge within his Lordshipps peculiar, In obedience to whose commands the present Governor hath with our advice and assistance commisionated certaine of the most sober and Judicious Clergy of the Country to enquire att a generall convocation of the rest of their function into the Lives and Conversations of the ministry as allso into their qualifications, abilities, and Maintenance and other matters which relate to the Ministry; of which his Lordshipp may expect a full and satisfactory account in due time.

2.   They desire an Honorable peace may be concluded with the Indians for the sake of their own Emergent necessities without which

---

10. The engrossment of enormous tracts of lands for speculative purposes certainly contributed to the outbreak of the rebellion. See Morgan, *American Slavery, American Freedom*, 220-221.

they could not possibly subsist as living in Continuall danger upon the fronteers.[11]

Ans.   A Peace is concluded with the Indians upon good, just, and honorable tearms, of which wee cannot in the least doubt but that itt will be a secure and lastinge one unless the English which God forbid should happen to be the first Infringers as heretorfore they have bin.

3.   If a warr happen they prepose and praye that the same may be soe managed that they of Rapahanock maye not sustaine the brunt and suffer under the like hard usage as of late they did more than any other Country in Virginia as wee are informed.

Ans.   In case of any warr with the Indians wee humbly conceive that this is a Business for the Assembly to order and regulate accordinge to Equalitie and Justice.

4.   They allso praye that upon any Indian warr this County beinge upon the fronteers is liable to much mischiefe by reason of the Indian incursions which in time of warr are soe frequent that they cannot att one time attend their crops of Corne and secure their own lives from the suddaine and surprizinge assaults of the Enimy; that therefore they maye be exempted from payinge any charge to the Warr, in which they are for these reasons more imployed than other Counties to defend themselves.

Ans.   Wee conceive that this is most proper and reasonable to be recommended to the Assembly, that soe this and such other frontier plantations, as bear the brunt of the Indian outrages, maye be exempted from the defrayinge the charge incumbent upon a Publick Warr with them

5 & 6.   Are of the same import in this as in the first and fourth articles in James Citty County grievances and soe not here incerted.

Ans.   The fifth and sixth articles are answered by the first and fourth in James Citty County Grievances:

---

11. For Indian affairs in Rappahannock County, see Helen C. Rountree, *Pocahontas's People: The Powhatan Indians of Virginia Through Four Centuries* (Norman: University of Oklahoma Press, 1990), 118-119.

7.   Article of this County grievances are consonant with the 8th article in James Citty grievances, & soe not here Incerted.

Ans.   The 8th Article of James City County grievances—the 7th article of the grievances of this County which also should have bin here incerted & answered.

8.   They desire that noe man maye hold more land than what he payes quitt Rent for; and that his Majestie will please to grant such concealed lands as are held by any person not payinge the same; to such as shall prove the fraud; and petition for such concealed lands.

Ans.   His Majestie and not wee, is alone to determine in this Matter; butt in our humble opinion itt is fitt and Just that every person should paye for what lands he holds.

9.   Thatt such assisted Bacon maye not be permitted to sitt as Judges in any Court.

Ans.   Wee are humbly of opinion that those person who have notoriously abetted the late rebellion, be for the Present Suspended from servinge in any place of Trust, till time have purged them of their former crimes; and they shall have approved themselves honest, quiet and loyall Persons to the Government.

10.   They would not have any office of publick trust conferred on any butt discreet & Knowing Gentlemen; and none of Slender education to sitt in the seat of Justice.

Ans.   Wee could hartily wish that none but persons of that Character might be the men in office of publick trust as is desired, but who or where those are; or who are fitt approvers or Judges of them wee know not.

11.   They desire that all shipps arrivinge in Virginia maye paye their Castle and fort duties in Powder and Bullet,[12] and that a Publick Magazine be raised for their defence.

---

12. The House of Burgesses, beginning in December of 1662, required masters of ships to pay their "fort duties in kind, vizt. halfe a pound of good merchantable musquett powder and three pounds of leaden shott for each tunn their shipp is off burden, to the captain of the fort." See Hening, ed., *Statutes at Large*, 2: 177-178.

Ans.   We humbly conceive itt fitt that the castle and fort duties be paid in Kind; if theire were Storehowses in every Countie to receive and secure the Same; else much better to be paid in money, into the hands of a just Treasurer towards the building a good fort att James Town

12.   They desire that for the future the Assembly may meet and all generall Courts maye be kept at a convenient place in the Countie of the Countrie; and that Care maye be had for the Erectinge towns in every County with all Speed possible.

Ans.   It is our most humble opinion that James City is the most proper place for all Publick conventions of the Country, both of Assembly and Generall Court, and if the Statehouse which was antiently there should be removed thence, itt would not only render the Erectinge a good fort there impracticable, but ruine the designe of buildinge that antient Town againe, for which there are much usefull materials remaininge, that will save the Country some thousand pounds charge; whereas the removal of itt was voted but by one Supernumery voice, and for noe other Reason or pretence— but only because some of the Inhabitants come over the River to James Town; and which others must doe the like from this other part, if the Statehowse be elsewhere scituated, & soe the Inconveniency will be only altered & not remedied by a removal: As for buildinge of Towns in every County, itt is here greatly to be desired and well to be encouraged.

13.   They desire that this County of Raphanock which hath bin a Bulwarke and defense to other Counties against the Indians, and thereby reduced to much poverty, maye have either a reparation of their losses from other parts or be taxed in their publick leavyes in regard of their great sufferings and loyalltie in the time of the late troubles.

Ans.   Wee doe humbly Judge itt proper for the Assembly to doe all that well maye be done for the ease of poor Rapahanock in their publick leavyes and that by a speciall Command from his most gratious majestie.

14.   They desire that the freemen of the Countie maye be admitted with the freeholders to give their votes att the Election of Burgesses.

Ans. Wee humbly suppose such election to be repugnant to the Laws of England & the peace of that Collony; the ill consequences of which were seen in the June Assembly, 1676, when freemen were both chosers and chosen Burgesses.

15. They desire to Know by whatt authority Col. George Mason & Major Geo. Brent went over into Maryland & killed severall Indians; Supposed by them the originall cause of the many murders committed in the County of Rapahanock.[13]

Ans. This wee have reported in our Narrative and spoke to itt perticularly there.[14]

Citterbourn Parish in Rapahanock County

1. The first article is meer matter of fact, and relates to the deplorable condition of those parts duringe the time of the late troubles.

Ans. Wee have made this part of our Narrative to which itt did properly relate, & requires noe answer.

2. They relate by the Second Article matters relatinge to and the manner of the proceedinge of the Indian Warr.

Ans. This wee have allso incerted in our Narrative; as more proper to be there recited than in this place.

3. They declare that in yeares 1674 & 1675 there hath bin leavyed upon each Tythable 52lbs. of which they desire an account.

Ans. For an account of these leavyes wee have recommended them to the Assembly.

4 , 5, 6. are the same here as the 1st, 2d: 8th articles in the grievances articles of James Citty County.

Ans. Articles are answered in the 8th, 1st, and 2nd articles in order, or else they should here have bin answered.

13. The men of Rappahannock County here refer to one of the critical events that set the stage for Bacon's Rebellion. See Oberg, *Dominion and Civility,* 198-199.
14. See Chapter 4, above.

7.   Article imports the same things here as doth the 11 article in Rapa-
         hanock grievances.

Ans.   The same answer will serve to the 7th Article here as to the 11 arti-
         cle of the Rapahanock grievances; to which wee doe therefore
         humbly referr.

8.   They complaine of the Penny impost upon all Tobacco shipped
         into any of his Majesties plantations to be an Injury to his Majes-
         ties Collony of Virginia, and this obstructs their trade and Supply
         from New England, who furnishes them with Supplies of corne
         and other necessarys att cheaper Rates than from other parts &c.

Ans.   In our humble opinion this Penny impost is soe necessarye an im-
         position, to prevent the defraudinge his Majesties Customes, by
         those of New England &c: that itt is not to be complained of, being
         layed by act of Parliament to that end: Besides, what they alleage
         concerninge New England is entirely untrue, and is to be rejected
         for that Reason.

9.   This article is the same in effect with the eight Article in the Rapa-
         hanock grievances.

Ans.   Wee humbly referr to the 8th Article of Rapahanock grievances as
         answeringe to the 9th in this.

10.   They desire that those men that are of the Militia, may not att same
         time sitt in the Courts of Judicature.

Ans.   Wee are humbly of opinion that none are more proper to sitt in
         Courts of Judicature than those Gentlemen of the Militia, being the
         most able and discreet persons of that Collony.

11.   They complaine of the approach of the Nensaticoe Indians within
         20 miles of the Plantation of Col. Cadwallader Jones and fear their
         Comittinge some outrages on them: [15]

Ans.   The late peace with the Indians has secured them from those feares
         and apprehensions of the Enimy.

---

15. The reference here is to the Nanzatico Indians. Cadwalladar Jones traded with Indians in the area. He was lieutenant colonel in the Stafford County Militia in 1680. He
lived at least until 1699.

12.   They complaine of the former murders committed in those parts, and that for want of due care taken to prevent such mischiefes as frequently happened by reason of their remote distances from all releife and succor from those forces they needed on such occasions; and desire that for the future that there maye be one Commander in cheife apointed by the Governor to raise men & armes to prevent the like miscarriages:

Ans.   Wee have mentioned this great defect in our Narrative relatinge to the former management of the Indian Warr, but this complaint is already answered by the peace concluded; yett in our humble opinion deserves due care upon any such like occasion which maye hereafter happen.

13.   They desire a proportionable part of those armes and ammunition sent into the Colony by his Majestie may be allotted to those parts they beinge in most likelihood to use them.

Ans.   This maye be thought reasonable when they shall first have provided a secure place for Keepinge them, and provided they maintaine their armes in good Kelter[16] against occasion, and renew att their own charge when broken, spoiled or lost:

14.   The last article concerns only what corse was taken to strengthen the weake plantations and of how smale a wall that corse proved to secure them against the Indian outrages.

Ans.   This last article is fallen off upon concluding the Peace lately made with the Indians:

Stafford County

1.   They begin with a Plea of Ignorance and Innocence of the Causes of the late Rebellion in Virginia.[17]

2.   They complaine of beinge very much burthened & oppressed by annuall assemblys; and desire remedy.

---

16. *kelter.* Good condition, order, state of health or spirits (OED).
17. The commissioners made no response to this statement.

Ans.   This pressure complained of is remedied in obedience to his Majesties Royall instructions in that behalfe given.

3.   They Complaine of the 2s. per pound

Ans.   This is answered in other grievances
     viz: Rapahanock County
             Citterbourn Parish
             James Citty County:

4.   They desire that Lord Baltimore, Proprietor of the province of Maryland, maye take that Corse with the Indians inhabitinge that province and soe near adjacent to this County of Stafford, that they maye not infest them in their Incursions.[18]

Ans.   The Governor of Maryland did by letter advise us that he beinge to make a peace with the Indians there the 12th July last would include those of Virginia in the Treaty wee havinge returned him a Coppy of our Articles.

5.   They complaine of payinge towards the buildinge of forts, &c.

Ans.   This is answered elsewhere:
     viz. James Citty County grievances, art: 2nd.

6.   They pray an account how the 50lb of tobacco per poll was imployed which was raised through the Country for Purchasinge this neck of land, &c.[19]

Ans.   Instead of this Purchase, they have a Royall promise of haveinge in the Grant without that charge, and the money raised to this intent returned them by their Treasurers therewith by them intrusted.

7.   They praye that the charge of the Indian Warr maye be defrayed & those Souldiers paid that served in that Expedition before the time of Bacons Rebellion.[20]

18. For the history of Indian-white relations in early Maryland, see Francis Jennings, "Indians and Frontiers in Seventeenth-Century Maryland," in *Early Maryland in a Wider World*, ed. David Beers Quinn (Detroit, MI: Wayne State University Press, 1982).
19. The Stafford County men here refer to the attempt by Governor Berkeley to purchase back from its proprietors the Northern Neck of Virginia.

Ans.   This last article haveinge bin under the consideration of the last assembly, wee conceive they have done them what is equitable to the agrievants.

Surrey County

1.   The first is information of the great Pressures of frequent Assemblys & the great charge of Assembly members salary.

Ans.   To this end his Majestie hath directed a Remedy and the same is accordingly effected.

2.   They Complaine that great quantities of tobacco have bin raised for buildinge of howses att James Citty which were not finished.

Ans.   The howses built att James Citty being now laid all in ashes that dispute is ended; however, if that tax was not laid by their own Representatives in the Assembly, the Law is open against them that leavyed itt:

3.   They complaine of the leavy laid & rased for buildinge of forts & the insufficiency of their defense.

Ans.   This Complaint is most true for the forts erected were of noe use or endurance.

4.   They complaine that there are great sums raised and quantities of ammunition paid in kind by shipps to maintaine a Magazine, & yet they are forced to buy their Powder and Shott att their own charge or else fined for default.

Ans.   There is noe magazine to receive or secure any stores of ammunition.

5.   They complaine that upon all emergent services they are summoned to James Citty, a place of vast expense, & are forced not only to bear their own Expence, but the Expenses of their Commanders: & allso to pay them for their Service.

---

20. This grievance refers to those men who joined in the abortive expedition to have been led against the hostile Indians by Sir Henry Chicheley.

Ans.   Wee know noe remedy for this Complaint the same thinge beinge practized not particularly there, butt in all parts of the Country; yett not complained of by any other Countie.

6.   They complaine of the imposition of 2s. per pound butt are mistaken in the intent of the Tax.

Ans.   This is answered to by the 1st Art: of James Citty County Grievances.

7.   They complaine of the Seizure of severall persons estates before the owner is convicted of any crime, notwithstandinge they lay hold of the Right Honorable the Governors Indempnity, and were admitted to take the oath of Allegiance *de novo*.

Ans.   These Complaints wee have often represented as unjust and illegall both by letter to Sir William Berkeley, and to his Majesties Right Honorable Secretaries of State.

8.   They declare that by the Assembly in June last they were injoyned upon a great Penaltie, to send men, Armes, ammunition & provisions to the late Rebell Nathaniell Bacon, Junior: the honorable Governor not contradictinge itt; also itt was sometime after the said Rebell had rebelliously forced his Commission; to our great loss and damage. They humbly praye that as they expect noe redress for their obedience to the said Assembly for their damages then received; that that Assembly may not increase their Sufferings by being chargeable to them.

Ans.   This article beinge a materiall Justification of our Narrative, wee have transcribed itt in their own very words; that some maye appeare to agree with our report given of this passage in the Narrative; and wee doe humbly conceive that the desire of the Complainants is reasonable.

9.   They allso declare that the erecting of forts togeather with the slackness of prosecutinge the Indian warr as allso the subtill Insinuations of Nathaniel Bacons pretences has bin the chief causes of the late Rebellion.

Ans.   This makes out another Part of our Narrative for which reason wee have here erected this article in their own words.

10.   That att the layinge of leavyes itt has bin the custome of countie
        courts, to withdraw into a private Room, whereby the poor people
        have bin kept Ignorant how theire Taxes comes soe high: They
        praye that for the future the County charges maye be laid pub-
        lickly in the open court Howse.

Ans.   Wee thinke itt most reasonable that all should know what all are
        concerned in.

11.   They complaine that they have layn under great Exactions of Sher-
        iffs and clerks fees, and pray that the same may be ascertained for
        the future under a great Penalties on such as shall exact.

Ans.   This wee believe was never complain'd of to the Secretary or his
        deputy, beinge confident he is soe just a person as he would have
        given them releife, Besides the laws have provided against Exorbi-
        tant fees & it must be their own faults if they doe not apply them-
        selves to such obvious Remedyes.

12.   They Complaine that contrary to the laws of England and that Col-
        lony, high sheriffs have continued two years and under sheriffs 3
        or 4 yeares, togeather.

Ans.   Wee have heard that formerly they did soe butt now that grievance
        is remedied both by law and practice.

13.   It is complained of as a grievance that men are forced to sue for
        very smale debts to the great charge of debtor and Creditor, they
        desire that for any debt under 450lb of tobacco and caske; a Justice
        of peace maye have Power to try and grant execution without any
        further trouble to the Court.

Ans.   This has bin before complained of and provided for in part by the
        35 Act of Assembly in the Printed booke for small debts; butt
        what they here desire is the contents of a whole hogshead of to-
        bacco which will deserve a Court.

14.   They desire a liberty to choose vestry men and that the whole par-
        ish maye have a free election which they have not had.[21]

---

21. Under Virginia law, vestrymen were to be selected "by the major part of the said
parish." See Hening, ed., *The Statutes at Large,* 2: 44.

Ans.   This wee referr to the generall usage of the Country.

15.   They desire that since his most gratious Majestie hath bin most mercifully pleased to pardon their late disloyalltie, they most earnestly and humbly praye, that an act of oblivion be made by the grand Assembly; that noe person maye be injured by the provokeinge Names of Rebell, Traytor and Rogues.

Ans.   This wee have here rendered in the peoples own words and doe joyne with the Petitioners in all humilitie to his Gratious Majestie that noe pretence maye obstruct the obtaininge what they most humbly implore; Since itt is like to be an effectuall meanes to secure the future quiet of that his Majesties Collony.

16.   They declare that the 60lb of tobacco per poll did much amuze, discontent & aggrieve the poor people whose pressure were before too heavy for them: Butt beinge well informed by Colonel Moryson of his Sacred Majesties Royall favour in this particular they are exceedingely well satisfied and yield his Most gratious Majestie all possible humble and hearty thanks for this transcendant goodness and only expect an account of the money in their Treasurers hands.

Ans.   An account answerable to their expectation will undoubtedly be given them of the Pattent money whereof the Assembly have disposed part to be paid by bills of Exchange charged on theire Treasurers.

17.   They plead extream poverty & pray that they maye not be sued or laid under Execution for their debts till next Cropp.

Ans.   Wee durst not Concern our selves in this matter beinge it must prove a stop of Justice.

18.   They complaine that divers persons are like to lose severall just debts due to them out of the Estates of persons Executed, fled and their Estates seized for the late rebellion; and praye that they may satisfie their debts out of the Estates soe seized.

Ans.   Wee are most humbly of opinion that it is most Just and reasonable that those debts be paid where the Estates will answer itt.

19.   That the Indians taken in the late warr maye be made slaves.

Ans.   This is contrary to the Articles of Peace with the Indians and as wee humbly conceive inconsistent with his Majesties Royall Goodness and Honor to grant.

Westmoreland County

1.   They desire there maye be a daye sett apart for thanksgiving for restoringe Virginia from the late rebellion, & that there maye be an order for degrading those of their titles assumed in the time of the Rebellion.

Ans.   This is left to the Care of the Governor & Councill and as for the degradinge the Rebells: itt is soe ordered by Governor Jefferys; that noe one that has had Command under the late rebel Bacon doe for the future presume to goe or Ride armed with Sword or Pistoll.

2.   They desire that effectuall means may be used for propagation of the Gospell; for remaininge scandalous ministers; and the strict observing of the Sabbath daye.

Ans.   This is provided for by the Pious care & Recommendation of the Right Reverend father in God, Henry, Lord Bishop of London in whose Diocese Virginia is.

3.   They desire that such persons as have bin disaffected to the Government & active in the late troubles maye Suffer accordinge to their demerritts; that the like Rebellion which God forbid maye not be Encouraged.

Ans.   Due enquiry & punishment have bin made & inflicted upon divers notorious abettors and promoters of the late Rebellion, accordinge to Justice and after the laws of England & their own demerritts.

4.   They declare that the Records of the Country by them supposed to be embezzled & burnt beinge lost greate care maye be taken for Settlinge as soon as maye bee every man in his Just rights; and Possession of lands and Estates.

Ans.   The Records were preserved by Mr. Drummond from burninge, and care is taken by Mr. Secretary whose office it is to keep them.

5.   They desire that an address may be made to his Majestie, in behalfe of the Country, begginge pardon for the late rebellion and

imploringe most humbly the Continuance of his Royall favors as formerly.

Ans. This has bin performed by a publick letter from the Assembly of Virginia att their last meeting att Green Spring.

6. They desire that the publick place of Judicature and meetinge of the Assembly maye be ordered in the most convenient place of the middle of the Country.

Ans. Wee humbly conceive the most convenient place to be James Citty, where the Statehowse formerly stood; and the walls and brick worke are yett standinge.

7. They supplicate that the Susquahanock charge maye be borne by the whole Country and the Counsellors Salarys & Tythables maye noe more be allowed them and noe Councellor to sitt Judge of any County Court.

Ans. As to the first itt has bin moved to the last Assembly. The Salary of the Councill are allso alleviated & order taken in the former, and wee are humbly of opinion that the Council should not properly sitt as Judges, butt in Circuits only; and then not to visit as Judges their own Countyes.

8. They desire that the Right Honorable the Governor maye be moved not to call too frequent Assemblys.

Ans. This grievance is taken awaye by his Majesties Speciall Command.

9. They desire a Peace with the Indians to the Best advantage, &c:

Ans. A good and Just Peace is lately concluded with the neighbour Indians.

10. That after a Peace made with the Indians noe person Keep an Indian to hunt for him or otherwise.

Ans. The Articles of Peace have provided for this.

11.   They desire that the Counties maye be divided across the neck:[22]

Ans.   This is proper in our humble opinion, for the antient inhabitants of
           those parts to represent and explaine to the Assembly.

12.   That whereas by the Assembly in June 1676 itt was ordered that a
           1000 men should be raised for the Indian warr out of the Respec-
           tive Counties in Virginia, each Countie to find their provisions and
           paye their souldiers, which act by the violence of Bacon being
           made null they desire that an act be provided to enable the Respec-
           tive Counties to paye their Souldiers, and for their provisions &c
           leavyed against the Indians:

Ans.   This has bin with the Assembly to consider:

Northampton County

1.   They present for settlement the former dividing of this County into
           two Countyes and desires theirs maye be enlarg'd answerable to
           that of Accomack.[23]

Ans.   This affaire has bin with the Assembly to determine, and is now
           before the Governor & Councill to Examine and Decide.

2.   They desire liberty to choose a new vestry.
Ans.   Referred to the antient usage & custome of the place.

3.   They pray that the act for killing wolves, Beares, wild catts &
           crowes maye be repealed, since noe man butt will for his owne
           security endeavour to destroye as many as they Cann, soe that the
           charge of payinge of this account maye be saved.

---

22. The "Northern Neck" counties, Westmoreland, Lancaster and Rappahannock, asked
the burgesses to divide the region into counties "by lynes running across from Rappahannock River to Potomacke River." The burgesses ordered in response that "the people in
each county in the whole Neck, be convened to meete and nominate two such persons, as
shall be thought Capable for each County to treate and Consult about it, Provided the
people shall judge it convenient to have such division made. See H. R. McIlwaine, ed.,
The Journals of the House of Burgesses, 1659/60-1693 (Richmond: Virginia State Library, 1914), 78.
23. For the issues between Accomack and Northampton Counties, see McIlwaine, ed.,
Journals of the House of Burgesses, 77-78.

Ans.   This act is repealed but in our humble opinion might well have bin continued since what wolves or wild creatures are Killed in any part of the Country thereby are the fewer in the whole.

4.   That any housekeeper payinge reasonable for the same maye have att any time of the clerke a list of Tythables.

Ans.   It was never denyed them to our Knowledge nor can wee Imagine the Clerks such enimys to their own interests as to refuse copies to any man that desire itt.

5.   They desire that noe person be sett tax free, bying magistrates particular favour to the oppression of other poore people.

Ans.   None are that ever wee heard of, nor doe wee in our humble opinion thinke it fitt or reasonable itt shold be soe.

6.   They desire itt may be gratned them to have a free choice of six howse-keepers without interposinge of any over-ruling magistrate, who maye be authorized to sitt vote, assess, and Examine the lists of Tythables yearely; at layinge of the Countie Leavyes to prevent future oppression and abuses, and they likewise crave that they having a Court of brothers, they may have liberty to make choice of two only out of the fower Brothers to sitt att the Assessment of the Countie leavye.[24]

Ans.   Wee conceive that the grantinge of what is desired would obstruct the speedy layinge of leavyes as occasion sometimes requires, by spinninge out the time in unnecessary disputes. As to the Court of Brothers (if any such be, as wee know nothinge of) wee believe itt best to be left to the Court to make choice which two, and noe more shall be present att the layinge the leavyes.

7.   They crave free access to search and take coppies of Records att the apointed place payinge the clerke his just fees.

Ans.   It is the peoples undeniable priveledge & the clerks Knowen profit, for theire Clients, to search and take out coppies of publick records which was never denyed them as wee Know of.

---

24. The commissioners did not understand the nature of the Northampton County request, and the meaning of it is no more clear today.

8.   They Complaine in Sundry instances of the undue keepinge the times of sittinge in Courts and reasonably pray that the same maybe regulated accordinge to act of Assembly, without often adjournment att Pleasure, which there is noe apparent cause for soe doinge.

Ans.   This Complaint if true is in our humble opinion worthy to be recommended to & rectified by the assembly; or by his Majesties Governor and Councill for the ease of the Publick.

9.   They crave liberty to apeale in any dubious case, though dependinge upon a fair final value than 3000lb of tobacco, which would not heretofore be permitted.

Ans.   The reason why this liberty of apeales was shutt up was for the generall ease of the people of this County, there beinge a sea of 7 leaugs which separates this part from the rest of the Collony; which however if found convenient for this County upon their complaint the Assembly will without doubt, lay appeales open to them as well as to other parts of the Country.

10.   They desire that noe drinke may be sould within a mile of the Court howse on the Court dayes for avoydinge the evill consequences by them in this article enumerated to accrue thereby.

Ans.   There are good Laws to restraine the abuses of drinkinge, & if not duly executed the fault maye be justly imputed to the Magistrates neglect & omission.

11.   They are against havinge any ordinary or tipplinge howse allowed in this County.

Ans.   Wee see noe reason to disallow the reasonable lawfull use of ordinaries & drinking houses.[25]

25. The burgesses on several occasions had passed laws designed to prevent "disorderly behavior and drunkenness." The burgesses required licenses to run a tavern, regulated prices, and, in 1668, attempted to limit "the exorbitant number of ordinaries and tipling houses" in the counties. The burgesses would permit no more than "one or two" in a county. In June of 1676, the Baconian Assembly suppressed all ordinaries unless built "in James Citty, and at each side of Yorke River, at the two great ferries of that river." See Hening, ed., *The Statutes at Large,* 2: 19-20, 234, 263, 268-269, 361.

12.   They complaine of the Magistrates being absent when orders are entered whereby many inconveniencys maye arise and Corruption is Practised, and that contrary to the usuall Course and Practice of Law orders are penn'd in private att the Magistrates howse, between him and the clerke, when as they ought to enter and examine all orders in open Court: They therefore desire that the act conceringe this be more strictly enjoyned, by a fine upon such defaults, to be committed for the future.

Ans.   If this Complaint be true wee humbly conceive itt fitt for the Assembly to enforce a stricter observance of a Printed law made to prevent the abuses complained of.

13.   They desire that sheriffs, clerks, Constables, Surveyers of high wayes, &c maye doe somethinge ex officio without fees.

Ans.   It is in our opinion unreasonable to desire or expect that sheriffs or clerks should performe Business *ex officio* without payinge them their due and just fees: Butt such fees as are Exorbitant to be left to the assembly to regulate if not already done by them.

14.   They propose that the Indians of the Easterne shore in Virginia maye be obliged to Kill a Certaine number of Wolves yearely for such satisfaction as may be thought fitt without the profit of particular men.[26]

Ans.   Wee Cannot in our humble Judgement thinke itt just to impose anythinge upon the Indians butt what they are by the articles of peace obliged to, butt if they maye be perswaded upon fitt encouragement to doe as is desired, wee Suppose itt maye be a very good service to the Country.

15.   They desire that noe Sheriff may officiate two yeares togeather.

Ans.   The article is provided for both by a Publick act and present practice to the contrary.

16.   They desire that noe person be admitted to bear any office till he shall have bin five yeares upon the place.

26. On the eastern shore Indians, see Helen C. Rountree and Thomas E. Davidson, *Eastern Shore Indians of Virginia and Maryland* (Charlottesville: University Press of Virginia, 1997).

Ans.   The last assembly have provided in this particular by a late act that none shall bear any public office under beinge 3 yeares Inhabitant in that Colony.

17.   They declare that whereas their shore is compassed with shoals insomuch that noe shipps but of small burden Can come to trade and those that Come butt few and Inconsiderable; itt maye be taken into Consideration and accordingly ordered, that noe person in this their County maye be suffered to ingrosse any Commodities as formerly to the great prejudice of the Commonaltie, that is to saye noe man shall within six weekes or what other time maye be thought convenient after the shipps or vessels morringe in the Creeke buy more than his own crop doth amount to att any Store.

Ans.   Wee have incerted this article att large in their own words, & doe hereby most humbly referr this business to the Right Honorable the Committee of trade to consider of.

Accomack County

1.   In the first place they Complaine of the great prejudice, expence and loss of many mens crops by watchinge and wardinge on all parts of the shore to hinder the rebells landinge, and protect the lives of the Right Honorable Sir William Berkeley and severall other loyall Gentlemen from the fury and rage of Bacon and Complices; they plead Ignorance of the cause and protest against the actings of the said Rebells.

Ans.   This County was all along to the last a most loyall place and the one Asilum of the Right Honorable the Governor and his party in the time of these troubles, to the great Prejudice and loss of many people there as is Complained of: But this only by the Courage, constancy, and loyalty of Major General Custis was kept up but when the Governor came to try the courage of the commonalty at James Citty itt proved the loss of the Town, but a few Gentlemen keepinge close to him, & the rest intent only on plunder.

2.   They desire his Majestie to Continue Sir William Berkeley Governor of Virginia as long as god shall spare him life.

Ans.   This Petitionary Article is become needless upon the late decease of the Right Honorable Governor.[27]

3.   The Right Honorable Governor haveinge promised that as well this County of Accomack as the rest of the Eastern Shore should be free from all County taxes for these one and twenty yeares to be issuinge, they therefore praye his Majestie will by his Royall Grant be gratiously pleased to confirme the same to them.

Ans.   Wee can doe noe more than most humbly to present to his Majestie this theire humble desires, and to assert the loyaltie, Services and great Sufferings of this County in the time of the late rebellion as most worthy his Majesties Royall Consideration, butt wee feare this Exemption will prove a Pressure to other Counties.

4.   They praye that beinge sensible of the great charge of this late unhappy warr & Rebellion, that they beinge in noe wayes the Cause of itt, maye be exempted from defrayinge any part of the charge thereof.

Ans.   Wee are humbly of opinion that they merit much of favour, in the mittigatinge & taking off such taxes, havinge borne more of the Burthen of the warr than any other County and approved themselves faithfull, loyall Subjects to his majesties Government; but theire is regard to be had to the other counties least they be over-burthened.

5.   They haveinge heared this his Majestie did gratiously intend to have given the Country their quitt Rents for many yeares to come; which they doubt this unhappy warr hath broke off, humbly praye that itt maye still remane good to them, beinge in noe wayes the cause or Knowinge of the late Rebellion.

Ans.   His Majestie hath an Eminent object for his Royall favours in this truly loyall County, which in all justice wee are found most humbly to recommend to his Majesties most gracious consideration; butt how his Majestie is determined concerninge this quitt Rents wee have not heard: but doe humbly conceive itt fitt to goe to the maintenance of a garrison if any of the souldiers be thought fitt to be Continued there.

27. Sir William Berkeley died on 9 July 1677 in England.

Lancaster County

1. They desire that the warr against the Indians be more speedily and effectually prosecuted than formerly and that such other corse be taken for the Security of the English as is by the Ensuinge articles propounded.[28]

Ans. To the fifth article all is answered by the Indian Peace.

5. They desire all loss and damages in the late ill times may be borne by the Sufferers and looked upon as the chance of warr.

Ans. This wee could wish might be otherwise, but are convinced that it cannot be for reasons alleaged the Povertie of the Countrie.

6. The delinquents' Estates be given to the poor and loyall sufferers.

Ans. This Contradicts the former and indeed this division is impracticall, should it be granted, and would leave the wives & children of those wretched men that have suffered death without bread to feed them.

7. For division of this County into two Counties.

Ans. This to be decided by the Major part of the Inhabitants of the whole Countie.

8. Concerninge the 2s. per pound.

Ans. Answered as in other grievances.

9. For Removeinge of James Citty to some part of Yorke River.

Ans. Wee conceive this an idle proposition only to save ferry money three times a yeare and laye itt upon other parts as many in Number, though not soe scattered on the other side of the River where they would have itt.

---

28. Wiseman and the Commissioners, apparently feeling that the Lancaster men had presented them with nothing new, did not include copies of their second, third, and fourth grievances.

10. For revivinge a law against hogg stealinge and makeinge itt felony as itt is by the Laws of England.

Ans. Fitt only to be offered to the Assembly.

11 & 12. For eneactinge laws for the Encouragement of Servants.

Ans. This allso to be left to the foregoinge examination.

13. Against the frequency of Assemblys and their long sittinge

Ans. Allready provided for and therefore the method prescribed falls off.

14. Complaininge of the uselessness of the forts found by Experience in the time of the late unhappy troubles.

Ans. Redressed by dismantlinge them upon the common complaints and clamorous commotions of the People against them.

Warwick County

The Preamble

A modest justification that all the time of the late Rebellion they had not taken up armes against his Majesties Government yet an humble acknowledgement withal that they stood in need of his Majesties gratious Pardon; since they had bin forced as well as others to take Bacons oath and doe other things they are now sensible were against their duty and allegiance, therefore withal thankfulness they most humbly imbrace and layehold of his Majesties most Gratious Pardon & forgiveness.

There desires are these thatt follow (viz.)

1. That noe tax maye be imposed on them butt by Assembly.

Ans. Wee never knew that itt was laid otherwise and therefore see noe cause for the feare.

2. That all persons maye be rated & taxed accordinge to their estates reall and Personall, but on their lands Especially.

Ans.   A thinge to be wished but never to be granted there; except enjoy-
         ned by Royall authority from hence; and if soe wee know not how
         itt will be relished by the landed men, since of Common usage has
         bin allwayes taxinge per poll.

3.   That noe persons maye have two places of publick profitt.

Ans.   Perhapps if this should be granted there would not be findable men
         sufficient singly to execute them.

4.   That Attorneys fees maye be limited.

Ans.   A thing difficult and dangerous to be attempted, since they must
         undertake all causes by the great, which will render them liable to
         the Penaltie of the Statute. [29]

5.   An account is desired of the 60lb of tobacco per poll in 1674 &
         1675.

Ans.   Often asked as often answered.

6.   All ordinaries to be putt down except for the Countries conven-
         iences.

Ans.   Thatt Conveniences to be left to the Justices of the County as in
         England.

7.   That Powder &c purchased with the Counties money maye remane
         in the County for a magazine.

---

29. In the codification of the colony's laws in 1662, the burgesses dictated fees chargeable by the colonial secretary (for depositions, or a "bond and recording itt," and for "Recording a will" and other matters); for the clerks of the county courts (for a deposition,
for instance, or a deed or subpoena); and for the clerk of the assembly (for militia commissions, for "copying the acts of assembly"); and for sheriffs. See Hening, ed., *The Statutes at Large*, 2: 144-146. The laws made pursuing justice in colonial courts an expensive undertaking. The Burgesses, in 1679, finally enacted a law stating "that noe attorney
or attorneys . . . take, demand, or receive from any person or persons, more for any cause
in the generall court and bringing the same to judgment, then five hundred pounds of
tobacco and caske, and for any cause in the county courts and bringing the same to judgment more than one hundred and fifty pounds of tobacco and caske." See Hening, ed.,
The Statutes at Large, 2: 479.

Ans.   Reasonable soe a place is provided to secure itt in.

8.   That all Clerks fees maye be regulated.

Ans.   This to be left to the Assembly, the proper Judges of Executions in that designe or else to the Secretary.

Isle of Wight County

In the Preamble:

They Excuse themselves for takinge up armes as being necessitated thereunto by these followinge Reasons:

1.   The great Taxes especially thatt of buildinge of forts on the fronteers, uselesse, Ruinous as they proved to the end they were erected.

2.   The Command from June Assembly 1676 to send 57 men under the Command of Bacon which was accordingly done with two months provisions.

3.   When their men were gonn out Sir William Berkeley endeavoured to raise men in Gloster County against them which that County refused to doe.

4.   The Governor and great men as they call them flyinge to Accomack leavinge them without a head under Bacons Power and Command.

Grievances and Answers

1.   The oppression of Colonel Joseph Bridger[30] in exactinge from the County 14 or 15 thousand weight of tobacco for 4 dayes entertaininge three Commissioners, viz. Colonel Cole[31], Colonel Chas.

30. Colonel Joseph Bridger (1628-1686) had been a member of Berkeley's council. He had been driven into exile in Maryland by Bacon, whose followers considered him one of their greatest oppressors. In December of 1676 Bridger returned to the colony with a vengeance aboard the fleet led by Captain Morris. He led militia forces loyal to the governor in attacks that combined plunder with a desire to crush the rebellion. His Isle of Wight neighbors hated him for his rapaciousness. See Stephen Saunders Webb, *1676: The End of American Independence* (New York: Knopf, 1984), 96.

31. Colonel William Cole (1638-1694), was one of Berkeley's most hated counselors. His "assertion" that the Pamunkey and Appomatox Indians were "Friends" of the colony who "we ought to defend with our blood" was specifically denounced in Bacon's "Manifesto." See Wilcomb E. Washburn, *The Governor and the Rebel: A History of Bacon's Rebellion* (Chapel Hill: University of North Carolina Press, 1957), 34.

Moryson;[32] & Colonel Mason[33] whoo mett att Bridgers howse about the devidinge of the County.

Ans.   This grievance was the more narrowly inquired into because one of the Commissioners entertained was a near relation to one of us; but wee find itt without cause complained of; for the tobacco was for a debt owinge Bridger for Soliticinge the Counties business 17 yeares toegather in which time he spent much more than the sum demanded.

2.   They complaine of Colonel Bridgers fineinge 2 men for not appearinge in armes, which amountinge to severall thousand pounds of tobacco they would know to what use itt was imployed.

Ans.   Colonel Bridger beinge a chiefe of the Militia imposed these mulcts[34] for neglect of duty as a thinge practicall by power of the Militia in other parts of the Country.

3.   The great taxes more than usuall laid by the assembly

Ans.   Of this they must aske their Representatives the reason that were privy & present at the imposinge them.

4.   The great quantities of tobacco leavyed for buildinge of howses of Publick use and reception at James Town, which were not habitable butt fell down before the finishinge them:

Ans.   They maye seeke their lawfull remedy against the undertakers and workemen for the defect complained of as they have just cause.

5&6.   For haveinge noe account nor use of the fort dutyes and that notwithstanding those duties they are forced to find themselves armes and ammunition att their own charge.

Ans.   Both these answered that it is for want of Magazeen howses to secure the Publick stores that the same are lost or misspent.

---

32. Colonel Charles Moryson, a nephew of the commissioner. Not surprisingly, the commissioners found that the charge that Moryson had misappropriated funds in Isle of Wight County was without merit. See Washburn, *The Governor and the Rebel*, 124.
33. Mason (1629-1686) earlier had led the attacks against the Doegs and Susquehannocks that to a great extent had precipitated the rebellion. See Chapter Four, above.
34. *mulcts.* Fines imposed for an offense or any other kind of penalty (OED).

7.   A complaint for sendinge out Indian forces to find out and apprehend their Xtian neighbours as they tearm them.

Ans.   Which in truth is to apprehend the worst of Rebells that are fled from his Majesties Justice or rather Mercy since pardoned if they had come in on time accordinge to Proclamation.

8.   The seizinge Estates before Conviction and of such as laid hold of the late Governors indemnity, and admitted to take the oath of allegiance.

Ans.   Complained of by many while wee were upon the Place, and as often Represented to the Governor as a corse contrary to law; in which he apealed to his Majestie and the learned Judges of England.

9.   A desire to their Burgesses to give noe more of their estates awaye by imposing of new Taxes.

Ans.   A thing to be wished butt wee Know not how it Cann be effected, consideringe the annuall occasions for raisinge taxes upon publick emergencies.

10.   A Complaint against Sheriffs continuing above one year in their office.

Ans.   This is not practized since those complaints whatever has bin done formerly.

11.   A wild proposition for a Continuall war with the Indians.

Ans.   and that they desire to be excused from payinge more taxes, not consideringe the charge that attends such a warr.

12.   Liberty desired to chose theire Vesterys without any member of Court to be Eligible.

Ans.   Referr'd to the Custome of other Counties.

13.   Noe Councillor to sitt in any inferior Court.

Ans.   Answered Before.

14.   They desire a land Tax only maye be laid.

Ans.   To be wisht but impracticall, otherwise than as wee have before propos'd by making every hundred above a thousand acres to paye equall with a tythable.

15.   Major Powell[35] haveinge 100lb. of tobacco a daye for dividinge the County as is complained of.

Ans.   Wee Know nothinge of itt butt believe hee might deserve itt.

16.   Allso that he had 12lb. per poll to buy the County ammunition which they never had any account of.

Ans.   Wee conceive hum liable to give an account when itt is required of him.

17.   They desire an account of the 2s. per pound.

Ans.   This is done every yeare in England, & wee beleve soe it is allso in Virginia, but the use they desire to have this imposition to, is wholy besides his Majesties Intentions and Instructions.

18.   They desire to have their County freed from all charges of buildinge those uselesse forts on the frontiers against the Indians, which they first find fault with.

Ans.   Since other Countyes complaine of the same thinge and as well deserve Exemption itt is not to be expected that their proportion of this County should be taken off from them and laid upon those other Counties, but that all should bear theire part if occasion were as none is like to be now.

19.   They desire an account of the 60lb. per poll.

Ans.   Answered often before.

20.   That the Publick leavyes maye be laid in open court and not privately.

---

35. Major John Powell, one of Governor Berkeley's most active supporters in the county, and a long-serving officer in the local militia. See John Bennett Boddie, *Seventeenth-Century Isle of Wight County, Virginia* (Baltimore: Southern Book Company, 1959), 161.

Ans.   Wee judge itt reasonable since all are concerned in them.

21.   They desire an account of Castle dutyes.

Ans.   Reasonable to be demanded and given in by the Assembly, butt not every particular person.

22.   That those duties maye be paid in Kind as heretofore in Powder and Shott.

Ans.   Reasonable allso soe ther be places of Security apointed & provided for Magazeens.

23.   A Complaint not against the abuse but against the amercements

Ans.   This laid by the laws of the Country as appears by the Printed booke.

24.   A desire that none should be exempt'd from leavyes.

Ans.   Provided for accordinge to their desire by the last assembly; the Councill themselves beinge allso made liable.

25.   A Justification of their takinge Bacons Oath by Example of theire Militia and Magistrates that tooke the same before them.[36]

There is remaininge in our hands a Protest against these grievances, as complained of without cause by another part of the same County.

New Kent County

1.   They complaine of the 60lb. per poll.

Ans.   This is already answered.

2.   The many Murders, Rapines, & depradations done by the Indians on their persons, stocks & estates, &c.

Ans.   Remedyed by the Peace with them.

36. The commissioners offered no answer to this particular grievance.

3.   The Extortions of sheriffs &c. complained of.

Ans.   Referred to the assembly and thought worthy of redress.

4.   They present as a grievance the sellinge of strong liquors where the County courts are kept.

Ans.   People that travill must have places of refreshment, but the abuse of drinkinge is by the laws provided against.

5.   They complaine of the fort duties as misemployed &c.

Ans.   If soe itt is for want of a fitt magazeen to keep them in; for want whereof they are often extravagantly expended att the Pleasure of the Storekeeper, &c.

6.   Of the 2s. per pound which they mistake as given by his Majesties favor to lessen their leavyes.

Ans.   It is intended and imployed to the Support of the Government; and as a stock for the raisinge and Encouraginge manufacturinge in that his Majesties Collony.

Elizabeth City County

1.   They present as their grievance the great charge occurringe to their Small County by the frequent meeting of Assemblys.

Ans.   The first is already remedied by his Majesties Speciall Command and instructions, under the Privy Signett and signe manuall, lately sent over to the Governor of Virginia.

2.   They complaine that beinge in this County not above 300 tythables which in the Publick leavy amounts to above 30lb of tobacco per poll in this County; when other Counties pay not above 6lb or 8lb a tobacco a head by reason of their great number of Tythables; they praye that their charg maye be putt in the Publick leavye that they maye pay proportionable onely to their small number.

Ans.   As to this latter grievance it must of necessity be left to the assembly since the Regulation of Tythables, beinge of a publick concern, other Counties might also happen to receive prejudice by that they here desire to be redressed.

Henrico County

Grievances and Answers

1.   They complaine that it is a most unsupportable grievance and oppression that the Indian Trade is Monopolized, and that in favor of
the monopolisers the people are betrayed to the Indians.

Ans.   Wee conceieve this a reall grievance & allso a great occasion of
the warr with the Indians. Therefore in the articles of peace wee
have left itt as worthy of the next assembly's Consideration to remedy.

2.   A Complaint that noe satisfaction hath bin had for the abundance
of blood spilt by the Indians for many years past, and that the
Erectinge of forts which proved defenceless against the Indians, &
that the Murders and Incursions rather increased after the erecting
them.

Ans.   These Complainants never considered that the breach of the peace
and occasion of blood shed has all bin on the side of the English;
which was publickly justified & affirmed in open Court in the face
of a very great Assembly & denyed by none. Butt this falls of by
the peace lately made with the Indians and the complaint against
the forts silenced by dismantling them.

3.   A complaint against the heavy taxes imposed especially the 60lb
per poll.

Ans.   Noe taxes imposed but by the Assembly where they had represent-
tatives; and for the 60lb per poll it is returned back with advantage:
viz: a gratious Royall Promise that the Country shall have the patents called in without charge which were prejudiciall to them.

4.   It is theire desire and request to have an imediat warr with all Indians in Generall; and that the charge maye be borne by voluntary
aydes and contributions of men and provisions and Commanders
apointed, who have interest in the Peoples affections to encourage
and forward this designe.

Ans.   A wild request to have a warr with all the Indians of a Continent,
and this by voluntary contribution proposed to be caryed on; when
if those very requestors were to be tryed upon any just occasion

they should be the first that would cry out of the charge and be unwillinge to paye 6d towards itt: [37] But God be thanked, there is now noe need to try them, since wee have a good peace with the Indians: Besides, by the desire of haveinge Commanders such as have interest in the peoples affections they shew their old mutinous humors, and in effect to desire new Bacons to head them.

5.   A Complaint, the major part of the Commissioners of their County courts are akin to one another, and desire noe County nor parish taxes be leavyed without att least six of the Comonaltie be joined to the Commissioners at the layinge the leavye.

Ans.   Wee know not how this can be helped in soe little choice, butt sure kindred must agree there better than with us if they be allwaies of one mind: for joyneinge six of the Commonaltie to the layinge the leavy, the consequence wee believe will be, noe leavyes will be laid, butt the time spin out in disputes and wranglings: Butt that it should be laid in open Court wee thinke most reasonable.

6.   A Complaint for beinge prohibited of haveinge ammunition & of their want thereof to defend themselves against their Indian Enimies.

Ans.   This is now remedied both by the law that restrained itt, which beinge but *pro tempore* is fallen off and by the Present Peace made with the Indians.

Yorke County

1.   A very modest preamble, Justifyinge Sir William Berkeley; that noe oppression of his was the rise and occasion of the late destractions but that the same proceeded from some disaffected persons spurninge against authority, and that the Pretence of the Dilatory Proceedings against the Indians was only taken up for a cloake and referrs to the acts made in the March Assembly before to shew what provision was made.

For the first part wee have charity to beleave itt, for before the warr with the Indians wee Can find noe Considerable grievance arisinge from the Governor, to give the people any Just cause of complaint of his management.

37. 6 pennies.

Butt for the latter part which concerns the dilatory proceedings for the Security of the people from the frequent murders and Depradations of the Indians; Since the same thing is Complained of by all other counties, and wee find the acts referred to very ineffectuall, for the defence of the Country, wee must still be of opinion that there were great and fatall Errors Committed in the Management of the Indian warr both by the Assembly and Governor.

Grievances and Answers

1. The too frequent meetinge of Assemblies; and the great allowance to Burgesses complained of as a grievance, &c.

Ans. This has bin Complayned of by divers other Counties and is Remedyed by his Majesties immediate Command & Instructions for restraininge the first and retrenchinge the latter.

2. Thatt the chiefe and only towne in Virginia beinge now burned maye be removed and built att middle Plantation as beinge which in land and farther off a river side &c.

Ans. This is just as if Middlesex should have petitioned that London might have been new built on high gate hill, and removed from the grand River that brings them in their trade.

3. An humble request for freedom to transport wheat or other commodities of the Countrys growth, except tobacco to the Azores and Canarie Islands; and to returne with any Comodities of the product of these Islands, as allso to enjoye the like liberty which is granted in new England and Newfoundland to fetch salt from any port in Europe by the shippinge that soley belongs to his Majesties Collony of Virginia.[38]

Ans. This is the full of their desires in theire own words recited that, soe the right Honorable Commissioners of trade maye consider of itt, to whose cognaisance as wee humbly conceive itt most properly apertains.

4. Against extortions of fees by Clerks and Sheriffs and that the latter continue noe longer than one yeare in their office.

38. To clarify, to allow that salt to be shipped by any ships from the colony of Virginia.

Ans.   The first is provided against by laws in the Printed booke, and for the latter it's not now in practice; though used soe before for 3 or 4 yeares togeather.

5.   They humbly begg of his Majestie a parcel of land of 70 acres, late Thomas Hanford and now forfeited as they suppose, who was condemned by a Councill without a Jurie, and Executed before our arrival in Virginia, and this they desire for a court howse as given by his fathers will to that intent.[39]

Ans.   Wee most humbly referr this to his Majesties pleasure but hope that his Majestie will act most gratiously to restore the estates of those wretched men to their miserable wives & children which will be an act of great mercy.

6.   Thatt all tobacco markt for payment of just debts beinge seized be discharg'd therefrom.

Ans.   This wee thought reasonable and acquainted the Right Honorable Governor soe, and believe he ordered therein accordingly for the complaint seased.

7.   Thatt attorneys maye have noe more than 50lb of tobacco for pleadinge a cause.

Ans.   If they intend (*pro una vice*)[40] wee thinke itt reasonable; butt if the cause shall require oftener attendance, such retrenchments of fees would leave the poore people unable to express their cause and without any to speake for them att Courts.

8.   A desire of revivinge a law concerninge plantinge and orderinge of tobacco & for advancinge the price of that Comoditie.

---

39. Thomas Hanford had commanded Bacon's forces holding Jamestown. When Governor Berkeley returned there on September 7, Hanford knew that he did not have the strength to hold the town. His men fled, but Hanford rode out to notify Bacon of the governor's return. After Bacon's death in October, Hanford took command of rebel forces near Yorktown. He was captured on 13 November 1676, by Beverley while, reportedly, paying "his oblations in the Temple of Venus." He asked Berkeley for mercy, on the grounds that "he had never taken up arms, but for the destruction of the Indians, who had murthered so many Christians." The governor refused to hear his appeal, so Hanford asked to be shot, the fate of a soldier. Berkeley ordered him hanged as a rebel. See Washburn, *The Governor and the Rebel*, 80, 86-87; Webb, *1676*, 60, 85, 105.

40. *pro una vice.* In this one instance.

Ans.   Onely fitt and Proper for the Assembly to consider of and provide for.

9.   An account is desired of the occasion & disposal of the 60lb per poll.

Ans.   Often answered before in other Grievances.

10.   The like is desired of the 2s per pound.

Ans.   This allso answered againe & againe.

11.   That his Majesties Quitt Rents be paid in Tobacco att two pence per pound, as formerly accustomed.

Ans.   It was never paid otherwise but this beinge part of the Royall Revenue though never Accounted for into the Exchequer; is most humbly left to the Right Honorable the Lord High Treasurer of England.

12.   That Courts of Justice maye be opened and that all just debts of any delinquents maye be paid out of their estates; that his Majesties good subjects may not be prejudiced in their just rights & dues.

Ans.   The first was done upon our comminge in to the Country; and the other part of the Repetition wee cannot butt thinke reasonable and accordinge to Justice.

In Conclusion

An humble alliance in his Majesties Royall releife and favor
for the good of this whole Colony; and particular County of
Yorke: togeather with a free protest and promise to bear faith
and true allegiance to his Most Sacred Majestie &c.

Gloster County

Grievances and Answers

1.   A complaint that the imposition of the 2s per pound laid by act of Assembly about 17 yeares since on tobacco shipt in this Country is a grievance, unless itt maye be imployed to the uses pretended when first raised.

Ans.   Wee humbly conceive itt reasonable that an account be rendered to the assembly, which wee take to be the Body representative of the Country, of the overplus of this Imposition above 1000 per annum to the Governor for the time beinge, & wee hold the continuance of this law most fitt and necessary, beinge made by the Country and confirmed by his Majestie.

2.   They Complaine of the 60lb per poll as a Pressure that occasioned the first discontents among the people; they beg an account and restitution.

Ans.   This hath bin full answered to themselves while wee were upon the place butt upon the frequent complaints in the foregoinge grievances.

3.   A complaint that within 14 or 15 months past there has bin near 300 xtian persons barbarously murdered by the Indians, and that the forts erected and other provisions assigned was wholly insufficient to the end intended, and that this was the occasion of the Peoples risinge in armes for their own preservation; without Command or Permission of their Superiors, & gave opportunity to the Rebell Bacon to head them whom beinge among them reputed a witt was by the vulgar adheared to and havinge obtained and published his forced Commission to the Severall Counties as freely granted him by the grand assembly, many people were ignorantly deluded and drawn into his Party, that thought of noe other designe than the Indian Warr onely; most of which persons though never soe inocent were prosecuted with Rigour of which with the ill management of this warr they complaine as grievances.

Ans.   This hath reference to our Generall Narrative and confirms some particulars of itt wherefore wee thought it necessary to recite this article the more att large, & humbly referr the same to his Majesties Royall Consideration as being matter of fact; of the truth whereof wee are well satisfied.

4.   That severall grievances being presented to the June Assembly 1676: upon which many good laws were consented to by the Assembly; before the Rebell Bacon came and interrupted the same; they begg those good and wholesome laws maye be Confirmed.

Ans.   Those laws att that time Enacted are since annul'd and ordered to be repealed by his Majestie; however if any of them be laws fitt to be revived, for the publicke good they maye be againe propounded to their Burgesses for Reenactinge.

5.   A Complaint that in the time of the late Rebellion the Rebells have plundered divers mens estates; they praye that the Assembly will take some care for restitution of what is to be found in Specie.

Ans.   This was accordingly referred to the last assembly.

6.   A complaint that some particular persons neer about the Governor: haveinge commission to plunder the late rebells, have misemployed that power to imprisonment; and riflinge the Estates of divers of his Majesties good subjects convertinge the same to their own private uses in which they beg redresses.

Ans.   This complaint is not untrue for in the time of the late rebellion withal that were not with the Governor, but staid at home att their own plantations to be secure & quiett were accounted Rebells and treated as such especially such as Kept any guard att their howses though butt for self preservation against the Indians on the frontier parts & committed noe other act of hostility but what was defensive only.

7.   A Complaint against Major Robert Beverley that with this County had accordinge to order raised 60 armed men to be an outguard for the Governor who not findinge the Governor nor their appointed Commander they were by Beverley commanded to goe to worke to fall trees; and maurls[41] and toat railes; which many of them refusinge to doe, he presently disarmed them and sent them home att a time when this Country was infested with the Indians who had but a little before cutt of 6 persons in one family and attempted others; They beg reparation against the said Beverly and his Majesties and Governors Pardon.

Ans.   Wee conceive this dealinge of Beverly to be a notorious abuse, and grievance to take awaye the peoples armes, while their families were cutt off by the Indians, and they desire just reparation therein.

8.   They desire the grand assembly to take order that the arms and ammunition sent over by his Majestie to the Country maye be proportionably distributed in each County into the hands of persons of

41. Presumably to fertilize the soil.

trust, for the use of the Country against occasions and that they may not be lost as they complaine men armes were formerly used to be.

Ans.   This is in the assembly care and a secure Magazeen or storehowse will prevent & Remedy the matter complained of as to the loss of armes &c.

9.   A Complaint against the too frequent assemblys, and the high charges of Burgesses of assembly.

Ans.   This remedied in both particulars by his Majesties Express Command.

10.   A Complaint of considerable sum of money colected for fort duties, now lyinge in private mens hands, desiringe the same maye be laid out for a Magazeen for the good of the Publick.

Ans.   Wee thinke itt very reasonable that the Assembly take the account and doe therein as is desired; which will answer the 8th article above written.

11.   A Complaint that there is a Proclamation prohibiting all matters of shipps, and marchants from selling any gunns or ammunition to the Inhabitants of this Collony: the Indians then makeinge daily Incursions upon them.

Ans.   This was only a prohibition *pro tempore* duringe the continuance of the late rebellion butt wee now conceive they have or maye have the liberty desired as they had formerly, besides there is now a peace with the Indians which answers the conclusion of this article.

Lower Norfolk County

Grievances and Answers:

1.   They desire that a fort maye be erected att Point Comfort as beinge the most convenient place &c.

Ans.   Wee are of opinion that a fort at point Comfort will be very requisite if money and Materialls can be found, and men to Erect and keep itt, but wee thinke in our Judgement that it is Impracticall with all is done to be build, man or maintaine a good fort there.

2. A Complaint that theire has bin tobacco paid towards the raisinge of a Magazeene besides the fort duties, taken for that use yet noe provision made nor account thereof given by those intrusted to collect the same.

Ans. The magazeens are most necessary & the accounts desired reasonable and fitt to be given by the Collectors of the tobacco raised and paid for their publick use.

3. A complaint of the 60lb of tobacco per poll whereof they desire an account.

Ans. Answered in other grievances.

4. An humble request since those of this County have bin great Sufferers by, and in noe wise the cause of the late rebellion, they maye be exempted from all publick charge that hath risen or maye thereby arise.

Ans. Wee thinke there is little notice of this request to be taken by us; butt by the Assembly who are only concerned in layinge Taxes, there beinge none imposed by his Majestie on this account; nor as wee humbly conceive like to be.

5. An extravagant request for liberty to transport their tobacco to any of his Majesties plantations, without payinge the impost payable by act of parliament.

Ans. This head is wholly mutinous to desire a thing contrary to his Majesties Royall pleasure and benifitt, and allso against an act of Parliament.

6. A Complaint that itt hath bin the Common practice of this Country to putt persons that are meer strangers into places of great honor, profitt and trust, Who unduely officiating therein doe abuse and wrong the people &c as has bin manifested in those two great rebells Nathaniell Bacon and Giles Bland: who bred great discords among the people; they pray that for preventinge the like for the time to come this maye be remedied &c.

Ans. This the late assembly have remedied by an act against admittinge any to beare any publick place or office that have not bin 3 yeares inhabitant in the Country which answers the waye prescribed by this article of theirs.

7.   They desire that noe person within the Government of Virginia doe sell any ammunition for warr to the Indians.

Ans.   This must be referred to the articles of Peace as to the clause which concerns the restraininge or layinge open the trade with them and if Maryland be left att liberty in this particular, and Virginia not, they will ingross the Beaver trade and those of Virginia be deprived of that Benefitt and the Indians furnished with powder &c in as plentifull manner as now.

Nancymond County

Grievances First Presented Us and Answers

The Preamble: Information of the rise and occasion of the late distractions, Tumults, and disturbances in Virginia; with a due acknowledgement of & hearty thankful expressions of sorrow for their late disloyaltie.

The first thing they Complaine of is:

1.   The uselessness and charges of forts built in the woods against the Indians.
Ans.   Taken notice of in other grievances, & now redressed because demolished.

2.   They desire confirmation of the acts in June Assembly (76) because most of their grievances were by those acts redressed.

Ans.   Impudent and mutinous to aske seeinge his Majestie has by his instructions and proclamation declared all that assemblys Laws null and void, because of Bacons force att the time upon the Assembly then sittinge.

3.   A desire that they maye have a war with all nations and families of the Indians whatsoever without favoringe any.

Ans.   A wild proposition which Consideringe this would intaile a perpetuall warr, and consequently a perpetuall tax on the Country.

4.   An excuse for sendinge men to Bacons army beinge ordered soe by governor, Councill, & Burgesses and their own ignorance in not Knowinge his Commission to be violently extorted; with a Complaint against two levyes in generall words and never since any particular Charge laid on them but what triviall.

Ans.   Wee are perswaded that they were induced to beleve, as they sett forth in their grievances, for there was nothing of a good while to contradict the validity of Bacons forced Commission, and undeceive the ignorant & seduced people gone forth by the Governor.

5.   They desire Restitution of such armes as have bin taken from them and for things seized or taken from them, they express themselves content that every man should bear his own loss.

Ans.   Wee thinge both the first and latter reasonable, especially the bearinge everyone his own loss; since theire is noe redressinge the latter without charginge the publick.

6.   They desire they may paye noe Tax this yeare by reason of their great losses and heavy charges occasioned by the troubles last yeare.

Ans.   Those men that in the 3rd article before desired a perpetuall warr against the Indians in this desire an exemption from all Taxes this yeare; which is impossible, soe many Justifications after the rebellion requiringe itt.

7.   They desire that noe tobacco maye be given to any person for his reall or pretended services.

Ans.   Wee wish the assembly were not soe lavish in rewardinge the latter, and for the first it is very rare and therefore will not be burthensome.

8.   A charge against the Leavy for takinge awaye armes which was in the very highth of the rebellion and Center of the Rebells quarters.

Ans.   This is what themselves confess for in this very article they say they were resolved to defend themselves untill they heard from his Majestie, and that beinge wearyed and for want of Provisions, and for preservation they were induced to lay down theire armes;

which in ittselfe shows itts stubborne aversness to submit to the Governor.

9.   A complaint of an oath imposed on them by the Commissioners: that imposed Bacons oath before on them being an oath of fidelity to Sir William Berkeley there recited by them, and taken after their Subjection.

Ans.   The oath is noe other than what any honest, loyall person there would or ought to have tooke, and as wee conceive most proper to be att that time tendered to them.

10.   A desire that they may have leave to buy powder and shott.

Ans.   The Restraint was only *pro tempore* and is now taken off.

11.   A desire that they maye paye nothing towards the uselesse forts, or for what is already bought, and in store for that Purpose, beinge the same is of noe defence or Security to the Inhabitants.

Ans.   Wee conceive this request butt reasonable and that what is in store to that end, may either be better imployed or returned them.

12.   Thatt the Collectors for building a fort att Point Comfort maye be Called to an account.

Ans.   Thought reasonable, soe for all other Collections to do the same.

13.   They desire to know the Reason of Seizinge and Markinge all Tobacco after the warr was ended, to the detriment of trade and damage of divers Marchants.

Ans.   Wee Can shew noe reason for doeinge what is Complained of; though wee have often inquired into itt, and declared our dislike of itt.

14.   An account desired for the levyes annually raised to provide ammunition beinge in the hands of the militia, and they feigne to buy their own powder and shott themselves: They desire an account allso of the two shillings per pound.

Ans.   Reasonable that an account thereof be Rendered. The 2s per pound answered often before.

15.   They desire so for what use the 60lb per poll was leavyed.

Ans.   Answered in other Grievances. They and this article was a scandal wee Conceive to the governor, that he cal'd itt treason to enquire what use itt was for.

16.   They complaine that the Castle duties accustomed to be paid by the masters of shipps in Powder and shott for the Service and Security of the Country is now converted into shooes & stockins &c as best liketh the Collectors of itt and disposed of to their own Private advantage; They desire an account and that itt maye be paid as formerly in Powder and Shott &c.

Ans.   This Complaint if true is a reall grievance deservinge due redress, and an account thereof thought most reasonable as before.

17.   A Complaint against Justices, Clerks and Sheriffs, pleading in their own County courts they belong to.

Ans.   This is provided for by a law to bee seen in the Printed booke of acts of Assembly.

18.   A desire that noe Inhabitants exercizinge merchandise, maye be permitted to trade without due limitation of their gaines.

Ans.   A reasonable desire and not impracticall to be granted, itt beinge against trade.

19.   A Complaint Concerninge the Bounds of the County part beinge taken from this County and laid to Warwick creeke.[42]

Ans.   Fitt to be determined & rectified by a Jury of the Country.

---

42. In 1674 the House of Burgesses passed a law "ascertaining the bounds of the counties of Isle of Wight and Nanzemond." The burgesses described the boundary line between the counties, because "long disputes have arisen between the inhabitants of the Isle of Wight and Nanzemun counties concerning the divideing line and bounds betwixt them, which disputes have bin the more perplext by reason partly of the uncertainty found in these former acts . . . that have seemed to establish the limmits between them, and partly from the unacquaintance of those heretofore concerned with the true courses, windings, and extent of the creeks and runs, and of the lands remote in the woods." See Hening, ed., *The Statutes at Large,* 2: 318.

20.   A desire that one Justice maye grant an order upon a speciality, & execution to issue upon the same for any debt not exceeding 400lb of tobacco.

Ans.   This wee hold unreasonable to be practiced, and would for soe much introduce an arbitrary power when apeales as they allso aime att are taken awaye.

21.   They desire that Colonel Leare and Major Lear[43] maye give an account of what tobacco they have received of the Counties the last two yeares.

Ans.   Reasonable and wee believe never denied them.

22.   They desire the laws maye be irrevocable.

Ans.   A request not worthy consideration any further onely then as it intrenches on his Majesties Royall prerogative.

Nancymond County:
Second Grievances

Wee havinge received a Protest against the foregoinge Grievances
Signed with the hands of divers of his Majesties loyall subjects of that
County; wherein they most humbly begg his Majesties gratious
Pardon; condemninge those other persons who instead of soe
doeinge, doe rather seem to Justifie than humbly deplore
their late wicked defection; and in conclusion
declare by the said Protest that it is their greatest
grievance that ever they shold have occasion
of his Majesties gratious Pardon
which they all own they have in some
measure reason to beg and lay
hold of, and are most
humbly thanke full

43. John Lear came to Virginia in 1656, and he represented Nansemond County in the House of Burgesses from 1666 to 1676. He supported the governor ardently during the rebellion. He was among the first of the governor's supporters to meet the commissioners, and he told them that he had suffered heavily for his loyalty. The people of Nansemond hated Lear, and his brother, Mr. David Lear, for their monopoly over local office. The Nansemond complaints had no effect, for Major Lear in 1680 still served as justice of the peace and colonel in the county militia. On 23 May 1683, Governor Culpeper appointed him to the council, where he served until his death in 1695.

for:

Whereupon they have presented these followinge grievances as now Genuine than the former, beinge drawn up by a generall Consent of the Whole Countie of Nancemond.[44]

Grievances and Answers:

1. A complaint against the forts on the fronteers.

Ans. Answered in the first grievances.

2. That they were Pressed under Bacon by the lawfull magistrates, and such as refused forced thereto by the Militia officers.

Ans. This was the cause of many persons who Complained to us, of their being punished and ruin'd for actinge under a force they were unable to resist.

3. They declare that the militia officers were the persons that summoned them to take and administered Bacons oath to them, which with threats and menaces they induced them to take.

4. A Complaint against mens haveinge more than one office att a time instanced in Colonel Lear.

Ans. For what concerns Lear tis redressed who hath of himselfe laid down all.

5. They complaine against the great Taxes imposed these 3 or 4 yeares last past and they know not for what.

Ans. The fault if any lyes in their own Representatives, who both laid the taxes and ought to have satisfied their Electors upon what occasion they were laid.

---

44. Nansemond County reflects perfectly the divisions rending Virginia society. The 48 men who signed the second set of grievances claimed to be the loyal inhabitants of the county. They claimed not to have been consulted by the authors of the first set of grievances, men who in their view sought to justify their participation in Bacon's illegal rebellion. Both sets of grievances agree on several particulars, reflecting the widespread economic distress that had gripped the colony. See J. M. Sosin, *English America and the Restoration Monarchy of Charles II: Transatlantic Politics, Culture, and Kinship* (Lincoln: University of Nebraska Press, 1980), 193.

6.   They pray an account of the 60lb per pole.

Ans.   Answered often before in other Grievances.

7   The Price of Loyalty: Personal Grievances

Personall grievances of divers Inhabitants within his Majesties Collony of Virginia; proved before us his Majesties Commissioners, by oath, all which wee doe here with accordinge to their desires most humbly present in their own words as wee received the same, and doe give this short abstract as followeth (viz.)

No. 1:   The Petition of: Alexander Walker complaininge & provinge that 23 hogsheads of sweet sented tobacco were seized by the Right Honorable Sir William Berkeleys order, after the surrender of West point; which he marked in his Majesties name with the broad arrow head, and afterwards remarked the same anew with his own marke of *W:S:* and by order ship'd onboard Captain Martyns ship for the Governors use beinge the poor petitioners whole cropp of tobacco.[1]

Observations and opinions: The petitioners crime was for being guilty of takinge Bacons oath, which he was forced to doe, the same being administered to the petitioner by Colonel Thomas Ballard then being at the howse of Colonel Nathaniell Bacon.

No. 2:   The Complaint of Henry Jenkins of Sir William Berkeleys seizing 22 heads of cattle, for noe other cause but that the petitioner had saved & preserved with the best of his art; being by trade a tanner; some raw hides belonginge to the Governor which Bacons souldiers had taken and brought from green springe, and the petitioner kept and returned to Sir William Berkeley att his comminge back to Green Springe; the petitioner haveinge had five or six and 40 pairs of shoes ready made forcibly taken from him by Bacons party, the said Jenkins haveinge never bin in armes in the late Rebellion, nor any ways assisting to Bacon or his Party.[2]

---

1. A statement from the London merchant Robert Bristow supports Walker's petition. See Letters and Papers Concerning American Plantations, 5 February 1678/9–19 December 1679, C.O. 1/43, 35ro (VCRP).
2. We know little about Henry Jenkins, who practiced his trade in Surrey County.

Observations and Opinions: This seizure was after our cominge into the country, viz: on the 28 of March last and the complaint & proofe thereof made to us the 20th of Aprill followinge. The same night that the Complainant Henry Jenkins Tanner returne hime to James Town from us he was sent for very late that night to green Spring; where the Lady Berkeley told the Petitioner he should have his cattle return'd home to him, and the next daye they were all accordingly brought home except a cow; there beinge in all 10 cows, 6 calves & 6 steers at first taken from him by the Governors order, & before he petitioned about the same denyed to be restored to him by the Governor.

Butt howsoever the Governor ordered an action to be entered against him for more hides than ever he had after he had restored all he had as hee the complainant informed us:

No. 3:   **Petitions: Otho Throp.**[3] The Petitioner setts forth his great services and sufferings for the governor both in person and estate.

He personally attended the Governor att the siege of James Town.

His wife was one of those women Bacon forced from home, & sett on his Trenches before the Town.[4]

His Servants beinge vi in number all caryed awaye and his other estate to the value of 1200lb sterlinge plundered by the late Rebells.

That the Right Honorable Governor not mindinge the Petitioners faithfull Services and great losses but takinge advantage of some note or scroule[5] craftily obtained by Giles Bland from the Petitioner did not only cause his estate to be inventoried, his crop of tobacco to be marked with the broad arrow head; but allso seized the Petitioners

---

3. Captain Otho Throp of York County. His petition for redress from these losses was referred by the Privy Council to the Committee for Trade and Plantations on 22 December 1677. See Privy Council Register, 1677-1678, P.C. 2/66, 205, 212-213 (VCRP).

4. In September, when Bacon marched on Jamestown to lay siege to the governor's position, he took "the wives and female Relations of such Gentlemen as were in the Governor's service against him," and placed them "in the face of the Enemy, as Bulwarkes for their Battery." He put as well captive Pamunkey Indian prisoners on the entrenchments, reminding the governor's few remaining supporters in Jamestown that they risked their lives for an Indian-lover. See Stephen Saunders Webb, *1676: The End of American Independence*, (New York: Knopf, 1984), 64, and the Commissioners' Narrative, Chapter 4, above.

5. i.e., scrawl.

goods on board the Shipp *Planters adventure* to the value of 400lb sterling; whereby he was disabled to purchase tobacco to comply with his freight, taken on the said ship beinge 120 hogsheads.

Hee was thereupon constrained to pass his Bill to the Governor for 100lb stirling and to discharge Sir William Berkeley of a just debt of 96lb stirling:

And all this was imposed upon the Petitioner Otho Throp by reason of the aforesaid paper which Bland had treacherously gott of him when drinke had bereaved the Petitioner of his reason: The purpose of which paper was as the Petitioner was after informed his desistinge of the Governors raising of forces in Gloster County att such a time as Bacon had the force and strength of the whole Country in his Power and Command or to that effect.

Ve. Capt. Throps case upon oath; the depositions of Mr. Wm. Grice and Mr. Wm. Kerle.

Orders Opinion and Observation: Note that upon this Composition of Sir William Berkeley's the Governor, Sir William Berkeley, made an order of Restitution; releasinge his goods and tobacco for submittinge to this Censure past on him, and in assurance of his future loyaltie and good behavior. This Composition was made by Coll. Ludwell, and the Governor for the 100lb stirling had fowr Negros of Alderman Jefferys.

Another order of the same date, viz. January 20, 1676[6] was granted by the Governor to Captain Throp recitinge the loss of his whole estate by plunder of the late Rebells, and thereby requiring all persons who have any part of the Petitioners estate to make imediat returne and delivery thereof to him and to make search for the same, &c.

Note allso that the said Throp did on the 18th day of April last petition Sir William Berkeley to redeliver the said bill of a 100lb, and to paye him the 96:12:5[7] soe taken from him by unjust Composition and to prefix a daye & summon a Jury for the Legall Tryall of the Petitioners demerits. Butt the Governor answered he would prefix noe time for any tryall nor have nothinge to doe with itt.

6. Actually 1677.
7. 96 pounds, 12 shillings, four pence.

The said Throp thereupon presented this as a grievance to us prayinge that if upon Examination of the matter itt shall appear as itt is sett forth that wee would report the same to his Majestie for his Royall releife therein.

All which wee have accordingly Examined, upon oath, and doe herewith present to his Majesties most Royall Consideration.

No. 4: **Mr. Thomas Grindon of Charles Citty County, Merchant, by Petition:** Setts forth that in the time of his beinge in England, about his lawfull concerns duringe the late rebellion in Virginia, upon the bare allegation and suggestion, that the Petitioners wife Sarah Grindon had uttered some foolish and indiscreat words, one Lt. Colonel Edward Hill[8] of the said County by pretence of a warrant from the Right Honorable Governor did actually seize, Remove and carry awaye from the Petitioners plantations severall of his servants, oxen, sheep, silver Plate, and other estate to the value of neer 500lb Sterlinge togeather with 9 hogsheads of tobacco, and all his Bills and accompts for debts due to the Petitioner, amountinge to about nintie thousand pounds of tobacco: The Petitioner beinge thereby hindered of receivinge his said debts to comply with his freight & other concerns.

Which proceedings in the Petitioners remote absence beinge contrary to law, and the same is complained of as a great grievance and redress therein desired.

Orders, Observations &c.: Upon this Petition of the 23rd of March wee sent a summons to Lt. Col. Edward Hill to appear before us and answer the premises upon Mr. Grindons complaint.

His answer to us was that this seizure was by Sir William Berkeleys order, and did thereupon produce a warrant under the Honorable Governors hand:

---

8. On Hill, see Chapter 2, above. A "malicious busybody," in the view of Wilcomb Washburn, Sarah Grindon earned the hatred of Sir William Berkeley for being "the first great encourager and setter on of the ignorant vulgar" and one who was "an active aider, assistor, and abettor of the Rebells." "Newswives" like Grindon, Berkeley complained, convinced hundreds of people that the Governor "was a greater friend to the Indians than to the English." Sarah Grindon was excluded from all pardons by Governor Berkeley in February of 1677. See William Waller Hening, ed., *The Statutes at Large: Being a Collection of All the Laws from the First Session of the Legislature in the Year 1619*, 2nd ed., vol 2 (Richmond: R. & W. & G. Bartow, 1823), 371.

Upon sight whereof wee observed: That the words of the warrant were to seize the body and Estate of Sarah Grindon not Thomas Grindons and to bringe the same to the Governor, and is dated the 13: 9er 1676^9 Which warrant wee conceive was unduly executed for these reasons followinge:

1.   The Estate was not the Estate of Sarah Grindon as the order expresses, but of her absent husband Thomas Grindon.

2.   The said warrant bears date of 13 november 1676 at Accomack when the Country was in actuall Rebellion, and was not executed till the February followinge, which was after the Country was settled in Peace and allso after our arrivall in Virginia.

3.   That the speaking of some foolish words by a simple woman; the tendinge to disturbance in those ill times, was not presence sufficient to seize the estate of a husband soe far absent especially without due proofe and conviction.

Upon a second petition the 20th of April the said Master Grindon prayes that his wife maye Receave a legall Tryall and Examination before us, for that the Right Honorable Governor had refer'd the same to be tried before the Commission of Oyer and Terminer.

Whereupon wee appointed the 20th of May last to be the daye of hearinge att Charles Citty County Court whereupon a full hearinge and Examination of witnesses.

Upon a full hearinge of what could be alleaged against Mrs. Sarah Grindon wee found nothinge done or acted by her, but was what any woman in such a case might well enough have done to preserve her absent husbands estate, which was a trust att that time in her hands; though in the maine she showed a great deale of feare and a great deale of folly: feare of Bacons force & folly in talkinge too favorably of his proceedings for which she hath most humbly asked her Majesties Pardon and tooke the oath of obedience though not by our direction and advice, and hath given security for her good behavior.

9. 13 November, 1676.

The Report of the Attorney Generall of Virginia under his hand, Maye the 20th at Westover in Charles Citty County, 1677.

Upon the readinge and serious Examininge of all the Evidences taken, and allso upon what was testified by the witnesses brought into the Court before the Right Honorable the Governor and Commissioners of Oyer and Terminer: I find nothinge against Mrs. Sarah Grindon, the wife of Thomas Grindon, that maye be a sufficient ground whereupon to ground an Indictment to try her for her life, nor did any witness sweare positively to any act done by her, butt what was att that time the Common feares and follyes of many others as well men as women; and she haveinge laid timely hold of his Majesties most gratious Pardon, and haveinge given bond for her future loyaltie and good behavior, It is my opinion that she is Capable of benefit of the said Pardon, and that she ought to be noe further prosecuted. The which I have Subscribed the daye abovesaid.

George Jordan

Attorney General for the Time Present.

No. 5:   **Petition of Thomas and William Dudley, Sonns to William Dudley, Senior, of Pianketank in the County of Middlesex lately deceased.**[10]

Sett forth that whereas their late deceased Father was commanded & enforced in the time of the late Rebell Bacon to administer the oath imposed by the said Bacon; which yett he did with that caution of savinge of his and their true allegiance to his Majestie: That he had never taken or Plundered of a mans goods; and used his best indeavors to persuade the People to a Submission to his Majesties Governour.

That after the Country was reduced to its obedience, and the Governor returned home to Green Spring, the said decedent waited on the Governor there and obtained his Honors Pardon.

Yet notwithstandinge Sometime in January last all the said Dudleys tobacco, being 15 hogsheads sweet sented tobacco, was seized for the governors use of the Right Honorable Sir William Berkeley, and putt on board Captain Martins ship to the undoing of the Poor Petitioners,

---

10. The Dudleys were tobacco merchants whose crop had been seized by Governor Berkeley and his followers. In April they received word that the king had ordered that their tobacco be restored to their agent in England. See James Dudley, Thomas Dudley, William Dudley and Elizabeth Dudley to James Cary, 25 April 1677, Letters and Papers Concerning American Plantations, 20 April–22 June 1677, C.O. 1/40, 8-9 (VCRP).

and the poore widdow of the deceased who had nothinge else to subsist on.

They Pray to have their sadd cause presented to his Majestie that they may reap the benefit of his Royall redress, haveinge by two severall petitions besought Sir William Berkeley, but noe purpose as by the report of his answer on the Petitions upon oath apeares.

Observations:

To prove the truth of the particulars in the petition sett forth:
    See the oath of
        William Young
            &
        Thomas Williams

The mates receipt for the 15 hogsheads of tobacco for Sir William Berkeley's use dated 2nd of March last.

Whereupon a note which the Governor gained of Dudley by waye of Composition for his pardon was upon receipt of the Tobacco delivered up and is as followeth, viz:

"Upon Consideration the Right Honorable the Governors Pardon: I doe oblige myselfe to paye and deliver to the Right Honorable Governor upon demand 15 hogsheads of good merchantable tobacco, and caske of my own & my sonns Cropp: wittness my hand this 25th of January 1676/7.

          William Dudley, Senior"

Present:
        Gregory Walklate
        Henry Hartwell

No. 6: **By Petition of Mr. John Page in behalfe of John Jefferys of London, Esquire.**

Shewinge that the Petitioner did deliver by vertue of Sir William Berkeleys order for his Majesties Service 20 pipes of Plyall wine the same daye before that James Town was left; which was sold att 8lb sterlinge per pipe.

Now soe itt is that the last grand assembly have ordered for payment for two pipes of the said wine att 8lb per pipe, which was expended att James Town, and for the other 18 pipes but 4lb per pipe, alleaginge that if itt had not bin taken awaye, itt would have bin lost to the towne beinge after burnt by Bacon and for the want of due caution given to remove what wine there was att that time left in the Cellars beinge 63 pipes, one hogshead, and one quarter Caske Plyall wine;[11] belonginge to Alderman John Jeffreys the same was all lost.

Opinions and Observations: We havinge seen the order of the Assembly annext to the Petition of Mr. John Page, did not only look upon the same as very rediculous, drawn up, but very unjust for they urged for a reason of payinge but halfe price for 18 pipes of wine, that the same was taken from Town, and soe saved from the fire, and wee doe further observe:

1. That the said order have sett a price of 8lb per pipe for the same wines which were sold to the Right Honorable Governor beinge two pipes; and yet by a very ridiculos evasion would faine perswade halfe rates to be as they tearm itt Sufficient on the rest and conclude that it is by themselves thought fitt to allow but 4lb per pipe.

2. Butt this order beinge a good receipt for the whole twenty of pipes, and in itt selfe ascertaining a full Rate for the two first pipes; Wee are of opinion that itt is most just and reasonable that Mr. John Jefferyes true owner of the said wines should and ought to receive full satisfaction for the whole twenty pipes after the Rate of 8lb per pipe; and that the preservinge them to the publick use, is noe reason against but rather for payment of the latter pro rato, which the first two pipes, and that they do thinke itt a sufficient loss to lose 63 pipes, one hogshead and one quarter caske of wine which timely notice of removal might have secured from being burnt upon the leavinge of James Town.

Wee have therefore by our Answer to the said Petition Most humbly refer'd the same to his Majesties most Royall consideration that the same maye be paid here in England out of the Publick moneys of the Country, the debt being contracted on the Publick account and by order for his Majesties Service.

---

11. "Pipe," in this sense, could mean simply a cask or a specific unit of measurement equivalent to 105 imperial gallons.

No. 7: **By Petition of Anne Hunt widow and relict of William Hunt of Charles City County, deceased, on behalfe of herselfe & two children.**[12]

Complaininge that the Honorable Governor beinge falsly informed that the said Hunt the Petitioners husband had bin actually in the late rebellion did after his death and without any indictment, tryall or conviction seize the estate of the Petitioner and her children, which had bin getting 25 yeares by the honest pains & hard labour of the decedent and the aged petitioner and the same removed and caryed to green Springe.

That the Better to Color the said doeings the Governor hath caused a Bill of Attainder to pass the last grand Assembly,[13] whereby the Petitioners Estate without soe much as haveinge the Petitioner or any other for her is adjudged forfeited to his Majestie.

Now for as much as the said William Hunt was never in armes against his Majestie or authority nor ever encouraged, aided or abeted the same; and ever a peaceable and good Subject of his Majestie.

And for that by the laws of England a man slaine or otherwise dyinge in open Rebellion before attainder forfeits noe part of his Estate: And the Petitioner beinge informed that this Plantation of Virginia cannot or ought not to make any laws repugnant to those of his Majesties Realme of England

The Poor Petitioner humbly Implores his Majestie would be pleased to putt a stopp to or cause the said act of attainder to be taken of as to your Petitioners said Estate, and that his Majestie in his Royall Mercy will be gratiously pleased to permit her and her children to enjoye the same for their Support and Maintenance and without which they are most miserable.

12. William Hunt's goods had been aboard Nicholas Prynne's ship, the *Richard and Elizabeth*, at the time of his death. Prynne, in an undated petition, requested that the goods in question be returned to him. See C.O. 1/40, 32 (VCRP).
13. The same act by the February 1677 Assembly that attainted Bacon specifically identified Hunt as a "principal ayder and abetter of the said Nathaniel Bacon" who, like the rebel, "dyed alsoe before the rebells were reduced to their allegiance to his majestie by which said meanes the said Nathaniell Bacon, junr. . . and William Hunt have escaped their due and just demerits for their wicked and unheard of treasons and rebellions." See Hening, ed., *The Statutes at Large*, 2: 375.

Observations: Note that the said William Hunt dyed at his own howse of a Naturall death; about the middle of October 1676: allso itt is proved upon oath that the said Hunt was never in armes against the Governor or ever assisted the late Rebells and that beinge solicited to take up Armes and offer'd A comission to be a Captain under the Rebell which the said Hunt refused to doe or accept, and sent back the Commission, &c.

See the Depositions of John Arnold and William Gibbon[14]

It is also proved by oath of others that well and long knew Mr. Hunt that he was not in Armes against the Right Honorable Governor or any of his forces, but on the contrary did on sundry times and occasions has bin herd to declare his dislike and abhorrence of the proceedings of the late rebel Bacon, &c.

See the Depositions of James Minge and Thomas Plaiton[15]

Allso there is an other oath that the Governor was indebted to Mr. Hunt: 18000lb of tobacco, a coppy of which account is annexed and was shewn Sir William Berkeley and demanded of him, who answered he must stay till he came againe and the Governors booke Keeper owned the said account to be true, &c.

See the oath of William Hunt to prove this as allso the Character of Mr. Hunts honesty & peaceable nature & moderation by Colonel Jordan and Major Home[16] subscribed in the booke of forfeited estates which is attested under their own hands and in their own words.

---

14. Not included in Wiseman's Book of Record.

15. James Minge migrated to Virginia from Wales, likely as an indentured servant, several decades prior to the rebellion. He lived in Charles City County on a plantation he called "Brandon." He served as a clerk in the House of Burgesses in 1673. He was friends with Nathaniel Bacon, and an outspoken critic of the rapacity of the governor's supporters after the rebellion. Thomas Plaiton could not be identified further.

16. On 1 May 1677, the commissioners requested Jordan and Major Theophilus Hone to "make an enquiry into all forfeitures, careying away of goods and cattle in the counties of James River, New Kent, and York," and to report their findings. See the Commissioners to Colonel George Jordan and Major Theophilus Hone, 1 May 1677, C.O. 1/40, 121 (VCRP). The commissioners did ultimately send to the king Jordan's and Hone's report, though the original is extremely difficult to read owing to the illegibility of the writer's script. See the Proceedings and Reports of the Commissioners for Enquiring into Virginian Affairs and Settling Virginian Grievances, 1677, C.O. 5/1371, 217-250 (VCRP).

No. 8: **By Petition of Nicholas Prynne of the ship *Richard and Elizabeth* of London.**

Settinge forth that Alderman Booth of London and Company beinge owners of the said ship, consigned to one William Hunt their factor in Virginia a cargoe of goods to the value of 265lb sterling to make sale and returne of for their proper account; for which goods the Petitioner Mr. Prynn gave bill of ladinge and is thereby accountable for the same.

Prayes restitution of the goods and Redress of the wrong and damage.

The Commissioners' Answer: Mr. Nicholas Prynne made oath before us that he had delivered the invoice of goods and other Papers to Colonel Ballard, and left the same in his hands, and never since received the same againe.

No. 9: **By Petition of Thomas Palmer Carpenter[17]**

Complains that he did build a howse for one Thomas Hansford who was indebted upon that account to the Petitioner 3800lb of tobacco and caske, due the 10th October 1675, which Hansford was executed for a Rebell att Accomack by Marshall law in which time Hansfords wife paid the Petitioner 7 hogsheads of tobacco:

Which the governor ordered the sherife of Yorke County to seize and upon the Petitioners application to Sir William Berkeley to discharge the same his Honors answer was that he would keep those 7 hogsheads and that the Petitioner should be paid out of the said Hansfords Estate, which will not amount to paye his just debts.

The Petitioner Humbly prays reliefe herein or else is like to be ruined.

Our Humble Opinion is that this Seizure is Illegall, the said Hansford haveinge noe Tryall or conviction by a Lawfull Jury.

No. 10: Wee have allso a true Coppie of a Warrant to the Sheriffe of Surry County to seize and send over to the Right Honorable Governor to Green Spring the Sheep of Robert Kay and to secure his other Estate

---

17. Little more is known about Palmer than that which is included in his petition.

which warrant was Executed and Returned the 30th of January, 1676/7.[18]

No. 11: **By Petition of Landes Knowles of Gloster County Planter.**[19]

Complaininge that although he was not in armes, aidinge or abettinge to the late Rebellion but continued peaceable upon his Plantation in the management of his crop only that he was seduced to take that unlawfull oath imposed by that Grand Rebell Bacon.

Yet about the 20 of October last Major Robert Beverley with armed men Came to the Petitioners howse; and carried him thence to Acco-mack, and then allso seized and tooke away 3 Negros and 5 English servants with his household goods and other Estate to the value of 400lb sterling;[20] Kept the Petitioner in Prison 3 months att Acco-mack and then sett the Petitioner att liberty upon bayle to appear upon Summons.

That the Petitioner hath since laid hold of his Majesties gratious Pardon, taken the oath of obedience and given bond for his future good behavior.

And the Petitioner most humbly conceivinge that his Majesties gratious pardon extends as well to the acquittal of his goods as life.

---

18. Robert Kay had been implicated in the rebellion, and for that suffered Governor Berkeley's wrath. Berkeley signed a warrant on 24 January 1677 to seize his estate and to send his sheep to Green Spring. The warrant can be found in Letters and Papers Concerning American Plantations, 4 January–19 March 1676/7, C.O. 1/39, 24 (VCRP). On livestock in early Virginia, see Virginia De John Anderson, "Animals into the Wilderness: The Development of Livestock Husbandry in the Seventeenth-Century Chesapeake," *William and Mary Quarterly*, 59 (April 2002), 377-408.

19. Surely the commissioners here refer to Lands Knowles. In Wiseman's original, this and the following petition appear without identifying numbers.

20. The inventory of "goods" seized from Knowles's estate reveals Virginia's gradual transition from a labor system based on white indentured servitude to one based on race-based African slavery. For a sampling of the huge literature on this subject, see Winthrop D. Jordan, *White Over Black: American Attitudes Toward the Negro, 1550-1812* (Chapel Hill: University of North Carolina Press, 1968); Edmund S. Morgan, *American Slavery, American Freedom: The Ordeal of Colonial Virginia* (New York: Norton, 1975); and, most recently, Anthony S. Parent, *Foul Means: The Formation of a Slave Society in Virginia, 1660-1740*, (Chapel Hill: University of North Carolina Press, 2003).

Implores the full benefitt thereof and to have his remedy for his seized Estate.

Deposition in Behalfe of the Petitioner

> See the oath of Henry Singleton
> See an Inventory of the goods taken by Beverley.[21]

No. 12: By Petition of William Howard

Complaininge that on the 10th of December which was about ten dayes before the first treaty for cessation of armes Mr. Robert Beverley entered the Petitioners howse under pretence to search for the Petitioners sonn-in-law John Harris who was then in Bacons army; and by force of armes Ransacked the poor aged Petitioner of servants and goods to the value of near 500lb sterling. Now Since the Petitioner was noe waies concern'd in the late Rebellion, but hath allways bin and still is a loyall Subject to his Majestie:

And for that the Petitioner will be left destitute of future support for himselfe and aged wife.

Prayes what remedy maye bee by us granted.

Ordered as in the Case of Master Richard Clerke; George Seaton and Lands Knowles, that an Inventory given with security against Wast, Sale, or Embezelment of the said goods or Servants till his Majesties Gratious Pleasure be Known, and not to dispossess the parties in possession of the Same. The order follows recited att large in the Clarkes case.[22]

No. 13: By Petition of John Deane of James City County, Planter[23]

Confessinge and Repentinge his breach of the law for takinge Bacons unlawfull oath & shewinge that he doth humbly laye hold of his Majesties Pardon and hath taken the oath of obedience.

---

21. Neither of these documents was included in Wiseman's compilation.

22. See below, 271-273

23. John Deane signed the James City County grievances. Little more is known about him than what appears in his petition. See also C.O. 1/40, 7 (VCRP).

Complaines that his whole crop of tobacco beinge 4 hogsheads was lately seized by Mr. William Hartwell; and marked with the broad arrow, without soe much as a warrant or cause for doeinge the same, soe that his wife and fower small children are without necessaryes for Support.

Prayes Remedy.

Response: An oath indorsed of the manner of the Seizure.

Personall Grievances Against William Hartwell, Servant to the Governor

John Williams of James City County, Planter: For imprisoninge 10 dayes and forceinge him by hard usage to a Composition of 2 hogsheads of tobacco & 6 barrills of Indian Corne to the value of 16lb Sterlinge.

Response: Proved by Williams his deposition & Hartwells own confession.

Thomas Bobby: That he was imprisoned by the said Hartwell, and by him forced to pay a Composition of 500lb of Porke, 200lb of Bacon & 100lb of Butter, &c.

Response: This allso owned by Hartwell himselfe and proved upon oath against him.

Nicholas Toope: Complaines against Hartwell for imprisoninge him 5 weekes after he was in the Kings service, and forcinge him to give a Bill for 20 pair of shoes.

John Johnson and James Barrow: Complain Against Hartwell imprisoninge them and forcinge from them a composition of ten thousand shingles.

Response: Owned by Hartwell and by him said to be by the Governors order.

William Hoare: Against Hartwell for deteininge him prisoner 10 dayes and takeinge from him his Cattle, hoggs & other goods. And for demandinge 10000lb to save his life.

Response: Proved & allso confessed to be true by James Gery the Governors servant.

Edward Lloyd a Mulatto:[24] Against Hartwell for imprisoninge him 3 weekes, and in that time some of the Governors servants went & seized the complainants goods, and att the same time soe affrighted the poor petitioners wife beinge then great with child, that she presently fell into Labour & dyed. And although nothinge was alleaged against the Petitioner he was denyed his Enlargement untill he passed by Bill his obligation to paye the Captain of the Guard 400lb of tobacco.

Response: This Complaint is certified to us upon oath:

> See the Midwifes deposition concerninge the Death of
> Lloyd's Wife
> As allso the oath of another woman to the same purpose.

Thomas Glover, Complainant: Against Hartwell for Imprisoninge him 5 weekes, & forceinge him to give a horse for his discharge, which horse was of the value of 1200lb of tobacco

Response: An oath that Mr. Ballard advised the Petitioner to give a horse for Composition.
Note: That the Petitioner was pressed by Hartwell to serve under Bacon, and was encouraged to goe by Mr. Ballard, who told him Bacons Comission was truly granted &c.
See the Depositions of Thomas Glover and Francis Robinson about Ballard.

Andrew Godeon, Complainant: Against Hartwell for Imprisoninge him 10 dayes, untill he passed an obligation for five months worke.

William Rowland: That he was pressed into Bacons Service, imprisoned and forced to paye or secure to be paid 8 thousand pounds of tobacco for his Enlargement.

---

24. Little is known about Lloyd. His existence in the records indicates again that a rigid slave society had not yet emerged in seventeenth-century Virginia. Nonetheless, the House of Burgesses had begun the process of legally defining who could be sold as slaves, and who could own them. Mulattoes like Lloyd could purchase Indian and African slaves, but they could not own English servants. See Hening, ed., *The Statutes at Large,* 2: 281.

Thomas Lushington: Against Hartwell for Imprisoninge the Petitioner, strippinge off his cloaths from his back and takeinge his papers out of his Pocketts, &c.

Response: To this Hartwell Confessed that when others were plundering the Petitioner he thereupon plundered too; and in Excuse said that what he did was by order of his Colonel, Colonel Ballard, and that the other party did the like.

Note: That Hartwell had bin on both sides both Bacons and the Governors.

Note those severall Complaints against Hartwell for Imprisonment of Persons after the Country was reduced to obedience; without any warrant that could be by him produced or proved, but the pretence only of haveinge the Governors verball order, or Colonel Ballards; and that the Governor received the severall compositions before Complained of, & not he the said Hartwell.

Personall Grievances

By Petition of Richard Clerke: Settinge forth that the Petitioner though he was seduced into that late unhappy Rebellion, of which he truly repenteth himselfe, yet for that this Petitioner hath laid hold & doth most humbly Implore his Majesties gratious Pardon; for that he never wronged any man, or tooke any mans goods, but Continued quietly under his own roofe.

Nevertheless on the first daye of January last severall armed men belonging to the late Governor under the Command of one Roger Potter & Bryan Smith came to the Petitioners howse, and thence in Company of William Hartwell, Richard Auborne, & Samuell Mathews took and carryed awaye:

> fower English Servants
> Seaven Negro slaves
> Six hogsheads tobacco, and all the petitioners household goods, bedding, linen & other Estate by a moderate Composition amountinge to at least 400lb Sterling.

Two of which English Servants and the said seaven negro slaves are in the possession of Major Robert Beverley, and one other of the said

English Servants is allso Kept and detained from the Petitioner by Mr. Bryan Smith.[25]

The Petitioners prayer is that if upon Examination itt shall apear a grievance to make such order therein & report thereof to his Majestie as shall seem Expedient.

Response: This complaint is certified to us upon oath annexed to the said Petition, & taken before us the 29 daye of Maye 1677 to which oath wee Humbly referr, as beinge a more ample state of the Petitioners case.
Whereupon we made this followinge order upon the said Petition, viz.

> "That Roger Potter, Robert Beverly and Bryan Smith doe severally giveth good security for such goods and servants of the Petitioner, Richard Clerke, as are in their or any of their possession or custody, togeather with a true Inventory of the same; to be registered on Record in the Secretarys office, as allso security against any willfull wast or Embezzlement of the said Estate or any part thereof, and to be answerable and accountable for the meane profits untill his gratious Majesties Royall pleasure be Known; which Bond for performance hereof, is to be given before the next Justice of the Peace, where the Party lives, in whose possession the said goods, servants, or other Estate of the said Clerke is or shall be found.
>
> > Herbert Jefferys
> > Francis Moryson"

Which order was served on the said Beverly &c. and was not to dispossess the parties in possession but to secure his Majesties right in the forfeitures, till his Royall pleasure could be herein Known & declared. Butt that the said Beverly thinking himselfe Injured hereby hath made a Scandalous complaint against our proceedings, which he calls an answer to the Complaint of the Petitioners, which wee doe freely and fairely laye before his Majestie, tho the same be against

---

25. Smith was one of Hartwell's henchmen, whom he aided in the plunder of Clerk's estate. Planters from New Kent County, including Robert Lowden, John Cocker, and Robert Porter complained to the commissioners that Smith had taken from them 4,250 pounds of tobacco. Their undated petition can be found in C.O. 1/40, 28 (VCRP).

ourselves, and not Cominge to our hands before wee were just ready to Saile for England, beinge both of us upon board.

By Petition of George Seaton:[26] Settinge forth that the Petitioner had all his goods and plate to the value of 150lb sterlinge by Major Robert Beverly & a party with him, seized and taken awaye from the Petitioner.

Prayes that the persons in whose possessions the said goods are or maye be found, to give Security before two Justices of the Peace against wast, till his Majesties most gratious pleasure be further known.

Response: Wee havinge Examined severall testimonys upon oath concerninge the Petitioners behavior in the time of the late Rebellion, and find noe other Crime laid to the Petitioners charge save only the takinge and givinge of Bacons oath:

And this itt seemed to us that the Petitioner was compelled by force to take that unlawfull oath; yett severall persons did Sweare that the Petitioner did not force itt upon any other.

Whereupon wee were induced to make the like generall rule or order, as is before recited in the Case of mr. Richard Clarke.

By Petition of Lands Knowles: Shewinge that Mr. Robert Beverly had seized and taken from the Petitioner:

> Three Negro slaves
> One shallopp
> five English servants & other goods to a Considerable value;
> to the utter Ruine of the Petitioner and his poore family.

Prayes the same Reliefe herein, as is by the Petition of mr. George Seaton desired.

Response: Wee haveinge examined into the Petitioners demerits by oaths of Persons sworne before us and the Petitioner haveinge bin fully admitted to the Benefitt of his Majesties Gratious Pardon; upon his

---

26. George Seaton, yet another planter preyed upon and dispossessed by the governor's supporters, was allowed by the commissioners to reclaim his lands. For his trial before the governor's council, see H. R. McIlwaine, ed., *Minutes of the Council and General Court of Colonial Virginia,* 2nd ed. (Richmond: Virginia State Library, 1979), 459.

humble Petition, Submission & due conformity to; and performance of his Majesties Commands enjoyned him:

Wee thereupon made the like Generall Rule or order, as in the Cases of Clarke, Howard & Seaton before recited, till his majesties pleasure were Known and noe otherwise.

Characters of the Severall Commanders of Shipps Togeather with a Perticular account of their respective Services to his Majestie in the time of the late Rebellion in Virginia.

1.   Captain Thomas Gardner, Commander of the ship *Adam and Eve* of London, who was the person ordered and imployed by Sir William Berkeley for the taking that grand Rebell Nathaniel Bacon, whome he seized with 4 armed men in his sloop in James River, and delivered Bacon and his guard of 40 men Prisoners to the Governor at James Town.

For which signall service, instead of a Reward Bacon was sett free upon his own parole; and Gardner clapt into Prison upon an order of that Assembly passed against him (before the force) for 70lb damage for the loss of Bacons sloop which Perished on the shore by neglect of others. He continued Prisoner till the Governors Returne from Accomack, and his ship then ordered down to the Governors assistance, in which service he Continued to the time of our arrival in Virginia, his ship beinge a Receptacle for the loyall Party and a Goale for the late Rebells, and is now as wee are Informed taken from him by his owners by reason of the neglect and losses occasioned by the Service aforesaid.

2.   Captain Larrimore, the Command of whose ship the *Rebecka* was usurped from him by Bland and Carver, and by them Caryed awaye to Accomack, where by Larrimore's advice privately sent to the Governor att that Instant when Carver with some men were gonn on shore to treat with Sir William Berkeley, the Governor sent severall of his own Party off in boats, whome Larrimore enteringe on board him at the Gunroom ports, Surprized Bland first, and afterward Carver and his Crew as they returned on board; and putt the ship and men againe into the Governors Service: In which ship after this fortunate Reprizall he Came up to James Town.

3.   Captain John Consett, Commander of the ship *Mary* of London, a very active resolute person, who did not only serve the Governor with his

ship, butt allso in his own person on shore, and with his own hand shott
that grand Rebell Groves,[27] and with a few seamen disarmed and routed
his whole party whereby the whole Southern Shore of James River was
reduced to its former obedience which was esteemed by the Governor
and others a very singul Peece of service.

4.   Captain Morris Commander of the ship *the young Prince* wherein he
        served the Governor under appointment of Admiralty and was very
        Instrumentall in discomfitinge the Rebells by assistinge with his ship
        and seamen the Loyall Party.

5.   Captain Nicholas Prynne, Commander of the ship *Richard and
        Elizabeth* who allso assisted the Governor upon all occasions, and
        went on shore with Captain Consett, and was Instrumentall in seizinge
        the Rebells, and after went and beat up a guard of the Rebells party att
        Cheepoke Creeke which he tooke, and Continued in the service with
        his shipp In James River untill the Country was reduced.

6.   These are to Certifie that Captain Thomas Grantham, Commander of
        the Shipp *Concord* of London, was a person most Eminently con-
        cerned, active and usefull in reducinge those Rebells that stood out
        against his Majesties Governor of Virginia after Bacons death and to
        whose management the Governor solely intrusted the Treaty for the
        surrender at West Point, the chiefe Rendezvous and Magazeen of the
        Rebells, Which Captain Grantham with good Caution, faithfull
        Conduct, great Expence & Emminent Danger of his life, effected with
        happy success, after haveinge Expended in Caryinge on this designe as
        wee are credibly Informed above 70lb Sterlinge in Brandy & other
        strong liquors; and was also in Jeopardy of beinge killed by the Negroe
        slaves who were dissatisfied with the said Treaty beinge in distrest of
        their hoped for liberty, and would not quietly laye downe their armes
        beinge about 100 in number, but threatened to kill Captain Grantham
        att the Generall Surrender then made by the Rest, of their armes,
        Colours, Ammunition, &c.[28]

27. Groves commanded Bacon's forces in Isle of Wight County. The battle in question
took place at "Burwell's Bay" in Isle of Wight on Christmas Day, 1676. See Webb,
1676, 96-97.
28. As he had done with the surrenders at West Point, Grantham told the assembled rebels, black and white, that the king had commissioners on the way to redress their grievances. He promised as well to grant the servants and slaves their freedom, a promise that
he ultimately could not keep. The servants and slaves were returned to their masters.
Their presence in rebel ranks is significant nonetheless. Servants and slaves made up

Which signall service of Captain Grantham was a means for the Resettlement of the Peace of that his Majesties Collony of Virginia: All which wee doe testifie and believe to be truth as much as itt is possible for us to doe that were not our Selves present and eye wittnesses of the same.

A List of the Names of those worthy persons whose Services & Sufferings by the Late Rebell Nathaniell Bacon Junior and his Party have been reported to us most Signall and Eminent duringe the late unhappy troubles In Virginia and particularly of Such whose Approved Loyalltie, Constancy and Courage, hath Rendered them most deservinge of his Majesties Royall Remarke (as followeth) viz:

1. The Right Honorable Sir William Berkeley his Majesties then Governor of Virginia, who suffered very much by the Rebell Bacon and his Complices beinge both persecuted in his Person, and plundered and dispoyled in his Estate: How he was Reimbursed or repaired wee Cannot certainly give an account, Butt most humbly Referr that to an article of Inquiry and (in Part) to the Personall grievances herwith presented.

2. Sir Henry Chichely, Barbarous imprisoned and Treated by Bacon and his Party for many months togeather and much damnified in his Estate. This worthy person was Imployed by the Governor on the Indian Expedition to disarme and Subject them butt beinge upon the very point of Execution was (on a Suddaine) countermanded by the Governor, and noe effectuall Care taken therein: In which Service had he proceeded he had in all likelihood Ended the warr as soon as began.

    Wee humbly present his Services and Sufferings to his Majesties Royall Consideration.

3. Colonel Nathaniell Bacon the Elder, the first that was plundered by his unnatural Kinsman Nathaniell Bacon the Rebell, to the value of att least 2000lb Sterlinge as wee have heard: A most steadfast Loyall subject to

two-thirds of Bacon's active forces during the closing months of the rebellion. See Webb, *1676*, 121; Morgan, *American Slavery, American Freedom*, 269.

his Majestie: Maugre[29] all the malice and Severe Treatment of the Rebells.

He is Said to have bin a person soe desirous and Industrious to divert the evill consequences of his Rebell Kinsmans Proceedings, that at the Beginninge he freely proposed and promised to invest him in a Considerable part of his Estate att present, and to leave him the Remainder in Reversion after his and his wifes death; and to leave him other advantages upon condition he would laye down his Armes; and become a good subject to his Maejstie that the Collony might not be disturbed or destroyed, nor his own family stained with soe foule a Blott.

4.   Colonel Philip Ludwell one that was constantly in the Governors Service & was not onely plundered in his own Personall Estate, but allso of an Estate of an orphan committed to his Trust;[30] for the losse whereof he seems more concerned than for his own.

5.   Colonel Augustine Warner, speaker of the Howse of Burgesses in the late Assembly & now Sworne one of his Majesties Councill of Virginia. [31] An honest worthy person and most Loyall Sufferer, by the late Rebells, who was plundered as much as any; & yet speakes as little of his losses; though they were very great.

---

29. Or, in other words, the king looks with ill will on the poor treatment accorded Nathaniel Bacon the elder by the rebels.

30. The burgesses did enact some regulations governing the protection of orphans and their property. In the 1662 codification of the colony's laws, the burgesses required county courts to take "care that the lands in the county belong to any orphants be not aliened sold or taken up as deserted land by any person during the minority of the orphant, and that the guardians or overseers of any orphants doe not let, set, or farme out any land belonging to any orphant, for longer terme, then till the oprhant be at age, and that an especiall care be had that the tenant shall improve the plantation by planting an orchard and building a good house, and that the tenant shall be bound to maintaine a good fence about the orchard, and keep the house in sufficient repaire and leave it tenantable at the surrender. See Hening, ed., *The Statutes at Large*, 2: 94-95.

31. Berkeley reported that Augustine Warner was dead in a letter to Philip Ludwell, dated 1 April 1676 (Letters and Papers Concerning American Plantations, 7 March 1675/6–30 May 1676, C.O. 1/36, 67-68 [VCRP]) but Warner was indeed alive to complain of the seizure of his property by William Byrd in September of 1676. A general court held at James City voted in June of 1678 to grant Warner £1000 for his losses (Letters and Papers Concerning American Plantations, 2 January 1677/8–13 December 1678, C.O. 1/42, 178-179 [VCRP]). He lived in Abbington Parish in Gloucester County. See also John Thornbush's petition on Warner's behalf. (C.O. 1/43, 29ro [VCRP]).

6.   Mr. Thomas Ludwell, Secretary of Virginia, whose stock was utterly ruined and taken awaye by the Rebells; though att the same time he was actinge here in England as the Country's agent att his own charge he never having six pence allowed him for itt by the Country, that ever wee upon our Enquiry could hear of.

7.   Colonel Daniell Parks, then allso in England and one of the Treasurers for the Countries money, who was plundered accordinge to the Computation wee have had made to us of att least 1500lb Sterling.[32]

8.   Colonel William Cole, a very honest Gentleman and one of the Councill who was all along constant to the Governor, and with him in all his Troubles.

9.   Colonel Joseph Bridger, a very resolute Gentleman, who tho forced to fly in the heat of the warr from his own County into Maryland, yet on his Returne was very active & Instrumentall in Reducinge to their obedience the South part of James River, and in his absence was as wee have heard plundered of his cattle &c. to a good vallue.

10.   Colonel Nicholas Spencer, an honest active worthy Gentleman, who did the Country very good service against the Rebells; in that hee affected part of the Country where he resided, and as wee are credibly informed, by his Correspondence here is much Impaired in his Estate by the late Rebells.[33]

11.   Mr. Ralph Wormely, a truly honest loyall Gentleman & one of the Councill who by his constant adhearance to the Governor was (as wee

---

32. Daniel Park first appeared as a member of the governor's council in 1665. He had been born in England, but died in Virginia on 6 March 1679. See William Glover Stanard and Mary Newton Stanard, *The Colonial Virginia Register* (Baltimore: The Genealogical Publishing Company, 1965), 39. His account of events in Virginia, sent to Secretary Joseph Williamson, and dated 30 January 1678, is at C.O. 1/42, 46-47 (VCRP).

33. Spencer first appeared as a member of the governor's council in 1671. Born in England, he resided in Westmoreland County. He died in Virginia on 23 September 1689. See Stanard and Stanard, *Colonial Virginia Register*, 40. Spencer continued to worry about the safety and security of Virginia after the rebellion. In 1682 he wrote to Sir Lyonel Jenkins (Letters and Papers Concerning American Plantations, 29 July–6 October 1682, C.O. 1/49, 106-107, [VCRP]), arguing that the Plant-cutting rebellion in the colony had been influenced by Bacon's Rebellion. On the plant-cutting problems and Spencer's fears, see Morgan, *American Slavery, American Freedom*, 286; Webb, *Governors-General*, 407-410.

have heard) much worsted and Ruined in his Estate by the late Rebells in Virginia.[34]

12.   Colonel Christopher Wormely, a person very loyall; who accordinge to a Perticular account given in to the last assembly lost 500lb Sterlinge by the Rebellion.[35]

Captain Walter Whitaker, a considerable sufferer and very loyall Gentleman who with the two worthy persons forenamed was imprisoned after Bacons death.[36]

13.   Major Richard Lee, a loyall discreet person worthy of the place to which he was lately advanced of beinge one of his majesties Councill of Virginia and as to his losses by the Rebills wee are Credibly Informed they were very great, and that he was imprisoned by Bacon above seaven weekes togeather att least 100 miles from his own beinge; whereby he received great prejudice in his health by hard usage, and very greatly by his absence in his whole Estate.[37]

14.   Colonel Thomas Ballard: Both of which as wee have heard
                                        lost considerably by the Rebell
                                        Party; the first of whome both
                                        tooke and gave Bacons unlawfull
       and   oath and the latter Edward Hill
                                        allwaies adhered to Sir William
                                        Berkeley; though in some things
15.   Lt.Col. Edward Hill: too much as maye apear in the case
                                        of Grendon & others.

---

34. Ralph Wormely, (1650-1703) had been born in England. He appears as a member of the House of Burgesses in 1674, and was appointed to the governor's council in 1677. Wormeley collected customs along the Rappahannock River. He would remain active in colonial affairs until his death, early in the next century. His home, "Rosegill," was located along the Rappahannock River.
35. Christopher Wormely died in Virginia in 1701. He became a member of the governor's council after the rebellion, in 1683.
36. Walter Whitaker served as a justice of the peace and, later, high sheriff of Middlesex County. Approximately 40 years old at the time of the rebellion, he died on 27 July 1692. See *Virginia Magazine of History and Biography,* 22 (1914), 50.
37. Major Richard Lee (1647-1714), from Mount Pleasant in Westmoreland County. A member of Berkeley's council, and a man respected by the Crown and commissioners. See Washburn, *The Governor and the Rebel,* 155; and C.O. 1/36, 56 (VCRP).

16.   Major Robert Beverly; Clerke of the Assembly, a person very active &
       Serviceable in surprizinge & beatinge up of Quarters & Small guards
       about the Country; and as himselfe sayes and wee have noe reason to
       believe the Contrary, a sufficient sufferer by the late Rebellion. Butt as
       wee allso believe the only person that gott by those unhappy troubles,
       in Plunderinge (without distinction) of honest mens Estates from
       others, as will be found when accounts are adjusted: and was one that
       had the Confidence to saye in hearinge of Mr. Wiseman our clerke, he
       had not plundered enough, soe that the Rebellion ended too soon for his
       Purpose.   Besides wee have observ'd him to have bin the evill
       Instrument that fomented the Ill humors between the two Governors
       then on the Place, and was a great occasion of their Clashinge and dif-
       ference.[38]

17.   Colonel Matthew Kemp, a Gentleman of an honest loyall family, a very
       deservinge person and much a Sufferer by the Rebells.[39]

18.   Colonel William Claiborne the older, and his sonns were all of them
       reported to us under a Character of Loyalltie, and obedience to his
       Majesties Governor; and losers both in stock and goods.[40]

19.   Captain Otho Thorpe, a signall sufferer by Bacon and his Party as
       apeares by oaths taken before us & Sir William Berkeleys own order
       for restitution of his plundered Estate, after the Governor had made a
       Composition with him of near 200lb Sterlinge for his Pardon for
       signinge a paper Extorted by menaces, and obtained by Giles Bland,

38. For the clashes between Berkeley and Jeffreys, see Chapter 2.
39. Colonel Matthew Kemp had been explicitly named by Bacon as an enemy of the
people, one of the governor's "wicked, pernitious Councellors, Aiders, and Assisters
against the Commonalty in these our Cruell Commotions." See "Proclamations of Nathaniel Bacon," *Virginia Magazine of History and Biography*, 1 (1894), 60. Kemp also
served as a justice of the peace in Middlesex County and as Speaker of the House of Burgesses. See Stanard, *Colonial Virginia Register*, 41.
40. Claiborne had arrived in Virginia in 1620. For information on his many exploits in
the colony, see J. Frederick Fausz, "Present at the Creation: The Chesapeake World that
Greeted the Maryland Colonists," *Maryland Historical Magazine*, 79 (1984), 7; Idem.,
"Profits, Pelts and Power: English Culture in the Early Chesapeake, 1620-1652," *Maryland Historian*, 15 (1983), 19-20; J. Mills Thornton III, "The Thrusting Out of Governor
Harvey: A Seventeenth-Century Rebellion," *Virginia Magazine of History and Biography*, 76 (1968), 19. A very old man, he almost entirely stayed out of the rebellion. He
died in 1677, approximately 90 years old. His sons actively sided with Berkeley during
the rebellion.

when Thorp was by drinke bereaved of common reason; Soe that this
Person maye be most truly said a great Sufferer by both sides.

20.   Mr. Phillip Lightfoote, a great loser and Sufferer in Estate & person
           beinge both plundered & imprisoned by the Rebells.[41]

21.   Colonel John Smith, received great loss by Rebells in his stock & other
           Estate taken and destroyed by them.[42]

22.   Major Lawrence Smith, a great sufferer in his Estate, & person beinge
           plundered and imprisoned by the Rebells.[43]

23.   Colonel John West, a person greatly impaired in his stock and goods by
           the Rebells; and a most constant Loyall Gentleman duringe the late
           Rebellion; and was for some time Imprisoned after Bacons death by the
           Rebell Party.[44]

24.   Major John Lewis, a sufferer in the same kind as the former.[45]

25.   Mr. John Ascough[46]
26.   Mr. Henry Whitinge [47]   Great Losers by the Rebells both in their
27.   Mr. Humprhey Gwyn[48]   stock & other Estates.

41. Philip Lightfoote served as a militia officer in Gloucester County. On his family
history, see "Lightfoot Family," *William and Mary Quarterly,* 1st ser., 3 (1894-1895),
104-105.
42. John Smith came to Virginia in 1652. He was a lieutenant colonel in the Gloucester
County militia, and sided with the governor during the rebellion.
43. A Royalist veteran of England's civil war, Lawrence Smith energetically defended
the interests of Governor Berkeley. In May of 1676 he had tried to organize the defenses
of Citterbourne Parish in Rappahannock County, and was captured and imprisoned there
by Bacon's followers. See Webb, *1676,* 109.
44. Colonel John West owned a large plantation in the Pamunkey Neck. According to
local tradition, he was the father of Cockacoeske's son, Captain John West, who had
signed the 1677 treaty. Both mother and son made their marks with a character that re-
sembled a "W." See Helen C. Rountree, *Pocahontas's People: The Powhatan Indians of
Virginia Through Four Centuries* (Norman: University of Oklahoma Press, 1990), 112.
45. I could find no information on Major Lewis.
46. Little more is known of Ascough than that he owned land in New Kent County. See
the *Virginia Magazine of History and Biography,* 14 (1907), 125.
47. Whitinge served variously as a burgess, a justice of the peace, and a militia officer in
Gloucester County.
48. Little is known about Humprhey Gwyn, of Gloucester County.

28.   Mr. Richard Whitehead[49]

        and   Great Sufferers in Estate by plunderinge
                                    and in person by Imprisonment.
29.   Mr. Edmond Gwyn[50]

30.   Mr. Thomas Royston & Doctor Cames,[51] Sufferers in the like manner
        in their Estates and Persons.

31.   Mr. Charles Roan,[52] one that had his dwellinge howse and other
        howses burnt down to the ground; and most part of his goods and
        provision destroy'd or caryed awaye by a Party of Rebells commanded
        by Gregory Walklate after Bacon's death.

32.   Mr. Thomas Deacon, a looser in his Estate and Sufferer in his Person
        by Imprisonement.
        Major John Burnham, Imprisoned by the Rebells & otherwise a sufferer
        by them.

33.   Major Powell, an honest loyall person who was wounded by the
        Rebells in his legg att James Town Engagement, and as wee have
        heard, was a great sufferer in his stock & otherwise,

34.   Major John Page

        and   Great loosers in their stocks & otherwise

35.   Mr. John Braye[53]

36.   Colonel John Leare, a person allwaies with the Governor in the late
        troubles who in his absence from his howse lost much in his stock at
        home and otherwise, and was the first person of Virginia that came on
        board us at our arrival and gave us an account of the condition of that
        place.[54]

---

49. I could find no information on Whitehead.
50. Edmund Gwyn, of Gloucester County.
51. I could find no information on Dr. Cames.
52. Charles Roan came to Virginia sometime around 1664 and established himself as one of the largest landholders in Gloucester County. See the *Virginia Magazine of History and Biography*, 16 (1908), 66-69.
53. Wiseman here refers to James Bray.
54. Of Nansemond County. See Chapter 6, above.

37.   Colonel Charles Moryson, a Gentleman of a constant & approved
        loyalty who was never from the Governor, but very serviceable and
        active upon all occasions, as well in his own person as by his Servants,
        & one that hath bin much burthened & impaired in his stock, by beinge
        att a great & frequent Expence in furnishinge Sir William Berkeley &
        his party with suplyes of provisions, and allso by beinge plundered by
        the Rebells, besides he hath bin att noe small charge, in entertaininge
        both the Governors att his own howse with the Traine that attended
        them with great freedome and openness to all Comers and goers.

38.   Captain William Diggs, sonn to mr. Edward Diggs deceased, a gallant
        Briske younge Gentleman; who in a Single dispute betwixt him and
        Hanford one of the cheifest Champions of the Rebells side, Cutt off one
        of Hansfords fingers, and forced him to fly, and maintained the
        Governors cause against the Rebells with great Constancy, till he was
        forced to fly to Maryland; whose mother suffered considerably in her
        Estate for her sonns Loyaltie.[55]

Inhabitants, Sufferers by the Burninge of James Town amongst whome the most Eminent were:

39.   Colonel Thomas Swann, who had a howse burnt & the goods in itt.

40.   Major Theop. Hone, who had allso a howse & goods destroyed.

41.   Mr. William Sherwood, and the orphan of one Mr. James, whose howse
        was burnt down by the Rebell Lawrence, & the loss Estimated att at
        least a 1000lb Sterlinge:

        There are divers other poor Persons, Inhabitants, whose particular
        names & losses wee cannot give in, that were great sufferers by this
        calamity that befell James Citty.[56]

55. Little more is known about Colonel William Diggs than what appears here in the
Commissioners' report.
56. Reliable population figures for seventeenth-century Virginia are elusive. Edmund
Morgan has estimated that in 1674, 5,000 individuals lived along the James River, 3,943
lived along the York, 1,869 lived along the Rappahannock, 1,561 along the Potomac, and
1,018 on the Eastern Shore. See Morgan, *American Slavery, American Freedom,* 414.
For the Chesapeake Region as a whole, historians John J. McCusker and Russell R.
Menard have arrived at the following figures (in thousands):

In Accomack

The Gentlemen of this province were very loyall to his Majestie & faithfull & constant to the Governor, and must therefore of Consequence be great Sufferers, since this place was the only shelter for the Governor & his party duringe the Troubles in the other Parts of his Majesties Colony of Virginia from which this is Seperated Seaven leauges distance.

The Persons of Perticular Eminency were these:

Colonel Stringer, Colonel Littleton, Mr. Foxcraft, Captain Juniper and in the first place:[57]

> Major Generall John Custis, whose howse was Sir William Berkeleys continued quarters, a person who att all times & places, boldly assert and Supported to his Power the Governors Honor & cause in his Majesties Behalfe against the Rebells.
>
> This worthy Gentleman upon consultinge Severall of the most Eminent & able persons of Virginia for victualinge his Majesties ships there most frankely proffered and Ingaged to lend the Kinge a thousand Pounds Sterling upon his own account to promote & advance the doeing hereof if itt could possibly have bin performed, answerable to his Majesties Service on the then Exigency which none would undertake to doe.

Year	Maryland	Virginia	White	Black	Total
1670	11.4	29.6	38.5	2.5	41.0
1680	20.0	39.9	55.6	4.3	59.9
1690	26.2	49.3	68.2	7.3	75.5

See John J. McCusker and Russell R. Menard, *The Economy of British America, 1607-1789* (Chapel Hill: University of North Carolina Press, 1985).

57. Colonel John Stringer planted on the Eastern Shore and served as a county justice of the peace. He served, as well, as customs collector in Accomac County. Elements of his career were reconstructed from J. Douglas Deal, *Race and Class in Colonial Virginia: Indians, Englishmen, and Africans on the Eastern Shore During the Seventeenth Century* (New York: Garland, 1993). Colonel Southy Littleton, a militia officer and planter in the county who was still a young man in 1677. Isaaac Foxcroft planted on the Eastern Shore. He died in 1702. The final name almost certainly is Captain Daniel Jenifer who, according to Berkeley, "hath fully approved himself a good and loyall subject of his Most Sacred Majesties Governor, being always ready to serve and obey me his Majesties Governor in suppressing the present Rebellion." Berkeley quoted in Frank P. Brent, "Some Unpublished Facts Relating to Bacon's Rebellion in Accomac County, Virginia," *Proceedings of the Virginia Historical Society,* ser. 3, 11 (1892), 183-184.

Major Robert Bristoll, a Gentleman of good Estate and an eminent Sufferer in his Stock, provisions, armes, ammunition, Marchants goods, & considerable quantities of strong Liquors: as allso in his person beinge kept prisoner untill Bacons death and afterwards he hath had a generall Knowledge of most Passages in the late unhappy troubles; and is able not only to Justifie most Perticulars of our Narrative, Butt allso is a person very fitt & necessary to be Examined to divers particulars relatinge to the Grievances both Generall and personall, Beinge a man of good understandinge in the Virginia affairs, and a Person of Integrity and Moderation, Soe that wee Could wish he might be sent for when there shall be occasion & use of him in any of the aforesaid affaires.[58]

The Good Queen of Pamunkey, a faithfull frend & lover of the English and their Interest, whose Sufferings by the late Rebells have bin much many wayes, beinge driven into the wild woods, and there almost famished; Plundered of all she had, her People taken Prisoners and Sold; allso Robbed her of Rich Match-coats for which she had great value, and offered to Redeem att any Rate.

Wee could not therefore but present her case to his Majestie, who though he maye nott att present soe easily provide remedies or rewards for the other worthy Suffers: Yett since a Present of small price maye highly oblige & gratifie this poor Indian Queen, Wee humbly Supplicate his Majestie to bestow itt on her.

---

58. Major Robert Bristow returned to England very shortly after the Rebellion, where he died in 1707. A copy of his will appeared in the *Virginia Magazine of History and Biography*, 13 (1906), 59-60. Sir John Berry thought highly enough of Bristow that he encouraged the Privy councilors to consult with him about matters in the colony.

Index

CPSIA information can be obtained at www.ICGtesting.com
Printed in the USA
LVOW10*0819210713

343876LV00004B/128/P